Eleventh Edition

CONTEMPORARY LOGISTICS

Eleventh Edition

CONTEMPORARY LOGISTICS

Paul R. Murphy, Jr.

A. Michael Knemeyer

Boston   Columbus   Indianapolis   New York   San Francisco   Upper Saddle River
Amsterdam   Cape Town   Dubai   London   Madrid   Milan   Munich   Paris   Montreal   Toronto
Delhi   Mexico City   Sao Paulo   Sydney   Hong Kong   Seoul   Singapore   Taipei   Tokyo

Editor in Chief: Stephanie Wall
Acquisitions Editor: Mark Gaffney
Program Manager Team Lead: Ashley Santora
Executive Marketing Manager: Anne Fahlgren
Project Manager Team Lead: Judy Leale
Project Manager: Tom Benfatti
Operations Specialist: Nacy Maneri
Creative Director: Jayne Conte

Cover Designer: Suzanne Behnke
Digital Production Project Manager: Lisa Rinaldi
Full-Service Project Management: Abinaya Rajendran, Integra Software Solutions.
Printer/Binder: Courier
Cover Printer: Lehigh-Phoenix Color/Hagerstown
Text Font: 10/12 Minion Pro

Credits and acknowledgments borrowed from other sources and reproduced, with permission, in this textbook appear on appropriate page within text.

Many of the designations by manufacturers and seller to distinguish their products are claimed as trademarks. Where those designations appear in this book, and the publisher was aware of a trademark claim, the designations have been printed in initial caps or all caps.

Library of Congress Cataloging-in-Publication Data

Murphy, Paul Regis.
  Contemporary logistics / Paul Murphy, Michael Knemeyer.—Eleventh edition.
    p. cm.
  ISBN-13: 978-0-13-295346-7 (alk. paper)
  ISBN-10: 0-13-295346-3 (alk. paper)
  1. Physical distribution of goods. 2. Business logistics. I. Title.
  HF5415.5.J6M87 2014
  658.5—dc23   2013028876

10 9 8 7 6 5 4 3 2 1

ISBN 10: 0-13-295346-3
ISBN 13: 978-0-13-295346-7

BRIEF CONTENTS

CONTENTS

PREFACE

This edition of *Contemporary Logistics* reflects a business landscape that is characterized by geopolitical tensions in various parts of the world, steadily increasing trade among countries and across continents, supply chain vulnerabilities caused by severe natural disasters, and an unabated pace of technological advancement. Although these and other events present both challenges and opportunities for logistics managers, the logistics discipline still remains fun, exciting, and dynamic—characteristics that are reflected in our revision.

WHAT'S NEW IN THIS EDITION?

This edition reflects input from reviewers, adopters, and other interested parties in terms of structure, presentation, and content. Specific modifications include the following:

- This edition welcomes a new coauthor, A. Michael Knemeyer, currently Associate Professor of Logistics at the Fisher College of Business, The Ohio State University. Mike's impressive blend of practical, academic, and consulting experience in logistics and supply chain management provides this edition with fresh insights and perspectives.
- This edition contains one new end-of-chapter case, Case 9-1 ("All-Indian Logistics Services"), and modifications of several other cases. For example, some case content, as well as several discussion questions, have been changed in Cases 7-1 ("Handy Andy, Inc."), 11-1 ("Let There Be Light Lamp Shade Company"), and 14-1 ("Nürnberg Augsburg Maschinenwerke (N.A.M.)").
- Each chapter in this edition has been revised and incorporates new examples and references. For example, Chapter 1's discussion of the globalization of trade reports the average growth rate of world trade between 1991 and 2011 (as opposed to between 1997 and 2007 in the tenth edition). As another example, Chapter 14's discussion of Incoterms reflects the revisions associated with Incoterms 2010, which were effective at the beginning of 2011.
- New content has been added throughout this edition. For example, Chapter 1 now includes a discussion of the rapidly emerging topic of humanitarian logistics. In addition, the "Logistics Activity Measures" section in Chapter 3 contains an expanded discussion of warehousing and inventory management performance measurements. Chapter 6 has added a subsection, "Procurement Portfolio Approach," that highlights Kraljic's Portfolio Matrix.
- Tables and figures containing country and industry data have been either revised or updated. Examples include Table 1-1, "The Cost of the Business Logistics System in Relation to a Country's Gross Domestic Product"; Figure 10-3, "2012 Liberty Mutual Workplace Safety Index Findings"; and Table 12-1, "Infrastructure Statistics in Several Countries."
- The list of Key Terms at the beginning of each chapter has been modified in the eleventh edition, and each key term is defined in the Glossary. New Key Terms in this edition include humanitarian logistics, big data, Logistics Uncertainty Pyramid Model, near-sourcing, and total cost of ownership, among others.
- The end-of-chapter Suggested Readings in the eleventh edition have been revised and over 60 percent of them have been published since 2009.

INSTRUCTOR SUPPLEMENTS

Supplements are available for adopting instructors to download at www.pearsonhighered.com/irc. Registration is simple and gives the instructor immediate access to new titles and new editions. Pearson's dedicated technical support team is ready to help instructors with the media supplements that accompany this text. The instructor should visit http://247.pearsoned.com/ for answers to frequently asked questions and for toll-free user support phone numbers. Supplements include the following:

- Instructor's Manual
- PowerPoint Slides

The current edition of *Contemporary Logistics* has been prepared by Paul Murphy and Mike Knemeyer, and they welcome your comments and suggestions at drmurphy@jcu.edu (Paul) and knemeyer_4@fisher.osu.edu (Mike). Paul and Mike gratefully acknowledge the important contributions that the late Donald F. Wood, James C. Johnson, and Daniel L. Wardlow made to earlier editions.

PART 1

OVERVIEW OF LOGISTICS

Part 1 of *Contemporary Logistics* introduces the many dimensions of the complex and dynamic subject of logistics. Chapter 1 presents an overview of logistics and introduces you to what logistics is and why it is important. The chapter covers the economic impact of logistics and discusses how logistics interacts with other functions, such as marketing, in an organization.

Chapter 2 provides an overview of the general types of information management systems that are applicable across each business function, and it provides examples of how these general types of information systems are specifically applied in logistics management. Chapter 2 also explores the Internet's influence on logistics and looks at some of the challenges associated with information technology.

Chapter 3 discusses the strategic financial outcomes influenced by logistics decisions. It uses the strategic profit model to highlight how logistics activities influence the key corporate financial measures of net income, capital employed, and return on capital employed.

Chapter 4 examines organizational and managerial issues in logistics. The chapter begins by looking at organizational structure and organizational design for logistics. Chapter 4 also discusses select managerial issues in logistics such as productivity, theft and pilferage, and the impact of terrorism on logistics systems.

1 | AN OVERVIEW OF LOGISTICS

ECONOMIC IMPACTS OF LOGISTICS

Although the logistics discipline today is vastly different than when the first edition of this book was published in the 1970s, one thing that remains constant is the economic impact of logistics. Before defining what logistics is, we believe that it's important to discuss the economic aspects of logistics and you might be surprised at its significant economic impact. From a macroeconomic perspective, Table 1.1 presents logistics costs in relation to gross domestic product (GDP) for a select group of countries. Although absolute and relative logistics costs in relation to GDP vary from country to country, logistics is most definitely an important component in any country's economy.

More specifically, logistics can play an important role in a nation's economic growth and development. For example, a poor transportation infrastructure and high levels of inventory are two key drawbacks that have limited the expansion of Vietnam's economy.[1] In a similar fashion,

---

[1] No author. "High Logistics Costs Stifle Vietnam's Economic Growth," *eyeforTransport*, February 24, 2009.

Table 1.1	The Cost of the Business Logistics System in Relation to a Country's Gross Domestic Product

Country	Logistics as a Percentage of GDP
United States	8.5
South Africa	12.7
India	13.0
Thailand	15.2
Brazil	15.4
People's Republic of China	17.8
Finland	19.0
Vietnam	22.5

Sources: "South Africa: Logistics costs as percentage of GDP improves," TradeMark SA; http://siteresources.worldbank.org/BRAZILINPOREXTN/Resources/3817166-1323121030855/FreightLogistics.pdf?resourceurlname=FreightLogistics.pdf; "Heavy logistics costs weigh on China's economy: report—Xinhua," English.news.cn; Autocar Professional; "Logistics cost to GDP declines," The Nation; "Vietnam high logistics costs lower businesses' competitiveness," TalkVietnam; http://www.panostaja.fi/index.php?id=150; 24th Annual State of Logistics Report, *Council of Supply Chain Management Professionals*, 2013.

relatively high logistics costs (as a percentage of GDP) in the People's Republic of China (China) continue to restrict the country's economic development, and in particular the high costs of highway transportation have severely constrained the growth of China's e-commerce market.[2]

Apart from the previous examples of macro-level economic impacts, the economic impacts of logistics can affect individual consumers such as you. These impacts can be illustrated through the concept of **economic utility**, which is the value or usefulness of a product in fulfilling customer needs or wants. The four general types of economic utility are possession, form, time, and place, and logistics clearly contributes to time and place utilities.

Possession utility refers to the value or usefulness that comes from a customer being able to take possession of a product. Possession utility can be influenced by the payment terms associated with a product. Credit and debit cards, for example, facilitate possession utility by allowing the customer to purchase products without having to produce cash or a cash equivalent. Likewise, automotive leases allow customers to take possession of a more desirable model than would be possible with conventional automotive loans.

Form utility refers to a product's being in a form that (1) can be used by the customer and (2) is of value to the customer. Although form utility has generally been associated with production and manufacturing, logistics can also contribute to form utility. For example, to achieve production economies (i.e., lower cost per unit), a soft drink company may produce thousands of cases of a certain type of soft drink (e.g., diet cola). You're not likely to purchase diet cola by the thousands of cases (unless you're having a really big social event!) but rather in smaller lot sizes, such as a six- or twelve-pack. Through *allocation*, logistics can break the thousands of cases of diet cola into the smaller quantities that are desired by customers.

Place utility refers to having products available *where* they are needed by customers; products are moved from points of lesser value to points of greater value. Continuing with the diet cola example, place utility is increased by moving the soda from a point of lesser value (e.g., stored in a warehouse) to a point of greater value (e.g., on a supermarket shelf).

Closely related to place utility is **time utility**, which refers to having products available *when* they are needed by customers. It's important to recognize that different products have

[2]Hua Wang, "High Logistics Cost, Toll Road and Institutional Factors Countermeasure in China," *Journal of Modern Accounting and Auditing* 7, no. 11 (2011): 1301–1306.

different sensitivities to time; three-day late delivery of perishable items likely has more serious consequences than three-day late delivery of nonperishable items.

Simultaneously achieving possession, form, place, and time utility goes a long way toward facilitating—but not guaranteeing—customer satisfaction. Consider the experience of a former student who placed an online order of Valentine's Day flowers for his out-of-state girlfriend. The seller facilitated possession utility by allowing the student to pay by credit card, and a healthy arrangement of the correct bouquet (form utility) arrived at the girlfriend's residence on Valentine's Day (place and time utility). Although the seller provided possession, form, place, and time utility, the buyer was quite unsatisfied with his purchase. The problem: The greeting card that accompanied the flowers had a wrong name for the girlfriend (but the right name for the boyfriend)!

LOGISTICS: WHAT IT IS

Now that you have been introduced to select economic impacts of logistics, it's important to define what **logistics** is. This book adopts the current definition promulgated by the Council of Supply Chain Management Professionals (CSCMP), one of the world's most prominent organizations for logistics professionals. According to the CSCMP, "Logistics management is that part of supply chain management that plans, implements, and controls the efficient, effective forward and reverse flow and storage of goods, services, and related information between the point of origin and the point of consumption in order to meet customers' requirements."[3]

Let's analyze this definition in closer detail. First, logistics is part of supply chain management. We'll talk about supply chains and supply chain management in greater detail in Chapter 5, but the key point for now is that logistics is part of a bigger picture in the sense that the supply chain focuses on coordination among business functions (such as marketing, production, and finance) within and across organizations. The fact that logistics is explicitly recognized as part of supply chain management means that logistics can affect how well (or how poorly) an individual firm—and its associated supply chain(s)—can achieve goals and objectives.

The CSCMP definition also indicates that logistics "plans, implements, and controls." Of particular importance is the word *and*, which suggests that logistics should be involved in all three activities—planning, implementing, controlling—and not just one or two. Some suggest, however, that logistics is more involved in the implementation than in the planning of certain logistical policies.[4]

Note that the CSCMP definition also refers to "efficient and effective forward and reverse flows and storage." Broadly speaking, effectiveness can be thought of as, "How well does a company do what it says it's going to do?" For example, if a company promises that all orders will be shipped within 24 hours of receipt, what percentage of orders are actually shipped within 24 hours of receipt? In contrast, efficiency can be thought of as how well (or poorly) company resources are used to achieve what a company promises it can do. For instance, some companies use premium or expedited transportation services—which cost more money—to cover for shortcomings in other parts of their logistics systems.

With respect to forward and reverse flows and storage, for many years logistics focused only on forward flows and storage, that is, those directed *toward* the point of consumption. Increasingly, however, the logistics discipline has recognized the importance of reverse flows and storage (*reverse logistics*), that is, those that *originate* at the point of consumption. Although the majority of the discussion in this book focuses on forward logistics, many companies today recognize the tactical and strategic implications of reverse logistics.[5] Indeed, reverse logistics

---

[3]www.cscmp.org
[4]Paul R. Murphy and Richard F. Poist, "Socially Responsible Logistics: An Exploratory Study," *Transportation Journal* 41, no. 4 (2002): 23–35.
[5]M. Jose Alvarez-Gil, Pascual Berrone, F. Javier Husillos, and Nora Lado, "Reverse Logistics, Stakeholders' Influence, Organizational Slack, and Managers' Posture," *Journal of Business Research* 60, no. 5 (2007): 463–473.

continues to grow in importance as individual companies, and select supply chains, recognize it as an opportunity for competitive advantage.[6]

The CSCMP definition also indicates that logistics involves the flow and storage of "goods, services, and related information." Indeed, in the contemporary business environment, logistics is as much about the flow and storage of information as it is about the flow and storage of goods. The importance of information in contemporary logistics is captured by Fred Smith, CEO and chairman of FedEx (a leading logistics service provider), who believes that "information about the package is as important as the package itself."[7] Furthermore, social media such as Facebook (launched in 2004), Twitter (launched in 2006), and LinkedIn (launched in 2007) are becoming key informational tools in contemporary logistics management.

Finally, the CSCMP definition indicates that the purpose of logistics is "to meet customer requirements." This is important for several reasons, with one being that logistics strategies and activities should be based on customer wants and needs, rather than the wants, needs, and capabilities of manufacturers or retailers. Advances in information technology have facilitated, and continue to facilitate, an understanding of customer wants and needs, and these technological advances increasingly allow for interactive communication with customers—a key to meeting customer requirements.

A second reason for the importance of meeting customer requirements is the notion that because different customers have different logistical needs and wants, a one-size-fits-all logistics approach (**mass logistics**)—in which every customer gets the same type and levels of logistics service—will result in some customers being overserved while others are underserved. Rather, companies should consider **tailored logistics** approaches, in which groups of customers with similar logistical needs and wants are provided with logistics service appropriate to these needs and wants.[8]

The principles in this textbook are generally applicable not only to for-profit situations, but also to governmental and not-for-profit situations. From a governmental perspective, logistics is quite germane to the armed forces, which shouldn't be surprising, given that logistics was first associated with the military. Consider, for example, the potential consequences of a supply chain disruption—a challenge faced by many for-profit organizations—in a war zone. For example, the United States military has been forced to shift supply routes to support its troops in Afghanistan whenever Pakistan closes its border crossings into Afghanistan.[9]

A community food bank provides one example of the relevance of logistics to not-for-profit situations. As an example, the Food Bank of New York City is responsible for delivering nearly 75 million pounds of food annually to more than 1,000 food assistance programs such as homeless shelters and food pantries. From a logistical perspective, the Food Bank of New York City is responsible for collecting, storing, repacking, and distributing food from its 90,000 square-foot warehouse.[10]

Furthermore, **humanitarian logistics** represents an emerging application of logistics to not-for-profit situations. Briefly, humanitarian logistics can be defined as the process and systems involved in mobilizing people, resources, skills, and knowledge to help people who have been affected by either a natural or a human-made disaster.[11] For example, natural disasters such as a catastrophic earthquake require food and medicinal supplies to be located, collected, transported, and distributed—and sooner, rather than later. Because of the increasing frequency (and severity) of disasters over the past 50 years, humanitarian logistics is likely to be an important topic into the foreseeable future.

---

[6]C. Clifford Defee, Terry Esper, and Diane Mollenkopf, "Leveraging Closed-Loop Orientation and Leadership for Environmental Sustainability," *Supply Chain Management: An International Journal* 14, no. 2 (2010): 87–98.

[7]Jonathan Reiskin, "Carriers Invest in Web Sites, Software, Networks," *Transport Topics*, May 8, 2006, 10.

[8]Joseph B. Fuller, James O'Conor, and Richard Rawlinson, "Tailored Logistics: The Next Advantage," *Harvard Business Review* 71, no. 3 (1993): 87–98.

[9]Agency Group 09, "Military Logistics Strained, but Healthy, Official Says," *FDCH Regulatory Intelligence Database*, January 10, 2012.

[10]www.foodbanknyc.org

[11]Luk N. Van Wassenhove, "Humanitarian Aid Logistics: Supply Chain Management in High Gear," *Journal of the Operational Research Society* 57 (2006): 475–489.

THE INCREASED IMPORTANCE OF LOGISTICS

The formal study of business logistics, and predecessor concepts such as traffic management and physical distribution, has existed since the second half of the twentieth century. Quite frankly, from approximately 1950 to 1980, limited appreciation was shown for the importance of the logistics discipline. Since 1980, however, increasing recognition has been given to business logistics, in part because of tremendous—and rapid—changes in the discipline and several key reasons are discussed next.

A Reduction in Economic Regulation

During the 1970s and the 1980s, widespread reductions in economic regulation (commonly referred to as *deregulation*) relaxed government control of carriers' rates and fares, entry and exit, mergers and acquisitions, and more. These controls were particularly onerous in the U.S. transportation industry in the sense that price competition was essentially nonexistent, and customers were pretty much forced to accept whatever service the carriers chose to provide. This meant that logistics managers had relatively little control over one of the most important cost components in a logistics system.

Reductions in economic regulation in the U.S. airfreight, railroad, and trucking industries allowed individual carriers flexibility in pricing and service. This flexibility was important to logistics for several reasons. First, it provided companies with the ability to implement the tailored logistics approach discussed earlier, in the sense that companies could specify different logistics service levels, and prices could be adjusted accordingly. Second, the increased pricing flexibility allowed large buyers of transportation services to reduce their transportation costs by leveraging large amounts of freight with a limited number of carriers.

Although the preceding discussion has focused on lessened economic regulation in the United States, it appears that deregulation has had similar effects in other countries. For example, lessened economic regulation of transportation among European countries has resulted in lower prices for truck shipments in these countries.[12] Likewise, privatization of commercial airports has been found to improve their operational efficiency relative to government owned and/or operated airports.[13]

Changes in Consumer Behavior

A common business adage suggests that "change is the only constant." Although changes in consumer behavior are commonly the purview of the psychology and marketing disciplines, such changes have important logistical implications as well. Several examples of changes in consumer behavior (customized customer, changing family roles, and rising customer expectations) and their possible logistical implications are discussed next.

The *customized customer* signifies that the customer desires a product offering that is highly tailored to the customer's exact preferences. One approach for addressing the customized customer is through mass customization, which refers to the ability of a company to deliver highly customized products and services that are designed to meet the needs and wants of individual segments or customers. The customized customer will not accept a "one size fits all" approach, and this means that logistics systems must be flexible rather than rigid. As an example, logistics service providers such as FedEx and UPS offer a variety of delivery options to prospective customers. FedEx and UPS customers can choose same-day delivery, next-day delivery by noon, next-day delivery by the close of business,

---

[12]Francine LaFontaine and Laura Malaguzzi Valeri, "The Deregulation of International Trucking in the European Union: Form and Effect," *Journal of Regional Economics* 35, no. 1 (2009): 19–44.
[13]Tae H. Oum, Jia Yan, and Chunyan Yu, "Ownership Forms Matter for Airport Efficiency: A Stochastic Frontier Investigation of Worldwide Airports," *Journal of Urban Economics* 64, no. 2 (2008): 422–435.

second-day delivery by noon, among others. As a general rule, the earlier the delivery time, the more expensive the transportation cost.

In terms of *changing family roles*, 40 years ago less than 45 percent of U.S. adult women were in the workforce; today, by contrast, approximately 60 percent are in the working world.[14] Moreover, approximately 30 percent of U.S. children live in a single-parent household. One consequence of these changing family roles has been an increasing emphasis on the convenience associated with a family's grocery shopping experiences. This convenience is manifested in various ways to include extended store hours, home delivery of purchased items, and ready-to-eat/ready-to-cook foods, and each of these has logistics-related implications. With extended store hours—some stores are now open 24 hours—retailers must address issues such as the optimal delivery times for replenishment trucks and when to replenish merchandise. For example, it wouldn't be a good idea for a 24-hour grocery store to replenish the shelves when its stores are crowded with customers.

Although home delivery could be convenient to the purchaser, the time-sensitive nature of grocery products means that delivery should be made when the purchaser is at home. As such, scheduling home deliveries to coincide with the purchaser's availability is paramount to avoiding dissatisfied customers.[15] Finally, the growth in ready-to-eat/ready-to-cook foods means that some food processors have added high-volume cooking systems at their production facilities. From a logistics perspective, food processors continue to experiment with packaging alternatives that will extend the shelf life of ready-to-cook foods.

As for *rising customer expectations*, it should come as no surprise that customer expectations tend to increase through time, which means that a satisfactory level of performance in the past might not be considered as so today. An excellent example of rising customer expectations is provided by Toyota Motor Company's North American Parts Operations. In an effort to retain customers and to reduce losing customers to other automotive repair facilities, Toyota now offers same-day delivery (rather than one-day delivery) of automotive parts to certain Toyota dealerships located in major metropolitan areas. This same-day delivery has been facilitated by a redesign of Toyota's automotive parts distribution network.[16]

Technological Advances

Prior to the start of every academic year, Beloit College in Wisconsin releases its annual Mindset list that details the worldview of incoming first-year college students.[17] The class of 2017, which assumes a 1995 birth date, is particularly noteworthy because it has never lived in the non-Internet world. Tremendous technological advances during the course of your lifetime—from desktop computers to tablets, from second-generation mobile phones to fourth-generation mobile phones—have profoundly influenced business management and, by extension, business logistics. The following paragraphs will discuss several examples of the logistical impacts of technological advances.

Technological advances have influenced channel design by allowing companies to offer an alternate distribution channel (or alternate distribution channels) to already existing channels. In some cases, this alternate channel is direct (i.e., no intermediaries between the producer and final customer) in nature because the final customer orders directly from the producer rather than through an intermediary. The removal of intermediaries between producer and consumer—called **disintermediation**—can clearly affect the design of logistics systems in the sense that there could be changes in both the number and location of fixed facilities such as

[14]http://www.bls.gov/spotlight/2011/women/pdf/women_bls_spotlight.pdf
[15]Jane Hiback, "Alternative Retailing Strategies," *Natural Food Merchandiser*, August 2011, 18–19.
[16]http://toyotadriverseat.com/pr/tds/same-day-parts-deliveries-help-230692.aspx
[17]http://www.beloit.edu/mindset/

warehouses and distribution centers. In addition, the logistical considerations of a retailer's online store (e.g., orders from numerous customers; orders for small quantities) are quite different from that retailer's brick-and-mortar stores (e.g., orders from a defined customer base; orders in larger quantities).[18]

Technological advances can also improve the productivity of the order picking process, which we'll discuss in greater detail in Chapter 7. Order picking traditionally involved paper pick tickets that listed the particular item(s) and quantity to be picked—and not necessarily the item's location in a facility. Locating the items to be picked could be quite time consuming, and paper picking often resulted in picking errors in part because of illegible pick orders. Today, by contrast, order picking can utilize radio frequency (RF) devices, voice-directed picking, as well as robotic picking. Although these technological picking advances are more costly than paper picking, they can lead to substantial improvements in picking efficiency. For example, RF terminals can reduce pick errors by approximately 60 percent compared to paper picking.[19]

Shipment tracking provides another example of how technological advances have impacted logistics management. When one of the authors worked for a U.S. trucking company in the early 1980s, shipment tracking was a time-consuming, labor-intensive process that sometimes did not yield a location for the shipment in question. If we fast-forward to today, global positioning systems can provide real-time location information about a shipment (sometimes to within *10 feet* of its exact location), as well as providing information about the vehicle's temperature, humidity, and vibrations. Such information can be especially important to pharmaceutical and health-care companies.[20]

The Growing Power of Retailers

Another influence on logistics involves the growing power of retailers relative to manufacturers in channels of distribution. Indeed, a 2011 study indicated that both manufacturers and retailers agree that retailers wield greater power in the manufacturer–retailer arrangement, and both parties agree that the retailers' power will increase in the future.[21] So-called **big-box retailers**—stores with large amounts of both floor space and products for sale—such as Walmart, Costco, and Dick's Sporting Goods provide an excellent example of the growing power of retailers.

Many big-box retailers explicitly recognize superior logistics as an essential component of their corporate strategies, and because of this, their logistical practices are often viewed as a barometer for emerging logistics trends. In the 1990s, for example, Walmart and Warner-Lambert were the first two companies to explore collaborative planning, forecasting, and replenishment (CPFR), a practice in which trading partners share planning and forecasting data to better match up supply and demand. Since then, there have been hundreds of successful (e.g., increased sales, reduced inventory levels) CPFR initiatives, although, to be fair, not all CPFR initiatives have been successful.

Big-box retailers have also been trendsetters with respect to environmental and social issues in logistics. For example, Target is committed to reducing its carbon footprint and does so with transportation by choosing the proper transport modes, reducing the number of transportation miles that freight is moved, and improving vehicle loading practices by maximizing space utilization.[22] In a similar fashion, two of Best Buy's sustainability goals for 2020 are to recycle one billion pounds of consumer goods and reduce its carbon footprint by 20 percent (relative to 2009 performance).[23]

---

[18]Shelly Banjo, "Wal-Mart's E-Stumble with Amazon," *The Wall Street Journal*, June 18, 2013, B1.

[19]Kristi Montgomery, "Tips for Quicker Product Picking," *Multichannel Merchant*, December/January 2012, 28–29.

[20]Ian Putzger, "Apps Mania," *CT&L*, April 2012, 32–33.

[21]No author, "Kantor Study Dissects Category Management," *Drug Store News*, June 27, 2011, 30–34.

[22]http://hereforgood.target.com/environment/efficient-operations/

[23]http://sustainability.bby.com/management-approach/product-stewardship

Globalization of Trade

Although countries have traded with each other for thousands of years, globalization's impact is greater today than ever before. Consider that world trade grew at an average annual rate of approximately 5.5 percent between 1991 and 2011, including the worldwide economic slowdown in 2008 and 2009.[24] Looking forward, the annual growth in world trade is forecast to be approximately 3.8 percent through 2017.[25] Many factors, such as rising standards of living and multi-country trade alliances, have contributed to the growth of global trade; logistics has played a key role, too. Indeed, the shipping **container**—a uniform sealed reusable metal box in which goods are shipped—is often championed as an important catalyst for the growth in global trade.

We'll look at international logistics in much greater detail in Chapter 14, but for now one should recognize that international logistics is much more challenging and costly than domestic logistics. With respect to challenges, the geographic distances between buyers and sellers are often greater (which may translate into longer transit times), and monitoring logistics processes is sometimes complicated by differences in business practices, culture, and language. As for costs, the greater geographic distances tend to result in higher transportation costs, and documentation requirements can be quite costly as well.

THE SYSTEMS AND TOTAL COST APPROACHES TO LOGISTICS

Logistics is a classic example of the systems approach to business problems. From a company-wide perspective, the **systems approach** indicates that a company's objectives can be realized by recognizing the mutual interdependence of the major functional areas of the firm, such as marketing, production, finance, and logistics. One implication of the systems approach is that the goals and objectives of the major functional areas should be compatible with the company's goals and objectives. This means that *one logistics system does not fit all companies* because goals and objectives vary from one firm to another. As such, the logistics system of an organization that emphasizes customer satisfaction is likely different from the logistics system of an organization that emphasizes cost minimization.

A second implication is that decisions made by one functional area should consider the potential implications on other functional areas. For example, one consequence of pursuing the marketing concept, which focuses on satisfying customer needs and wants, is often a marked increase of the number of **stock-keeping units (SKUs)** or line items of inventory (each different type or package size of a good is a different SKU) offered for sale by many companies. An increased number of SKUs provides customers with more choices, which today's customer often wants.

Alternatively, from a logistics perspective, the proliferation of SKUs creates challenges such as more items to identify, more items to store, and more items to track, which increases the chances of mistakes—which today's customers don't like. An example of misidentification involves a consumer products company that mistakenly assigned the *same product code* to a 3-pack, 6-pack, and 12-pack of a particular product it sold. Imagine the reaction of the customer who ordered a 3-pack of the product, only to receive a 6-pack or a 12-pack of it!

Just as the major functional areas of a firm should recognize their interdependence, so too should the various activities that comprise the logistics function (what we'll call *intrafunctional logistics*). The logistics manager should balance each logistics activity to ensure that none is stressed to the point where it becomes detrimental to others.

This can be illustrated by referring to Figure 1.1, which indicates that business logistics is made up of **materials management** (movement and storage of materials into a firm) and **physical distribution** (storage of finished product and movement to the customer). Intrafunctional

---

[24]http://www.wto.org/english/news_e/pres12_e/pr658_e.htm
[25]HSBC Global Connections, "Trade Forecast Update: Global," February 2012.

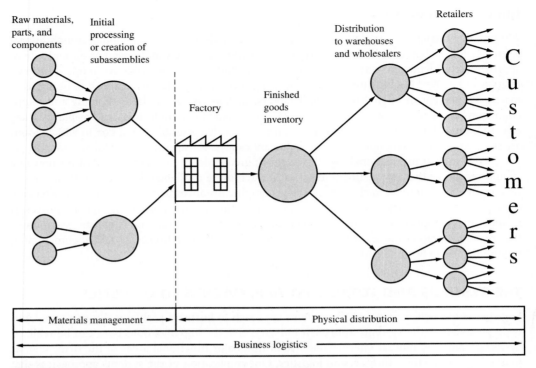

Raw materials, parts, and components

Initial processing or creation of subassemblies

Factory

Finished goods inventory

Distribution to warehouses and wholesalers

Retailers

Customers

← Materials management →   ← Physical distribution →

← Business logistics →

FIGURE 1.1 Control Over the Flow of Inbound and Outbound Movements
In this drawing, the circles represent buildings where inventories are stored, and the lines with arrows represent movement performed by carriers, a stop-and-start process. Current thought deals more with flows, possibly in different volumes and at different speeds, but without the inventory standing still. The supply chain extends to both the left and right of this diagram and includes the suppliers' suppliers and the customers' customers.

logistics attempts to coordinate materials management and physical distribution in a cost-efficient manner that supports an organization's customer service objectives.

Materials management and physical distribution can be coordinated in many ways. One way is by using the same truck to deliver materials and component parts and to pick up finished goods. Although this may appear to be little more than common sense—and the authors believe that *common sense is one of the keys to being an effective logistics manager*—consider the case of the company that used the same trucking company to deliver materials and parts to one of its production plants as well as to take finished products from the facility. Unfortunately, one truck would arrive early in the morning to deliver the materials and parts, and another truck would arrive in the late afternoon to pick up the finished products. How could this happen? Quite simply: The inbound logistics group and the outbound logistics group were unaware that they were using the same trucking company—the two groups never communicated even though they worked in the same building!

Logistics managers use the **total cost approach** to coordinate materials management and physical distribution in a cost-efficient manner. This approach is built on the premise that all relevant activities in moving and storing products should be considered as a whole (i.e., their total cost), not individually. Use of the total cost approach requires an understanding of **cost trade-offs**; in other words, changes to one logistics activity cause some costs to increase and others to decrease. Importantly, an understanding of logistical cost trade-offs recognizes that the costs of certain logistical activities generally move in opposite directions. As an example, a decrease in transportation costs is often associated with an increase in warehousing costs.

The key to the total cost approach is that all relevant logistical cost items are *considered simultaneously* when making a decision. For example, expedited transportation, such as air freight, will increase a company's transportation costs. At the same time, expedited transportation leads to a faster order cycle, which allows the receiving company to hold lower levels of inventory, thus reducing both its inventory carrying costs and warehousing costs. The total cost approach evaluates if the decreased inventory and warehousing costs are greater than the increased costs of expedited transportation. If so, the company might consider using expedited transportation (assuming that customer satisfaction isn't negatively impacted), because the total logistics costs (consisting, in this example, of transportation, inventory, and warehousing costs) are less than the total costs of the existing system.

When used in the logistics decision-making process, the total cost concept approach forms what is commonly called the *total logistics concept*. This concept is unique not because of the activities performed, but because of the integration of all activities into a unified whole that seeks to minimize distribution costs in a manner that supports an organization's customer service objectives. The total logistics concept can be extended to include a firm's suppliers and customers, such as in supply chain management, which will be covered in Chapter 5.

LOGISTICAL RELATIONSHIPS WITHIN THE FIRM

From a companywide perspective, the system and total cost approaches to logistics require an understanding of logistics and its relationships with other functional areas. Because Chapter 6 is devoted specifically to procurement (purchasing), our discussion here focuses on logistical relationships with finance, production, and marketing.

Finance

The finance staff is often charged with the responsibility of allocating the firm's funds to projects desired by the various operating departments. As such, the finance department is often instrumental in approving capital budgeting decisions that affect logistics, such as the acquisition of materials handling equipment (e.g., forklifts) and packaging equipment (e.g., a shrink-wrap machine). In such situations, finance personnel may decide to either purchase or lease the relevant equipment, assuming they have approved the decision to acquire it.

Inventory is another area where finance and logistics can interact. A basic challenge for the two areas is that the finance department often measures inventory in terms of its cost or value in dollars, whereas logistics tends to measure inventory in terms of units. The differing ways of measuring inventory can create potential friction between the two groups, as illustrated in the following example. From a cash flow perspective, the finance department might prefer to sell 2 boxes of hair dryers worth $1,000 dollars than to sell 15 boxes of hair shampoo worth $900. Alternatively, from a productivity perspective such as the number of boxes handled per worker, the logistics department might prefer selling the 15 boxes of hair shampoo rather than the 2 boxes of hair dryers.

In addition, in times of inflation, identical items added to inventory at different times means that each unit has a different cost, and even though inventory levels are not affected, it makes a difference whether an organization uses historic cost or current value as an indicator of the inventory's total value. Or, consider the concept of depreciation, which reduces the monetary value of inventory by a certain amount per period of time, even though the actual quantity of inventory may be unchanged. Indeed, the authors have consulting experiences with companies that showed a particular SKU to be fully depreciated, with an accounting value of $0—while the companies' warehousing facilities contained several hundred units of physical inventory of the particular SKU.

Production

One of the most common interfaces between production and logistics involves the length of production runs. In many cases, the production people favor long production runs of individual products because this allows the relevant fixed costs to be spread over more units, thus resulting in a lower production cost per unit. Having said this, long production runs generate large amounts of inventory, and it is often the logistician's responsibility to store and track the inventory. It's generally much easier to store and track five units of a product that it is to store and track 500 units of the product.

Another consideration with long production runs is that sometimes excess inventory for particular products occurs because of limited (or no) demand for them. At a minimum, these products add to a company's inventory carrying costs and also take up space that could be used to store other products. Slow-selling (or nonselling) products may also increase a company's handling costs, as illustrated by a situation in which forklift drivers would periodically move 150 refrigerators from one warehouse area to another, just to ensure that the company's managers would not see the refrigerators sitting in the same place for an extended period of time! You may find it difficult to believe that these 150 refrigerators were moved throughout the warehouse for nearly five years before managers were alerted to the behavior.

Increasing utilization of the **postponement** concept (the delay of value-added activities such as assembly, production, and packaging until the latest possible time[26]) also influences the interface between production and logistics. More specifically, some value-added activities (e.g., case packing, case labeling) that were traditionally performed at a production plant are now performed in warehousing facilities. As a result, warehousing facilities are adding new types of equipment and being configured differently to allow specific value-added activities to take place.

Marketing

Contemporary marketing places a heavy emphasis on customer satisfaction, and logistics strategies can facilitate customer satisfaction through reducing the cost of products, which can translate into lower prices as well as bringing a broader variety of choices closer to where the customer wishes to buy or use the product. Logistics strategies offer a unique way for a company to differentiate itself among competitors, and logistics now offers an important route for many firms to create marketing superiority. The following discussion about the interactions between logistics and marketing focuses on the marketing mix, sometimes referred to as the *four Ps* of marketing (place, price, product, and promotion).

PLACE DECISIONS   Decisions regarding place involve two types of networks, namely, logistics and the marketing channel (which is discussed in greater detail later in this chapter). Logistics decisions concern the most effective way to move and store the product from where it is produced to where it is sold. An effective logistics system can provide positive support by enabling the firm to attract and utilize what it considers to be the most productive channel and supply chain members. Channel members are frequently in a position to pick and choose which manufacturer's products they wish to merchandise. If a manufacturer is not consistently able to provide a certain product at the right time, in the right quantities, and in an undamaged condition, the channel members may end their relationship with the supplier or cease active promotion of the supplier's product.

From a marketing perspective, place decisions may also involve new strategies for reaching customers. A popular contemporary marketing strategy involves **co-branding**, which refers to an alliance that allows customers to purchase products from two or more name-brand retailers at one store location. Examples of co-branding include Starbucks coffee shops located with Marriott hotels, Subway restaurants located within some Walmart stores, and colocated Dunkin' Donuts and Baskin-Robbins stores. From a marketing perspective, co-branding offers potential customers convenience by allowing for one-stop shopping as well the opportunity to purchase

[26]John J. Coyle, Edward J. Bardi, and C. John Langley, *The Management of Business Logistics: A Supply Chain Perspective*, 7th ed. (Mason, OH: South-Western, 2003).

brand-name, rather than private-label (proprietary), products.[27] From a logistical perspective, one decision involves product delivery to the particular retail locations. Should, for example, each co-branding party deliver its respective products to a particular location, or should the co-branding parties co-load vehicles to minimize the number of deliveries that arrive at a particular location? While the former might result in higher delivery costs because of multiple deliveries, the latter requires a higher degree of coordination between the co-branding parties.

PRICE DECISIONS   A key price-related decision for marketers involves how a product's transportation costs should be reflected in its selling price, and this has proved to be a particularly vexing issue for some online merchants. For example, should a company's selling price reflect its product's **landed costs**, which refer to the price of a product at the source plus transportation costs to its destination? On the one hand, a selling price that is based on a product's landed cost allows the seller to offer "free" delivery of the product to prospective customers, because the transportation costs associated with delivery are captured in the landed cost. On the other hand, a selling price that is based on a product's landed cost could result in a substantial increase in a product's selling price, and a higher selling price tends to decrease buyer demand for most products. One way that some online merchants address this conundrum is to require a minimum order amount (e.g., $50) to qualify for "free" delivery.

In addition to transportation considerations, logistics managers may play an important role in product pricing. They are expected to know the costs of providing various levels of customer service and therefore should be consulted to determine the trade-offs between costs and customer service. Because many distribution costs produce per unit savings when larger volumes are handled, the logistics manager can also help formulate the firm's quantity discount pricing policies.

PRODUCT DECISIONS   A number of potential interfaces are possible between marketing and logistics in terms of product decisions. For example, as noted earlier, the marked increase in product offerings—which allows for more customer choice—creates logistical challenges in terms of identification, storage, and tracking.

Another product interface between marketing and logistics involves the amount of particular SKUs to hold. Marketers often prefer to carry higher quantities of particular items because this reduces the likelihood of **stockouts** (being out of an item at the same time there is demand for it). However, from a logistics perspective, higher quantities of inventory (1) necessitate additional storage space and (2) increase inventory carrying costs.

Product design, which is often the purview of marketers, can also have important implications for logistical effectiveness and efficiency. For example, long-necked glass beverage containers might be more distinctive than aluminum cans; however, from a logistics perspective, long-necked bottles take up more space and are more likely to be damaged than aluminum cans.

In addition, marketers' growing emphasis on offering **sustainable products**—products that meet present needs without compromising the ability of future generations to meet their needs—can also impact logistical decisions. Consider, for example, *fair trade products*, or those that guarantee a better deal for producers in the developing world through fair and stable prices as well as teaching farming methods that are environmentally sustainable.[28] From a marketing perspective, customer demand for fair trade products such as coffee or chocolate has resulted in some companies establishing distinct fair trade brands.[29] From a logistical perspective, an organization's commitment to selling fair trade products, such as coffee or chocolate, may result in changed sourcing requirements for the necessary raw materials.

---

[27]Marilyn Odesser-Torpey, "Co-Branding: Positives and Pitfalls," *Convenience Store Decisions*, April 2012, 46–48.
[28]Derek Townsend, "Fair Trade Future?" *Food Service*, June 2008, 27.
[29]No author, "More Chocolate Manufacturers Moving to Ethical Sourcing," *Candy Industry*, April 2010, 10–12.

PROMOTION DECISIONS   Many promotional decisions require close coordination between marketing and logistics. One important situation concerns the availability of highly advertised products, particularly when a company is running pricing campaigns that lower the price of certain items. Few things are more damaging to a firm's goodwill than being stocked out of items that are heavily promoted in a sales campaign. In addition, in some instances imbalances of product supply and demand can be viewed as *bait and switch tactics*—that is, enticing customers with the promises of a low-priced product, only to find that it is unavailable, but that a higher-priced substitute product is readily available.

Moreover, once a decision is made to promote the introduction of a new product, the logistics staff assumes responsibility for having the product in place on the scheduled release date—not earlier, not later. The complexity of so doing is well illustrated by looking at some of the activities associated with the release of *Harry Potter and the Deathly Hallows*, the final book in the *Harry Potter* series, which went on sale at midnight on July 21, 2007. The book's author, J.K. Rowling, finished writing *Harry Potter and the Deathly Hallows* in Edinburgh, Scotland, in early 2007. Mark Seidenfeld, who was in charge of bringing the manuscript to New York to begin the publishing process, made sure the manuscript was safe by *sitting on it* during his airplane flight to the United States! Barnes and Noble, a large book retailer, hired an outside security firm to guard the padlocked trucks that contained its copies of the *Deathly Hallows*.[30]

MARKETING CHANNELS

Another concept that is useful to studying the marketing relationships between and among firms is to look at **marketing channels**, which refer to "a set of institutions necessary to transfer the title to goods and to move goods from the point of production to the point of consumption and, as such, which consists of all the institutions and all the marketing activities in the marketing process."[31] The principal, traditional institutions in the marketing channel are the manufacturer, the wholesaler, and the retailer. These channel members work together in several different channel arrangements—*ownership channel, negotiation channel, financing channel, promotions channel*, and *logistics channel*—and we'll look more closely at how manufacturers, wholesalers, and retailers interact in these five channels.

The *ownership channel* covers movement of the title to the goods, and the goods themselves might not be physically present or even exist. If a good is in great demand, one might have to buy it before it is produced, such as a commissioned piece of art or a scarce new consumer product. Sometimes, a product will not be made until there are sufficient financial commitments, which is often the case with new models of commercial airplanes. The party owning the good almost always has the right to trade or sell it and bears the risks and costs associated with having it in inventory. Also, while owning the good, one can use it as collateral for a loan, although this may place some restrictions on its use or movement.

The *negotiations channel* is the one in which buy and sell agreements are reached. This could include transactions face-to-face or by telephone, e-mail, electronic data interchange, or almost any other form of communication. In many situations, no actual negotiations take place; the price for the product is stated, and one either buys at that price or does not. In some trades, auctions are used; in others, highly structured, organized trading takes place, such as markets for some commodities. One part of the negotiations covers how activities in the other channels are to be handled. For example, each buying party will specify the point and time of delivery and the point and time of payment. Even packaging design may be negotiated. (An old Henry Ford story is that suppliers of some parts were directed to ship in wooden crates built of good lumber and to

---

[30]Lev Grossman, Andrea Sachs, Kristine Dell, and Laura Fitzpatrick, "Harry Potter and the Sinister Spoilers," *Time*, July 9, 2007, 49–52.
[31]American Marketing Association Dictionary, www.marketingpower.com

very exacting specifications. It turned out that the empty crates were then partially disassembled and became floorboards in Ford Model Ts.)

The *financing channel* handles payments for goods. More importantly, it handles the company's credit. The multiple participants in the channel have different financial strengths, and often one must help another to keep the entire channel alive. For example, a newly opened retail store may have some of its goods placed on consignment, meaning that the wholesaler, not the store, owns them. The retailer will reimburse the wholesaler only for goods sold; the wholesaler bears nearly all the financial risks. Sometimes, in an effort to develop what it believes is a necessary new product line, a wholesaler will assist the manufacturer by putting up cash in advance along with an order. Alternatively, the wholesaler will place a large, guaranteed order, and the manufacturer can take that order to a bank and use it as a basis for receiving a loan.

Credit is important to all parties in the channel, who frequently receive or extend it, and credit becomes an integral part of the negotiations. If bills are not paid when due or if credit is overextended, collection becomes a financing channel function. Indeed, one aftereffect of the 2007–2009 economic recession is that some large companies are taking longer to pay their bills. More specifically, some larger companies now pay their bills within 90 days, as opposed to 30–60 days prior to the recession. While beneficial to the larger companies, these lengthened payment cycles negatively impact their suppliers.[32]

The *promotions channel* is concerned with promoting a new or an existing product, and can be related to the financing channel because monetary allowances are often part of the promotion effort. In addition, the promotions channel and the logistics channel are linked in several ways. First, there may be special advertising materials, such as coupon books, floor advertising posters, or displays, which must be distributed with the promoted product. Second, some of the cartons or consumer packs may have special labeling, and their placement at retailers must coincide with other promotional efforts. Third, because logistics personnel handle order processing, they have instantaneous records of actual sales, which indicate the initial success of the promotional efforts.

As mentioned previously, the *logistics channel*, its components, and its functioning are the main topics of this book. The most significant contribution that the logistics channel makes to the overall channel process is the **sorting function**, which bridges "the discrepancy between the assortment of goods and services generated by the producer and the assortment demanded by the consumer."[33] The sorting function has four steps, and these are important to understanding the concept of goods flowing through the logistics channel:

- *Sorting out* is sorting a heterogeneous supply of products into stocks that are homogeneous.
- *Accumulating* is bringing together similar stocks from different sources.
- *Allocating* is breaking a homogeneous supply into smaller lots.
- *Assorting* is building up assortments of goods for resale, usually to retail customers.

These steps take place between the manufacturer and the consumer, which means that they are performed by the wholesaler, the retailer, or specialist intermediaries.

In addition to the major actors or primary participants in a logistics channel, many less-well-known actors, called *facilitators* or *channel intermediaries*, play minor but essential roles. Intermediaries make the entire system function better and should only be used when they add value to a transaction. They spring up and flourish in areas where communications and other interactions between major parties are not well meshed. In international transactions, for example, translators may be an important intermediary. Intermediaries also function in areas needing orderly routines, such as order processing, and in searching, for example, when customers are looking for products or producers are looking for customers. Intermediaries fill niches, they are very well focused, and they serve as buffers between various channel members. Usually, they do not take an ownership position in the products or goods being handled.

[32]Angus Loten, "Big Customers Are Taking Longer to Pay," *The Wall Street Journal*, June 7, 2012, B7.
[33]American Marketing Association Dictionary.

The five channels discussed previously show where intermediaries function and fit. For example, in the ownership channel, a common intermediary is the bank or finance company, which may assume temporary or partial ownership of goods as part of an ongoing transaction. Often, this is a condition for the extension of credit. Banks routinely loan funds to all parties in a channel, making it possible for goods to be manufactured, marketed, and sold.

Brokers, who are associated with the negotiation channel, are independent contractors paid to arrange a particular transaction. A broker can be used by either a buyer or seller and is often used to arrange truck transportation for either the buyer (shipper/receiver) or seller (trucker). A broker can add value for a trucker in the sense that an individual trucker believes that his or her time is more profitably spent driving, rather than being on the phone or Internet trying to negotiate for the next load. In a similar fashion, a broker adds value for a shipper/receiver because of the broker's knowledge of potential transportation options.

Banks and finance companies are prominent intermediaries in the financing channel and both parties supply the credit necessary for a deal to be finalized. For big-ticket items, such as ships or warehouses, the buyer almost always borrows money to finance part of the purchase. Sometimes insurance is also a requirement in the agreement, so insurance companies may also serve as intermediaries.

The promotions channel has intermediaries that aid with promotions, such as firms that design, build, and transport product exhibits for display at trade shows. Advertising agencies can handle the preparation and media placement of advertising materials, and firms often use public relations agencies to represent them to the news media. Some companies choose to outsource their personal selling functions by hiring an intermediary to provide them with a contract sales force. These promotion efforts handled by intermediaries must be coordinated with the firm's overall marketing communication activities.

The logistics channel has many intermediaries, and many are mentioned in this book. A commonly used intermediary is the freight forwarder, whose function is to assemble small shipments into larger shipments and then tender them in truckload or rail carload quantities to truck lines or to railroads. In international logistics, intermediaries abound, and more than a hundred different types could be listed. One example is cargo surveyors who specialize in coffee; these specialists examine and arbitrate damage claims involving shipments of coffee beans.

ACTIVITIES IN THE LOGISTICAL CHANNEL

To successfully apply the systems and total cost approaches to logistics, it is essential to understand the various logistics activities. Keep in mind that because one logistics system does not fit all companies, the number of activities in a logistics system can vary from company to company. Activities that are considered to be logistics related include, but are not limited to, the following:

Customer service	Demand forecasting
Facility location decisions	International logistics
Inventory management	Materials handling
Order management	Packaging
Procurement	Reverse logistics
Transportation management	Warehousing management

Customer Service

There can be many definitions of customer service, such as "keeping existing customers happy." Customer service involves making sure that the right person receives the right product at the right place at the right time in the right condition and at the right cost. Customer service is discussed in greater detail in Chapter 7.

Demand Forecasting

Demand forecasting refers to efforts to estimate product demand in a future time period. The growing popularity of the supply chain concept has prompted increasing collaboration among supply chain partners with respect to demand forecasting. Such collaboration can enhance efficiency by reducing overall inventory levels in a supply chain. We discuss demand forecasting in Chapter 7.

Facility Location Decisions

It's often said that the success of a retail store depends on three factors: location, location, and location. It can also be said that the success of a particular logistics system is dependent on the location of the relevant warehousing and production facilities. Facility location decisions are increasingly important as the configuration of logistics systems is altered due to the impacts of multinational trade agreements. Facility location decisions are covered in Chapter 9.

International Logistics

International logistics, which refers to the logistics activities associated with goods that are sold across national boundaries, is much more costly and challenging than domestic logistics. We'll take a closer look at international logistics in Chapter 14.

Inventory Management

Inventory refers to stocks of goods that are maintained for a variety of purposes, such as for resale to others, as well as to support manufacturing or assembling processes. When managing inventory, logisticians need to simultaneously consider three relevant costs—the cost of carrying (holding) product, the cost of ordering product, and the cost of being out of stock. Chapter 8 provides further discussion concerning inventory management.

Materials Handling

Materials handling refers to the short-distance movement of products within the confines of a facility (e.g., plant, warehouse), and materials handling considerations are presented in Chapter 11.

Order Management

Order management refers to management of the activities that take place between the time a customer places an order and the time it is received by the customer. As such, order management is a logistics activity with a high degree of visibility to customers; order management is discussed in Chapter 7.

Packaging

Packaging can have both a marketing (consumer packaging) and logistical (industrial packaging) dimension. Industrial (protective) packaging refers to packaging that prepares a product for storage and transit (e.g., boxes, crates), and packaging has important interfaces with the materials handling and warehousing activities. As such, Chapter 11 discusses packaging in conjunction with materials handling.

Procurement

Procurement refers to the raw materials, component parts, and supplies bought from outside organizations to support a company's operations.[34] Procurement's direct link to outside

---

[34]Donald J. Bowersox, David J. Closs, and M. Bixby Cooper, *Supply Chain Logistics Management* (Boston, MA: McGraw-Hill Irwin, 2002).

organizations means that its strategic importance has increased as supply chain management has become more popular. Procurement is discussed in more detail in Chapter 6.

Reverse Logistics

Products can be returned for various reasons, such as product recalls, product damage, lack of demand, and customer dissatisfaction. The challenges associated with reverse logistics can be complicated by the fact that returned products often move in small quantities and may move outside forward distribution channels. Reverse logistics is examined in Chapter 4.

Transportation Management

Transportation can be defined as the actual physical movement of goods or people from one place to another, whereas transportation management refers to the management of transportation activities by a particular organization. Transportation can account for up to 50 percent of a firm's total logistics costs and thus represents the most costly logistics activity in many organizations. The transportation system is discussed in Chapter 12, and transportation management is discussed in Chapter 13.

Warehousing Management

Warehousing refers to places where inventory can be stored for a particular period of time. As noted previously, important changes have occurred with respect to warehousing's role in contemporary logistics and supply chain systems. Warehousing is discussed in Chapter 10.

LOGISTICS CAREERS

The logistics manager has a highly complex and challenging position, in part because the logistician needs to be both a generalist and a specialist. As a generalist, the logistician must understand the relationship between logistics and other corporate functions, both within and outside the firm. As a specialist, the logistician must understand the relationships between various logistics activities and must have some technical knowledge of the various activities.

Despite the current tepid economic conditions, the job market for logisticians continues to be strong at both the undergraduate and MBA levels. Indeed, the magazine *U.S. News & World Report* highlighted has "logistician" as one of the 50 best careers and suggested that logistics employment should increase by 20 percent through 2018.[35] Logistics-related jobs include, but are not limited to, logistics analyst, consultant, customer service manager, purchasing manager, transportation manager, and warehouse operations manager.[36] In the United States, compensation levels for entry-level positions requiring an undergraduate degree in logistics can range from the upper $30K to the mid-$50K level.

Because of the growing importance of logistics, a number of professional organizations are dedicated to advancing the professional knowledge of their members. One rationale for these professional associations is that the state of the art is changing so rapidly that professionals must educate and reeducate themselves on a regular basis. Several prominent professional logistics organizations are summarized in Appendix 1.

---

[35]Liz Wolgemuth, "The 50 Best Careers of 2010," *U.S. News & World Report*, December 28, 2009.
[36]www.cscmp.org

Summary

This chapter introduced the topic of logistics, which the CSCMP defines as "that part of Supply Chain Management that plans, implements, and controls the efficient, effective forward and reverse flow and storage of goods, services, and related information between the point of origin and the point of consumption in order to meet customers' requirements."

The economic impacts of logistics were discussed along with reasons for the increased importance of logistics since 1980. Systems and total cost approaches to logistics were discussed, as were logistical relationships within a firm, with a particular focus on various interfaces between marketing and logistics. A short description of a number of logistics activities was presented, and the chapter concluded with a brief look at logistics careers.

Questions for Discussion and Review

1.1 Did it surprise you that logistics has such an important economic impact? Why or why not?

1.2 Distinguish between possession, form, time, and place utility.

1.3 How does logistics contribute to time and place utility?

1.4 How can a particular logistics system be effective but not efficient?

1.5 Explain the significance of the fact that the purpose of logistics is to meet customer requirements.

1.6 Explain how an understanding of logistics management could be relevant to your favorite charitable organization.

1.7 How has a reduction in economic regulation contributed to the increased importance of logistics?

1.8 Discuss the logistical implications associated with the increased emphasis on the convenience associated with a family's shopping experience.

1.9 Explain how big-box retailers are logistical trendsetters.

1.10 What is the systems approach to problem solving? How is this concept applicable to logistics management?

1.11 Distinguish between materials management and physical distribution.

1.12 Explain what is meant by the total cost approach to logistics.

1.13 Define what is meant by a cost trade-off. Do you believe that this concept is workable? Why or why not?

1.14 What are several areas in which finance and logistics might interface?

1.15 Discuss the postponement concept as it relates to the production and logistics interface.

1.16 Define what is meant by a landed cost and explain its relevance for pricing decisions.

1.17 Discuss several possible interfaces between marketing and logistics in terms of product decisions.

1.18 Briefly discuss the ownership, negotiations, financing, promotions, and logistics channels.

1.19 Discuss five activities that might be part of a company's logistics department.

1.20 Logistics managers must be both generalists and specialists. Why is this true? Does this help to explain why there tends to be an imbalance in the supply of, and demand for, logistics managers?

Suggested Readings

Day, Jamison M., Steven A. Melnyk, Paul D. Larson, Edward W. Davis, and D. Clay Whybark. "Humanitarian and Disaster Relief Supply Chains: A Matter of Life and Death." *Journal of Supply Chain Management* 48, no. 2 (2012): 21–36.

Genchev, Stefan E. "Reverse Logistics Program Design: A Company Study." *Business Horizons* 52, no. 2 (2009): 139–148.

Jon, Seong-Jong, Hokey Min, Ik-Whan G. Kwon, and Heboong Kwon. "Comparative Efficiencies of Specialty Coffee Retailers from the Perspectives of Socially Responsible Global Sourcing." *International Journal of Logistics Management* 21, no. 3 (2010): 490–509.

Larson, Paul D., Richard F. Poist, and Arni Halldosson. "Perspectives on Logistics vs. SCM: A Survey of SCM Professionals." *Journal of Business Logistics* 28, no. 1 (2007): 1–24.

Lynch, J. and L. Whicker. "Do Logistics and Marketing Understand Each Other? An Empirical Investigation of the Interface Activities between Logistics and Marketing." *International Journal of Logistics: Research & Applications* 11, no. 3 (2008): 167–178.

Ozment, John and Scott Keller. "The Future of Logistics Education." *Transportation Journal* 50, no. 1 (2011): 65–83.

Perego, Alessandro, Sara Perotti, and Ricardo Mangiarcina. "ICT for Logistics and Freight Transportation: A Literature Review and Research Agenda." *International Journal of Physical Distribution & Logistics Management* 41, no. 5 (2011): 457–483.

Spillan, John E., Michael A. McGinnis, Ali Kara, and George Liu Yi. "A Comparison of the Effect of Logistic Strategy and

Logistics Integration on Firm Competitiveness in the USA and China." *International Journal of Logistics Management* 24, no. 2 (2013).

Stank, Theodore P., J. Paul Dittman, and Chad W. Autry. "The New Supply Chain Agenda: A Synopsis and Directions for Future Research." *International Journal of Physical Distribution & Logistics Management* 41, no. 10 (2011): 940–955.

Tan, Vinh V. "Competency Requirements for Professionals in Logistics and Supply Chain Management." *International Journal of Logistics: Research and Applications* 15, no. 2 (2012): 109–126.

CASE

CASE 1.1   KiddieLand and the Super Gym

KiddieLand is a retailer of toys located in the Midwest. Corporate headquarters is in Chicago, and its 70 stores are located in Minnesota, Wisconsin, Michigan, Illinois, Indiana, Ohio, Iowa, and Kentucky. One distribution center is located in Columbus (for Kentucky, Indiana, Michigan, and Ohio) and one in Chicago (for Illinois, Iowa, Minnesota, and Wisconsin).

KiddieLand markets a full range of toys, electronic games, computers, and play sets. Emphasis is on a full line of brand-name products together with selected items sold under the KiddieLand brand. KiddieLand's primary competitors include various regional discount chains. The keys to KiddieLand's success have been a comprehensive product line, aggressive pricing, and self-service.

Donald Hurst is KiddieLand's logistics manager. He is responsible for managing both distribution centers, for transportation management, and for inventory control. Don's primary mission is to make sure all stores are in stock at all times without maintaining excessive levels of inventory.

One morning in late January, while Don was reviewing the new year's merchandising plan, he discovered that starting in March, KiddieLand would begin promoting the Super Gym Outdoor Children's Exercise Center. Don was particularly interested that the new set would sell for $715. In addition, the Super Gym is packaged in three boxes weighing a total of 450 pounds. "Holy cow!" thought Don. "The largest set we have sold to date retails for $159 and weighs only 125 pounds."

"There must be some mistake," thought Don as he walked down the hall to the office of Olga Olsen, KiddieLand's buyer for play sets. Olga was new on her job and was unusually stressed because both of her assistant buyers had just resigned to seek employment on the West Coast.

As soon as Olga saw Don, she exclaimed, "Don, my friend, I have been meaning to talk to you." Don knew right then that his worst fears were confirmed.

The next morning Don and Olga met with Randy Smith, Don's transportation manager; A. J. Toth, general manager for KiddieLand's eight Chicago stores; and Sharon Rabiega, Don's assistant for distribution services. Because the previous year had been unusually profitable, everyone was in a good mood because this year's bonus was 50 percent larger than last year's.

Nevertheless, A. J. got to the point: "You mean to tell me that we expect somebody to stuff a spouse, three kids, a dog, and 450 pounds of Super Gym in a small sedan and not have a conniption?"

Randy chimed in, "Besides, we can't drop ship Super Gyms from the manufacturer to the consumer's address because Super Gym ships only in quantities of 10 or more."

Olga was now worried. "We can't back out of the Super Gym now," she moaned. "I have already committed KiddieLand for 400 sets, and the spring–summer play set promotion went to press last week. Besides, I am depending on the Super Gym to make my gross margin figures."

"What about SUVs?" asked Toth. "They make up half the vehicles in our parking lots. Will the three packages fit inside them?"

By now the scope of the problem had become apparent to everyone at the meeting. At 3 P.M. Don summarized the alternatives discussed:

1. Purchase a two-wheeled trailer for each store.
2. Find a local trucking company that can haul the Super Gym from the KiddieLand store to the customer.
3. Stock the Super Gym at the two distribution centers and have the truck that makes delivery runs to the retail stores also make home deliveries.
4. Charge for delivery if the customer cannot get the Super Gym home.
5. Negotiate with the Super Gym manufacturer to ship directly to the customer.

When the meeting adjourned, everyone agreed to meet the following Monday to discuss the alternatives. On Thursday morning a record-breaking blizzard hit Chicago; everyone went home early. KiddieLand headquarters was closed on Friday because of the blizzard. By Wednesday, the same group met again.

Don started the meeting. "Okay," Don began, "let's review our options. Sharon, what did you find out about buying trailers for each store?"

"Well," Sharon began, "the best deal I can find is $1,800 per trailer for 70 trailers, plus $250 per store for an adequate selection of bumper hitches, and an additional $50 per year per store for licensing and insurance. Unfortunately, bumpers on the newest autos cannot accommodate trailer hitches."

"Oh, no," moaned Olga, "we only expect to sell 5.7 sets per store. That means $368 per Super Gym for delivery," she continued as she punched her calculator, "and $147 in lost gross margin!"

Next, Randy Smith summarized the second option. "So far we can get delivery within 25 miles of most of our stores for $38.21 per set. Actually," Randy continued, "$38.21 is for delivery 25 miles from the store. The rate would be a little less for under 25 miles and about $1.50 per mile beyond 25 miles."

A. J. Toth chimed in, "According to our marketing research, 85 percent of our customers drive less than 25 minutes to the store, so a flat fee of $40 for delivery would probably be okay."

Randy continued, "Most delivery companies we talked to will deliver twice weekly but not daily."

Sharon continued, "The motor carrier that handles shipments from our distribution centers is a consolidator. He said that squeezing an 18-wheeler into some subdivisions wouldn't make sense. Every time they try, they knock down a couple of mailboxes and leave truck tracks in some homeowner's lawn."

Olga added, "I talked to Super Gym about shipping direct to the customer's address, and they said forget it. Whenever they have tried that," Olga continued, "the customer gets two of one box and none of another."

"Well, Olga," Don interrupted, "can we charge the customer for delivery?"

Olga thought a minute. "Well, we have never done that before, but then we have never sold a 450-pound item before. It sounds like," Olga continued, "our choice is to either absorb $40 per set or charge the customer for delivery."

"That means $16,000 for delivery," she added.

"One more thing," Don said. "If we charge for shipping, we must include that in the copy for the spring–summer brochure."

Olga smiled. "We can make a minor insert in the copy if we decide to charge for delivery. However," she continued, "any changes will have to be made to the page proofs—and page proofs are due back to the printer next Monday."

Questions

1. List and discuss the advantages and disadvantages of purchasing a two-wheeled trailer for each store to use for delivering Super Gyms.
2. List and discuss the advantages and disadvantages of having local trucking companies deliver the Super Gym from the retail stores to the customers.
3. List and discuss the advantages and disadvantages of stocking Super Gyms at the distribution centers, and then having the truck that makes deliveries from the distribution center to the retail stores also make deliveries of Super Gyms to individual customers.
4. List and discuss the advantages and disadvantages of charging customers for home delivery if they are unable to carry home the Super Gym.
5. Which alternative would you prefer? Why?
6. Draft a brief statement (catalog copy) to be inserted in the firm's spring–summer brochure that clearly explains to potential customers the policy you recommended in Question 5.
7. In the first meeting, A. J. asked about SUVs, but there was no further mention of them. How would you follow up on his query?

APPENDIX 1

Logistics Professional Organizations

APICS—The Association for Operations Management (www.apics.org)

APICS "builds and validates knowledge in supply chain and operations management." APICS offers three certification programs: Certified in Production and Inventory Management (CPIM), Certified Fellow in Production and Inventory Management (CFPIM), and Certified Supply Chain Professional (CSCP).

American Society of Transportation and Logistics (AST&L) (www.astl.org)

AST&L strives "to promote and ensure a highest level of global standards through professional certification in the field of transportation and logistics." It offers four certification programs: Certified in Transportation and Logistics (CTL), Professional Designation in Logistics and Supply Chain Management (PLS), Distinguished Logistics Professional (DLP), and Global Logistics Associate (GLA).

Council of Supply Chain Management Professionals (CSCMP) (www.cscmp.org)

Formerly known as the Council of Logistics Management, the CSCMP's mission aims to be at the forefront of supply chain knowledge and research. CSCMP offers a three-level certification program, SCPro™.

International Society of Logistics (SOLE) (www.sole.org)

The International Society of Logistics, formerly the Society of Logistics Engineers, is a "non-profit international professional society composed of individuals organized to enhance the art and science of logistics technology, education and management." It has several certification programs: the Demonstrated Logistician Program (DL Program), the Certified Professional Logistician Program (CPL), and the Certified Master Logistician Program (CML).

The Chartered Institute of Logistics and Transport in the UK—CILT (UK) (www.ciltuk.org.uk)

CILT (UK) "is the preeminent independent professional body for individuals associated with logistics, supply chain and all transport throughout their careers." CILT offers the Chartered Membership designation, which reflects educational achievement as well as significant practical experience.

Warehousing Education and Research Council (WERC) (www.werc.org)

WERC is a "professional organization focused exclusively on distribution and warehousing management and its role in the supply chain." It emphasizes education and learning, research into industry issues, and networking opportunities.

2 LOGISTICS AND INFORMATION TECHNOLOGY

The logistics discipline has been through many changes since the first edition of this book was published in the mid-1970s. The first edition, for example, primarily focused on physical distribution management, and the corresponding definition emphasized the *movement and storage of goods.* The current edition of this book, by contrast, is focused on logistics and its role in supply chain management. Moreover, the corresponding definition of logistics (see Chapter 1) mentions the *flows and storage of goods, services, and related information.*

The effective and efficient utilization of information can be quite beneficial to logistics and supply chain management, and four of the more prominent benefits include the following:

- Greater knowledge and visibility across the supply chain, which makes it possible to replace inventory with information
- Greater awareness of customer demand via point-of-sale data, which can help improve planning and reduce variability in the supply chain

- Better coordination of manufacturing, marketing, and distribution through enterprise resource planning (ERP) systems
- Streamlined order processing and reduced lead times enabled by coordinated logistics information systems.[1]

Successful implementation and exploitation of the right information technologies is critical to maintaining competitiveness.[2] Additionally, the effective and efficient use of information allows organizations to simultaneously reduce their costs and improve customer satisfaction in the sense that organizations stock the inventory that will be demanded by customers. For example, several U.S.-based grocery chains have carefully studied Hispanic consumers and learned that they place greater emphasis on fresh produce than do other ethnic groups. As such, grocery stores located in heavily Hispanic areas often stock more fresh produce than do grocery stores located in other areas.

Before proceeding further, it's important to distinguish between **data** and **information**: "data are simply facts—recorded measures of certain phenomena—whereas information is a body of facts in a format suitable for decision making."[3] Advances in technological hardware and software now allow logisticians access to abundant amounts of data in relatively short periods of time. In attempting to manage this data, managers must first determine which data are relevant for their purposes. Next the data need to be organized and analyzed; once analyzed, managers should make the appropriate decision or decisions. In today's competitive business environment, these actions must be completed in as short a time period as possible.

One contemporary issue for logisticians to consider is the emergence of what industry has termed **big data**—the collection of large amounts of near-real-time data collected through a variety of sources, such as sensors, smart phones, RF tags and business-to-business data exchanges. Logisticians will need to develop strategies for how they can manage the flood of data that will be available to help them manage assets, increase visibility and enhance communications across the supply chain. The opportunity will be to use this data to sense changes in demand and then use logistics activities to effectively and efficiently respond to these changes.[4]

The next section of this chapter will provide an overview of general types of information management systems that are applicable across each business function. In addition, examples of how these general types of information systems might be specifically applied in logistics management are provided. This will be followed by an explanation of the Internet's influence on logistics, and the chapter will conclude with a look at select information technology challenges.

GENERAL TYPES OF INFORMATION MANAGEMENT SYSTEMS

Professor Steven Alter has identified six different types of information systems that are applicable to every business function.[5] These six categories, summarized in Figure 2.1, form the basis of this section.

---

[1]Stephen M. Rutner, Brian J. Gibson, Kate L. Vitasek, and Craig G. Gustin, "Is Technology Filling the Information Gap?" *Supply Chain Management Review,* March/April 2001, 58–63.
[2]Benjamin T. Hazen and Terry Anthony Byrd, "Toward Creating Competitive Advantage with Logistics Information Technology," *International Journal of Physical Distribution & Logistics Management* 42, no. 1 (2012): 8–35.
[3]William G. Zikmund and Michael d'Amico, *Marketing,* 7th ed. (Cincinnati, OH: South-Western, 2001), p. 125.
[4]Robert F. Byrne, "Driving Profitable Growth with Big Data and Better Forecasts," *Supply Chain Europe* 21, no. 1 (2012): 40–41.
[5]The framework in this section is adapted from S. Alter, *Information Systems,* 4th ed. (Upper Saddle River, NJ: Prentice Hall, 2002).

System type	Logistics examples
Office automation system: provides effective ways to process personal and organizational business data, to perform calculations, and to create documents	Spreadsheet applications to calculate optimal order quantities, facility location, transport cost minimization, among others
Communication system: helps people work together by interacting and sharing information in many different forms	Virtual meetings via computer technology Voice-based order picking
Transaction processing system (TPS): collects and stores information about transactions; controls some aspects of transactions	Electronic data interchange Automatic identification technologies such as bar codes Point-of-sale systems
Management information system (MIS) and executive information system (EIS): converts TPS data into information for monitoring performance and managing an organization; provides executives information in a readily accessible format	Logistics information system
Decision support system (DSS): helps people make decisions by providing information, models, or analysis tools	Simulation Application-specific software such as warehouse management systems Data mining
Enterprise system: creates and maintains consistent data processing methods and an integrated database across multiple business functions	Logistics modules of enterprise resource planning systems

FIGURE 2.1 General Types of Information Management Systems   *Source:* Taken from Steven Alter, *Information Systems,* 4th ed. (Upper Saddle River, NJ: Prentice Hall, 2002), p. 191.

Office Automation Systems

Office automation systems provide effective ways to process personal and organizational business data, to perform calculations, and to create documents.[6] Included in office automation systems are general software packages—word processing, spreadsheet, presentation, and database management applications—that most of you probably learned in an introductory computer class.

The most relevant general software package for logisticians is the spreadsheet. Whereas early spreadsheet programs for personal computers were little more than speedy calculators, today's spreadsheets have a multitude of capabilities that allow managers to solve a variety of complex business problems relatively quickly and inexpensively.

Indeed, logistics spreadsheet applications into the early 1990s tended to reflect the rather limited capabilities of the existing software packages. For example, representative topics included economic order quantity (EOQ) calculations, warehouse sizing, transportation modal and carrier decisions, production planning, and center of gravity location decisions, among others.[7] As we moved through the 1990s, increased spreadsheet capabilities allowed organizations to analyze issues that had traditionally been solved by specially designed computer programs. In this vein, the classic issue of transportation cost minimization—transporting products from multiple

---

[6]Alter, *Information Systems,* p. 191.
[7]John E. Tyworth and William L. Grenoble, "Spreadsheet Modeling in Logistics: Advancing Today's Educational Tools," *Journal of Business Logistics* 12, no. 1 (1991): 1–25.

sources to multiple destinations, at a minimum transportation cost—could be analyzed using spreadsheet software.[8]

Today spreadsheets have developed to the point that they are able to solve for basic logistics optimization models. **Logistics optimization models** utilize spreadsheet software and add-ins to help logisticians make complex judgments and decisions about key logistics issues at strategic, tactical, operational and collaborative levels.[9] For example, at a strategic level global consumer products company P&G uses spreadsheets with the add-in package "What's Best" to help them make decisions regarding plant location and size decisions.[10] Logistics optimization models differ from traditional operations research in that they are typically focused on the practical implementation instead of pure optimization.[11] Thus, the use of spreadsheets provides a method for logisticians to conduct a variety of "what-if" analyses in support of their logistics decision making.

Communication Systems

Communication systems help various stakeholders—employees, suppliers, customers—work together by interacting and sharing information in many different forms.[12] From a logistical perspective, the importance of well-defined and well-executed communication systems was highlighted by the events of September 11, 2001, especially for companies that use or provide airfreight services. Because of the total shutdown of the U.S. aviation system for several days following the terrorist attacks, many air shipments were diverted onto trucks, thus delaying many deliveries. As such, airfreight providers such as FedEx worked feverishly to inform customers when their shipments would be arriving.[13]

Many advances in telecommunication technology—such as fax machines, personal computers, electronic mail, cellular phones, tablets and smart phones, among others—have occurred since the first edition of this book was published in the 1970s. As recently as the 1990s, some of these technologies were considered workplace "luxuries." Today, by contrast, many of these technologies are essential for enabling the contemporary logistician to perform in the workplace.

Electronic data interchange, or EDI (to be discussed in the next section), was viewed by many experts as the measuring stick for logistics information technology in the 1990s. By contrast, **wireless communication** emerged as the measuring stick during the first decade of the twenty-first century.[14] For our purposes, wireless communication refers to communication without cables and cords and includes infrared, microwave, and radio transmissions, among others.

Although wireless communication has many logistical applications, we'll take a look at one of the more popular types, namely, global positioning systems. **Global positioning systems**, or GPS, refer to a network of satellites that transmits signals that pinpoint the exact location of an object. You might be familiar with global positioning systems in the form of personal navigation devices that provide maps or voice instructions as you drive your automobile.

Global positioning systems have become quite valuable to the transportation component of logistics because of high fuel costs and the relentless pressure to improve efficiency and productivity. Indeed, transportation companies that have implemented global positioning systems have reported an increase in worker productivity, reduced operating costs, and improved customer

---

[8]Brian J. Parker and David J. Caine, "Minimizing Transportation Costs: An Efficient and Effective Approach for the Spreadsheet User," *Transport Logistics* 1, no. 2 (1997): 129–137.

[9]Michael R. Bartolacci, Larry J. LeBlanc, Yasanur Kayikei, and Thomas A. Grossman, "Optimization Modeling for Logistics: Options and Implementations," *Journal of Business Logistics* 33, no. 2 (2012): 118–127.

[10]G. Anthes, "Modeling Magic: IT-Based Operations Research Builds Better Supply Chains at Procter & Gamble," http://www.computerworld.com/s/article/99484/ModelingMagic.

[11]Bartolacci et al., "Optimization Modeling for Logistics."

[12]Alter, *Information Systems*, Chapter 5.

[13]Kristen S. Krause, "FedEx's 9–11 Response," *Traffic World*, September 9, 2002, 12–13.

[14]Roger Morton, "Working Without a Wire," *Logistics Today*, February 2005, 29–33.

relations. More specifically, one study found that GPS implementation allows transportation companies to recapture nearly one hour per day of their drivers' time, which translates into labor savings of approximately $5,500 per employee. The same study also reported that GPS implementation allows companies to reduce vehicle travel by about 230 miles per week, for an annual fuel savings of approximately $52,000.[15]

Tablets, such as Apple's iPad, are also becoming important contributors to logistics decision making. The use of these types of consumer-grade mobile devices in an industrial setting, such as a warehouse or port, may require the device to become "ruggedized" in order to withstand the conditions that exist in these locations.[16] For example, Markley Enterprises, a manufacturer of marketing support products, uses iPads along with third-party apps to enhance the productivity of their warehouse workers, improve pick accuracy, and eliminate paperwork.[17] Similarly, Cleveland-based Arhaus Furniture placed iPads in their delivery trucks, which has led to savings in paperwork costs, increased truck utilization, and improved customer service.[18]

Continuing advances in hardware and software have resulted in dramatic cost reductions for wireless communication, and one implication is that the technology is no longer limited to those companies with the deepest financial resources. Moreover, hardware and software cost reductions have shortened the relevant investment payback period and GPS implementations can pay for themselves within one year.[19]

Transaction Processing Systems (TPS)

A *transaction processing system*, or TPS, collects and stores information about transactions and may also control some aspects of transactions. The primary objective of a TPS is the efficient processing of transactions, and to this end, organizations can choose to do batch or real-time processing.[20] With batch processing, data are collected and stored for processing at a later time, with the later time perhaps being based on schedule (e.g., process every six hours) or volume (e.g., process once 25 transactions have accumulated) considerations. Real-time processing, not surprisingly, means that transactions are processed as they are received. Although batch processing might be somewhat out of step with the contemporary emphasis on speed and time reduction, it can be quite effective when real-time processing is not necessary. Moreover, in comparison with real-time systems, batch processing tends to be less costly and easier for employees to learn.

A prominent example of a logistics-related TPS is **electronic data interchange (EDI)**, the computer-to-computer transmission of business data in a structured format. Because EDI provides for the seamless transmission of data across companies (assuming technological compatibility), it can facilitate the integration of, and coordination between, supply chain participants. Thus, firms with strong EDI links to both suppliers and customers might have a substantial advantage over supply chain arrangements without such implementations. Common uses of EDI include invoicing, submission of purchase orders, pricing, advanced shipment notices, electronic funds transfer, and bill payment.

EDI has a number of benefits, including reductions in document preparation and processing time, inventory carrying costs, personnel costs, information float, shipping errors, returned goods, lead times, order cycle times, and ordering costs. In addition, EDI may lead to increases in cash flow, billing accuracy, productivity, and customer satisfaction. Potential drawbacks to EDI include a lack of awareness of its benefits, high setup costs, lack of standard formats, and incompatibility of computer hardware and software.

---

[15]Bridget McCrea, "The Golden Age of Wireless," *Logistics Management*, October 2008, 47–50.
[16]Mary Shacklett, "Supply Chain Technology Prospects for the Warehouse," *World Trade: WT 100* 25, no. 3 (2012): 24–28.
[17]Andrew K. Reese, "iPad in the Warehouse," *Supply & Demand Chain Executive* 11, no. 3 (2010): 14–17.
[18]Heath E. Combs, "Arhaus to Equip Trucks with iPads," *Furniture Today* 34, no. 47 (2010): 34.
[19]No author, "Remote Asset Management Worth the Cost," *GPSWorld*, January 2009, 27.
[20]Alter, *Information Systems*, Chapter 5.

Despite these drawbacks and a perception that EDI is an "old" technology,[21] EDI continues to be an important logistics technology tool in the twenty-first century. Moreover, while the Internet was viewed by some as a possible replacement or substitute for EDI, time has shown that the Internet can serve as a complement to, rather than a replacement or substitute for, EDI. For example, Walmart was one of the first companies to adopt Internet-based EDI (I-EDI) in place of Value Added Network (VAN)-based EDI. Importantly, I-EDI's significantly lower setup costs than VAN-based EDI make I-EDI more affordable for smaller companies, thus expanding EDI's scope.[22]

Automatic identification technologies, another type of logistics-related TPS, include optical character recognition (which can read letters, words, and numbers), machine vision (which can scan, inspect, and interpret what it views), voice-data entry (which can record and interpret a human voice), radio-frequency identification (which can be used where there is no line of sight between scanner and label), and magnetic strips.

Automatic identification systems are an essential component in point-of-sale (POS) systems and the idea behind POS systems is to provide data to guide and enhance managerial decision-making. Operationally, POS systems involve scanning Universal Product Code (UPC) labels, either by passing the product over an optical scanner or recording it with a handheld scanner. The UPC is read and recorded into a database that supplies information such as the product's price, applicable taxes, whether food stamps can be used, and so on. The specific price of each product and its description are also flashed on a monitor screen positioned near the counter. When all the products have been recorded, the customer receives verification that lists the products purchased, the price of each article, and the total bill.

Bar code scanners currently remain the most popular automatic identification system in use. They work to integrate suppliers and customers along the supply chain because all parties read the same labels; in addition, the transfer of goods between parties can be recorded by simple electronic means. Traditionally, laser scanners have been used to read bar codes. The scanners record inventory data and may be directly attached to a computer that uses the data to adjust inventory records and track product movement.

Radio-frequency identification (RFID) technology is another automatic identification technology that has received considerable attention in the first part of the twenty-first century. Conceptually, RFID involves the use of radio frequency to identify objects that have been implanted with an RFID tag. Operationally, RFID consists of three components, a scanning antenna, an RFID tag (chip) that conveys the relevant data, and a transceiver that interprets the data. As an RFID tag passes within the scanning antenna's range, the tag's data are picked up by the scanning antenna and interpreted by the transceiver. Compared to bar codes, RFID (1) does not require clear line of sight between an object and RFID hardware, (2) can store much larger quantities of data, and (3) can offer both read and write capabilities.

A major catalyst for RFID usage in logistics was a Walmart mandate that by January 1, 2005, its top 100 suppliers deploy RFID tags on shipments into one particular Walmart distribution center in Texas. While this goal has not been realized, Walmart's mandate jumpstarted a technology that had existed since the 1940s but that had not been widely used by organizations. As a result, there has been significant improvement in the technology and costs are coming down. The apparel and health care industries are approaching a critical mass of users. Many large retail companies are using RFID to track individual items of clothing and roughly 10 percent of hospitals in the United States have some form of RFID system installed.[23]

A number of benefits have been reported by adopters of RFID technology. For example, dramatic reductions (between 20 percent and 50 percent) in inventory stockouts have been

---

[21]Malcolm Wheatley, "A Question of Standards," *Automotive Logistics*, September/October 2008, 60–64.
[22]Zhenyu Hang, Brian D. Janz, and Mark N. Frolik, "A Comprehensive Examination of Internet-EDI Adoption," *Information Systems Management* 25, no. 3 (2008): 273–286.
[23]No author, "Will 2012 See Widespread Adoption of RFID?" *RFID Journal*, January/February (2012): 6–9.

reported by Walmart and some its suppliers.[24] In addition, RFID reduced the time needed to count inventory by 80 percent and improved the accuracy of inventory counts at one clothing retailer.[25] Despite the potential benefits associated with RFID, various challenges must be addressed before the technology becomes more widely used in logistics. A major drawback to more widespread RFID adoption involves the costs of installing the related hardware and software, which can range from $100,000 for smaller companies to $20 million for larger companies.

Another drawback to RFID involves privacy concerns, such as the inappropriate use of the technology. For example, a major retailer embedded RFID chips into a particular line of cosmetic products, and consumers who selected this product from the store shelf were beamed, via webcam, to the manufacturer's headquarters![26] Yet another drawback is that data accuracy can be lower in items with high moisture content, such as fruits and vegetables.

Management Information Systems (MIS) and Executive Information Systems (EIS)

These systems convert TPS data into information for monitoring performance and managing an organization, with the objective of providing managers and executives with the information they really need.[27] To this end, a **logistics information system** (LIS) can be defined as "the people, equipment, and procedures to gather, sort, analyze, evaluate, and distribute needed, timely, and accurate information to logistics decision makers."[28]

As shown in Figure 2.2, an LIS begins with a logistics manager requesting information and ends with the manager receiving regular and customized reports. For logistics managers to receive *needed* information, it's important that they be fairly specific when submitting requests. For example, a logistics manager who wants information about a specific warehouse or distribution center needs to request information on, say, "the Chicago warehouse," rather than information on "corporate warehouses."

Timely information would appear to be incumbent on the effectiveness and efficiency of a company's particular LIS and timely information can encompass several dimensions. However, *timely* can refer to the up-to-date status of information, which can be influenced by a company's collection and analysis procedures. Information collection should emphasize both internal and external sources; unfortunately, internal sources of logistics information are not always as plentiful

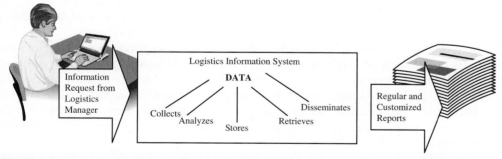

FIGURE 2.2 Structure and Function of a Logistics Information System *Source:* Adapted from Michael Etzel, Bruce Walker, and William Stanton, *Marketing,* 14th ed. (New York: McGraw-Hill Irwin, 2007), p. 172.

[24]John S. Webster, "Wall-Mart's RFID Revolution a Tough Sell," *Network World,* September 15, 2008, 34–36.

[25]Alan M. Field, "Tag, You're It!" *Florida Shipper,* October 13, 2008, 10–11.

[26]Tom Andel, "Big Brother in Aisle Five?" *Paperboard Packaging,* February 2006, 4.

[27]Alter, *Information Systems,* Chapter 5.

[28]Adapted from a definition of "marketing information system" provided by Philip Kotler and Gary Armstrong in *Principles of Marketing,* 11th ed. (Upper Saddle River, NJ: Prentice Hall, 2006), Chapter 4.

as desired. Indeed, research into the business value attributable to logistics discovered that "logistics measurement is happening much less frequently than one might imagine."[29] External sources focus on information from outside the company and include information about customers, competitors, and suppliers, along with information about economic, technological, political, legal, and sociocultural environments.

Timely also can refer to how quickly managers receive the information requested; this is affected by each company's retrieval and dissemination procedures. A manager's ability to quickly receive information can be influenced by technology hardware and software, and faster and more powerful technology has helped to reduce retrieval and dissemination times. Alternatively, retrieval and dissemination can be slowed by hardware and software glitches, including incompatible hardware or software, power outages, system crashes, and computer viruses.

Accurate information may also reflect the effectiveness and efficiency of a company's logistics information system. As such, an LIS must be concerned with the nature and quality of the relevant data; for instance, although the Internet can provide access to tremendous amounts of external information at a very low cost, the validity of some Internet information is suspect. Keep in mind the *GIGO*—garbage in/garbage out—principle: Information that is erroneous, misrepresented, or unclear will likely result in poor decisions by logisticians.

Decision Support Systems (DSS)

Decision support systems help managers make decisions by providing information, models, or analysis tools,[30] and they can be widely applied and used by logisticians. Specific uses of DSS in logistics include, but are not limited to, vehicle routing issues, inventory control decisions, developing automatic order picking systems, and optimization models for buyer–seller negotiations. Several of the more prominent logistics-related DSS techniques are discussed in the following paragraphs.

Simulation is a technique that models a real-world system, typically using mathematical equations to represent the relationships among the system's components. Simulation reliability is achieved by making the model as akin to the real world as possible. Although simulation can be a powerful analytic tool, a poorly constructed simulation involving bad data or inaccurate assumptions about the relationships among variables can deliver suboptimal or unworkable solutions to logistics problems.

The primary advantage of simulation is that it enables the firm to test the feasibility of proposed changes at relatively little expense. In addition, it prevents firms from experiencing the public embarrassment of making a major change in their logistics system that might result in a deterioration of customer service levels or an increase in total operating expense.

A second type of DSS is what can be broadly labeled as **application-specific software**, which has been developed to help managers deal with specific logistics processes or activities. Traditionally, application-specific software often involved customers purchasing a particular software package and then having the software installed (i.e., so-called "purchase and install") on their computer(s). The purchase and install option was (is) quite expensive in the sense that the software costs can approach $500,000 while implementation costs can run into the several millions of dollars.

An increasingly popular option for application-specific software is **on-demand software (also referred to as software-as-a-service** or **cloud computing**), or "software that users access on a per-use basis instead of software they own or license for installation."[31] A major advantage

[29]James S. Keebler, Karl B. Manrodt, David A. Durtsche, and D. Michael Ledyard, *Keeping Score: Measuring the Business Value of Logistics in the Supply Chain* (Oak Brook, IL: Council of Logistics Management, 1999), Chapter 2.

[30]Alter, *Information Systems*, Chapter 5.

[31]David Hannon, "On-Demand Brings Spend Control to the Masses," *Purchasing*, March 2, 2006, 40–42.

of on-demand vis-à-vis purchase and install software is on-demand's pay-per-use model allows customers to avoid high capital investment costs (we'll look more closely at on-demand software later in the chapter).

Transportation management systems (TMS) and **warehouse management systems (WMS)** are two prominent examples of logistics-related application-specific software. Indeed, an annual software survey conducted by *Logistics Management* magazine has consistently found that TMS and WMS software are the most likely applications to be purchased or upgraded.[32] Due to their importance as logistical decision support systems, we'll take a brief look at transportation management systems and warehouse management systems.

A transportation management system is a software package that automates the process of building orders, tending loads, tracking shipments, audits, and payments.[33] Table 2.1 presents a representative list of 15 tasks that might be performed by a TMS package. Organizations that have implemented TMS software have reported decreases in empty vehicle miles, reduced fuel consumption, and reduced transportation expenditures.

The demand for TMSs continues to grow driven by several factors. These factors include the following: older TMS systems needing upgrades, the growth of intermodal transportation, the improvement of TMS capabilities beyond just execution, the emergence of the previously described "big data", and a desire for more holistic solutions.[34] In addition, the use of a TMS is now seen as one way for an organization to improve the environmental sustainability of their logistics activities. By using the information provided, companies can get their freight to where and when it is needed in a more environmentally efficient manner.[35]

Warehouse management systems are software packages that provide oversight of the storage and flow of materials within a company's operations.[36] Activities that can be controlled by a WMS include inventory management, product receiving, determination of storage locations, order selection processes, and order shipping. Potential benefits to warehouse management system include dramatic reductions in data entry errors as well as dramatic reductions in the travel distances for order picking. Other benefits to WMS include reduced operating expenses, fewer stockouts, increased inventory accuracy, and improved service to customers.

Research has shown that firms that have adopted and implemented a WMS have significantly more efficient logistics processes than nonadopters. Adopters were found to spend less on

Table 2.1   Transportation Management Systems Task Capabilities

Task Capability	Task Capability
Asset tracking	Carrier selection
Claims management	Driver management
Freight payment	Load planning
Load tendering	Order or shipment visibility
Package delivery verification	Package pickup tracking
Pickup scheduling	Rating
Real-time route reporting	Route optimization
Shipment consolidation	

Source: "Transportation Management Systems Solution Selector," *Logistics Today,* September 2004, 76–80.

---

[32]Bridget McCrea, "Scrutiny Rules the Day," *Logistics Management,* April 2009, 38–40.

[33]Amy Zuckerman, "Transportation Management Systems Give Shippers Power to Make Smarter Trucking Choices," *World Trade,* January 2008, 34–38.

[34]Bridget McCrea, "5 Trends Driving TMS Growth," *Logistics Management* 51, no. 1 (2012): 42–44.

[35]Simon Kaye, "Green is the Color of Today's TMS," *Material Handling & Logistics* 67, no. 2 (2012): 33–34.

[36]Dave Piasecki, "Warehouse Management Systems," www.inventoryops.com.

their overall logistics processes, even though the costs of the WMS affected the costs of operating their warehouse. The results are largely driven by the increased visibility that is provided by the WMS.[37]

Because of the many different TMS and WMS options that are available to a logistics manager, it's important that an organization utilizes a software package that best suits its needs, as opposed to one from a "name" provider or one that offers many unneeded options. Moreover, the installation of a TMS or WMS can cause organizational upheaval in the sense that the organization will change its established approach to managing transportation and warehousing, and current employees will need varying degrees of training to become proficient with the new system.

Data mining, which can be defined as "the application of mathematical tools to large bodies of data in order to extract correlations and rules,"[38] is a DSS technique that has grown in popularity in recent years. Data mining utilizes sophisticated quantitative techniques to find "hidden" patterns in large volumes of data; these patterns allow managers to improve their decision-making abilities as well as enhance their organization's competitive advantage. Although data mining has been characterized as a "fishing expedition" of sorts—in the sense of applying sophisticated quantitative techniques merely to find relationships, whether meaningful or not—data mining, in reality, should follow a well-defined methodology.[39]

Efficient data mining is dependent on **data warehouses**, that is, a central repository for all the relevant data collected by an organization. Walmart, which is acknowledged to have one of world's foremost data warehouses, and its vendors make extensive use of data mining to improve logistical effectiveness and efficiency. For example, data mining has allowed Walmart to discover that when hurricanes are projected to hit the state of Florida, demand dramatically increases for two products, beer and Kellogg's Pop Tarts (a toasted pastry product)! So, when a hurricane is projected to hit Florida, Walmart makes sure that additional stocks of beer and Pop Tarts are available in its stores there.

Enterprise Systems

Enterprise systems, the final general type of information management system to be discussed, create and maintain consistent data processing methods and an integrated database across multiple business functions.[40] The most prominent example of enterprise systems is probably **enterprise resource planning (ERP)** systems, which "lets a company automate and integrate the majority of its business processes, share common data and practices across the enterprise, and produce and access information in a real-time environment."[41] In theory, ERP systems (such as those offered by Oracle and SAP) allow all prospective users access to a single database when making decisions. The attractiveness of ERP systems comes from their potential for lower costs (such as inventory reductions), as well as increased productivity and increased customer satisfaction.

Although contemporary ERP systems encompass a firmwide perspective, their origins can be traced back to logistics and manufacturing in the form of inventory control and materials requirement planning programs.[42] Unlike these earlier programs, today's ERP systems (conceptually, at least) provide an opportunity for all functional areas within a firm to access and analyze a common database—which might not have been previously possible because (1) certain data were proprietary to a particular functional area and (2) of insufficient or slow computing capabilities.

---

[37]Becky Partida, "WMS Can Produce Big Logistics Benefits," *Supply Chain Management Review* 16, no. 3 (2012): 51–53.
[38]Sam Joseph and Daniel Scuka, "AI," *Japan Inc.*, November 2001, 20–28.
[39]Michael S. Garver, "Try New Data-Mining Techniques," *Marketing News*, September 16, 2002, 31–33.
[40]Alter, *Information Systems*, Chapter 5.
[41]Joel D. Wisner, G. Keong Leong, and Keah-Choon Tan, *Principles of Supply Chain Management: A Balanced Approach*, 2nd ed. (Mason, OH: South-Western Cengage Learning, 2008), p. 507.
[42]Kuldeep Kumar and Jos van Hillegersberg, "ERP Experiences and Evolution," *Communications of the ACM* 43, no. 4 (2000): 23–26.

One of the most frequently mentioned shortcomings of ERP systems involves the costs of installation. It's common knowledge that ERP software is relatively expensive; however, the software is only one part of ERP implementation costs. For example, the vast amounts of data necessary for ERP systems may necessitate new or upgraded computer hardware. Other hidden or frequently overlooked costs of ERP implementation include employee training, data conversion (converting existing data into a usable and consistent format), integrating and testing a new system, maintenance costs, and consultant fees. Indeed, consultant fees can quickly ratchet up ERP implementation costs; there are suggestions that consultant fees may be three times more costly than the software itself.[43] When all relevant costs are factored in, ERP installation costs can easily reach into the tens of millions of dollars, and installation costs in the hundreds of millions of dollars are not out of the question.

A second shortcoming is that implementation of ERP systems can be a very time-consuming process. Indeed, many of the hidden costs of ERP implementation mentioned in the previous paragraph are the result of hidden time associated with ERP implementation. For instance, employee training, data conversion, and integrating and testing the new system all require time beyond the installation of the ERP software itself. A general rule of thumb is that actual time to implement ERP systems may range from two to four times longer than the time period specified by the ERP vendor.

A third shortcoming of ERP systems is that they initially lacked strong application-specific logistical capabilities such as TMS or WMS. Many companies addressed this challenge by adding so-called "best of breed" (i.e., the best product of its type) logistical applications to their ERP programs, but the process associated with adding the respective software could be costly and time consuming. In recent years, however, ERP vendors have begun to provide high-quality application-specific logistical capabilities, particularly with respect to WMS.[44]

Given the preceding discussion on time and implementation costs, it is not surprising that some ERP installations do not go as smoothly as desired, and these ERP glitches occasionally have a logistical component to them. For example, ERP implementation problems at a leading manufacturer of home medical products caused the company to lower its revenue estimates for several time periods. From a logistical perspective, the ERP-related problems meant that the company missed shipment deadlines, could not respond to customer inquiries, and had limited information about order status. The order-related problems, in turn, resulted in a higher-than-normal level of returns associated with incorrect orders, and the missed shipment deadlines caused the company to spend more money for expedited transportation.[45]

THE INTERNET'S INFLUENCE ON LOGISTICS

Although the Internet may appear to be a ubiquitous technology today, the reality is that only about 35 percent of the world's population currently uses the Internet, up from approximately 5 percent of the world's population at the beginning of the twenty-first century.[46] Just as the Internet's usage continues to expand during the twenty-first century, so does its influence on the logistics discipline. While it's not possible to present a comprehensive discussion of the Internet's influence on logistics, this section will discuss three specific influences—online retailing, cloud computing, electronic procurement—of the Internet on the logistics discipline.

Online Retailing

It should be noted that there are logistical similarities between online retailing and in-store retailing. For example, many logistical functions and activities—such as transportation, warehousing,

---

[43]Bob Violino, "Will a New Planning System Bust You?" *Baseline*, June 2005, 88.
[44]Bridget McCrea, "ERP: Gaining Momentum," *Logistics Management*, November 2008, 44–46.
[45]Marc L. Songini, "Faulty ERP App Results in Shortfall for Medical Firm," *Computerworld*, January 2, 2006, 8.
[46]www.internetworldstats.com

materials handling, and order management—occur in both. Likewise, both may use the same type of equipment and materials, such as bar coding and warehouse management systems.

Alternatively, powerful differences exist between online and in-store retailing with respect to the execution of logistics activities. For example, the orders associated with online shopping tend to be more plentiful and in much smaller quantities than those associated with in-store retailing. As such, online retailing requires an order management system capable of handling high volumes of orders, and it's also essential that the information management system be capable of correctly transmitting each order so that it can be filled in a timely fashion.

In addition, because of smaller order quantities, online shopping is characterized by open-case, rather than full-case, picking; open-case picking is facilitated by materials handling equipment, such as totes and push carts. Moreover, open-case picking necessitates that products be slotted (placed) in locations that facilitate picking effectiveness and efficiency. Not surprisingly, online retailing's smaller order quantities have important packaging implications as well, in the sense that companies need containers—small cartons, envelopes, bags—that are well suited to holding small quantities of product.[47] Some companies that engage in both online and in-store retailing choose to outsource online's pick-and-pack activities because they are so different than for in-store retailing.[48]

Two other key logistical considerations for online retailing involve transportation and returned orders. The smaller order quantities associated with online retailing tend to favor transport companies with extensive delivery networks and expertise in parcel shipments. This, in turn, suggests that outbound shipments tend to be picked up at a loading dock by small-capacity vehicles, such as delivery vans. Moreover, many online retailers are challenged by "last-mile" considerations (those related to delivering product to the customer) such as congestion, frequent stops, and return trips if the customer is not available to accept the delivery. Another emerging consideration is the use of same-day delivery of online orders. Companies such as Amazon, eBay, and Walmart are all looking at ways to offer their online customers the ability to receive their products the same day.[49] While still in the pilot stage, the logistical implications of this strategy are immense.

Although returned orders are an issue in all types of retailing, the return rates associated with online shopping tend to be much higher than with other types of retailing; one estimate suggests 10 percent return rates for traditional forms of retailing, compared to approximately 30 percent for online purchases.[50] Because many of these returns are from individual customers, not businesses or organizations, online retailers should attempt to make the return process as painless as possible. As such, when online customers receive their orders, they might also receive information on how to return the order, a return label, as well as a return container such as an envelope or bag. A relatively smooth and painless returns process not only improves return effectiveness and efficiency, but can also be an effective way of building and maintaining customer loyalty.[51]

Furthermore, it's important to note that a "one size fits all" logistics strategy is not likely to facilitate the effectiveness and efficiency of online shopping. Rather, a variety of logistics strategies might need to be applied, and it's important to recognize the potential trade-offs associated with the different strategies. For example, one way of addressing the last-mile issue of customer unavailability would be to install some type of receptacle (e.g., a drop box) for the product at the customer's residence. However, these receptacles might not be feasible for large items (such as a refrigerator), for perishable items (such as certain types of food), or for extremely valuable items (such as jewelry). The challenges of implementing the appropriate logistics strategy, or strategies,

[47]Norm Saenz, Jr., "Picking the Best Practices for E-fulfillment," *IIE Solutions* 33, no. 3 (2001): 37–40.
[48]William Hoffman, "One-Click Shopping," *Journal of Commerce*, February 20, 2006, 22–23.
[49]Tim Parry, "Walmart Testing Same-day Delivery Service," *Multichannel Merchant Exclusive Insight*, October 10, 2012, 2.
[50]Saenz, "Picking the Best Practices."
[51]Tim Parry, "Many Happy Returns?" *Multichannel Merchant*, February 2006, 37.

for online shopping are exacerbated by the fact that (1) a particular customer may require vastly different levels of service depending on the product ordered and (2) a particular product may require vastly different levels of service depending on the customer ordering it.[52]

Cloud Computing

The previously mentioned cloud computing (an umbrella term including both on-demand software and software as a service) has experienced meteoric growth since the beginning of the twenty-first century. In fact, the worldwide public cloud services market—where software, services, or information are shared via the Internet without the users having control over the technology infrastructure—grew almost 20 percent between 2011 and 2012.[53] There are myriad logistics-related applications for cloud computing, including collaborative forecasting and inventory optimization, with transportation management systems emerging as the most popular on-demand application.[54]

One reason for cloud computing's popularity is that its pay-per-use formula allows customers to avoid high capital investment costs, which speeds up return on investment for the software. In addition, because cloud computing involves operational as opposed to capital expenditures, it becomes a viable option for many companies that could not afford to purchase, install, and maintain application-specific software such as transportation management systems and warehousing management systems. Moreover, the worldwide economic slowdown that began in 2007 has caused many organizations to slash their information technology expenditures, thus benefitting cloud-based applications. Other advantages to cloud computing include faster and less-costly installation, a smaller information technology staff, and regular upgrades and updates from the software provider.[55] As such, companies such as Red Prairie, a provider of productivity software, are now offering cloud-based deployment of TMSs and WMSs.[56]

Although cloud computing appears to be quite attractive, particularly from a financial perspective, it has several potential drawbacks. For example, the regular software upgrades and updates mentioned earlier can sometimes be *too numerous* and *too frequent,* and customers can struggle to keep up with them. Moreover, cloud-based software allows for a limited amount of customization, meaning that customers need to fit what they're doing to what the software can achieve.[57] And, because the Internet is the primary transaction medium for cloud-based software, security issues such as data protection have been identified as a key concern.

ELECTRONIC PROCUREMENT   **Electronic procurement** (also known as **e-procurement**) uses the Internet to make it easier, faster, and less expensive for an organization to purchase goods and services. The types of benefits that come from electronic procurement include transactional benefits, compliance benefits, management information benefits, and price benefits. *Transactional benefits* measure the benefits of enhnaced transactional efficiency (e.g., a reduced invoice-to-payment time) associated with e-procurement. *Compliance benefits* focus on the savings that come from adherence to established procurement policies. *Management information benefits* encompass those that result from management information, customer satisfaction, and supplier satisfaction levels after implementation of electronic procurement. *Price benefits* are those that are given as the result of adopting e-procurement. For example, the electronic processing of invoices can save a great deal of money in terms of postage and stationery, and these savings can be passed on to the buyer.[58]

---

[52]Alberto Grando and Marco Gosso, "Avoiding the E-Commerce Trap," *EBF*, Summer 2004, 48–51.

[53]Bridget McCrea, "Cloud Breakthrough," *Logistics Management* 51, no. 11 (2012): 36–40.

[54]Bridget McCrea, "The State of On-Demand: CATCHING FIRE," *Logistics Management,* January 2009, 43–45.

[55]John Fontana, "What's Behind On-Demand's Software Rise," *Network World*, December 12, 2005, 1, 14.

[56]David Biederman, "Supply Chains Head to the Cloud," *Journal of Commerce* 13, no. 1 (2012): 186–189.

[57]Hannon, "On-Demand Brings Spend Control."

[58]David Eakin, "Measuring E-Procurement Benefits," *Government Procurement*, August 2002, 6–12.

Just as there are benefits to electronic procurement, there are important drawbacks as well. One concern with electronic commerce in general and e-procurement in particular, involves the security of information that is being transmitted; there is a risk that sensitive or proprietary information could end up in the wrong hands. Another concern is that electronic procurement can be impersonal in the sense that human interaction is replaced by computer transactions. Moreover, despite substantial hype about the potential benefits of e-procurement, one study discovered that only about 25 percent of the responding companies mandate the use of electronic procurement. The same study also found a dramatic drop in user confidence with respect to having the required skills and knowledge to use e-procurement tools.[59]

One activity that has been greatly facilitated by electronic procurement is online reverse auctions. You might be familiar with traditional auctions in which multiple buyers bid on a particular product, with the product being sold to the highest bidder. By contrast, in a **reverse auction**, a buyer invites bids from multiple sellers, and the seller with the lowest bid is generally awarded the business. As reverse auctions have evolved, so too have their parameters; in some situations a buyer is exempted from accepting the lowest bid, whereas in other situations a buyer does not have to accept any of the bids.[60]

Buyers tend to like reverse auctions because they aim to generate low procurement prices, and the online nature of reverse auctions allows buyers to drill down to a seller's low price very quickly. Alternatively, sellers are critical of reverse auctions because their primary emphasis is low price. However, reverse auctions can provide sellers with valuable information such as the number of other bidders. This can be important in the sense that a large number of bidders will likely lead to a great deal of price competition.[61]

INFORMATION TECHNOLOGY CHALLENGES

Thus far, this chapter has presented various challenges associated with specific types of information technology. We conclude this chapter with a discussion of several macro-level information technology challenges, or those challenges that might be faced regardless of the type(s) of information technology being utilized.

One macro-level challenge is the recognition that information technology *is a tool* that can help managers to address organizational problems and *is not a panacea* or a be-all/end-all solution for organizational problems. This can be illustrated by the situation of a senior manager whose disorganization caused him to often miss regularly scheduled meetings with various constituencies. The senior manager and his boss decided to "solve" the missed meeting problem by providing the manager with a smart phone that contained a calendar detailing the time and place of his various meetings. Unfortunately, the senior manager continued to miss regularly scheduled meetings because he occasionally failed to (1) carry the smart phone with him; (2) have the smart phone turned on; and (3) upload the meeting information into the smart phone's calendar. In this situation, the technological "solution" could not address—and may have actually exacerbated—the manager's disorganization.

Security concerns represent another macro-level information technology challenge, and these security concerns have many dimensions. For example, a 2006 study indicated that information security is the most important technology issue that companies face today.[62] Moreover, the theft of proprietary information for an "average" company is estimated to cost approximately $300,000 annually.[63] Moreover, increasing reliance on the Internet for logistics activities such as

[59]Maria Varmazis, "Buyers Become More Selective in Online Tools," *Purchasing,* September 15, 2005, 43–45.
[60]Bridget McCrea, "Going Once, Going Twice," *Industrial Distribution,* July 2005, 30–32.
[61]Ibid.
[62]Paul Demery, "Safe Driving? Is Your Lap Strapped in?" *Accounting Technology,* September 2006, 45–49.
[63]Ray Zambroski, "Think Before You Send," *Communication World,* May–June 2006, 38–40.

ordering and shipment tracking makes it essential that websites are as secure as possible from computer viruses or computer hackers that could compromise a customer's access to those websites.

Yet another security concern involves the decreasing size and increasing portability of technology devices such as laptop computers, flash drives, and smart phones. These smaller technology devices are more susceptible than larger technology devices to loss or theft, and it's important to recognize that the loss or theft of small, portable technology devices cause an organization to lose both the device *and* the data stored on the device. A particularly noteworthy example involved an intern for the state of Ohio who had a laptop computer, containing personal data on approximately 1 million residents of Ohio, stolen from her car.

A third information technology challenge involves human resource issues. Importantly, people-related factors such as employee resistance have been identified as a major cause of information technology implementation failure.[64] Technology addiction, another human resource issue, is perhaps best exemplified by the term "CrackBerry," which describes a person who uses a BlackBerry smart phone addictively or obsessively.[65] Underscoring the potential seriousness of technology addiction is whether an employer can be held liable for an employee's technology addiction.

Summary

This chapter discussed key issues of logistics and information technology. Six general types of information management systems were examined, with a particular emphasis on relevant logistical applications. Topics discussed include global positioning systems, electronic data interchange, application-specific software, and enterprise resource planning systems.

The chapter also looked at the Internet's influence on logistics in terms of three issues, online retailing, cloud computing, and electronic procurement. A discussion of information technology challenges—such as the recognition that information technology is a tool and not a panacea—concluded the chapter.

Questions for Discussion and Review

2.1 In what ways can information be helpful in logistics and supply chain management?

2.2 List the six general types of information management systems, and give one logistics application for each one that you've named.

2.3 Do you view the spreadsheet as the most relevant general software package for logisticians? Why or why not?

2.4 How can communication systems facilitate logistics management in the aftermath of situations such as terrorist attacks and natural disasters?

2.5 What advances in telecommunications technology do you view as being most beneficial to logistics management? Why?

2.6 Discuss how global positioning systems have become quite valuable in transportation management.

2.7 Discuss the benefits and drawbacks of EDI.

2.8 Discuss the relationship between automatic identification technologies and point-of-sale systems.

2.9 Why are some companies hesitant to adopt RFID technology?

2.10 Discuss the importance of timely and accurate information to a logistics information system.

2.11 What benefits are associated with transportation management and warehouse management systems?

2.12 What is data mining? How might it be used in logistics?

2.13 Discuss advantages and disadvantages of enterprise resource planning systems.

2.14 Refer back to the logistical activities listed in Chapter 1; pick two that you're interested in and research how they have been influenced by the Internet. Are you surprised by your findings? Why or why not?

---

[64]Tracey E. Rizzuto and Jennifer Reeves, "A Multidisciplinary Meta-Analysis of Human Barriers to Technology Implementation," *Consulting Psychology Journal: Practice and Research* 59, no. 2 (2007): 226–240.

[65]www.dictionary.com

2.15 From a logistical perspective, what are some of the differences between online and in-store retailing?

2.16 Why is a "one size fits all" logistics strategy not likely to facilitate effective or efficient online shopping?

2.17 Discuss the advantages and disadvantages of cloud computing.

2.18 Discuss the benefits and drawbacks to electronic procurement.

2.19 What is an online reverse auction? Why do buyers like them?

2.20 What are some of the macro-level information technology challenges that managers face?

Suggested Readings

Fawcett, Stanley E., Paul Osterhaus, Gregory M. Magnan, and Amydee M. Fawcett. "Mastering the Slippery Slope of Technology." *Supply Chain Management Review* 12, no. 7 (2008): 16–25.

Hazen, Benjamin T. and Terry Anthony Byrd. "Toward Creating Competitive Advantage with Logistics Information Technology." *International Journal of Physical Distribution & Logistics Management* 42, no. 1 (2012): 8–35.

Hurley, W. J. and Mathieu Balez. "A Spreadsheet Implementation of an Ammunition Requirements Model for the Canadian Army." *Interfaces* 38, no. 4 (2008): 271–280.

Kerr, John. "Technology Outlook: Getting by Without the Big Buys." *Supply Chain Management Review* 13, no. 1 (2009): 14–19.

Leonard, Lori N. K. and Christine Clemons. "Supply Chain Replenishment: Before-and-After EDI Implementation." *Supply Chain Management: An International Journal* 11, no. 3 (2006): 225–232.

Min, Hokey. "Application of a Decision Support System to Strategic Warehousing Decisions." *International Journal of Physical Distribution & Logistics Management* 39, no. 4 (2009): 270–281.

Moser, George and Peter Ward. "Which TMS is Right for You?" *Supply Chain Management Review* 12, no. 3 (2008): 50–56.

New, Steve. "The Transparent Supply Chain." *Harvard Business Review* 88, no. 10 (2010): 76–82.

Parry, Glenn and Andrew Graves. "The Importance of Knowledge for ERP Systems." *International Journal of Logistics: Research & Applications* 11, no. 6 (2008): 427–441.

Pearcy, Dawn H. and Larry C. Guinipero. "Using e-Procurement Applications to Achieve Integration: What Role Does Firm Size Play?" *Supply Chain Management: An International Journal* 13, no. 1 (2008): 26–34.

Rai, Arun, Paul A. Pavlou, Ghiyoung Im, and Steve Du. "Interfirm IT Capability Profiles and Communications for Cocreating Relational Value: Evidence from the Logistics Industry." *MIS Quarterly* 36, no. 1 (2012): 233–262.

Savitske, Katrina. "Internal and External Logistics Information Technologies: The Performance Impact in an International Setting." *International Journal of Physical Distribution & Logistics Management* 37, no. 6 (2007): 454–468.

Schoenherr, Tobias. "Diffusion of Online Reverse Auctions for B2B Procurement: An Explanatory Study." *International Journal of Operations & Production Management* 28, no. 3 (2008): 259–278.

White, Andrew and Mark Johnson. "RFID in the Supply Chain: Lessons from European Early Adopters." *International Journal of Physical Distribution & Logistics Management* 38, no. 2 (2008): 88–107.

CASE

CASE 2.1   Just-in-Time in Kalamazoo

Jim Ballenger was president of a medium-size firm that manufactured mini motor homes in Kalamazoo, Michigan. The firm had expanded from a local Midwest market to a national one, including Southern California and New England. As markets had expanded, so too had sources of supply for the company, with major suppliers located in Southern California, the Pacific Northwest, and Michigan. The decision to found the company in Michigan had been made for two reasons: Jim's former associates in the auto industry were there, and the largest single component of the mini—the truck or van chassis on which the rest of the vehicle is built—was purchased from one of the U.S. light-truck makers.

Like others in the field, Jim's company actually manufactured very few of its components. Virtually the entire product was assembled from components purchased from outside vendors. There was, however, a well-defined order in which the components could most efficiently be installed in the vehicle. Recently, it had become clear to Jim that transportation and inventory costs were a relatively large portion of his component parts expenses and that they might be ripe for a substantial reduction. He had been hearing about just-in-time (JIT) systems. According to some notes he had taken at a professional meeting, the JIT production system was developed by the Toyota Motor Company more than

50 years ago. It involves an approach to inventory that, in turn, forces a complementary approach to production, quality control, supplier relations, and distributor relationships. The major tenets of JIT can be summarized as follows:

1. Inventory in itself is wasteful and should be minimized.
2. Minimum replenishment quantity is maintained for both manufactured and purchased parts.
3. Minimum inventory of semifinished goods should be maintained—in this case, partially completed motor homes.
4. Deliveries of inputs should be frequent and small.
5. The time needed to set up production lines should be reduced to the absolute minimum.
6. Suppliers should be treated as part of the production team. This means that the vendor makes every effort to provide outstanding service and quality and that there is usually a much longer-lasting relationship with a smaller number of suppliers than is common in the United States.
7. The objective of the production system is zero defects.
8. The finished product should be delivered on a very short lead time.

To the U.S. inventory planner, vice president of logistics, and production planner, an operation run on the preceding principles raised a number of disturbing prospects. Jim Ballenger was very aware of the costs that might arise if a JIT production system were to be established. From the materials management standpoint, the idea of deliberately planning many small shipments rather than a few large ones appeared to ensure higher freight bills, especially from more distant suppliers, for which freight rates would make the most difference.

With regard to competition among suppliers, Jim often had the opportunity, in the volatile mini-motor-home market, to buy out parts and component supplies from manufacturers that were going out of business. Those components could be obtained at a substantial savings, with the requirement that inventory in the particular parts be temporarily increased or that purchases from existing vendors be temporarily curtailed. Perhaps the greatest question raised by JIT, however, had to do with the probability of much more erratic production as a result of tight supplies of components. Both with suppliers' products and with his own, Jim operated with the

(generally tacit) assumption that there would be some defective components purchased and that there would likely be something wrong with his product when it first came off the assembly line. For this reason, the Kalamazoo minis were extensively tested (Their advertising said, "We hope you'll never do what we do to your Kalamazoo mini."), as were the components prior to installation. To the extent that only a few of a particular type of component were on hand, the interruption in the production schedule would be that much greater. It might entail expensive rush orders for replacement components or equally expensive downtime for the entire plant.

Jim was also concerned about his relationship with his suppliers, as compared, say, to a large auto manufacturer. In the mini-motor-home business, generally the manufacturers are small and the component makers are large. In this situation, it was somewhat more difficult to see the idea of the supplier as a part of the production team, in the sense that the supplier would be expected to make a special effort in either quality control or delivery flexibility on behalf of one of its almost miniscule accounts.

Despite these concerns, Jim was painfully aware that he was using a public warehouse near his plant that usually contained between $500,000 and $1,000,000 in inventory, on which he paid more than 1.5 percent per month for the borrowed funds used to buy it, as well as expenses relating to the use of the warehouse itself. In addition, his firm was now producing so many different models (one with a bath, one with a shower only) and using so many different appliances (various types of radio, three varieties of refrigerator, etc.) that the costs of a safety stock for each component were going up every day.

As an aid to making his decision on whether to try a JIT orientation at his plant, Jim's executive assistant, Kathy Williams, drew up a table that summarized the anticipated impacts of a JIT system (see Exhibit 2.A). The figures are based on random samples of inventory items. The major component of any mini motor home—the chassis—would always be purchased on a one-at-a-time basis from Ford, Chevrolet, Dodge, or International. With rare exceptions, it would always be available on demand. It would be delivered through the local dealer. If the dealer did not have one in stock, one could easily be obtained from another area dealership.

Exhibit 2.A is a representative 10 percent sample of Ballenger's components inventory. It covers weekly

	Current System					Using JIT		
Item	Distance from vendor (in miles)	Average number of units used each week	Current lot size purchased	Unit cost	Average freight cost per unit	JIT lot size	Unit cost	Average freight cost per unit (surface)
Gas range	1,145	10	200	100	$20	10	$105	$22
Toilet	606	10	240	80	18	10	100	18
Pump	26	56	125	16	3	7	15	4
Refrigerator (large)	22	6	120	110	20	6	113	25
Refrigerator (small)	22	7	15	95	15	1	85	15
Foam cushion	490	675	1,500	8	2	75	7	3
DVD player (type D)	1,800	9	24	136	11	3	130	26
Dome lights	3	824	1,720	2	0	36	4	0
Awning Brackets	48	540	1,200	4	1	60	5	1
Insect Screens	159	570	1,240	7	1	50	7	2

EXHIBIT 2.A Ten Percent Random Sample of Component Inventory
Note: The plant operates 52 weeks per year and produces 10 mini motor homes per week.

use of each item, the current lot size purchased, and so on. Before figuring the total costs under the present and JIT systems, two additional facts must be noted. First, Ballenger's inventory carrying costs are assumed to be 20 percent per year on the average investment in inventory on hand, including its acquisition and transportation costs.

Second, under the current system, the number of units of each type of component kept in stock is calculated as follows: For those items purchased from vendors more than 500 miles away, a safety stock representing four weeks of use is maintained. For items from vendors between 100 and 500 miles away, a safety stock representing two weeks of use is maintained. For items from closer sources, a safety stock representing one week of use is maintained. In addition to safety stocks, the average inventory of any item is the current lot size purchased, divided by 2.

If you are familiar with Excel or other spreadsheet software, you might try using it here, although it is not necessary.

Questions

1. What is the total annual cost of maintaining the components inventory under the present system?
2. What would be the total annual cost of maintaining the components inventory under the JIT system (assuming no safety stocks)?
3. Should Ballenger take into account any other costs or benefits from the JIT system? If so, what are they?
4. If the JIT system is adopted, are there safety stocks of any item that should be maintained? If so, which ones and how much?
5. If the JIT system is adopted, what changes, if any, should occur in the relationships between Ballenger's firm and his suppliers of components? Discuss.
6. Assume that Ballenger has switched to the JIT system and that he receives a surprise phone call from a competitor who is going out of business. The competitor wants to sell Ballenger 7,000 dome lights of the type listed in Exhibit 2.A. Should Ballenger buy them? If so, at what price?
7. Carrying costs are 20 percent. Is there a level of carrying costs at which both Ballenger's present system and a JIT system have similar costs? If so, what is it?

3 STRATEGIC AND FINANCIAL LOGISTICS

KEY TERMS

- Assets
- Asset turnover
- Balanced scorecard (BSC)
- Balance sheet
- Cost leadership strategy
- Current ratio

- Differentiation strategy
- Expenses (costs)
- Focus strategy
- Income statement
- Liabilities
- Net profit margin

- Owners' equity
- Return on assets (ROA)
- Revenues (sales)
- Strategic profit model (SPM)

LEARNING OBJECTIVES

- To appreciate how logistics can influence an organization's strategic financial outcomes
- To review basic financial terminology
- To understand how the strategic profit model can demonstrate the financial impact of logistics activities

- To consider the value of utilizing the balanced scorecard approach for examining the performance of a logistics system
- To become aware of some of the common performance measures for logistics activities

As was highlighted in Chapter 1, an effective and efficient logistics function plays a crucial role within most organizations. Shorter product life cycles, increasing customer expectations, technological advancements, rising shareholder demands, and globalization are all pushing firms to develop efficient, effective, and differentiated logistics activities.[1] Research has continuously demonstrated that logistical activities can be an important consideration for achieving exceptional levels of customer service and ultimately contributing to firm financial performance.[2] For example, housewares retailer Williams-Sonoma was able to significantly increase their profits through logistics gains from implementing improved distribution accuracy programs that helped them enhance their customer service levels and reduced inventory shrinkage.[3]

---

[1]Brian S. Fugate, John T. Mentzer, and Theodore P. Stank, "Logistics Performance: Efficiency, Effectiveness and Differentiation," *Journal of Business Logistics* 31, no. 1 (2010): 43–62.
[2]Michael Tracey, "The Importance of Logistics Efficiency to Customer Service and Firm Performance," *International Journal of Logistics Management* 9, no. 2 (1998): 65–81.
[3]"Williams-Sonoma Profits from Logistics Gains," *Journal of Commerce* 11, no. 13 (2010): 6–7.

Management of reverse logistics provides another potential way for managers to make decisions that influence their firm's financial performance. Improvements to one's reverse logistics system could provide cost improvements and/or revenue enhancement opportunities. Depending on the industry and product type, reverse logistics costs as a percent of revenue can range between 3 and 6 percent.[4] Estée Lauder (a manufacturer of cosmetics, skin care, and fragrances) made an investment of $1.3 million to build a system of scanners and other technologies to assist its reverse logistics efforts. With respect to cost improvements, this system enabled Estée Lauder to sharply reduce the percentage of returned goods that it dumped into landfills while also providing half a million dollars in labor cost savings. In terms of revenue enhancements, the system is a key part of a $250 million product line based on returned cosmetics. Estée Lauder collects items and then sells them to seconds stores or to retailers in developing countries.[5]

This chapter provides an overview of how an organization's strategic financial outcomes are influenced by logistics decisions. We begin with a description of the connection of functional logistics strategy to overall corporate strategy and ultimately financial performance. Next, a general overview of key financial terminology will be presented. This is followed by an examination of how the strategic profit model can be used to highlight how logistics activities influence the key corporate financial measures of net income, capital employed, and return on capital employed. The chapter concludes with a description of the balanced scorecard and common logistics performance measures in the areas of transportation, warehousing, and inventory.

CONNECTING STRATEGY TO FINANCIAL PERFORMANCE

A recurring theme in the logistics research is that an organization's logistics capabilities need to be directly connected to objective (as opposed to subjective) firm performance measures. In addition, this research stream asserts that logistics managers must continue to find ways to effectively communicate how these logistics capabilities provide value and ultimately support corporate strategy and success in financial terms.[6] In fact, an international survey of manufacturing firms reported that logistics performance was important or very important for achieving competitive advantage by almost 70 percent of the respondents.[7]

Strategy can be formulated at a corporate level, a business unit level, and a functional level. Corporate-level strategy is focused on determining the goals for the company, the types of businesses in which the company should compete, and the way the company will be managed. Typically, organizations strive to create value by effectively managing a portfolio of businesses and ensuring that each of these businesses is financially successful.

Strategy at a business unit level is primarily focused on the products and services provided to customers and on finding ways to develop and maintain a sustainable competitive advantage with these customers. Renowned strategist Michael Porter has identified three generic strategies that can be pursued by an organization, namely, cost leadership, differentiation, and focus. A **cost leadership strategy** requires an organization to pursue activities that will enable it to become the

[4]Sumantra Sengupta, "10 New Ideas for Generating Value," *Supply Chain Management Review* 13, no. 4 (2009): 20–25.
[5]Andrew O'Connell, "Improve Your Return on Returns," *Harvard Business Review* 85, no. 11 (2007): 30–34.
[6]See for example, Edward A. Morash, Cornelia L.M. Droge, and Shawnee K. Vickery, "Strategic Logistics Capabilities for Competitive Advantage and Firm Success," *Journal of Business Logistics* 17, no. 1 (1996): 1–22; Douglas M. Lambert and Renan Burduroglu, "Measuring and Selling the Value of Logistics," *International Journal of Logistics Management* 11, no. 1 (2000): 1–17; Edward A. Morash, "Supply Chain Strategies, Capabilities, and Performance," *Transportation Journal* 41, no. 3 (2001): 37–54; Jeff Hoi Yan Yeung, Willem Selen, Chee-Chuong Sum, and Baofeng Huo, "Linking Financial Performance to Strategic Orientation and Operational Priorities: An Empirical Study of Third-party Logistics Providers," *International Journal of Physical Distribution and Logistics Management* 36, no. 3 (2006): 210–230; and Kenneth W. Green Jr., Dwayne Whitten, and R. Anthony Inman, "The Impact of Logistics Performance on Organizational Performance in a Supply Chain Context," *Supply Chain Management: An International Journal* 13, no. 4 (2008): 317–327.
[7]A. Harrison and C. New, "The Role of Coherent Supply Chain Strategy and Performance Management in Achieving Competitive Advantage: An International Survey," *Journal of Operational Research Society* 53, no. 3 (2002): 263–271.

low-cost producer in an industry for a given level of quality. A **differentiation strategy** entails an organization developing a product and/or service that offers unique attributes that are valued by customers and that the customers perceive to be distinct from competitor offerings. Finally, a **focus strategy** concentrates an organization's effort on a narrowly defined market to achieve either a cost leadership or differentiation advantage.[8] Logistics leverage can help firms achieve a competitive advantage from each of these strategies.[9]

The functional level of the organization is where logistics resides. The strategic issues at this level are related to business activities that support the achievement of the higher-level goals set by the business unit and corporation. This *hierarchy of strategy* entails the functional units of an organization providing input into the other levels of strategy formulation. This input could take the form of information on the resources and capabilities available to the organization. After the corporate-level and business unit strategies are developed, the functional units must translate these strategies into discrete action plans they must accomplish for the higher-level strategies to succeed.

Functional-level strategies will exist in such areas as marketing, finance, manufacturing, procurement, and logistics. Logistics strategy decisions involve issues such as the number and location of warehouses, the selection of appropriate transportation modes, the deployment of inventory, and investments in technology that support logistics activities. In addition to being influenced by the goals of the corporate and business unit strategies, logistics strategy is directly influenced by strategic decisions in the functional areas of marketing, finance, manufacturing, and procurement. Marketing goals in areas such as product availability, desired customer service levels, and packaging design directly influence logistics decisions that must be made to support achievement of these goals or to provide information for strategy formulation in these areas. Financial hurdle rates of return may affect the decision to manage one's own warehouse or use a third-party provider. Similarly, a strategic decision by manufacturing to implement a just-in-time system would affect logistics decisions in areas such as warehousing, transportation, and inventory management. In terms of the connection to procurement strategy, the decision to move from domestic to global sourcing would naturally affect logistics activities such as the potential use of new modes of transportation.

With respect to logistics organizational forms, Professors Bowersox and Daugherty identified three orientations that can be used in isolation or in combination when developing a logistics strategy. These orientations include the following: *process strategy* (management of logistics activities with a focus on cost); *market strategy* (management of logistics activities across business units with a focus on reducing complexity for customers); and *information strategy* (management of logistics activities with goal of achieving coordination and collaboration through the channel).[10] These strategies have been found to remain stable over time and provide a basis for meeting organizational goals. While most firms will have a dominant orientation that represents their strategic thrust, these forms are likely to interact.

The ability of the logistics function to ultimately influence the overall financial success of an organization is based on the ability of logistics managers to develop and implement strategies that are aligned with the overall corporate strategy. Research has shown positive affect of this alignment of functional level strategies with higher-level strategies on financial performance.[11] Specifically, logistics strategy must be designed to optimally support the requirements of the

---

[8]Michael Porter, *Competitive Strategy: Techniques for Analyzing Industries and Competitors* (New York, The Free Press, 1980).

[9]John T. Mentzer and Lisa R. Williams, "The Role of Logistics Leverage in Marketing Strategy," *Journal of Marketing Channels* 8, no. 3–4 (2001): 29–47.

[10]Donald J. Bowersox and Patricia J. Daugherty, "Emerging Patterns of Logistical Organization," *Journal of Business Logistics* 8, no. 1 (1987): 46–60.

[11]See for example, M. P. Joshi, R. Kathuria, and S. J. Porth, "Alignment of Strategic Priorities and Performance: An Integration of Operations and Strategic Management Perspectives," *Journal of Operations Management* 21, no. 3 (2003): 353–369; P. D. Cousins, "The Alignment of Appropriate Firm and Supply Strategies for Competitive Advantage," *International Journal of Operations and Production Management* 25, no. 5 (2005): 403–428; and Cristian Baier, Evi Hartmann, and Roger Moser, "Strategic Alignment and Purchasing Efficacy: An Exploratory Analysis of Their Impact on Financial Performance," *Journal of Supply Chain Management* 44, no. 4 (2008): 36–52.

business and the corporation in order to positively affect the financial outcomes of an organization. Thus, an appreciation for this interconnectedness and need for alignment of strategies is important for every logistics manager.

BASIC FINANCIAL TERMINOLOGY

Logistics managers in every organization are expected to use financial information to help them make decisions, allocate resources, and budget expenses. Having a basic understanding of financial terminology is important knowledge in assisting logistics managers to formulate intelligent questions for other functions as well as providing them an ability to understand and effectively communicate how logistical activities can help improve their company's financial performance. Some of the more important financial terms are described in the following sections.

Income Statement

The **income statement** shows revenues, expenses, and profit for a period of time; an example is presented in Figure 3.1. It can also be referred to as a profit and loss statement (P&L). In general, the income statement measures the profitability of the products and/or services provided by a company. It reports the revenues generated by company activities during a given period of time, the expenses associated with achieving these revenues, and the profit or loss that is a result of these activities. **Revenues**, also referred to as sales, provide a dollar value of all the products and/or services an organization provides to their customers during a given period of time. **Expenses**, also referred to as costs, provide a dollar value for the costs incurred in generating revenues during a given period of time.

Logistics managers need to understand how logistics costs influence the profits or losses being incurred by their firm so that they can make appropriate decisions. While it is not always possible for a logistics manager to directly correlate logistics service improvements with an increase in sales, superior logistics service can have a positive influence on an organization's financial performance.

More obvious direct correlations of logistics decisions occur across the expense categories of the income statement. Specifically, cost of goods sold may be influenced directly by procurement decisions and inbound transportation costs that are part of a product acquisition agreement. In addition, the potential to reduce several of the operating cost categories associated with logistics can be significant. Because a large percentage of costs for a typical organization

Income Statement 2012		
Sales		$200,000
Cost of goods sold		$130,000
Gross Margin		$70,000
Transportation cost	$6,000	
Warehousing cost	$3,000	
Inventory carrying cost	$1,000	
Other operating	$30,000	
Total operating cost	$40,000	
Earnings Before Interest and Taxes		$30,000
Interest		$11,000
Taxes		$6,000
Net income		$13,000

FIGURE 3.1 Example Income Statement

are driven by logistics decisions, many organizations spend considerable time focusing on this connection between logistics and financial performance.[12]

More efficient and effective decisions in the areas of transportation, warehousing, and inventory can offer logistics managers the ability to lower costs and directly influence overall financial performance. Referring to Figure 3.1, a decrease in transportation, warehousing, and/or inventory costs (assuming no change in logistics service performance) translates into lower total operating costs and higher earnings before interest and taxes. In addition, the ability of logistics managers to do *more with less* in areas such as inventory, plant, and equipment can ultimately affect the interest and tax expense categories on the income statement. As can be seen in Figure 3.1, the ability to lower these costs will fall directly to the bottom line (i.e., higher net income).

Balance Sheet

The **balance sheet** reflects the assets, liabilities, and owners' equity at a given point in time. The balance sheet equates assets with liabilities plus owners' equity. **Assets** are what a company owns and come in two temporal forms: *current assets* that can be easily converted to cash (such as stock) and *long-term assets* that have a useful life of more than a year (such as a company-owned warehouse). **Liabilities** are the financial obligations a company owes to another party. Similar to assets, liabilities come in two temporal forms: *current liabilities*, which need to be paid in less than a year, and *long-term liabilities*, which are due over an extended period of time. **Owners' equity** is the difference between what a company owns and what it owes at any particular point in time.

Figure 3.2 is an example of a basic balance sheet. As is the case with the income statement, logistics can affect the balance sheet of an organization in several distinct ways. Order cycle time, order completion rate, and invoice accuracy can influence the speed in which one's customers pay their invoices, thus directly affecting the cash and accounts receivables categories on the balance sheet. Clearly, inventory management decisions that raise or lower inventory levels show up in the inventory category. Expansion of company-owned warehouses and/or acquiring additional equipment to use in one's warehouses will flow through to the fixed assets category. In terms of liabilities, procurement's purchase order quantities are reflected in current liabilities and financing options for inventory, plant, and equipment could impact long-term debt levels.[13]

Balance Sheet 2012	
Assets	
Cash	$20,000
Accounts receivable	$35,000
Inventory	$15,000
Total current assets	$70,000
Net fixed assets	$80,000
Total assets	$150,000
Liabilities	
Current liabilities	$60,000
Long-term debt	$30,000
Total liabilities	$90,000
Shareholders' Equity	$60,000
Total Liabilities and Equity	$150,000

FIGURE 3.2 Example Balance Sheet

---

[12]Martin Christopher, *Logistics and Supply Chain Management,* 3rd ed. (Harlow, England, Prentice Hall—Financial Times, 2005).
[13]Ibid.

STRATEGIC PROFIT MODEL[14]

Several general measures of performance reflect on an organization's financial results and should be understood by logistics managers. As was discussed in the income statement section, profit is a basic financial measure that represents the difference between revenues and expenses. While a raw number such as profit would seem to be adequate, there are issues with reporting financial figures without an appropriate context. Therefore, many financial measures are reported as ratios that indicate the relationship of one number to another. Ratios provide a point of comparison and can provide management with more information than raw numbers alone. For example, the **current ratio**, which is calculated by dividing *total current assets* by *total current liabilities*, measures how well an organization can pay its current liabilities by using only current assets.

Profitability analysis is an important means of assessing logistics activities and proposed changes to a firm's logistical systems. Profitability analysis goes beyond just focusing only on logistics costs by attempting to also include the revenue effect of logistical activities. For example, an improved level of service provided by higher levels of safety stock should bring about increased revenue as customers respond to improved in-stock availability. These revenue effects must be built into the analysis of logistics performance.

A common measure of organizational financial success is return on investment (ROI), which can be measured by return on net worth (RONW) or return on assets (ROA). RONW measures the profitability of the funds that have been invested in the business, and is most likely of primary interest to investors. ROA provides a more operational perspective by providing insight on how well managers utilize operational assets to generate profits. Thus, ROA becomes a key managerial tool for logistics profitability analysis.

Return on assets (ROA) indicates what percentage of every dollar invested in the business ultimately is returned to the organization as profit. Logistics managers are inherently concerned with assets such as inventory and equipment used to support logistics activities. While these types of assets will show up on the balance sheet, ROA will allow managers to understand how effective their organization is in using these assets to generate profit. The formula for ROA is: ROA = net profit margin × asset turnover.

The **Strategic Profit Model (SPM)** provides the framework for conducting ROA analysis by incorporating revenues and expenses to generate net profit margin, as well as an inclusion of assets to measure asset turnover. **Net profit margin** measures the proportion of each sales dollar that is kept as profit, while **asset turnover** measures the efficiency of the capital employed to generate sales. Together, they form the basis for computing ROA. Figure 3.3 provides the general framework for how to develop an SPM to better understand how a logistics manager's decisions can impact net profit margin, asset turnover, and ultimately, ROA. Suppose, for example, that a logistics manager is able to eliminate some unnecessary inventory; this would reduce the value of current assets as well as total asset value. As a result, sales divided by total assets—asset turnover—would be higher, as would the organization's return on assets.

The SPM has the advantage of assisting logistics managers in the evaluation of cash flows and asset utilization decisions. It provides a way for managers to examine how a proposed change to their logistics system influences profit performance and ROA. However, it fails to consider the timing of cash flows, is subject to manipulation in the short run, and fails to recognize assets that are dedicated to specific relationships.[15]

---

[14]The material in this section is drawn from Drew Stapleton, Joe B. Hanna, Steve Yagla, Jay Johnson, and Dan Markussen, "Measuring Logistics Performance Using the Strategic Profit Model," *International Journal of Logistics Management* 13, no. 1 (2002): 89–107.
[15]Lambert and Burduroglu, "Measuring and Selling the Value of Logistics."

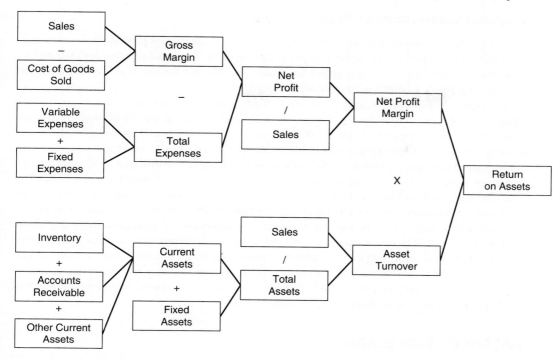

FIGURE 3.3 Strategic Profit Model

Logistics Connections to Net Profit Margin

Operationally, net profit margin is net profit divided by sales, and looking at net profit and sales, as reported on the income statement, suggests multiple ways in which net profit margin can be influenced by managerial decisions. The most relevant categories for logistics managers to consider are sales, costs of goods sold, and total expenses.

Sales are the dollar value of all the products or services an organization provides to its customers during a given period of time. The primary influence of logistics activities on sales would be through the improvement of customer service. For example, one logistics decision that could be made by an e-commerce company would be to provide overnight delivery to their customers at no cost. While this type of decision would need to consider the cost implications of providing this level of service, it would be expected that the move would have a positive influence on customer retention and sales.

Cost of Goods Sold is one category of expenses. It includes all the costs or materials and labor directly involved in producing a product or delivering a service. A significant part of this expense category is the cost of materials that are used to make a product. As such, logistics can influence these costs through procurement activities (e.g., purchasing at volume discounts, reverse auctions) or through any logistics-related efficiency improvements that enable labor to be more productive (e.g., enhanced materials handling processes on a production line).

Total Expenses are made up of the variable and fixed costs that are not directly related to making the product or delivering a service. This expense category could include logistics-related activities in areas such as transportation, warehousing, and inventory. For example, a logistics decision to reduce the number of less-than-truckload shipments through a consolidation strategy would show up in the transportation costs category that is part of variable expenses. A decision to sell a company-owned warehouse could directly affect the fixed expenses of running the facility. In addition to understanding the financial effects of a logistics cost reduction, any potential cost increases should also be analyzed. For example, a decision to increase inventory levels in response to a marketing request would increase inventory carrying costs that flow to the variable expense category.

Logistics Connections to Asset Turnover

Asset turnover is computed by dividing total sales by total assets and provides information on how efficiently capital is employed to support the business. The most relevant logistics asset is typically inventory. In addition, logistics decisions can influence the speed at which invoices are paid as reflected in accounts receivable on the balance sheet.

Inventory can represent a significant part of an organization's current assets. Logistics decisions affect all types of inventory within an organization from raw materials to work-in-progress inventory to finished goods. Logistics strategy on inventory levels and stocking locations will directly influence this category. For example, a decision by a retailer to move to a system of vendor managed inventory where a supplier of a product maintains control and ownership over an inventory item can result in a significant reduction of the amount of inventory on an organization's balance sheet. Similarly, the use of premium transportation may also enable a firm to reduce lead time and ultimately reduce pipeline inventory that would show up on the balance sheet.

Accounts receivable is the amount of money customers owe to an organization. It is all the promises to pay that have not been collected yet. Logistics decisions can influence this category by accurately communicating and completing transactions with customers. For example, a decision to invest in an EDI system that would increase invoice accuracy should enable customer payments to be received in a more timely fashion. Customers that receive inaccurate invoices will tend to hold payment until these issues are worked out.

BALANCED SCORECARD

The **balanced scorecard (BSC)** is a strategic planning and performance management system used extensively in industry, government, and nonprofit organizations. It is based on the belief that management should evaluate their business from four distinct perspectives: customers, internal business processes, learning and growth, and financial results. Performance measures are developed to address particular goals or capabilities under one of these four perspectives. For example, from the customer's perspective a goal might be to provide consistent, timely supply that could entail the use of a metric-like order fill rate. While there is no standard set of measures that firms should employee, using a concise yet comprehensive set of measures should provide an effective monitoring and management tool for an organization.[16]

When viewed from a logistics point of view, the BSC approach forces managers to look beyond traditional financial measures when conducting a strategic logistics analysis. While the financial perspective is still considered a good indicator of whether or not logistics strategy is being properly implemented and executed, the BSC pushes for a more holistic approach that includes the other three perspectives. To develop an effective logistics scorecard, management first defines the organization's vision and goals. Next, logistics strategies are designed to ensure achievement of this vision and goals. These strategies are then translated into specific tactical performance-enhancing activities, and, finally, appropriate measurements are established for each activity. The next section provides some common logistics measures that can be used in isolation or as part of a logistics BSC.

LOGISTICS ACTIVITY MEASURES

Performance measures are critical for effectively managing logistics activities. A continuing challenge for logistics managers is to develop and maintain an effective set of measures to help make decisions and support the achievement of financial success. As detailed in our description of

---

[16]Matthew J. Liberatore and Tan Miller, "A Framework for Integrating Activity-Based Costing and the Balanced Scorecard into the Logistics Strategy Development and Monitoring Process," *Journal of Business Logistics* 19, no. 2 (1998): 131–154.

the balanced scorecard, both financial and nonfinancial measures should be leveraged. In addition, the measures can be at a strategic, tactical or operational level.[17] While it is not possible to cover all potential logistics measures in this section, we will highlight some of the more common measures related to a few key areas of logistics management. The section will conclude by providing some guidance on how best to design and implement a system of logistics measures in an organization.

Logistics measurement systems have been traditionally designed to include information on five types of performance: (1) asset management, (2) cost, (3) customer service, (4) productivity, and (5) logistics quality.[18] Several measures are designed and implemented in each of these categories to manage logistics activities such as transportation, warehousing, and inventory management. Research suggests that leading-edge organizations are highly focused on performance measurement across these five areas, and this serves as a platform on which competitive position, value-adding capabilities, and supply chain integration can grow.[19]

Transportation Measures

The major transportation measures focus on such things as labor, cost, equipment, energy, and transit time. The diversity of equipment types, sizes, and products carried will complicate the performance measurement in this area of logistics. Measurements in this area include items such as return on investment (investments in transportation equipment), outbound freight costs, transportation labor productivity, on-time deliveries, and in-transit damage frequency, to name a few.

Many companies have turned to using scorecards to measure and improve transportation performance. In fact, one study found that while most of the companies they examined produced transportation scorecards monthly, Best in Class companies were twice as likely to be producing daily scorecards.[20] Use of these scorecards reduced shipper complacency and enabled shippers to increase competition on lanes that led to freight cost savings.

Warehousing Measures

Performance measurement in warehousing is used to identify design and operations options that provide benefits in terms of increased speed or reduced costs.[21] The primary warehousing measures include such things as labor, cost, time, utilization, and administration. As was the case with transportation, the diversity of warehouse types, sizes, and products carried will complicate the performance measurement in this area. Some common macro-level measurements focused on warehousing include return on investment (investments in warehousing facilities or equipment), warehouse order processing costs, and warehouse labor productivity.

Common operational activities in a warehouse include receiving, storage, picking, and shipping. There are a variety of metrics that could be used for each of these activities. For receiving, measures such as volume received per man-hour, cases processed per day or receiving dock door utilization percentage may be appropriate. In terms of storage, measures such as percentage of location and cube occupied, pilferage costs, or storage cost per item could be used. Cost of picking per order line, pick accuracy percentage, and order lines picked per hour are examples

[17]A. Gunasekaran, C. Patel, and E. Tirtiroglu, "Performance Measures and Metrics in a Supply Chain Environment," *International Journal of Operations & Production Management* 21, no. 1–2 (2001): 71–87.

[18]Donald Bowersox and David Closs, *Logistical Management, The Integrated Supply Chain Process* (New York, McGraw-Hill, 1996) and Donald Bowersox, Patricia Daugherty, Cornelia Droge, Dale Rogers, and Daniel Wardlow, *Leading Edge Logistics: Competitive Positioning for the 1990's* (Oak Brook, IL: Council of Logistics Management, 1989).

[19]Stanley E. Fawcett and M. Bixby Cooper, "Logistics Performance Measurement and Customer Success," *Industrial Marketing Management* 27, no. 4 (1998): 341–357.

[20]Aberdeen Group, *The Transportation Management Benchmark Report* (Boston, MA: Aberdeen Group Inc., 2006).

[21]Andrew Johnson and Leon McGinnis, "Performance Measurement in the Warehousing Industry," *IIE Transactions* 43, no. 3 (2011): 220–230.

of some of the picking measures that managers could track. Finally, measures such as shipping dock door utilization percentage, cases shipped per day, and cost of shipping per order could be utilized.

Inventory Measures

Inventory management measures tend to relate to the inventory service levels provided to customers as well as controlling inventory investment across an organization's logistics system. Some common performance measures include obsolete inventory, inventory carrying cost, inventory turnover, and information availability.

Two organizational-level performance measures directly connected to inventory are cash-to-cash cycle and gross margin return on inventory (GMROI). Cash-to-cash cycle looks at how long an organization's cash is tied up in receivables, payables, and inventory. It is equal to the number of receivable days plus the number of inventory days minus the number of payable days. In comparison, GMROI is a common metric used by retailers and distributors that examine inventory performance based on margin and inventory turn. The formula for GMROI is as follows: GMROI = (gross profit in dollars/sales in dollars) × (sales in dollars/ average inventory at cost).

Design and Implementation of Measures[22]

While the number and types of measures to use can seem daunting to a logistics manager, several suggestions have emerged from research to provide some guidance. Some of the key things to consider when applying performance measures to logistics activities include the following:

1. Determination of the key measures should be tailored to the individual organization and level of decision making.
2. Data collection and analysis are a major part of a performance measurement system in logistics. This complexity is increased in global settings.
3. Behavioral issues should be considered when establishing and implementing a system of logistics measures. Top management support can help tremendously in this area.
4. Frequent communication and constant updating of the measures is a necessary condition for ensuring they are supporting the stated goals of the organization.

Summary

This chapter focused on the connection between logistics strategy and an organization's financial performance. Beginning with a discussion of the connection between corporate strategy and logistics strategy, the chapter provided an overview of key financial concepts as they relate to forming a better understanding of how logistics decisions can influence financial results.

The chapter also discussed key financial tools, such as the income statement, the balance sheet, the strategic profit model, and the balanced scorecard. Various logistics performance measures were also presented. We also looked at some key considerations when implementing a performance measurement system focused on logistics activities.

---

[22]This section based on findings from Angappa Gunasekaran and Bulent Kobu, "Performance Measures and Metrics in Logistics and Supply Chain Management: A Review of Recent Literature (1995–2004) for Research and Applications," *International Journal of Production Research* 45, no. 12 (2007): 2819–2840.

Questions for Discussion and Review

3.1 Discuss the differences between corporate-level, business unit-level, and functional-level strategies.

3.2 Discuss the cost leadership, differentiation, and focus strategies.

3.3 What are the two key components of an income statement?

3.4 What are the three key components of a balance sheet?

3.5 What are the key components of the strategic profit model? How can it be used to examine the affect of logistics decisions?

3.6 Discuss how logistics decisions affect net profit margin in an organization.

3.7 Discuss how logistics decisions affect asset turnover in an organization.

3.8 Discuss some of the ways that inventory costs can be reduced in order to affect an organization's financial performance.

3.9 Do you agree or disagree that return on assets is a good way to examine operational efficiency? Why?

3.10 How does logistics strategy connect to overall corporate strategy? Is it a one-way or two-way connection?

3.11 Why is top management commitment necessary for establishing a successful logistics performance measurement system?

3.12 Most managers believe that while it is possible to connect logistics decisions to costs, the connection to revenue enhancement is difficult to impossible. Do you agree or disagree? Why?

3.13 What are some common logistics measures in transportation, warehousing, and inventory management?

3.14 Do you think corporate cultures are relevant for designing a logistics measurement system? Why or why not?

3.15 Why might performance measurement be more difficult in global logistics systems?

3.16 Describe how logistics decisions might affect an organization's cost of goods sold.

3.17 Describe the common types of information included in traditional logistics measurement systems.

3.18 What are the major parts of a balanced scorecard? Why are these parts needed?

3.19 Do you agree or disagree with the sentiment that logistics measurement systems need to include both financial and nonfinancial measures? Why?

3.20 Identify some of the key considerations for a logistics manager who is designing and implementing a logistics measurement system in their organization.

Suggested Readings

Bhatnagar, Rohit and Chee-Chong Teo. "Role of Logistics in Enhancing Competitive Advantage: A Value Chain Framework for Global Supply Chains." *International Journal of Physical Distribution & Logistics Management* 39, no. 3 (2009): 202–226.

Berman, Karen and Joe Knight. *Financial Intelligence: A Manager's Guide to Knowing What the Numbers Really Mean* (Boston, MA: Harvard Business School Press, 2006).

Caplice, Chris and Yossi Sheffi. "A Review and Evaluation of Logistics Metrics." *International Journal of Logistics Management* 5, no. 2 (1994): 11–28.

Davis, Thomas S. and Robert A. Novack. "Why Metrics Matter." *Supply Chain Management Review* 16, no. 4 (2012): 10–17.

Fugate, Brian S., John T. Mentzer, and Theodore P. Stank. "Logistics Performance: Efficiency, Effectiveness, and Differentiation." *Journal of Business Logistics* 31, no.1 (2010): 43–62.

Gunasekaran, Angappa and Bulent Kobu. "Performance Measures and Metrics in Logistics and Supply Chain Management: A Review of Recent Literature (1995–2004) for Research and Applications." *International Journal of Production Research* 45, no. 12 (2007): 2819–2840.

Green Jr., Kenneth W., Dwayne Whitten, and R. Anthony Inman. "The Impact of Logistics Performance on Organizational Performance in a Supply Chain Context." *Supply Chain Management: An International Journal* 13, no. 4 (2008): 317–328.

Hult, Thomas M., David J. Ketchen Jr., Garry L. Adams, and Jeannette A. Mena. "Supply Chain Orientation and Balanced Scorecard Performance." *Journal of Managerial Issues* 20, no. 4 (2009): 526–544.

Kaplan, Robert S. and David P. Norton. *The Balanced Scorecard: Translating Strategy into Action* (Boston, MA: Harvard Business Press, 1996).

Lambert, Douglas M. and Renan Burduroglu. "Measuring and Selling the Value of Logistics." *International Journal of Logistics Management* 11, no. 1 (2000): 1–17.

Keebler, James S. and Richard E. Plank. "Logistics Performance Measurement in the Supply Chain: A Benchmark." *Benchmarking: An International Journal* 16, no. 6 (2009): 785–798.

Neely, Andy. *Business Performance Measurement: Unifying Theory and Integrating Practice,* 2nd ed. (Cambridge, UK: University Press, 2007).

Slone, Reuben E., John T. Mentzer, and J. Paul Dittmann. "Are You the Weakest Link in Your Company's Supply Chain?" *Harvard Business Review* 85, no. 9 (2007): 116–127.

Stapleton, Drew, Joe B. Hanna, Steve Yagla, Jay Johnson, and Dan Markussen. "Measuring Logistics Performance Using the Strategic Profit Model." *International Journal of Logistics Management* 13, no. 1 (2002): 89–107.

Toyli, Juuso, Lotta Hakkinen, Lauri Ojala, and Tapio Naula. "Logistics and Financial Performance: An Analysis of 424 Finnish Small and Medium-Sized Enterprises." *International Journal of Physical Distribution & Logistics Management* 38, no. 1 (2008): 57–80.

Zacharia, Zach G., Nancy W. Nix, and Robert F. Lusch. "An Analysis of Supply Chain Collaborations and their Effect on Performance Outcomes." *Journal of Business Logistics* 30, no. 2 (2009): 101–124.

CASE

CASE 3.1   Brant Freezer Company

Located in Fargo, North Dakota, the Brant Freezer Company manufactures industrial freezers. These freezers come in one size and are distributed through public warehouses in Atlanta, Boston, Chicago, Denver, Los Angeles, Portland, and St. Louis. In addition, some space is used in the company's Fargo warehouse. Young Joaquin (J. Q.) Brant, with a fresh M.B.A. degree from the University of South Alabama, returned to the family firm, where he had once worked during summers. On his first day of work, J. Q. met with his father. His father complained that they were being "eaten alive" by warehousing costs. The firm's controller drew up a budget each year, and each warehouse's monthly activity (units shipped) and costs were tallied.

| | 2012 Figures | | | | 2013 Figures | | | |
| | Units Shipped | | Warehouse Costs | | Units Shipped | | Warehouse Costs | |
	12 Months Jan.–Dec.	5 Months Through May 31	12 Months Jan.–Dec.	5 Months Through May 31	Projected 12 Months Jan.–Dec.	Actual 5 Months May 31	Budgeted 12 Months Jan.–Dec.	Actual Costs Through May 31
Atlanta	17,431	4,080	156,830	35,890	18,000	4,035	178,000	40,228
Boston	6,920	3,061	63,417	27,915	7,200	3,119	73,000	29,416
Chicago	28,104	14,621	246,315	131,618	30,000	15,230	285,000	141,222
Denver	3,021	1,005[a]	28,019	8,600[a]	3,100	1,421	31,000	14,900
Fargo	2,016	980	16,411	8,883	2,000	804	17,000	9,605
Los Angeles	16,491	11,431	151,975	109,690	17,000	9,444	176,000	93,280
Portland	8,333	4,028	73,015	36,021	9,000	4,600	85,000	42,616
St. Louis	5,921	2,331	51,819	23,232	8,000	2,116	56,000	19,191

EXHIBIT 3.A Brant Freezer Warehouse Performance
[a]Denver warehouse closed by strike March 4–19, 2012.

Income Statement 2012		
Sales		$4,003,450
Cost of goods sold		$937,000
Gross Margin		$3,066,450
Transportation cost	$657,322	
Warehousing cost	$735,982	
Inventory carrying cost	$567,987	
Other operating	$345,876	
Total operating cost		$2,307,167
Earnings Before Interest and Taxes		$759,283
Interest		$110,000
Taxes		$69,000
Net income		$580,283

EXHIBIT 3.B Brant Freezer Company Income Statement

Exhibit 3.A shows actual 2012 figures for all warehouses, plus actual figures for the first five months of 2013. Projected 12-month 2013 budgets and shipments are also included. Exhibit 3.B shows the income statement for 2012. Exhibit 3.C is the 2012 balance sheet. If you are familiar with Excel or other spreadsheet software, you might try using it to answer the questions that follow.

Balance Sheet 2012

Assets	
Cash	$706,034
Accounts receivable	$355,450
Inventory	$1,590,435
Total current assets	$2,651,919
Net fixed assets	$803,056
Total assets	$3,454,975
Liabilities	
Current liabilities	$1,678,589
Long-term debt	$398,060
Total liabilities	$2,076,649
Shareholders' Equity	$1,378,326
Total Liabilities and Equity	$3,454,975

EXHIBIT 3.C Brant Freezer Company Balance Sheet

Questions

1. When comparing performance during the first five months of 2013 with performance in 2012, which warehouse shows the most improvement?
2. When comparing performance during the first five months of 2013 with performance in 2012, which warehouse shows the poorest change in performance?
3. When comparisons are made among all eight warehouses, which one do you think does the best job for the Brant Company? What criteria did you use? Why?
4. J. Q. is aggressive and is going to recommend that his father cancel the contract with one of the warehouses and give that business to a competing warehouse in the same city. J. Q. feels that when word of this gets around, the other warehouses they use will "shape up." Which of the seven should J. Q. recommend be dropped? Why?

5. The year 2013 is nearly half over. J. Q. is told to determine how much the firm is likely to spend for warehousing at each of the eight warehouses for the last six months in 2013. Do his work for him.
6. When comparing the 2012 figures with the 2013 figures shown in the table, the amount budgeted for each warehouse in 2013 was greater than actual 2012 costs. How much of the increase is caused by increased volume of business (units shipped) and how much by inflation?
7. Use the 2012 income statement and balance sheet to complete a strategic profit model for J. Q.
8. Holding all other information constant, what would be the effect on ROA for 2013 if warehousing costs declined 10 percent from 2012 levels?

4

ORGANIZATIONAL AND MANAGERIAL ISSUES IN LOGISTICS

KEY TERMS

- "C-level" position
- Centralized logistics organization
- Container security initiative (CSI)
- Customs Trade Partnership Against Terrorism (C-TPAT)
- Decentralized logistics organization
- Excess capacity
- Fragmented logistics structure

- Importer security filing (ISF) rule
- ISO 9000
- Lean Six Sigma
- Logistics service quality
- Logistics social responsibility
- Logistics uncertainty pyramid model
- Malcolm Baldrige National Quality Award
- Pilferage

- Productivity
- Reverse logistics
- Six Sigma
- Tachograph
- Theft
- Transportation worker identification credential (TWIC)
- Unified logistics structure

LEARNING OBJECTIVES

- To examine organizational structure for logistics
- To learn about traditional and contemporary organizational design for logistics
- To explore productivity issues in logistics
- To explore quality issues in logistics

- To learn about ways to manage theft and pilferage
- To introduce you to the concept of logistics social responsibility
- To discuss issues associated with reverse logistics
- To describe programs designed to lessen the impact of terrorism on logistics systems

---

This chapter focuses on organizational and managerial issues in logistics, and with respect to organizational issues the degree to which logistics activities are fragmented or unified can play a key role in determining an organization's logistical effectiveness and efficiency. Likewise, logistical effectiveness and efficiency can be enhanced by successfully addressing the wide variety of managerial issues faced by today's logistician.

This chapter first looks at organizing logistics within the firm, with a specific focus on organizational structure for logistics as well as organizational design for logistics. The chapter also looks at select managerial issues in logistics, with a particular emphasis on productivity, quality, risk, sustainability, and complexity.

ORGANIZING LOGISTICS WITHIN THE FIRM

The organization of logistics activities within a firm depends on a number of factors, including the number and location of customers, as well as an organization's size, among others.[1] For example, the number and location of customers might influence whether a firm adopts a centralized or

---

[1]David J. Bloomberg, Stephan LeMay, and Joe B. Hanna, *Logistics* (Upper Saddle River, NJ: Prentice Hall, 2002).

decentralized logistics organization (to be more fully discussed in the "Organizational Structure for Logistics" section that follows). A company's size might influence the organizing of logistics activities in the sense that there are limitations in the degree of specialization of managerial talent in small firms. In such situations, one consideration in organizing might be to even out the workloads of each manager. Thus, one manager might have transportation-related responsibilities, another manager might be responsible for ordering and inventory management, and a third manager might be assigned warehousing responsibilities.

It's not possible to present a comprehensive description of the many organizational topics associated with logistics. As a result, we'll focus on two key organizational topics, namely, organizational structure for logistics and organizational design for logistics.

Organizational Structure for Logistics

Organizational structure focuses on how work roles and administrative mechanisms are allocated in an effort to integrate and control work.[2] Two basic organizational structures are associated with logistics, namely, fragmented and unified. In a **fragmented logistics structure**, logistics activities are managed in multiple departments throughout an organization. For example, a company might assign outbound transportation, demand forecasting, warehousing management, and customer service to the marketing department, whereas procurement, inbound transportation, packaging, and materials handling might be the responsibility of the manufacturing department. A fragmented logistics structure might also see order management under the control of the accounting department, and inventory management might be under the auspices of the finance department.

Although the example in the previous paragraph suggests logistics activities that are spread across four distinct departments, a fragmented logistics structure can come in all shapes and sizes. In a fragmented structure, it's possible for the various logistics activities to be managed in two, three, four, or more departments. Likewise, although our example assigns particular logistics activities to certain departments, there is no established template for which logistics activities are assigned to which departments. For example, an organization might divide inventory management into three categories—raw materials, work-in-process, and finished goods; raw materials and work-in-process inventories might be managed by the manufacturing department, whereas finished goods inventory might be the purview of the marketing department.

One problem with a fragmented logistics structure is that because logistics activities are scattered throughout the firm, they likely remain subservient to the objectives of the department (e.g., marketing, manufacturing) in which they are housed. Moreover, because effective and efficient logistics is predicated on a high degree of coordination among logistics activities, such coordination can become difficult when the logistics activities are spread throughout an organization.

In a **unified logistics structure**, multiple logistics activities are combined into, and managed as, a single department. The unified structure can be further classified based on the number and type of activities assigned to the department. A basic unified logistics structure might have responsibility for transportation, inventory management, and warehousing. A more progressive unified structure would include these basic activities plus several additional logistics activities such as order management and customer service. An advanced unified structure would include both the basic and progressive activities, along with several other logistics activities such as demand forecasting and procurement.

Regardless of how many, or what type, of logistics activities are managed, the unified logistics structure should be better positioned than the fragmented structure to achieve coordination

---

[2]J. Child, "Organizational Structure, Environment and Performance: The Role of Strategic Choice," *Sociology* 6, no. 1 (1972): 1–22.

across the various activities. For example, efficient and accurate communication among inbound and outbound transportation, warehousing, inventory management, procurement, and so on should be facilitated when they are combined into one department. Indeed, so-called leading-edge logistics companies—firms with demonstrably superior logistical capabilities—exhibit different logistics organizational structures than do other organizations. For example, leading-edge organizations are more likely to use a unified, as opposed to fragmented, logistics organizational structure. In addition, leading-edge companies tend to manage more types of logistics activities than do other companies, including less-traditional logistics activities such as demand forecasting and procurement.[3]

An important issue in terms of organizational structure is whether the logistics department should be centralized or decentralized. A **centralized logistics organization** implies that the company maintains a single logistics department that administers the related activities for the entire company from the home office. A **decentralized logistics organization**, in contrast, means that logistics-related decisions are made separately at the divisional or product group level and often in different geographic regions.

There are advantages to both approaches, with a primary advantage of centralization being its relative efficiency, whereas a primary advantage of decentralization is its customer responsiveness. Centralization allows an organization to take advantage of the cost savings that can arise from volume-creating opportunities. Suppose, for example, that an organization has four distribution facilities that annually generate 125,000 pounds of outbound freight, for a total outbound volume of 500,000 pounds. A centralized logistics organization should be able to achieve lower transportation rates for 500,000 pounds of volume than the individual facilities could each achieve for 125,000 pounds of volume.

Advocates of decentralization question the ability of a centralized logistics unit to provide the required levels of customer responsiveness. Indeed, the contemporary marketplace is made up of heterogeneous customers who aren't necessarily well served by centralized logistics practices. For instance, an organization with a mixture of consumer and business-to-business product lines might benefit from decentralization because of differing logistical requirements of consumer and business-to-business segments. Likewise, many global firms need to decentralize operations because of geographic and time distances from the home office. As an example, the time difference between the United States and China (at least 12 hours depending on one's location in the United States) doesn't readily lend itself to timely resolution of issues if managed under a centralized approach.

Another important issue in logistics organization structure is the job title or corporate rank (e.g., manager, director, vice president, chief) of the top logistics person; indeed, one attribute of leading-edge organizations is that logistics tends to be headed by senior-level (vice president, chief) personnel.[4] Although in recent years logistics has assumed greater importance in many organizations in the sense that the top logistics person holds a vice president title, to date logistics has generally been excluded from holding a **"C-level" position**, which refers to corporate officers such as a chief executive officer (CEO), a chief operating officer (COO), or a chief financial officer (CFO). In other words, there are few companies in which a person holding the position of chief logistics officer (CLO) leads the logistics function. One exception is Green Mountain Coffee Roasters, a leader in specialty coffee and coffee makers. Driven by the complexity of their multichannel business, they have established a CLO for their organization.

---

[3]Donald J. Bowersox, Patricia J. Daugherty, Cornelia Dröge, Dale B. Rogers, and Daniel Wardlow, *Leading Edge Logistics: Competitive Positioning for the 1990s* (Oak Brook, IL: Council of Logistics Management, 1989).
[4]Bowersox et al., *Leading Edge Logistics.*

Organizational Design for Logistics[5]

Organizational design is much broader than the familiar series of boxes and lines that detail reporting relationships in an organization. Organizational design is also concerned with issues such as who makes work-related decisions and the appropriate communication channels between workers and managers, among other things. Broadly speaking, three primary types of organizational design are used: hierarchical (also called functional), matrix, and network.

Hierarchical, or functional, organizational design has its foundations in the command-and-control military organization, where decision making and communication often follow a top–down flow. One advantage to hierarchical design is flexibility in exercising command in the sense that no one manager commands more than a "limited" number (e.g., 10, 20, 25) of employees. In addition, each employee reports to one, and only one, supervisor. One disadvantage of hierarchical design is that societal changes, such as individuality and questioning authority, are not easily accommodated in a command and control philosophy.

In a matrix design, one employee might have cross-functional responsibilities. For example, the category manager of small appliances at a particular organization might report to logistics, marketing, and production executives and this manager would have responsibility for the production, marketing, and logistics of small appliances. One advantage of this design is that the category manager (such as the small appliance manager in our example) can be very responsive to customer requirements. One disadvantage is that a matrix organization tends to be more costly because more managerial-level employees are necessary in comparison to a hierarchical organization.

Both the hierarchical and matrix forms of organization are well suited for environments dominated by costly information and restricted communication—constraints that have been lessened by the Internet. Moreover, hierarchical and matrix organizations flourish when there are a limited number of decision alternatives as well as limited time constraints on making a decision. However, the contemporary business environment is increasingly characterized by a myriad of decision alternatives and shorter time windows for making decisions. To this end, a network organization design attempts to create an organization that is responsive to the parameters of the contemporary business environment.

A key attribute of a network organizational design is a shift from function to process. In a functional–hierarchical philosophy, products and processes were divided into easy-to-complete tasks. A process philosophy, by contrast, focuses on combining tasks into *value-creating products and activities*. For example, effective and efficient order management is a process designed to produce satisfied and loyal customers, and order management consists of a number of different tasks such as order receipt, order entry, credit check, order triage, order picking, and so on. It's only when these tasks work in concert that value is created.

The network organization's emphasis on process and value creation has important implications for organizational design. Because processes and value creation tend to be customer focused, organizational design should facilitate an organization's interaction with its customers. For example, one way to facilitate customer interaction is to move decisions as close as possible to the point at which action is required, which requires empowering lower-level employees and managers with the authority to make decisions. You should recognize that the concept of worker empowerment is directly opposed to the specifications of hierarchical organizational design.

Moreover, from a logistics perspective, a network organizational design is manifested in terms of relevancy, responsiveness, and flexibility. *Relevancy*, which refers to satisfying current and emerging customer needs, can be facilitated by developing mutually beneficial relationships with key customers; at a minimum, these relationships should provide an understanding of customer needs and wants. *Responsiveness* reflects the degree to which an organization can accommodate

---

[5]Much of the material in this section is drawn from G. Bruce Friesen, "Organization Design for the 21st Century," *Consulting to Management* 14, no. 3 (2005): 32–51.

unique or unplanned customer requests; responsiveness can be achieved when the appropriate decision makers are provided with both relevant information and the authority to address unique or unplanned requests. *Flexibility*, which can be defined as an organization's ability to address unexpected operational situations, is predicated on avoiding early commitment to an irreversible course of action. One example of logistics flexibility would be the postponement of assembly, labeling, and so on until exact customer requirements are known.[6]

MANAGERIAL ISSUES IN LOGISTICS

The logistics discipline would be relatively easy if it entailed simply organizing a logistics system and then putting it into operation. However, well-run companies recognize that logistics systems must not only be organized, but they must also be managed. Although the remaining chapters will discuss managerial issues associated with particular logistics activities (e.g., procurement-specific managerial issues, warehousing-specific managerial issues, and so on), the following sections will focus on overarching managerial issues affecting logistics managers that are not activity specific.

Productivity

Productivity is an important managerial issue because it provides insight into the efficiency (or inefficiency) with which corporate resources are being utilized. At a basic level, **productivity** can be defined as the amount of output divided by the amount of input. An understanding of this relationship leads to the recognition that there are but three ways to improve productivity—reduce the amount of input while holding output constant, increase the amount of output while holding input constant, or increase output while at the same time decreasing input.

Understanding the three ways to improve productivity is important to the logistics manager because several logistics activities, particularly warehousing and transportation, are heavily dependent on human labor. For productivity purposes, human labor is considered an input (i.e., workers receive wages or salaries), and most humans are resistant to productivity suggestions that focus on reducing their wages or salaries (i.e., input). As such, productivity improvement efforts in logistics are often directed toward *increasing the amount of output while holding input constant.*

Moreover, in some geographic locations logistics operating employees (e.g., warehouse workers, truck drivers) are unionized, and the union contracts can provide a challenge to improving productivity. This is because union work rules are often very specific in the sense that job descriptions spell out in exacting detail the responsibilities associated with a particular job. Thus, if an order picker's forklift were to malfunction, the order picker might be prohibited from remedying the situation because forklift repairs are the responsibility of another group of workers. Although detailed job specifications help create additional employment opportunities, the relative lack of worker flexibility can potentially hinder productivity by increasing inputs (e.g., additional workers, hence additional labor costs) while also decreasing output. For example, the order picker with the malfunctioning forklift may have to delay order picking until the forklift is repaired or another forklift becomes available for use.

Many warehousing facilities have clearly articulated work rules that serve a number of purposes, the most important of which is to keep the workforce in general, and individual employees in particular, from engaging in unproductive and potentially destructive activities. It's simply not enough to have a set of clearly articulated work rules—to be effective, the work rules must be enforced.

A distinction needs to be made between warehousing and trucking when discussing the management of labor productivity in logistics. In warehousing, supervisors can be physically

---

[6]Donald J. Bowersox, David J. Closs, and Theodore P. Stank, *21st Century Logistics: Making Supply Chain Integration a Reality* (Oak Brook, IL: Council of Logistics Management, 1999), Chapter 3.

present and are expected to be on top of nearly any situation. When a worker in a warehouse falls behind schedule, it is usually noticed relatively quickly, and corrective action can be taken in a timely fashion.

However, once on the road, truck drivers are removed from immediate supervision, and their work becomes more difficult to evaluate. Truck drivers can fall behind schedule or be delayed for a variety of reasons such as traffic conditions, a bottleneck at a loading dock, or perhaps too much time socializing with fellow drivers at a particular truck stop. Initially, a manager has little choice but to accept the driver's explanation for the delay. As such, it is necessary to have control mechanisms so that drivers who often encounter uncontrollable delays (e.g., traffic conditions) can be distinguished from those who encounter controllable delays (e.g., socializing with fellow drivers).

Technological considerations play an increasingly important role in managing truck drivers and their productivity. For example, some firms photograph or videotape drivers making pickups at their loading docks. Moreover, activity can be recorded by a **tachograph**, a recording instrument that is installed inside a truck and produces a continuous, timed record of the truck, its speed, and its engine speed. From the information on a tachograph chart, one can tell how efficiently the truck and driver are being used. If the driver works on a regular route, it may be possible to rearrange the stops so that the driver can avoid areas of traffic congestion. Bad driving habits, such as high highway speeds and excessive engine idling, can also be detected. In case of an accident, a tachograph chart is invaluable in reporting and explaining what occurred just prior to the crash.

The interfaces involving wireless communications, global positioning systems (GPS), and graphical information systems (GIS) offer tremendous technology-related opportunities to improve driver productivity. Global positioning systems use satellites that allow companies to compute vehicle position, velocity, and time, whereas graphical information systems allow companies to produce digital maps that can drill down to site-specific aspects such as bridge heights and customer locations. GPS and GIS are evolving toward a situation in which instant updates can be provided to GIS databases—data that can be leveraged to provide real-time route planning that can direct drivers away from accidents and other traffic bottlenecks.

Thus far this section has focused only on worker productivity, but asset productivity is also an important consideration for logistics managers. One asset-related productivity concern involves space utilization, or the percent of available space that's actually being used. **Excess capacity**, or unused available space, can be unproductive because it may result in the purchase of additional equipment or facilities—a situation that adds to costs (input) but not necessarily to output, thus resulting in lower productivity.

Consider the example of a company that built an approximately 700,000 square foot warehouse as a replacement for a smaller storage facility. A review of the new warehouse one year after its opening revealed that only 55 percent of the available space was actually being utilized and the company concluded (reluctantly) that it could have satisfied current and future demand with a 450,000 square foot facility. The 700,000 square foot facility caused the company to purchase additional real estate, incur higher construction costs, and incur higher materials handling costs (in the form of storage racks and forklifts) when compared to a 450,000 square foot facility. From a managerial perspective, the 700,000 square foot facility handled the same amount of product (output), at a higher cost (input), as could a 450,000 square foot facility—thus resulting in decreased productivity.

A second asset-related productivity concern focuses on improving the output from existing assets. Southwest Airlines, for example, is able to fly more trip segments per day with its airplanes than many of its competitors because Southwest's planes spend less time parked at airport gates. Another way of improving the output from existing assets involves extending their revenue-producing lifespan. For example, one of the authors worked for a trucking company that regularly utilized 25-year-old tractors to serve certain customers. From one perspective, the 25-year-old tractors were extremely productive in the sense that a fully depreciated asset was generating revenues. Having said this, the 25-year-old tractors lacked certain safety features found on newer-model tractors, incurred higher maintenance costs and were less fuel-efficient than newer-model tractors.

Quality

Logistics service quality relates to a firm's ability to deliver products, materials and services without defects or errors to both internal and external customers.[7] However, it's important that we operationalize "quality" before beginning our description of logistics service quality. Consider that the American Society of Quality, which bills itself as the world's leading membership organization focused on quality, notes that quality is a subjective term.[8] Each person will have his or her own definition. Although there are somewhat stringent definitions of quality, such as a product or service that is free from defects, deficiencies, or errors, we will take a more flexible approach and define quality as conformance to mutually agreed upon requirements.

The issue of quality in logistics often represents a delicate balancing act for the involved organizations. That is, if an organization provides logistics services of inferior quality when delivering their products, it runs the risk of lowering the customer's perceived value of the seller's product. If an organization provides higher levels of logistics service quality than their customer values or requires, it may be paying for something that is not needed. This increased cost without an associated perception of value can affect the competitiveness of a firm's offering. In short, organizations designing their logistics service offerings must understand issues of quality and strive to match the quality levels of the logistics services they provide with the expectations of their customers and the competitive landscape in which they operate.

Today, vendors are expected to have quality programs, and many have worked for years to achieve a good reputation for quality. One way for vendors to convince potential buyers that they are committed to quality is through a program known as ISO (International Standards Organization) 9000 certification. **ISO 9000** is a set of generic standards used to document, implement, and demonstrate quality management and assurance systems. Applicable to manufacturing and service industries, these standards are intended to help companies build quality into every core process in each department. Firms demonstrating a commitment to quality through training, reviews, and continuous improvement can receive ISO 9000 certification. After achieving ISO 9000 certification, organizations are audited each year and can be recertified every three years. Among logistics managers, ISO 9000 certification is credited with increasing customer service, improved order accuracy, and enabling enhanced costs analysis.[9]

Another quality-related concept or practice relevant for logistics managers is known as **Six Sigma**, which emphasizes the virtual elimination of business errors. Those who remember the normal distribution (curve) from their statistics class will recall that Sigma's are related to standard deviations from the mean. The higher the number of deviations included, the more area under the normal curve that is covered. In the case of Six Sigma, or six standard deviations, the area covered is 99.99966 percent, leaving a tiny area, .00034, uncovered. More specifically, the Six Sigma approach suggests that there will be 3.4 defects, deficiencies, or errors per one million opportunities—obviously a very high standard. These standards can be applied to various logistics activities such as order picking.

From a North American perspective, Six Sigma is a relatively new approach in the sense that it really didn't begin to achieve widespread acceptance—and adoption—until the mid 1990s. Indeed, a recent worldwide Six Sigma study indicated that only about 10 percent of the responding organizations had established a structured performance improvement program prior

---

[7]E.A. Morash, C. Droge, and S. Vickery, "Strategic Logistics Capabilities for Competitive Advantage and Firm Success," *Journal of Business Logistics* 17, no. 1 (1996): 1–22.

[8]www.asq.org

[9]Paul D. Larson and Stephen G. Kerr, "ISO and ABC: Complements or Competitors?" *International Journal of Logistics Management* 13, no. 2 (2002): 91–100.

to 1995. This same study also found that the most significant benefits from Six Sigma have been reduced costs, reduced errors and waste, and reduced cycle time, whereas the key drawbacks have involved overcoming business cultural barriers, investing the required resources (both human and money), and gaining top management commitment.[10]

While traditionally seen as rival initiatives, the integration of Six Sigma with the Lean approach, so-called **Lean Six Sigma**, is an area of emerging focus within many companies. Lean Six Sigma integrates the goals and methods of these two approaches in pursuit of quality. What sets Lean Six Sigma apart from its individual components is the recognition that organizations cannot focus only on quality or speed. There needs to be an organizational focus on improving quality as it relates to responsiveness. Halliburton, an oilfield services provider, has implemented Lean Six Sigma concepts both internally as well as pushing the concept out to their suppliers in an effort to better align their supply base with Halliburton's increasing demand and supply expectations.[11]

Another quality-related initiative is the **Malcolm Baldrige National Quality Award**, which was established in the late 1980s to recognize U.S. organizations for their achievements in quality and performance. Initially only manufacturers, services, and small businesses were eligible for this award, but eligibility was expanded to include health care and educational institutions in the late 1990s. Research has show that several factors included in the Baldridge critieria are important to the improvement of logistics processes.[12]

The Baldrige Quality Awards, which are restricted to organizations headquartered in the United States, require interested parties to submit a formal application that is evaluated by a committee largely made up of private-sector experts in business and quality. Applications are evaluated for achievement and improvement across seven categories: business results; customer and market focus; human resource focus; leadership; measurement, analysis, and knowledge management; process management; and strategic planning.[13] Importantly, organizations that choose not to apply for a Baldrige Award can use these seven categories as a template for evaluating the quality of current and prospective suppliers.

There are substantive differences between ISO 9000 and the Baldrige Award; ISO 9000 essentially allows an organization to determine if it complies with its specific quality system. In contrast, the Baldrige Award is more heavily focused on the actual results from a quality system as well as on continuous improvement.[14] The Baldrige Award also tends to be more externally focused in the sense that organizations benchmark themselves against organizations from outside their particular industry.

Risk

Logistics systems are complex networks of companies and activities that are constantly exposed to potential unpredictable disruptions. Risk can be viewed as susceptibility to disruptions that could lead to a loss for a firm, and this risk can take a variety of forms as it relates to the management of logistics activities. For example, regularly occurring risks involve things such as variability in demand or the potential for a damaged shipment, whereas catastrophic risks such as earthquakes or terrorist attacks can also unexpectedly affect a logistics system.[15] The **Logistics Uncertainty Pyramid Model** has been established to identify uncertainty sources that can affect the risk

---

[10]"Exclusive Worldwide Six Sigma Survey Reveals…" *Business Credit*, October 2005, 48–51.
[11]William Atkinson, "Halliburton Pushes Lean Six Sigma to Its Supply Base," *Purchasing* 138, no. 3 (2009): 18–20.
[12]Ronald D. Anderson, Roger E. Jerman, and Michael C. Crum, "Quality Management Influences on Logistics Performance," *Transportation Research—Part E* 34, no. 2 (1998): 137–148.
[13]www.quality.NIST.gov
[14]Ibid.
[15]A. Michael Knemeyer, Walter Zinn, and Cuneyt Eroglu, "Proactive Planning for Catastrophic Events in Supply Chains," *Journal of Operations Management* 27, no. 2 (2009): 141–153.

exposure for logistics activities.[16] The model identifies several types of uncertainty including shipper, customer, carrier, control systems, and external. The model can help logistics managers structure their examination of potential risks that could influence their firm's logistics system. While space limitations restrict us from discussing all potential risks that could arise in these areas of uncertainty, we will describe one operational risk and one catastrophic risk in greater detail. Namely, the remainder of this section will focus on two risks that can impact logistics activities in a firm, namely, terrorism and theft/pilferage.

Terrorism can be viewed as an illegal use of or threat of force or violence made by a group or an individual against a person, a company, or someone's property with a goal of menacing the target, often grounded in politics or ideology.[17] Although terrorism is often viewed by the media through a political or ideological lens, it can have important implications for commerce and for managing logistics systems.

It's no exaggeration to state that the terrorist attacks in the United States on September 11, 2001, were a defining moment that brought terrorism considerations to the forefront of logistics management. The September 11 terrorist attacks have profoundly impacted logistics practices on a worldwide basis, and processes, procedures, and activities that might have been given minimal attention prior to September 11 are now viewed from an entirely different perspective.

Consider the storage and transport of hazardous materials, which prior to September 11 were primarily managed from a safety perspective. Although safety remains an important perspective, the storage and transport of hazardous materials in today's world are also managed with an eye to potential terrorist considerations. For example, there are continuing efforts to reroute rail shipments of hazardous materials—because of terror concerns—away from major U.S. population centers, as oceangoing petroleum tankers have the potential to be used as mobile bombs.

One response to the September 11 attacks involved the creation of a new federal agency in the U.S., the Department of Homeland Security (DHS); two of its major aims are to prevent terrorist attacks in the United States as well as to reduce the vulnerability of the United States to terrorism. A total of 22 separate U.S. government entities were incorporated into the DHS, with the Transportation Security Administration (TSA) and Customs and Border Protection (CBP) being two of the most important from a logistics perspective.

The Transportation Security Administration is responsible for the security of the U.S. transportation system. You might be familiar with the TSA because it is the agency that conducts the passenger screening at U.S. commercial airports. The TSA also plays a number of roles with respect to freight security, such as using dogs to screen airfreight. In addition, the TSA was responsible for developing a **Transportation Worker Identification Credential** (TWIC) which is a common credential used to identify workers across all modes of transportation. One of the key attributes of TWIC is that the corresponding card contains both personal and biometric data, with the biometric data being used to exclude certain workers from secure areas at ports and terminals. The TWIC program became fully operational in early 2009, and while implementation has been relatively smooth, several problems, such as lengthly processing time for credentials, have surfaced.[18]

Customs and Border Protection is responsible for securing U.S. borders to protect the American people and the U.S. economy. One key CBP function is inspecting cargo, and a number of high-profile CBP initiatives have affected the management of logistics systems. The Trade Act of 2002, which required submission of advanced electronic data on all shipments entering

---

[16]V. Sanchez-Rodrigues, D. Stantchev, A. Potter, M.M. Naim, and A. Whiteing, "Establishing a Transport Operation Focused Uncertainty Model for the Supply Chain," *International Journal of Physical Distribution & Logistics Management* 38, no. 5 (2008): 388–411.

[17]Terrorism. *The American Heritage® Dictionary of the English Language,* 4th ed. (n.d.). Retrieved from Dictionary.com website: http://dictionary.reference.com/browse/terrorism.

[18]R.G. Edmonson, "TWIC's Forgotten Few," *Journal of Commerce*, April 20, 2009, 20.

Table 4.1	Timeline for Presenting Electronic Advance Manifest Information

Inbound to the United States

Mode	Timeline
Air and courier	Four hours prior to arrival in the United States, or "wheels up" from certain nearby airports
Rail	Two hours prior to arrival at a U.S. port of entry
Ocean vessel	24 hours prior to lading at foreign port
Truck	Free and Secure Trade (FAST): 30 minutes prior to arrival in the United States; non-FAST: one hour prior to arrival in the United States

Outbound from the United States

Mode	Timeline
Air and courier	Two hours prior to scheduled departure from the United States
Rail	Two hours prior to the arrival of the train at the border
Ocean vessel	24 hours prior to departure from U.S. port where cargo is laden
Truck	One hour prior to the arrival of the truck at the border

Source: Erlinda Byrd, "Rules for Improving Cargo Security," *Customs and Border Protection Today,* March 2004.

and leaving the United States, is aimed at identifying high-risk shipments that might threaten U.S. safety and security. Table 4.1 summarizes the manifest times for inbound and outbound shipments involving air, rail, water, and truck.

In particular, oceangoing containers destined for the United States are receiving much greater scrutiny today than prior to September 11. One of the things learned after the 2001 terrorist attacks was that a relatively small percentage of containers that arrived at U.S. ports was scanned to learn about their actual contents. This alarmed some U.S. legislators, and the result was a series of proposals that culminated in legislation requiring 100 percent scanning of U.S.-bound containers by 2012.

This scanning, which is to be done prior to a container being loaded onto ships at non-U.S. ports, has the potential to be quite disruptive to international trade because a number of nondomestic ports currently do not have the technology required to inspect containers. These ports would have to acquire and install the relevant scanning technology (which is quite expensive), discontinue sending containers to the United States, or route containers through other nondomestic ports that are equipped with the relevant technology. However, in early 2009, DHS Secretary Janet Napolitano suggested that the 2012 scanning deadline probably would not be achieved, in part because of difficulties in achieving agreements with all nondomestic ports that ship containerized cargo to the United States.[19]

Another example of the CBP's emphasis on containerized shipments is the **Container Security Initiative** (CSI), an agreement in which some of the world's ports agree to allow U.S. customs agents to identify and inspect high-risk containers bound for the United States before they are loaded onto ships. Approximately 60 international ports, including such major ports as Hong Kong, Singapore, Shanghai, and Rotterdam, currently participate in the CSI.

One of the best-known CBP programs enacted since September 11 is the **Customs Trade Partnership Against Terrorism** (C-TPAT), in which public (CBP) and private (e.g., retailers

---

[19]R.G. Edmonson, "DHS's New Boss," *The Journal of Commerce,* March 9, 2009, 16.

and manufacturers) organizations work together to prevent terrorism against the United States through imports and transportation. Private organizations apply to Customs and Border Protection for C-TPAT certification, and the process involves demonstrating that organizations have improved the physical security of their containerized shipments as well as the ability to track people who have access to the containerized shipments. Although the government-provided benefits to C-TPAT certification include fewer security inspections of inbound containers along with faster processing time through Customs, many companies have discovered that the C-TPAT process has also led to a reduction in cargo theft, pilferage, and loss.[20]

As if logistics managers aren't potentially overwhelmed by TWIC, CSI, C-TPAT, and other terrorism-related acronyms, Customs and Border Protection is also responsible for implementing and enforcing the **Importer Security Filing (ISF)** rule, also known as "10 + 2," which went into effect in early 2009. The "10 + 2" moniker refers to the fact that importers are required to file 10 pieces of information, and carriers two pieces of information, before cargo is loaded at non-U.S. water ports; Table 4.2 lists the "10 + 2" information requirements.

The initial feedback on "10 + 2" suggests that while erroneous filings have declined from 30 percent to less than 5 percent, some importers struggle to get timely, accurate, and complete information for their 10 required pieces of information. In addition, importers are concerned with the costs of "10 + 2" compliance, which can include the cost of upgrading their information systems, the actual cost of filing the 10 pieces of information, and potential monetary penalties for erroneous information or failure to file the information.[21]

Theft (stealing), which can be defined as the taking and removing of personal property with the intent to deprive the rightful owner of it,[22] is another logistics risk issue that confronts many managers. Unfortunately, it is often difficult to accurately quantify the impact of theft, in part because some companies are hesitant to report this data because a reported theft serves as direct evidence of a logistics system shortcoming. Having said this, anecdotal evidence suggests that cargo theft increased as U.S. economic conditions began to deteriorate in late 2007.[23]

Table 4.2   Information Required for 10 + 2 Rule

Importer:
1. Manufacturer's name and address
2. Seller's name and address
3. Buyer's name and address
4. Ship to name and address
5. Scheduled container stuffing location
6. Consolidator's name and address
7. Importer of record
8. Consignee identification number
9. Country of origin
10. Harmonized tariff schedule at minimum six-digit level

Carriers:
1. Vessel stow plan
2. Container status message

Source: R.G. Edmonson, "10 + 2 = Now," *The Journal of Commerce,* June 1, 2009, 13.

---

[20]Christine Blank, "Cruise through Customs," *Multichannel Merchant,* August 2006, 46–47.
[21]R.G. Edmonson, "10 + 2 = Now," *The Journal of Commerce,* June 1, 2009, 10–13.
[22]www.m-w.com/dictionary
[23]Barry Tarnef, "Into Thin Air," *World Trade,* September 2008, 50–52.

You might be wondering why logisticians would be concerned about theft, particularly because many organizations carry insurance to compensate themselves in cases of theft. However, even though insurance may reimburse an organization for the market value of the stolen items, the time and costs (e.g., documentation) associated with theft tend not to be covered by insurance. A second logistical concern is that theft results in the planned flow of goods being interrupted and can lead to stockouts.

In addition, theft can factor into the facility location decision in the sense that some organizations will avoid locating their facilities in areas characterized by high crime rates.[24] It's also possible for the stolen products to reappear in the market at a lower price to compete with products that have moved through traditional channels. Indeed, there are suggestions that approximately 2 percent of the products available on Internet auction sites are actually stolen goods.[25]

Pilferage, which refers to employee theft, cannot be eliminated, and both warehousing and transportation operations are especially vulnerable to pilferage. Managing pilferage can be challenging for the logistics manager, and the managing begins with the hiring process. In fact, one of the best ways to manage pilferage is to avoid hiring people who are predisposed to steal, such as people with credit, alcohol, or drug problems. Some organizations utilize psychological tests as part of the hiring process in an effort to identify prospective employees who might pilfer.

Organizations can better manage pilferage if they have clearly articulated and enforced pilferage-related policies. To this end, experts recommend that the best pilferage policy should be based on zero tolerance because problems inevitably arise for those companies that tolerate a "small amount" of pilferage. For example, there may be disagreement in terms of how to operationalize "amount"—are we concerned with the number of units or the dollar value of items? Once this has been established, then what is meant by "small"—does, say, five units or $75 qualify as "small"? Quite simply, a zero-tolerance policy means that pilferage exceeding zero units or zero dollars is unacceptable.

One of the most effective methods of protecting goods from theft or pilferage is to keep them moving through the system. Goods waiting in warehouses, in terminals, or to clear customs are more vulnerable to theft than goods that are moving. No list of methods for protecting goods is complete; determined thieves are likely to overcome almost any safeguard placed in their way. However, a few suggestions are offered here, mainly to reflect the breadth of measures that might be taken:

- Decals are required for autos in employee parking lots, and nonemployees may be required to park in designated areas as well as to register with a company receptionist. This makes it more difficult for outsiders to access an organization's facilities.
- Forklifts in warehouses are locked at night, making it difficult to reach high items or to move heavy items.
- Seals (small wirelike devices that once closed cannot be reopened without breaking) are used more and more, with dispatchers, drivers, and receiving personnel all responsible for recording the seal number and inspecting its condition. Figure 4.1 shows a seal used for truck trailer or container doors.
- Electronic tags or strips are embedded in products at the time of their manufacture, and they can activate alarms at warehouse or retail store doors.
- Organizations should take a proactive approach to theft; waiting until theft reaches "unacceptable" levels might mean that certain dysfunctional behavior has been permitted for so long that it has come to be viewed as typical or acceptable.
- Experts suggest that companies should facilitate an employee's ability to report theft and other aberrant behavior, such as through a hotline that guarantees anonymity as well as protection from potential retaliation or retribution.

---

[24]Perry A. Trunick, "To Catch a Thief," *Logistics Today,* July 2005, 35–40.
[25]Julia Kuzeljevich, "The Seven Deadly Sins in Warehouse Security," *Canadian Transportation & Logistics,* April 2006, 44.

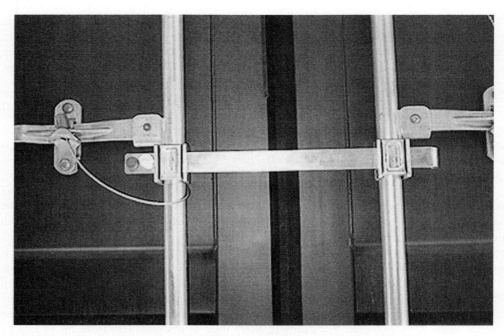

FIGURE 4.1 The Small Wire Shown on the Left Will Break if the Trailer Door Latch Is Opened. The Plug at its Upper End Is Marked with a Unique Number *Source:* CGM Security Solutions, Inc.

Note that many of the preceding suggestions are common sense in nature (e.g., decals, locked forklifts); indeed, common sense is viewed as a basic foundation for controlling theft. Importantly, commonsense approaches to system security are often no cost, or low cost, in nature.[26]

The discussion to this point has been primarily focused on domestic theft and pilferage. When goods move in international commerce, particularly by ship, they are much more vulnerable to theft and pilferage. Piracy attacks on ships have become a major concern in the twenty-first century, and unlike the somewhat romanticized pirates of movies and literature who wore eye patches and carried swords, contemporary pirates use speedboats, smart phones, global positioning systems, and automatic weapons. In addition, approximately 20 percent of all pirate attacks in recent years have involved petroleum tankers, which is of concern because of the potential for an environmental accident as well as the fact that tankers could be used as bombs in a terrorist attack.

To underscore the seriousness of pirate attacks for today's logistics manager, the International Maritime Bureau, an arm of the International Chamber of Commerce, reported 240 pirate attacks worldwide in the first six months of 2009 compared to 114 pirate attacks during the same time period in 2008.[27] Much of the 2009 increase was due to a surge in pirate attacks off the Somalian coast, and managerial responses to these attacks included outrunning the pirates, rerouting vessels away from Somalia, vehicle escort services, and armed professionals. The cost of these responses to pirate attacks—just for Somalia—has been estimated at approximately *$500 million annually!*[28]

[26]Michael Imlay, "Off-Highway Robbery," *Off-Road Business*, November 2005, 55–57.
[27]www.ics-ccs.org
[28]Robert R. Frump, "Danger at Sea," *The Journal of Commerce*, February 16, 2009, 20–24.

Sustainability

Logistics has an inherent connection to sustainability. A common definition of sustainability centers on the concept of the "triple bottom line," which was introduced in the mid-1990s and refers to the interaction of social, environmental, and economic dimensions. While most attention to date has focused on the environmental dimension, the social and economic dimensions are also critical to consider.[29] As such, this section will discuss logistics social responsibility as well as environmental issues associated with reverse logistics. The environmental dimension while not specifically examined underlies managerial decisions in both of these areas. In order to be truly sustainable, logistics managers must consider the economic impact of their sustainability-related decisions on their firm's bottom line.

The social responsibility concept suggests that an organization's obligations transcend purely economic considerations such as profit maximization. While corporate social responsibility concept has existed since the early 1970s, the concept of **logistics social responsibility**, or corporate social responsibility issues that relate directly to logistics,[30] did not emerge until the mid-1990s.

Potential logistics social responsibility dimensions include the environment, ethics, diversity, safety, philanthropy, and human rights, among others, and myriad activities or practices can be used to assess each of these dimensions. In terms of the environment, for example, organizations might focus on reusing and recycling products, reducing the amount of packaging, improving energy efficiency, and reducing various types of pollution. Ethical considerations include improperly sharing information, as well as bribes and gift giving, whereas diversity might evaluate the use of minority and female suppliers. Safety-related activities or practices include the safe movement and storage of products, particularly those of a hazardous nature, preventive vehicle maintenance, and proper workplace equipment (e.g., hardhats, goggles). Philanthropic logistics activities might include the donation of excess or obsolete inventory to charitable organizations, and sweatshop labor continues to be a preeminent human rights consideration.

Energy efficiency is a prominent logistics social responsibility issue for many organizations, and we'll take a closer look at energy efficiency in the following paragraphs. Warehousing and transportation represent two logistics activities where most energy costs occur and where energy-saving measures should be focused. For instance, design, lighting, and roofing represent three possible energy control areas in warehousing. With respect to design, facilities might be positioned so that dock doors aren't placed on the north side of a building (most cold winds blow from the north). Lighting provides a variety of opportunities for managing energy consumption; skylights, large windows that incorporate solar energy, and high-efficiency lighting can reduce electricity usage between 20 and 60 percent. In addition, high-efficiency lighting generally provides better lighting quality, and thus potentially improves workplace safety (another logistics social responsibility issue).

Roofing, which tends to be the largest exposed surface of a warehouse facility, is often overlooked as an area for energy control. White roof material, for example, tends to reflect sun-generated heat, while darker roof colors such as black and gray tend to absorb sun-generated heat, which causes increased electricity consumption to cool the interior areas of a warehouse. Moreover, some warehousing facilities are being designed with grass roofs, which lower energy consumption during the summer months.

---

[29]Marc Winter and A. Michael Knemeyer, "Exploring the Integration of Sustainability and Supply Chain Management—Current State and Opportunities for Future Inquiry," *International Journal of Physical Distribution & Logistics Management* 43, no. 1 (2013).

[30]Craig R. Carter and Marianne M. Jennings, "Logistics Social Responsibility: An Integrative Framework," *Journal of Business Logistics* 23, no. 2 (2002): 145–180.

Transportation is a second logistics activity where considerable energy savings can take place, particularly because transportation is a primary consumer of energy. Indeed, transportation accounts for approximately two-thirds of all petroleum consumption in the United States. As a result, many transportation providers are actively searching for ways to reduce their fuel consumption, which in turn will reduce their fuel costs. The U.S. Environmental Protection Agency's Smart Way Transport Partnership, established in 2004, helps companies to address environmental challenges such as fuel consumption. Results have been promising, as illustrated by Kohl's Department Stores, which has reduced empty truck movements by nearly 4 million miles since joining the partnership.[31]

You might be surprised to learn that the annual cost of **reverse logistics**, which refers to the process of managing return goods, exceeds $100 billion in just the United States. In addition, reverse logistics can be four to five times more expensive than forward logistics and the reverse logistics process can take 12 times as many steps (e.g., assessing the returned product and repairing the returned product) as the forward logistics process.[32]

The reverse logistics process focuses on three critical factors: (1) why products are returned, (2) how to optimize reverse logistics, and (3) whether reverse logistics should be managed internally or outsourced to a third party.[33] With respect to the first factor, products are returned for a variety of reasons, such as the customer making an error in ordering or the shipper making an error when filling an order. Goods may also be returned because of a product recall, which occurs when a hazard or defect is discovered in a manufactured or processed item, and its return is mandated by a government agency.

The second factor in managing returned goods, optimizing reverse logistics, involves a number of strategic and tactical considerations. One basic decision concerns the design of the reverse logistics system, such as whether return operations should be incorporated into existing warehousing and production facilities. If so, how will returned products be segregated from other products in an effort to reduce loss of returned product, to prevent mixing returned and nonreturned goods, and to prevent returned products from mistakenly being shipped out of the particular facility?[34]

Optimizing reverse logistics is incumbent on goods being carefully counted and the appropriate records (e.g., accounting, inventory) being adjusted. After a returned item has been received, it is important to evaluate the item in terms of a series of questions:

- Is the product damaged and unsalable, or can it be refurbished and resold?
- Was it returned as part of an overstock arrangement with a retailer?
- Is it a product that is being recalled?
- Is the item in an unopened package that can go into inventory for immediate resale?
- Does the item need to undergo special testing?
- What is the item's worth?
- How do the company's returned goods policies apply to this item?[35]

The scope of the preceding questions indicates that returned goods should not be managed as an afterthought. This leads directly to the third critical factor in managing reverse logistics—whether reverse logistics should be managed internally or outsourced to a third party. If a company decides to internally manage returned goods, there must be recognition that one or more employees will have returned goods as their primary, if not only, job

---

[31]Marianne Wilson, "Green Transport," *Chain Store Age*, January 2009, 55.

[32]David Blanchard, "Moving Ahead by Mastering the Reverse Supply Chain," *Industry Week*, June 2009, 58–59.

[33]John Paul Quinn, "Are There Ever Any Happy Returns?" *Logistics Management*, June 2005, 63–66.

[34]Ibid.

[35]Ibid.

responsibility. Because reverse logistics can be so different (e.g., irregular flow of product, small shipments) from forward logistics, the outsourcing of reverse logistics continues to grow in popularity.[36]

Complexity

The degree of complexity in a logistics system is largely a function of the dynamic, global, diverse, and highly uncertain nature of relationships and activities that are involved in today's business environment. Logistics managers are increasingly faced with the challenge of managing this complexity both within their firms and across the network of relationships that exist in their supply chain. The increased data challenges, decision-making variability, and relationship intricacy pose difficult situations for logistics managers. While space limitations will inhibit us from examining all of the various manifestations of complexity in logistics systems, we will take a look at some of the most relevant types affecting logistics decision making. Specifically, we will explore the role of network complexity, process complexity, and range complexity on logistics activities.

Network complexity refers to the growing number of nodes and the associated changes to the links in logistics systems. For example, a decision to outsource manufacturing activities to a country like China will necessarily increase the complexity of logistics activities associated with managing the flow and storage of materials and information from this facility. New modes, new carriers, customs issues, and exchange rate considerations are only a few examples of how logistics activites are affected by this change. In addition, with the increased use of outsourcing over the past decade, an associated increase in network complexity has occurred. Often, managers have been overly influenced by the promise of potential labor cost savings without fully considering the increased logistics costs that result from this more dispersed network. As labor rates have increased, this appreciation has begun to emerge.

Process complexity centers on the haphazard development of processes, additions and modifications to processes over time, and/or changing process requirements. For example, take a logistics process associated with pick and pack operations in a warehouse environment. Logistics implications of increased process complexity could emerge due to an increased amount of time required to pick an order resulting from changes in the number of steps or changes in the handling requirements that the warehouse worker needs to complete. These changes could be caused by safety, regulatory, or even customer considerations.

Range complexity centers on the implications associated with the increasing number of products that most companies continue to face in an effort to differentiate themselves with their customers. This so-called issue of stock-keeping unit (SKU) proliferation will typically result in increased levels of inventory and warehousing costs. In addition, the ability to realize scale economies in areas of transportation and procurement could also be affected by this type of complexity. Logistics managers must work not only to reduce the complexity they face but also to communicate the costs of increased complexity to the firm.

Summary

A diverse set of organizational and managerial issues affect today's logisticians. The chapter began by examining how logistics is organized within a firm, with a specific focus on organizational structure and design approaches.

The chapter concluded by looking at general managerial issues facing logistics managers. These issues included productivity concerns, quality management, risk considerations, sustainability concerns and complexity management.

---

[36]Bob Trebilcock, "Outsourcing Reverse Logistics," *Modern Materials Handling*, June 2008, 18–20.

Questions for Discussion and Review

4.1 Discuss several issues that influence the organization of logistics activities within a firm.

4.2 Compare and contrast the fragmented and unified logistics organizational structures.

4.3 What are the differences between a centralized and a decentralized logistics department?

4.4 Describe the hierarchical and matrix organizational design.

4.5 From a logistics perspective, how is network organizational design manifested in terms of relevancy, responsiveness, and flexibility?

4.6 Define what is meant by productivity and discuss the ways in which productivity can be improved.

4.7 In what ways can a unionized workforce be a challenge to improving worker productivity?

4.8 Discuss how technological considerations can help in managing truck drivers and their productivity.

4.9 What are some potential challenges to improving productivity by getting more output from existing assets?

4.10 Discuss the reasons why logisticians might be concerned with theft.

4.11 How can logistics managers attempt to control pilferage?

4.12 Explain why piracy attacks on ships are a potentially serious issue for today's logistics manager.

4.13 Describe some potential logistics social responsibility dimensions.

4.14 How can warehouses control their energy usage in terms of design, lighting, and roofing considerations?

4.15 Discuss reasons why products might be returned.

4.16 What questions should be asked after a returned item has been counted and recorded?

4.17 What are some ways in which the Transportation Security Administration is attempting to improve the security of the U.S. transportation system?

4.18 In what ways is the legislation requiring 100 percent scanning of U.S.-bound containers likely to be disruptive to international trade?

4.19 Discuss the Customs Trade Partnership Against Terrorism (C-TPAT).

4.20 What are some types of complexity that are affecting logistics activities in a firm?

Suggested Readings

Ashenbaum, Bryan, Peter A. Salzarulo, and W. Rocky Newman, "Organizational Structure, Entrepreneurial Orientation and Trait Preference in Transportation Brokerage Firms." *Journal of Supply Chain Management* 48, no. 1 (2012): 3–23.

Autry, Chad W., Zach G. Zacharia, and Charles W. Lamb. "A Logistics Strategy Taxonomy." *Journal of Business Logistics* 29, no. 2 (2008): 27–51.

Bernon, Michael and John Cullen. "An Integrated Approach to Managing Reverse Logistics." *International Journal of Logistics: Research & Applications* 10, no. 1 (2007): 41–56.

Cantor, David E. "Workplace Safety in the Supply Chain: A Review of the Literature and Call for Research." *International Journal of Logistics Management* 19, no. 1 (2008): 65–83.

Daugherty, Patricia J., Haozhe Chen, and Bruce G. Ferrin, "Organizational Structure and Logistics Service Innovation." *International Journal of Logistics Management* 22, no. 1 (2011): 26–51.

Ekwell, Daniel. "The Displacement Effect in Cargo Theft." *International Journal of Physical Distribution & Logistics Management* 39, no. 1 (2009): 47–62.

Gamelas, Theophilos and Mark Johnson. "A Systems Approach to Transportation Security." *Journal of Transportation Law, Logistics & Policy* 74, no. 2 (2007): 156–180.

Goldsby, Thomas J. and Robert O. Matichenko. *Lean Six Sigma Logistics: Strategic Development to Operational Success* (Boca Raton, FL: J. Ross Publishing, 2005).

Kraska, James and Brian Wilson. "Maritime Piracy in East Africa." *Journal of International Affairs* 62, no. 2 (2009): 55–68.

Kumar, Sameer and Janis Verruso. "Risk Assessment for the Security of Inbound Containers at U.S. Ports: A Failure, Mode, Effects, and Criticality Analysis Approach." *Transportation Journal* 47, no. 4 (2008): 26–41.

Maloni, Michael J. and Michael E. Brown. "Corporate Social Responsibility in the Supply Chain: An Application in the Food Industry." *Journal of Business Ethics* 68, no. 1 (2006): 35–52.

McKinnon, Alan, Sharon Cullinane, Michael Browne, and Anthony Whiteing. *Green Logistics: Improving the Environmental Sustainability of Logistics* (London, UK: Kogan Page, 2010).

Pettit, Timothy J., Joseph Fiksel and Keely L. Croxton. "Ensuring Supply Chain Resilience: Development of a Conceptual Framework." *Journal of Business Logistics* 31, no. 1 (2010): 1–21.

Sanchez-Rodrigues, Vasco, Andrew Potter and Mohamed M. Naim. "Evaluating the Causes of Uncertainty in Logistics Operations." *International Journal of Logistics Management* 21, no. 1 (2010): 45–64.

Spence, Laura and Michael Bourlakis. "The Evolution from Corporate Social Responsibility to Supply Chain Responsibility: The Case of Waitrose." *Supply Chain Management: An International Journal* 14, no. 4 (2009): 291–302.

Stock, James R. and Jay P. Mulki. "Product Returns Processing: An Examination of Practices of Manufacturers, Wholesalers/Distributors, and Retailers." *Journal of Business Logistics* 30, no. 1 (2009): 33–62.

Whitfield, Gwendolyn, and Robert Landeros. "Supplier Diversity Effectiveness: Does Organizational Culture Really Matter?" *Journal of Supply Chain Management* 42, no. 4 (2006): 17–29.

CASE

CASE 4.1 Red Spot Markets Company

The Red Spot Markets Company operates a chain of grocery stores in New England. It has a grocery distribution center in Providence, Rhode Island, from which deliveries are made to stores as far north as Lowell, Massachusetts, as far west as Waterbury, Connecticut, and as far northwest as Springfield, Massachusetts. No stores are located beyond the two northernmost points in Massachusetts. Stores to the west are supplied by a grocery warehouse located in Newburgh, New York. The Providence grocery distribution center supplies 42 Red Spot retail stores.

Robert Easter, Red Spot's distribution manager, is responsible for operations at the Newburgh and Providence distribution centers. By industry standards, both centers were fairly efficient. However, of the two, the Providence center lagged in two important areas of control: worker productivity and shrinkage. Warehouse equipment and work rules were the same for both the Newburgh and Providence centers, yet the throughput per worker hour was 4 percent higher for the Newburgh facility. Shrinkage, expressed as a percentage of the wholesale value of goods handled annually, was 3.6 percent for the Newburgh center and 5.9 percent for the Providence center. Jarvis Jason had been manager of the Providence distribution center for the past three years and, at great effort, managed to narrow the gap between the performance rankings of the two Red Spot facilities. Last week he requested an immediate reassignment, and Easter arranged for him to become the marketing manager for the Boston area, which would involve supervising the operations of 11 Red Spot markets. The transfer involved no increase in pay.

Easter needed a new manager for the Providence distribution center, and he picked Fred Fosdick for the task. Fosdick graduated from a lesser Ivy League college, where he majored in business with a concentration in logistics. He had been with Red Spot for two years and had rearranged the entire delivery route structure so that two fewer trucks were needed. As part of this assignment, he also converted the entire system to one of unit loads, which meant everything loaded on or unloaded from a Red Spot truck was on a pallet. Fosdick was familiar with the operations of both the Providence and Newburgh centers. He has been in each facility at least 50 different times. In addition, he spent two weeks at the Providence center when the loading docks were

redesigned to accommodate pallet loading. Fosdick was surprised that Jason had requested his reassignment to a slot that did not involve an upward promotion. That was his first question to Easter after Easter asked whether he was interested in the Providence assignment.

"I'm sorry you started with that question," said Easter to Fosdick. "Now we'll have to talk about the troublesome aspects of the assignment first, rather than the positive ones. To be frank, Fred, one of the union employees there made so much trouble for Jason, he couldn't stand it."

"Who's the troublemaker?" asked Fosdick.

"Tom Bigelow," was Easter's answer.

Fosdick remembered Bigelow from the times he had been at the Providence center. Thomas D. Bigelow was nicknamed T. D. since his days as a local Providence high school football star. Fosdick recalled that during work breaks on the loading dock, Bigelow and some of the other workers would toss around melons as though they were footballs. Only once did they drop a melon. Fosdick recalled hearing the story that Bigelow had received several offers of athletic scholarships when he graduated from high school. His best offer was from a southern school, and he accepted it. Despite the fact that the college provided a special tutor for each class, Bigelow flunked out at the end of his first semester and came back to Providence, where he got a job in the Red Spot warehouse.

In the warehouse, Bigelow was a natural leader. He would have been a supervisor except for his inability to count and his spotty attendance record on Monday mornings. On Mondays, the day that the warehouse was the busiest because it had to replenish the stores' weekend sales, Bigelow was groggy, tired, and irritable. On Mondays, he would sometimes hide by loading a forklift with three pallets, backing into any empty bay, and lowering the pallets in position (which hid the lift truck from view), and he would fall asleep. The rest of the week Bigelow was happy, enthusiastic, and hardworking. Indeed, it was he who set the pace of work in the warehouse. When he felt good, things hummed; when he was not feeling well or was absent, work dragged.

"What did Bigelow do to Jason?" Fosdick asked Easter.

"Well, as I understand it," responded Easter, "about two weeks ago Jason decided that he had had it with

Bigelow and so he suspended him on a Monday morning after Bigelow showed up late, still badly hung over. It was nearly noon, and he told Bigelow to stay off the premises and to file a grievance with his union shop steward. He also told Bigelow that he had been documenting Bigelow's Monday performance—or nonperformance— for the past six months and that Red Spot had grounds enough to fire Bigelow if it so chose. He told Bigelow to go home, sober up, and come back on Tuesday when they would discuss the length of his suspension. Bigelow walked through the distribution center on his way out, and I'm sure Jason felt he had control of the matter."

"However," continued Easter, "by about one o'clock, Jason realized he had a work slowdown on his hands. Pallet loads of bottled goods were being dropped, two forklifts collided, and one lift truck pulled over the corner of a tubular steel rack. At 4:00 P.M. quitting time, there were still three trucks to be loaded; usually they would have departed by 3:30. Rather than pay overtime, Jason let the workforce go home, and he and the supervisor loaded the last three trucks."

"On Tuesday, Bigelow did not show up, and the slowdown got worse. In addition, retail stores were phoning with complaints about all the errors in their orders. To top it off, at the Roxbury store, when the trailer door was opened, the trailer contained nothing but empty pallets. Tuesday night somebody turned off the switches on the battery chargers for all the lift trucks, so on Wednesday, the lift-truck batteries were dying all day. I got involved because of all the complaints from the stores. On Wednesday, Jason got my permission to pay overtime, and the last outgoing truck did not leave until 7:00 P.M. In addition we had to pay overtime at some of our retail stores because the workers there were waiting for the trucks to arrive. While I was talking to Jason that afternoon, he indicated that he had fired Bigelow."

Easter lit his cigar and continued, "On Wednesday, I decided to go to Providence myself, mainly to talk to Jason and to determine whether we should close down the Providence center and try to serve all our stores out of Newburgh. This would have been expensive, but Providence was becoming too unreliable. In addition, we had a big weekend coming up. When I showed up in Providence, Jason and I had breakfast together in my hotel room Thursday morning, and he told me pretty much the same thing I've been telling you. He said he knew Bigelow was behind all the disruption and that today, Thursday, would be crucial. I've never seen Jason looking so nervous. Then we drove to the distribution center. Even from a distance, I could tell things were

moving slowly. The first echelon of outgoing trucks, which should have been on the road, was still there. Another 20 of our trucks were waiting to be loaded. On the other end of the building, you could see a long line of arriving trucks waiting to be unloaded; usually there was no line at all. I knew that our suppliers would start complaining because we had established scheduled unloading times. However, I decided not to ask Jason whether he had begun receiving phone calls from them."

"Inside the center, the slowdown was in effect. Lift-truck operators who usually zipped by each other would now stop, turn off their engines, dismount, and carefully walk around each other's trucks to ensure there was proper clearance. Satisfied of this, they would then mount, start their engines, and spend an inordinate amount of time motioning to each other to pass. This was only one example. When we got to Jason's office, he had a message to phone Ed Meyers, our local attorney in Providence, who handles much of our labor relations work there. He called Meyers and was upset by the discussion. After he hung up, he told me that Meyers had been served papers by the union's attorney, charging that Wednesday's firing of Bigelow was unjustified, mainly because no provable grounds existed that Bigelow was behind the slowdown. Meyers was angry because, in firing Bigelow on Wednesday, Jason may have also blown the suspension of Bigelow on Monday. Jason and I started talking, even arguing. I talked so much that my cigar went out," said Easter, "so I asked Jason, who was sitting behind his desk, for a match. He didn't carry matches but looked inside his center desk drawer for one. He gasped, and I didn't know what was the matter. He got up, looking sick, and walked away from his desk. He said that a dead rat had been left in his desk drawer, and he wanted a transfer. He was in bad shape and the distribution center was in bad shape, so I had the opening in the Boston area and I let him have it. Actually, right now he and his family are vacationing somewhere in Eastern Canada. He needs the rest."

Fosdick was beginning to feel sorry that he knew all the details, but he persisted. "Then what?" he asked Easter.

"Well, I took over running the distribution center. I phoned Meyers again, and he and I had lunch. He thought that Jason had blown the case against Bigelow and that we should take him back. So on Friday, Meyers, Bigelow, the union attorney, the shop steward, Bigelow's supervisor, and I met. Jason, of course, was not there. It was a pleasant meeting. Everything got blamed on poor Jason. I did tell Bigelow that we would be documenting his performance and wanted him to know that Jason's successor, meaning you, was under my instructions to tolerate no nonsense. Bigelow was so pleasant that day that I could not imagine him in the role of a troublemaker. The amazing thing was that, when he went out into the center to resume work, a loud cheer went up and all the drivers started blowing their lift-truck horns. For a moment, I was afraid all the batteries would run down again. But I was wrong. They were plain happy to see Bigelow back. You know, the slowdown was still in effect when Bigelow walked onto the floor. I'd say it was 10:00 A.M. and they were an hour behind. Well, let me tell you what happened. They went to work! By noon we were back on schedule, and by the end of the shift we were a half-hour ahead of schedule. In fact, the last half-hour was spent straightening up many of the bins that had been deliberately disarranged during the slowdown. I tell you, Tom Bigelow does set the work pace in that warehouse!"

"So what do you suggest I do at the center?" asked Fosdick.

"Well, the key is getting along with Bigelow. Talk to Meyers about the kind of records you should keep in case you decide to move against Bigelow. Be sure to consult with Meyers before you do anything irreversible. Frankly, I don't know whether Bigelow will be a problem. We never had trouble with him that I knew about before Jason was there. According to Bigelow and the union attorney, Jason had it in for Bigelow. If I were you, I'd take it easy with Bigelow and other labor problems. See what you can do instead about the inventory shrinkage."

On the next Monday morning, Fosdick showed up at the Providence distribution center. After gingerly looking in all his desk drawers, he had a brief meeting with his supervisors and then walked out to meet the entire workforce on a one-to-one basis. Many remembered Fosdick from his earlier visits to the facility. Because it was a Monday morning, he had not expected to encounter Bigelow, who was present, clear-eyed, alert, and enthusiastic. Bigelow was happy to see Fosdick and shook his hand warmly. Bigelow then excused himself, saying he had to return to work. The truck dispatcher said that the workforce was ahead of schedule again: It was 11:00 A.M., and they were about 15 minutes ahead. Fosdick returned to his office, and there was a phone message from Ed Meyers. Meyers asked to postpone their luncheon for that day until Tuesday noon. Then Robert Easter called to ask how things were going on Fosdick's first day. Easter was pleased that things were going smoothly.

It was lunchtime. Fosdick decided to walk to a small café where he had eaten at other times. It was two blocks from the distribution center and on the side away from the office. So he walked through the center, which was quiet since it was closed down for lunch. He walked by the employees' lunchroom and heard the normal sounds of 50 people eating and talking. Just outside the lunchroom was one lift truck with an empty wooden pallet on it. As Fosdick watched, one of the stock clerks came out of the lunchroom with an opened case of sweet pickles from which three jars had been taken. Next came another stock clerk with an opened carton of mustard from which two bottles had been removed. One of the clerks suddenly saw Fosdick and said weakly, "We take these opened cases to the damaged merchandise room." Fosdick went into the lunchroom. There, on the center table were cases of cold meat, cheese, soft drinks, mayonnaise, and bread. All had been opened and partially emptied to provide the workers' lunches.

Bigelow was making himself a large sandwich when he saw Fosdick approach. "Don't get uptight," he said to Fosdick. "You've just come across one of the noncontract fringe benefits of working at the Red Spot Providence distribution center. May I make you a sandwich?"

Questions

1. How should Fosdick respond to the immediate situation?
2. What controls, of the types discussed in this chapter, might have been used by Red Spot Markets to reduce or eliminate the problems discussed in the case?
3. What longer-range steps should Fosdick take to control the operations of the Providence distribution center?
4. What longer-range steps should Fosdick take to improve the Providence distribution center's productivity?
5. What longer-range steps can Fosdick take to reduce the distribution center's high rate of shrinkage?
6. Assume that Fosdick decides that the practice of free lunches from the opened cases of goods must be stopped. Develop and present the arguments he should give in a meeting with the union shop steward.
7. (This is a continuation of Question 6.) Assume, instead, that you are the union shop steward. Develop and present your argument that the free lunches represent a long-standing employee benefit enjoyed by the distribution center's employees and that management's attempt to stop them is a breach of an unwritten contract and will be resisted.
8. Much of the situation described in the case seems to evolve around the personality of T. D. Bigelow. How should he be treated? Why?

SUPPLY CHAIN MANAGEMENT

Because supply chain management and procurement are inextricably linked with logistics management, Part II of *Contemporary Logistics* takes a closer look at these two topics. Chapter 5 examines supply chain management, which is a distinct concept from logistics management. Supply chain management focuses on business process integration that requires contributions from logistics as well as the other functional areas. In addition, supply chain management provides the structure for the network of interorganizational relationships that form one's supply chain. Also covered are enablers and barriers that affect one's ability to integrate their network of relationships.

Chapter 6 examines procurement, a business function responsible for ensuring an efficient and effective supply of materials in support of manufacturing and marketing strategies. It will examine key aspects of this essential linkage between suppliers and buyers, and the mechanism that initiates the movement of materials into one's logistics system. In addition, logistics considerations that can potentially affect procurement decisions are detailed.

5 | THE SUPPLY CHAIN MANAGEMENT CONCEPT

As pointed out in Chapter 1, the contemporary view is that the logistics is a key part of **supply chain management (SCM)**, and there are many examples of the importance of the logistics function to SCM. Research on underperforming supply chains, defined as those exhibiting poor service, unproductive assets, or high variable operating costs, suggests that logistical considerations can be crucial to achieving desired levels of supply chain performance. For example, damaged goods resulting from shoddy materials handling practices might result in poor service. Poor inventory turnover, an indicator of unproductive asset utilization that can negatively affect firm performance, can be addressed by consolidating stocking points and eliminating slow-moving items. Finally, high transportation costs, one example of margin-reducing operating costs, call for an examination of modal or carrier selection policies as well as of transportation routing decisions.[1]

This chapter provides an overview of the SCM concept and begins with a description of its evolution and establishes its definition. Next, descriptions of two prominent SCM process

---

[1]Foster Pinley and Chap Kistler, "Fixing an Underperforming Supply Chain," *Supply Chain Management Review* 9, no. 8 (2005): 46–52.

frameworks are provided. An examination of key enablers that can influence a firm's ability to implement SCM, such as the leveraging of technology for enhanced visibility and communication, will follow this. Next comes an overview of select barriers to SCM implementation, and the chapter concludes with a look at supply chain integration approaches.

EVOLUTION OF SUPPLY CHAIN MANAGEMENT

SCM is a relatively new concept in the sense that it was rarely mentioned in either the academic or practitioner communities prior to 1990. According to Professor Mentzer and colleagues, "the supply chain concept originated in the logistics literature, and logistics has continued to have a significant impact on the SCM concept."[2] More specifically, a dominant logistical philosophy throughout the 1980s and into the early 1990s involved the integration of logistics with other functional areas of an organization in an effort to achieve the enterprise's overall success.[3] The early to mid-1990s witnessed a growing recognition that there could be value in coordinating the various business functions not only within organizations but *across* organizations as well—in what can be referred to as an SCM philosophy.

Since the early to mid-1990s academics, practitioners and industry associations have suggested a number of definitions for both a supply chain and SCM. As was the case when defining logistics, it's important to have a common understanding of what is meant by *supply chain* and *SCM* in order to support management efforts in this area.

A **supply chain** can be liberally viewed as a combination of processes, functions, activities, relationships, and pathways along which products, services, information, and financial transactions move in and between enterprises from original producer to ultimate end-user or consumer.[4] Figure 5.1 presents illustrations of several generic types of supply chains, and it's important to note several key points. First, supply chains are not a new concept in that most organizations traditionally have been dependent on suppliers, and organizations traditionally have served

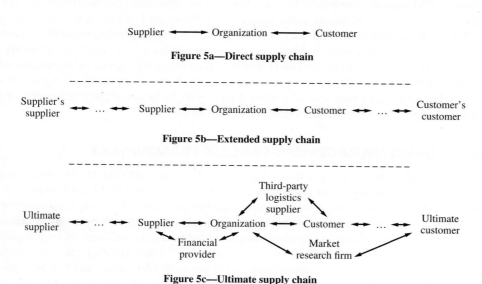

FIGURE 5.1 Different Supply Chain Configurations   *Source:* John T. Mentzer et al., "Defining Supply Chain Management," *Journal of Business Logistics* 22, no. 2 (2001): 1–25.

---

[2]John T. Mentzer et al., "Defining Supply Chain Management," *Journal of Business Logistics* 22, no. 2 (2001): 1–25.
[3]Richard F. Poist, "Evolution of Conceptual Approaches to Designing Business Logistics Systems," *Transportation Journal* 25, no. 1 (1986): 55–64.
[4]John Gattorna, "Supply Chains Are the Business," *Supply Chain Management Review* 10, no. 6 (2006): 42–49.

customers. For example, Procter & Gamble (P&G), a prominent multinational company that produces consumer packaged goods, needed raw materials to make soap, as well as customers for the soap, when it was founded in 1837; today, P&G still needs raw materials to make soap—as well as customers for the soap.

Figure 5.1 also points out that some supply chains can be much more complex (in terms of the number of participating parties) than others, and coordinating complex supply chains is likely to be more difficult than doing so for less-complex supply chains. Moreover, complex supply chains may include "specialist" companies, such as third-party logistics (3PL) providers, to facilitate coordination among various supply chain parties. Note also that customers are an integral component in supply chains, regardless of their complexity.

With respect to the relationship between logistics and supply chain management, the Council of Supply Chain Management Professionals (CSCMP) views logistics activities as being part of managing one's supply chain. In addition, activities involved in sourcing, procuring, and manufacturing are also involved. Consistent with Figure 5.1, CSCMP also asserts the need to work with multiple parties, including suppliers, third-party service providers, and end customers as an organization integrates supply and demand management internally and with other companies in the supply chain.

The CSCMP view goes on to establish that SCM has a leading role for connecting business functions and business processes internally and across companies so as to ensure coordination and high performance across the supply chain.[5] As such, SCM is inclusive of logistics management activities and logistics managers can contribute to the success and benefit from involvement in SCM.[6] Moreover, although nearly any organization can be part of a supply chain, SCM must be specifically managed by the organizations operating within the supply chain.[7]

Successful SCM requires companies to adopt an enterprise-to-enterprise point of view, which can cause organizations to accept practices and adopt behaviors that haven't traditionally been associated with buyer–seller interactions (as will be seen later in this chapter). Moreover, successful SCM requires companies to apply the systems approach (previously mentioned in Chapter 1) across all organizations in the supply chain. When applied to supply chains, the systems approach suggests that companies must recognize the interdependencies of the decisions made in major functional areas and business processes within, across, and between firms. In turn, the goals and objectives of individual supply chain participants should be compatible with the goals and objectives of other participants in the supply chain. For example, a company that is committed to providing a high level of customer service might be out of place in a supply chain comprising companies whose primary goal is cost containment.

SUPPLY CHAIN MANAGEMENT PROCESS FRAMEWORKS

The Supply Chain Council [Supply Chain Operations Reference (SCOR) Model—www.supply -chain.org] and the Supply Chain Management Institute [Global Supply Chain Forum (GSCF) Model—www.scm-institute.org] have established the two prominent SCM process frameworks. The prominence of these models is attributable to the fact that they identify business processes in such a way that the processes can actually be implemented, and thus evaluated, by organizations; each of the models are also supported by major corporations.[8] A primary distinction between the models is the degree of cross-functional involvement prescribed by each, with the GSCF model

[5]Ibid.

[6]Douglas M. Lambert, Sebastian J. Garcia-Dastugue, and Keely L. Croxton, "The Role of Logistics Managers in the Cross-Functional Implementation of Supply Chain Management," *Journal of Business Logistics* 29, no. 1 (2008): 113–132.

[7]Mentzer et al., "Defining Supply Chain Management."

[8]Douglas M. Lambert, Sebastian J. Garcia-Dastugue, and Keely L. Croxton, "An Evaluation of Process-Oriented Supply Chain Management Frameworks," *Journal of Business Logistics* 26, no. 1 (2005): 25–51 and Christopher R. Moberg, Kate Vitasek, Theodore P. Stank, and Abre Pienaar, "Time to Remodel," *Supply Chain Quarterly* 2, no. 3 (2008): 32–44.

Table 5.1	Six Processes in the Supply Chain Operations Reference (SCOR) Model
SCOR Process	**Definition**
Plan	Processes that balance aggregate demand and supply to develop a course of action which best meets sourcing, production, and delivery requirements.
Source	Processes that procure goods and services to meet planned or actual demand.
Make	Processes that transform product to a finished state to meet planned or actual demand.
Deliver	Processes that provide finished goods and services to meet planned or actual demand, typically including order management, transportation management, and distribution management.
Return	Processes associated with returning or receiving returned products for any reason. These processes extend to post delivery customer support.
Enable	Processes that manage relationships, performance, and information for a supply chain. These processes interact with all other internal and external processes associated with supply chain.

Source: SCOR Model, Version 11.0, Pittsburgh, PA: Supply Chain Council, Inc. (www.supply-chain.org)

involving all business functions. In contrast, the SCOR model is focused on the logistics, operations, and procurement functions. The proposed models are briefly described next.

The **SCOR model** identifies six processes—*Plan, Source, Make, Deliver, Return,* and *Enable*—associated with SCM (see Table 5.1). Moreover, closer analysis of the six processes, and their definitions, indicates the important role of logistics in SCM. It can be argued that logistics has some involvement in both sourcing and making; for example, with respect to making, recall the narrative in Chapter 1 about the concept of postponement resulting in value-added activities being performed in warehousing facilities. Alternatively, logistics can be involved in delivering and returning; the definition of the deliver process specifically mentions the logistics components of order management, transportation management, and distribution management. Logistics is also a key area of consideration within SCOR's planning and enabling processes. In terms of planning, logistics is a key contributor to understanding capacity constraints that could inhibit the ability to meet delivery requirements. With respect to the enable process, logistics assets such as trucks and warehouses are scheduled and maintained in order to enable the ultimate deliver process.

The **GSCF model** comprises eight processes (see Table 5.2)—*customer relationship management, supplier relationship management, customer service management, demand management, order fulfillment, manufacturing flow management, product development and commercialization,* and *returns management.* Unlike the SCOR model, the GSCF model includes the involvement of all business functions. However, as was the case with the SCOR model, logistics plays an important role in the processes associated with the GSCF model.[9] For example, logistics considerations such as on-time pickup and delivery could arise within the order fulfillment process as well as being monitored by the customer service management process. The logistics function can contribute to customer relationship management and supplier relationship management processes in terms of outbound or inbound material flow being part of a product and service agreement with a key customer or supplier. Logistics decisions in support of a new product might surface in the manufacturing flow (inbound flows of new raw materials), demand management (forecasted transportation requirements for a product rollout), or product development and commercialization (packaging considerations) processes. Moreover, reverse logistics is a key consideration for the returns management process.[10]

---

[9]Douglas M. Lambert, Garcia-Dastuge, Sebastian J. and Croxton, Keely L., "The Role of Logistics Managers in the Cross-Functional Implementation of Supply Chain Management." *Journal of Business Logistics* 29 no. 1, 113–132.

[10]Douglas M. Lambert, Editor, *Supply Chain Management: Processes, Partnerships, Performance,* 4th ed., Ponte Vedra Beach, FL: Supply Chain Management Institute, 2014. (www.scm-institute.org)

Table 5.2 Eight Processes in the Global Supply Chain Forum (GSCF) Model	
GSCF Process	**Definition**
Customer Relationship Management	Provides the structure for how relationships with customers will be developed and maintained.
Supplier Relationship Management	Provides the structure for how relationships with suppliers will be developed and maintained.
Customer Service Management	Deals with the administration of the PSAs developed by customer teams as part of the Customer Relationship Management process.
Demand Management	Balances the customers' demand with the capabilities of the supply chain. Process includes forecasting, synchronizing supply and demand, reducing variability and increasing flexibility.
Order Fulfillment	Involves filling orders as well as all activities necessary to design a network and enable a firm to meet customer requests while maximizing its profitability.
Manufacturing Flow Management	Deals with all activities necessary to obtain, implement and manage manufacturing flexibility as well as product movement into, through and out of plants.
Product Development and Commercialization	Provides the structure for developing and bringing to market products jointly with customers and suppliers.
Returns Management	Involves activities associated with returns, reverse logistics, gatekeeping, and avoidance.

Source: Douglas M. Lambert, Editor, *Supply Chain Management: Processes, Partnerships, Performance*, 4th ed. (Ponte Vedra Beach, FL: Supply Chain Management Institute, 2014), pp. 10–13. (www.scm-institute.org)

ENABLERS OF SCM IMPLEMENTATION

A variety of enablers can influence a firm's ability to implement SCM, including managerial understanding of the implications of increased customer power, establishing appropriate relationship structures, leveraging technology for enhanced visibility and communication, and the use of supply chain facilitators. Although each of these is discussed in the following paragraphs as discrete entities, interdependencies exist among them. For example, advances in technology could facilitate enhanced communication across organizations in support of a collaboration initiative between a company and one of their third-party logistics providers.

Understanding the Implications of Increased Customer Power

You are probably familiar with the adage that "information is power." In recent years, the customer has gained tremendous power over buying decisions, in large part because of greater access to information.[11] This access, largely enabled by the Internet, allows the consumer to become highly knowledgeable about an individual organization and its products—as well as also becoming aware of competing organizations and their products.

This increased power of customers has important implications for the design and management of supply chains. For example, because customer needs and wants can change relatively quickly, supply chains are increasingly required to be fast and agile, rather than slow and inflexible. A **fast supply chain** emphasizes a speed and time component, whereas an **agile supply chain**

---

[11]Glen. L. Urban, "Customer Advocacy: A New Era in Marketing," *Journal of Public Policy and Marketing* 24, no. 1 (2005): 155–159.

focuses on an organization's ability to respond to changes in demand with respect to volume and variety.[12] Failure to be fast and agile can result in decreased market share, reduced profitability, lower stock price, or dissatisfied customers for supply chain members. The drive to be fast and agile has even resulted in some e-commerce firms such as Amazon to begin offering same-day delivery services in select markets.[13]

Furthermore, the customer power concept suggests that traditional factory-driven, push supply chains should be replaced by customer-centric, pull-oriented ones. And where traditional supply chains focused on internal cost metrics (measures) such as labor costs and freight costs, customer-centric supply chains are increasingly concerned with metrics that take a more holistic perspective. Take for example, the **perfect order** (i.e., *simultaneous* achievement of relevant customer metrics such as on-time delivery, damage free and correct order quantity) metric that examines the total impact of an incorrect order in a single metric via a multiplier effect. This metric has been shown to help diagnose problems within a supply chain and improve satisfaction by looking at orders from the customer's perspective.[14]

However, firms must focus on both effectively and efficiently designing their supply chains according to market needs/characteristics. While an agile supply chain may be most appropriate in contexts where customer demand is volatile, and their requirements for variety are high.[15] In cases where customer demand is relatively stable and the need for variety is low, establishing a **lean supply chain** may be a more appropriate goal. Lean supply chains are focused on eliminating all waste, including time, and to ensure a level schedule. A hybrid approach used in practice, sometimes referred to as **leagility**, combines aspects of both lean and agile as a way to focus part of one's supply chain on a timely response to fluctuating customer orders and/or product variety and another part of the supply chain on leveling out the planning requirements to smooth production output.[16]

Logistics decisions such as mode selection, warehouse design, facility location and inventory levels can directly influence the ability to achieve the goals of any of these approaches. For example, attempts to "lean out" the supply chain through a better-controlled flow of inventory with lower levels of expensive inventory "lumps" along the way can be a daunting task. In this situation, managerial focus is on reducing the so-called **bullwhip effect**, which is characterized by variability in demand orders among supply chain members—the end result of which is inventory *lumps*.[17] In short, one aspect of inventory control that could be influenced by a lean approach is to move from a pattern of stops and starts to a continuous flow.

Another goal of a lean approach could center on reducing the amount of inventory in the supply chain. Inventory can be reduced in a number of ways, such as smaller, more frequent orders; the use of premium transportation; demand-pull, as opposed to supply-push, replenishment; and the elimination or consolidation of slower-moving product, among others. However, prominent supply chain disruptions in the early part of the twenty-first century—terrorist attacks (such as September 11, 2001), natural disasters (such as the earthquake in Haiti or the hurricanes that hit New Orleans and the Northeast part of the United States), and health pandemics [such as sudden acute respiratory syndrome (SARS) and swine flu (H1N1)] have caused some supply chains to reassess the risk implications of this approach.

---

[12]Martin Christopher, "The Agile Supply Chain," *Industrial Marketing Management* 29, no. 1 (2000): 37–44.

[13]David Biederman, "Overnight Sensation," *The Journal of Commerce* 13, no. 32 (September, 17, 2012): 4A–10A.

[14]Joseph Tiliman and Kate Vitasek, "The Perfect Order Christmas Story," *Material Handling & Logistics* 66, no.11 (2011): 38–40.

[15]Denis Towill and Martin Christopher, "The Supply Chain Strategy Conundrum: To be Lean Or Agile or To be Lean And Agile," *International Journal of Logistics: Research and Applications* 5, no.3 (2002): 299–309.

[16]J. Ben Naylor, Mohamed M. Naim, and Danny Berry, "Leagility: Integrating the Lean and Agile Manufacturing Paradigm in the Total Supply Chain," *International Journal of Production Economics* 62 (1999): 107–118.

[17]Hau L. Lee, V. Padmanabhan, and Seungin Whang, "The Bullwhip Effect in Supply Chains," *Sloan Management Review* 38, no. 3 (1997): 93–102.

Establishing Appropriate Relationship Structures

Well-run supply chains improve the long-term performance of the individual companies and the supply chain as a whole. This perspective suggests that companies should consider employing a long-term as opposed to a short-term orientation with key members—suppliers, customers, intermediaries, and facilitators—of their supply chain. Importantly, a long-term orientation tends to be predicated on **relational exchanges**, whereas a short-term orientation tends to focus on **transactional exchanges**. For relational exchanges to be effective, a transactional "What's in it for me?" philosophy needs to be replaced by a relational "What's in it for us?" philosophy. Relational exchanges tend to be characterized by a far different set of attributes than are transactional exchanges, including—but not limited to—trust, commitment, dependence, joint investment, and shared benefits.[18]

At a minimum, relational exchanges may result in individual supply chain members having to rethink (and rework) their approaches to other supply chain members. Commitment, for example, suggests that supply chain members recognize the importance of maintaining the relationship that has been established, as opposed to regularly changing sources to take advantage of short-term bargains. Moreover, relational exchanges—and by extension, SCM—cannot be successful without information sharing among key members. However, this is much more easily said than accomplished, in part because the previously mentioned business adage, "Information is power," can make supply parties somewhat hesitant to share information, lest they jeopardize their competitive advantages or expose organizational shortcomings.

Given a primary objective of SCM is to optimize the performance of the supply chain as a whole, rather than optimizing the performance of individual organizations, collaboration among supply chain members across both transactional and relational exchanges is essential. While collaboration between functions within an organization (internal collaboration) can sometimes be problematic, the benefits from organizations successfully collaborating with other supply chain members (external collaboration) drop directly to the bottom line and can increase the competitiveness of one's supply chain.[19]

A great deal has been written about supply chain collaboration in recent years, and a review of what's been written might leave the reader confused in the sense that some writings indicate that supply chain collaboration is currently more wishful thinking than practical reality, that few organizations engage in collaboration, and those that do haven't experienced much improvement in performance. Alternatively, other writings indicate that supply chain collaboration is widely applied, and participating organizations experience noticeable performance-related improvements. One reason for the widely divergent views of supply chain collaboration is that there are myriad definitions of it. For our purposes, **supply chain collaboration** will be defined as cooperative relationships between members of a supply chain—formal or informal—between companies and their suppliers or customers, established to enhance the overall business performance of all parties.[20]

In addition, some writers believe that supply chain collaboration is strategic in nature (a "narrower" view), whereas others view collaboration as ranging from transactional to strategic behaviors (a "broader" view). We'll take the broader view, which suggests that supply chain collaboration can be classified as transactional, tactical information sharing, or strategic in nature (summarized in Figure 5.2). According to this rubric, although transactional and tactical information sharing are currently the most prevalent types of collaboration, strategic collaborations are increasing and offer the best opportunity for improving supply chain performance.[21]

---

[18]Robert M. Morgan and Shelby D. Hunt, "The Commitment–Trust Theory of Organizational Commitment," *Journal of Marketing* 58, no. 3 (1994): 20–38.

[19]Mary Shacklett, "Collaboration-It's Now Closer Than Ever," *World Trade* 25, no. 11 (2012): 24–28.

[20]John Matchette and Andy Seikel, "How to Win Friends and Influence Supply Chain Partners," *Logistics Today*, December 2004, 40–42.

[21]Ibid.

Relationship Type	Definition	Examples of Data Exchanged
Transactional	Integrate and automate the flow of information to align with product flow	Purchase orders; invoices
Tactical information sharing	Share information before or after a purchase is made	Order status; product prices
Strategic	Joint buyer/seller processes, decision making and measurement (often proprietary)	Forecasts; fulfillment processes

FIGURE 5.2 **Levels of Supply Chain Collaboration** *Source:* John Matchette and Andy Seikel, "How to Win Friends and Influence Supply Chain Partners," *Logistics Today,* December 2004, 41.

An example of a strategic collaboration could be the formation of a formal **supply chain-partnership**, defined as a tailored business relationship between two supply chain members. Key characteristics of supply chain partnerships include, but are not limited to, high interdependence among the partners, an increased willingness to share information, compatible goals, mutual trust, and buying decisions based on value as opposed to cost or price. Recent research has empirically demonstrated favorable relationships between the formation of supply chain partnerships and performance-related outcomes such as cost reduction, improved profits, and revenue growth.[22] Organizations should establish systematic processes for identifying, developing, implementing, and continuously improving the key relationships in their supply chain.[23]

Leveraging Technology for Enhanced Visibility and Communication

It is argued that technology has been at the center of changes taking place that affect the supply chain, and that two key factors—computing power and the Internet—have sparked much of this change.[24] With respect to the former, supply chains can be complex entities consisting of multiple organizations, processes, and requirements. As such, attempts at applying mathematical modeling techniques to supply chains in an effort to maximize shareholder wealth or minimize costs (1) were not very practical prior to the advent of computers and (2) took a great deal of time, even after computers were introduced. However, the introduction and continued advancement of computing power now allows for fast, low-cost mathematical solutions to complex supply chain issues.

Business futurists Joseph Pine and James Gilmore have referred to the Internet as "the greatest force of commodization known to man, for both goods and services."[25] With respect to supply chains, the Internet can facilitate efficiency and effectiveness by providing opportunities for supply chains to simultaneously improve customer service and reduce their logistics costs.[26]

It's important to recognize that the Internet has important implications for both business-to-consumer links and business-to-business links within supply chains. (These implications are more fully discussed in Chapter 2.) In today's business environment, the Internet can allow one

[22]Rachel Duffy and Andrew Fearne, "The Impact of Supply Chain Partnerships on Supplier Performance," *International Journal of Logistics Management* 15, no. 1 (2004): 57–71.
[23]Douglas M. Lambert and A. Michael Knemeyer, *Building High Performance Business Relationships* (Sarasota, FL: Supply Chain Management Institute, 2009).
[24]Barbara Rosenbaum, "The Technology-Enabled Supply Chain Network," *Industrial Management* 43, no. 6 (2001): 6–10.
[25]B. Joseph Pine and James H. Gilmore, *The Experience Economy* (Boston: Harvard Business School Press, 1999).
[26]George Gecowets and Michael J. Bauer, "The Effect of the Internet on Supply Chain & Logistics," *World Trade* 13, no. 9 (2000): 71–80.

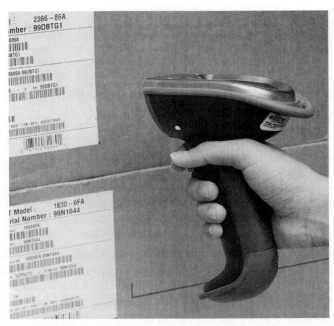

FIGURE 5.3 Information Supplied by the Truck Driver Is Recorded and Then Transmitted by the Small Computer *Source:* Photo courtesy of the Telxon Corporation.

supply chain party to have virtually instantaneous visibility to the same data as other parties in the supply chain. Such instantaneous visibility offers the opportunity for supply chains to become more proactive and less reactive, which can translate into lower inventories and improved profitability throughout the supply chain.[27]

Because supply chains depend on huge quantities of real-time information, it is essential that this information can be seamlessly transmitted across organizations. For example, retail point-of-sale information can be transmitted directly to suppliers and translated into orders for replenishment of product. Alternately, vendors may allow customers to query vendor inventory records to determine what products are in stock and where the stocks are located. The enhanced communication across organizations is dependent on both technological capabilities and a willingness to share information (part of a long-term orientation). Figure 5.3 shows a handheld computer with a radio-frequency connection used to communicate some real-time inventory information regarding a truck and its contents. Customers could use this information for tracking anticipated delivery of their orders and suppliers may use the same information to trigger replenishments. Companies are investing more aggressively in technology to achieve supply chain visibility in pursuit of this "single version of truth" about what is going on inside of their supply chain.[28]

Use of Supply Chain Facilitators

In Figure 5.1, we saw that the ultimate supply chain contains several types of organizations (e.g., financial provider, third-party logistics supplier, market research firm), which exist to facilitate coordination among various supply chain members. Because this is a logistics textbook, the most relevant facilitator for our purposes is the third-party logistics provider, so it is especially relevant to examine its impact on logistics and supply chains.

---

[27]Rosenbaum, "The Technology-Enabled Supply Chain Network."
[28]Mary Shacklett, "Supply Chain Visibility: Eliminating the Invisible," *World Trade* 23, no.11 (2010): 24–27.

Third-party logistics, also called **logistics outsourcing** or **contract logistics**, continues to be one of the most misunderstood terms in logistics and SCM. As we have seen with other supply chain concepts (e.g., collaboration, SCM), there is no commonly accepted definition of third-party logistics. Some definitions, for instance, take a "broad" perspective by suggesting that any logistics activity not performed in-house is representative of third-party logistics. Other definitions, in contrast, emphasize that 3PL arrangements involve a long-term perspective between buyer and seller and that the parties have a relationship, as opposed to transactional, perspective.

Regardless of whether one takes a broad or narrow perspective, the general idea behind third-party logistics is that one company (say, a manufacturer) allows a specialist company to provide it with one or more logistics functions (e.g., warehousing, outbound transportation). Some well-known 3PL providers include Exel Logistics , Kuehne and Nagel, Schenker Logistics, and UPS Supply Chain Solutions. A great deal of consolidation has occurred among 3PL providers in recent years (e.g., Deutsche Post acquired Exel, UPS Supply Chain Solutions acquired Menlo Logistics, among others), and this consolidation is expected to continue into the future. Although these consolidations could provide customers a broader range of supply chain services, consolidation could also lead to fewer competitive options.[29]

3PL customers can demand a number of different activities, with some of the most common involving inbound and outbound transportation, carrier negotiation and contracting, and freight consolidation.[30] Moreover, some 3PL providers have begun to offer so-called supplemental services—such as final product assembly, product installation, and product repair, among others—that are beyond their traditional offerings. As noted in Chapter 1, these supplemental 3PL services can blur traditional distinctions among supply chain members (e.g., product assembly has generally been performed by the manufacturing group). Importantly, however, this blurring of distinctions may actually facilitate supply chain integration, in that there is less emphasis on functional issues and more emphasis on cross-functional processes.[31]

The decision to use 3PL services can be driven by strategic considerations, in the sense that an organization believes that one or more aspects of its supply chain(s) need to be transformed. Alternatively, the decision to use 3PL services could be more tactical in nature; an organization might have an inefficient distribution network, an inability to control internal costs, a costly or inflexible workforce, outdated warehousing facilities, or outdated information systems. Whether strategic or tactical in nature, the use of 3PL services is driven by recognition that an organization does not have sufficient internal capabilities to address the issue, or issues, in question.[32]

Although logistics outsourcing has the potential to improve both the effectiveness and efficiency of supply chains, 3PL arrangements can easily result in failure (i.e., an inability for one party to provide what is expected by the other party). One common cause of 3PL failure is unreasonable and unrealistic expectations, generally from the user's perspective; for example, it might be unrealistic (and unreasonable) for a customer to expect a 3PL provider to cut the user's annual transportation expenditures by 50 percent. Another cause of failure in 3PL arrangements involves a lack of flexibility. Regardless of how thoroughly the provider and customer have prepared for a 3PL arrangement, unexpected issues and challenges are bound to arise. Has the arrangement been structured so that unexpected occurrences can be dealt with in a timely and satisfactory manner?[33]

One measure of the pervasiveness of outsourcing in SCM can be seen in the evolution of **fourth-party logistics (4PL)**, or the **lead logistics provider (LLP)**, concept, which emerged in the mid-1990s. Because 4PL/LLP is still relatively young, there is disagreement as to what it

[29]Jeff Berman, "Recent Deals Drive Logistics Industry Consolidation," *Logistics Management*, January 2006, 14–16.
[30]A. Michael Knemeyer, Thomas M. Corsi, and Paul R. Murphy, "Logistics Outsourcing Relationships: Customer Perspectives," *Journal of Business Logistics* 24, no. 1 (2003): 77–109.
[31]Remko I. van Hoek, "The Contribution of Performance Measurement to the Expansion of Third-Party Logistics Alliances in the Supply Chain," *International Journal of Operations & Production Management* 21, no. 1/2 (2001): 15–29.
[32]Brooks Bentz, "So You Think You Want to Outsource?" *Logistics Today*, May 2006, 24–27.
[33]James A. Tompkins, "The Business Imperative of Outsourcing," *Industrial Management*, January/February 2006, 8–12.

should be called as well as how it should be defined. With respect to the former, lead logistics provider appears to be emerging as the moniker of choice, but some providers, such as UPS Supply Chain Services, don't use either term to describe their services. And although an exact definition is elusive, for our purposes 4PL/LLP will refer to a company whose primary purpose is to ensure that various 3PLs are working toward the relevant supply chain goals and objectives. In order to be successful at managing other 3PLs, a 4PL/LLP needs to have the expertise to consider supply chain solutions and potential trade-offs, make constant objective decisions across a broad set of value-adding activities, and be viewed as neutral.[34] Whatever one calls it, by one estimate, 4PL/LLP currently accounts for approximately 20 percent of total logistics outsourcing expenditures, and revenues are projected to continue growing in the future.[35]

BARRIERS TO SCM IMPLEMENTATION

Although implementation of SCM may sound attractive from a conceptual perspective, a number of barriers can block its effectiveness, and these are discussed in the following paragraphs.

Regulatory and Political Considerations

Several decades ago, many of the supply chain arrangements in use today would have been considered illegal under certain regulatory statutes. In the United States, for example, cross-business coordination was fostered by the passage of the National Cooperative Research and Development Act of 1984. Long-term commitments, which are one of the bedrocks of SCM, may stifle competition to the extent that they make it more difficult for others to enter particular markets. Although the overall global climate for business has shifted toward allowing more cooperation among firms, it still would be wise to seek sound legal advice before entering into future supply chain arrangements.

Political considerations such as war and governmental stability can also act as a barrier to SCM. With respect to war, the first decade of the twenty-first century have witnessed ongoing tensions in the Middle East, increasing tensions between Pakistan and India (both with nuclear weapon capabilities), industry nationalization by the Venezuelan government, and wars in Iraq and Afghanistan, as well as civil and political unrest in various parts of Africa. These political uncertainties might cause some organizations to shy away from joining or developing supply chains that rely on companies located in these areas of the world. Governmental stability is also a key consideration, because SCM is so dependent on interorganizational coordination. Governmental policies that either discourage such coordination or discourage doing business with certain countries would obviously have a negative impact on supply chain efficiency.

Lack of Top Management Commitment

Top management commitment is regularly cited as an important component when individual companies attempt to initiate and implement new initiatives, programs, and product introductions. Because of SCM's interorganizational focus, top management commitment is absolutely essential if supply chain efforts are to have any chance of success. Top management has the ability to allocate the necessary resources for supply chain endeavors and the power to structure, or restructure, corporate incentive policies to focus on achieving organizational and interorganizational (as opposed to primarily functional) objectives.

Unfortunately, recent research presents a "mixed bag" of sorts with respect to top management commitment to SCM. More specifically, although senior management tends to be aware of SCM, actual senior management commitment to SCM occurs in only one of every three

---

[34]Ben Hill, "Appeal of 4PL: Proliferation and Differentiation as a 5PL," *Logistics & Transport Focus* 13, no. 8 (2011): 42–45.
[35]David Biederman, "Inside the Supply Chain: Fourth-Party Logistics," *The Journal of Commerce*, June 6, 2005, 28–31.

organizations.[36] Top management may be hesitant to fully commit to SCM because it is uncomfortable with (or does not understand) one or more of its underpinnings. For example, some companies may be uncomfortable with the concept of customer power in supply chains. Alternatively, other companies may be hesitant to enter into long-term relationships because such relationships might be perceived as limiting their operational flexibility or potentially increasing costs.

Reluctance to Share, or Use, Relevant Information

One tenet of SCM is that well-run supply chains are characterized by information sharing among their members. Nevertheless, some organizations are reluctant to share information, particularly information that might be considered proprietary in nature. However, this reluctance can contribute to supply chain problems because members may be making decisions based on erroneous data or assumptions. For example, one cause of the bullwhip effect is asymmetrical information among supply chain members.

Furthermore, advances in computer hardware and software now permit significant amounts of information to be processed and analyzed relatively quickly. To this end, **supply chain analytics** combines technology with manual employee effort to identify trends, perform comparisons, and highlight opportunities in supply chain processes, even when large amounts of data are involved. Supported by technology, supply chain analytics help decision makers in areas such as sourcing, inventory management, manufacturing, quality, sales, and logistics. Supply chain analytics leverage enterprise applications, the Internet, data warehouses, and information obtained from external sources to locate data patterns. For example, frequent shopper cards, such as those offered by grocery chains, offer the opportunity to develop highly detailed profiles of individual customers. Some companies, however, are reluctant to fully utilize the information that comes from these data; they believe that the highly detailed data that can be provided by the cards—what was purchased, when it was purchased, where it was purchased, how it was purchased—potentially violate the customer's right to privacy.

Incompatible Information Systems

Twenty years ago, a major barrier to interorganizational collaboration was incompatible computer hardware; today, by contrast, software compatibility is likely the more pressing issue. A key software question involves the decision between a single integrator approach and a best-of-breed approach. Organizations pursuing a single integrator approach rely on a single vendor to provide all relevant software applications (e.g., inventory management, transportation management, warehouse management). One advantage to the single integrator approach is that there should be coordination across the various applications.[37]

Alternatively, a best-of-breed approach chooses the best application for a particular function, so that an organization could have transportation management software from one company and warehouse management software from another company.[38] However, best-of-breed solutions often require additional software packages to coordinate these different applications—and these integrations don't always proceed smoothly. One well-known example of a not-so-smooth integration involved Hershey Foods' effort to integrate several specialized supply chain software packages. The growing pains of this integration included unfilled candy orders for Halloween and Christmas, longer delivery times, increased inventory levels, and upset customers.[39]

[36]Stanley E. Fawcett, Jeffrey A. Ogden, Gregory M. Magnan, and M. Bixby Cooper, "Organizational Commitment and Governance for Supply Chain Success," *International Journal of Physical Distribution & Logistics Management* 36, no. 1 (2006): 22–35.
[37]Joel D. Wisner, G. Keong Leong, and Keah-Choon Tan, *Principles of Supply Chain Management: A Balanced Approach* (Mason, OH: South-Western Publishing, 2005), Chapter 7.
[38]Ibid.
[39]Craig Stedman, "Failed ERP Gamble Haunts Hershey," *Computerworld*, November 1, 1999, 1–2.

Incompatible Corporate Cultures

Because SCM can involve a long-term orientation and partnerships between various members, it is important that the parties be comfortable with the companies they will be working with. In a broad sense, corporate culture refers to "how we do things around here" and reflects an organization's vision, values, and strategic plans. It's important to recognize that compatible corporate cultures don't require all organizations to be the same. Rather, organizations should identify potential differences that could negatively affect supply chain effectiveness and efficiency. For example, an organization with a participative management style might not mesh very well with an organization that has an autocratic management style.[40]

All manifestations of corporate culture may provide important clues about the ability of companies to work together. For instance, one of the more notable supply chain failures in past years involved the dissolution of the relationship between Office Max and Ryder Integrated Logistics. Although a number of reasons explain why this relationship didn't succeed, the two companies had quite different dress codes. Indeed, a Ryder manager told one of the authors that it was clear from the first face-to-face meeting that the companies were going to have difficulty working together—in large part because of their vastly different dress codes!

Globalization Challenges

Although much of the discussion so far has focused on domestic supply chains, one should recognize that supply chains are becoming increasingly global in nature. Reasons for the increased globalization of supply chains include lower-priced materials and labor, the global perspective of companies in a supply chain, and the development of global competition, among others.[41] Supply chain integration can be challenging in a domestic setting, but integration challenges are even greater in global supply chains due to cultural, economic, technological, political, spatial, and logistical differences.

Global supply chains translate into both longer and more unpredictable lead times (time from when an order is placed until it is received) for shipments, which increases the chance that customer demand might not be fulfilled, due to a potential out-of-stock situation. In addition, recent research indicates that glitches are routine occurrences in global supply chains; causes include, but are not limited to, documentation errors, packaging errors, routing errors, incomplete shipments, and failure to follow order guidelines. These and other global supply chain glitches drive up supply chain costs and potentially jeopardize customer satisfaction.[42]

SUPPLY CHAIN INTEGRATION

An individual firm can be involved in multiple supply chains at the same time, and it's important to recognize that expectations and required knowledge can vary across supply chains. For example, food manufacturers may sell to grocery chains, institutional buyers, specialty firms (which might position the food items as gifts), and industrial users (which might use the product as an ingredient in another product that they manufacture). It seems reasonable to assume that the packaging expectations of specialty firms might be more demanding than those of industrial users.

---

[40]Douglas M. Lambert and A. Michael Knemeyer, "We're in This Together," *Harvard Business Review* 82, no. 12 (2004) 114–122.

[41]Pedro Reyes, Mahesh S. Raisinghani, and Manoj Singh, "Global Supply Chain Management in the Telecommunications Industry: The Role of Information Technology in Integration of Supply Chain Entities," *Journal of Global Information Technology Management* 5, no. 2 (2002): 48–67.

[42]Beth Enslow, "Best Practices in Global Trade Management Stress Speed and Flexibility," *World Trade*, January 2006, 36–40.

Supply chains are integrated by having various parties enter into and carry out long-term mutually beneficial agreements. These agreements are known by several names, to include *partnerships*, *strategic alliances*, *third-party arrangements*, and *contract logistics*. Whatever they are called, these agreements should be designed to reward all participants when collaborative ventures are successful, and they should also provide incentives for all parties to work toward success. In a similar fashion, the participants should share the consequences when cooperative ventures are less successful than desired.

When an organization enters into a long-term agreement with a supplier or customer, the organization must keep in mind how this arrangement could affect the rest of the supply chain. Ideally, all participants in the supply chain will establish whatever agreements are necessary to ensure that the entire supply chain functions in the most desirable manner.

To integrate a particular supply chain, the various organizations must recognize the shortcomings of the present system and examine channel arrangements as they currently exist and as they might be. All this is done within the framework of the organization's overall strategy, as well as any logistics strategies necessary to support the goals and objectives of the firm's top management.

Broadly speaking, organizations can pursue three primary methods when attempting to integrate their supply chains. One method is through *vertical integration*, where one organization owns multiple participants in the supply chain; indeed, the Ford Motor Company of the 1920s owned forests and steel mills and exercised tight control over its dealers. The most common examples of vertical integration today are some lines of paint and automotive tires. It's important to recognize that regulations (often in the form of state laws) may limit the degree of vertical integration that will be permitted in particular industries.

A second possible method of supply chain coordination involves the use of *formal contracts* among various members. One of the more popular uses of contracts is franchising, which attempts to combine the benefits of tight integration of some functions along with the ability to be very flexible while performing other functions. From a supply chain perspective, a franchiser may exert contractual influence over what products are purchased by a franchisee, acceptable vendors (suppliers) of these products, and the distribution of the product to the franchisee. For example, the Martin-Brower Company handles distribution for some McDonald's franchisees in the United States (e.g., food, beverage, and store supplies). A third method of supply chain coordination involves *informal agreements* among the various organizations to pursue common goals and objectives, with control being exerted by the largest organization in the supply chain. Although this method offers supply chain participants flexibility in the sense that organizations can exit unprofitable or unproductive arrangements quickly and with relative ease, organizations should be aware of potential shortcomings. For one, the controlling organization may be so powerful that the supply chain becomes more like a dictatorship than a partnership. Moreover, the same flexibility that allows for exiting unprofitable or unproductive arrangements also allows parties the ability to switch supply chains when presented with what appears to be a better deal.

Summary

This chapter focused on the supply chain concept and began by defining supply chain and SCM. Supply chains consist of a number of different parties and can include the end consumer; SCM requires companies to adopt an enterprise-to-enterprise point of view.

The chapter also discussed two of the most prominent SCM process frameworks. Key enablers of SCM, such as and understanding of the implications of increased customer power and leveraging technology for enhanced visibility and communication, were identified and described. Various barriers to SCM, such as lack of top management commitment and reluctance to share, or use, relevant data, were also presented. The chapter concluded with a look at issues around and approaches for supply chain integration.

Questions for Discussion and Review

5.1 Discuss the differences between a supply chain and supply chain management.

5.2 Discuss the SCOR and GSCF models of supply chain management.

5.3 Discuss how the logistics function contributes to the supply chain management processes established in the SCOR and GSCF models.

5.4 What are four key enablers of supply chain management implementation?

5.5 What is the difference between a lean and an agile supply chain? Under what circumstances is each an appropriate supply chain approach to pursue?

5.6 Discuss some of the ways that inventory can be reduced in the supply chain.

5.7 What is the difference between relational and transactional exchanges? Which is more relevant for supply chain management? Why?

5.8 Do you agree or disagree that supply chain collaboration can be classified as transactional, tactical information sharing, or strategic in nature? Why?

5.9 This chapter suggests that technology has been at the center of changes taking place that affect the supply chain. Do you agree or disagree? Why?

5.10 Discuss the impact of the Internet on supply chain management.

5.11 How might regulatory and political conditions act as barriers to supply chain management?

5.12 Why is top management commitment necessary for successful supply chain management?

5.13 Some companies are hesitant to use frequent shopper cards because the data provided could violate the customer's privacy. Do you agree or disagree? Why?

5.14 Discuss the best of breed and single integrator approaches.

5.15 Do you think corporate cultures are relevant for supply chain management? Why or why not?

5.16 Why is supply chain integration so difficult in global supply chains?

5.17 Discuss the strategic and tactical considerations that can drive a company to use the services of a 3PL.

5.18 What are some reasons that third-party logistics arrangements aren't always successful?

5.19 What is the difference between a 3PL and a 4PL/LLP?

5.20 Discuss the three primary methods that organizations can use to integrate their supply chains.

Suggested Readings

Bagchi, Prabir K. and Tage Skjoett-Larsen. "Supply Chain Integration: A European Survey." *International Journal of Logistics Management* 16, no. 2 (2005): 275–290.

Fawcett, Stanley E., Amydee M. Fawcett, Bradlee J. Watson, and Gregory M. Magnan. "Peeking Inside the Black Box: Toward an Understanding of Supply Chain Collaboration Dynamics." *Journal of Supply Chain Management* 48, no. 1 (2012): 44–72.

Fawcett, Stanley E., Lisa M. Ellram, and Jeffrey A. Ogden. *Supply Chain Management: From Vision to Implementation* (Upper Saddle River, NJ: Prentice Hall, 2007).

Gibson, Brian J., John T. Mentzer, and Robert L. Cook. "Supply Chain Management: The Pursuit of a Consensus Definition." *Journal of Business Logistics* 26, no. 2 (2005): 17–25.

Giguere, Mike and Brad Householder. "Supply Chain Visibility: More Trust than Technology." *Supply Chain Management Review* 16, no. 6 (2012): 20–25.

Jacoby, David. *Guide to Supply Chain Management* (Canada: The Economist Newspaper Ltd., 2009).

Lambert, Douglas M., Editor, *Supply Chain Management: Processes, Partnerships, Performance,* 4th ed. (Ponte Vedra Beach, FL: Supply Chain Management Institute, 2014). (www.scm-institute.org)

Lambert, Douglas M., A. Michael Knemeyer, and John T. Gardner. *Building High Performance Business Relationships* (Sarasota, FL: Supply Chain Management Institute, 2009).

Lambert, Douglas M., Sebastian J. Garcia-Dastugue, and Keely L. Croxton. "An Evaluation of Process-Oriented Supply Chain Management Frameworks." *Journal of Business Logistics* 26, no. 1 (2005): 25–51.

Lambert, Douglas M., Sebastian J. Garcia-Dastugue, and Keely L. Croxton. "The Role of Logistics Managers in the Cross-Functional Implementation of Supply Chain Management." *Journal of Business Logistics* 29, no. 1 (2008): 113–132.

Lee, Hau. "Don't Tweak your Supply Chain-Rethink It End to End." *Harvard Business Review* 88, no. 10 (2010): 62–69.

Lieb, Robert C. "The North American Third-Party Logistics Industry in 2011. The Provider CEO Perspective." *Transportation Journal* 51, no. 3 (2012): 353–367.

Reeve, James M. and Mandyam M. Srinivasan. "Which Supply Chain Design Is Right for YOU?" *Supply Chain Management Review* 9, no. 4 (2005): 50–57.

Slone, Reuben, J. Paul Dittmann, and John T. Mentzer. *New Supply Chain Agenda: The 5 Steps That Drive Real Value* (Boston, MA: Harvard Business Review Press, 2010).

Wisner, Joel D., Keah-Choon Tan, and G. Keong Leong, *Principles of Supply Chain Management: A Balanced Approach,* 3rd ed. (Mason, OH: South-Western Publishing, 2011).

CASE

CASE 5.1   Johnson Toy Company

Located in Biloxi, Mississippi, the Johnson Toy Company is celebrating its seventy-fifth year of business. Amy Johnson, who is president, and Lori Johnson, who is vice president, are sisters and are the third generation of their family to be involved in the toy business. The firm manufactures and sells toys throughout the United States. The toy business is very seasonal, with the majority of sales occurring before Christmas. A smaller peak occurs in the late spring–early summer period, when sales of outdoor items are good.

The firm relies on several basic designs of toys—which have low profit margins but are steady sellers—and on new designs of unconventional toys, whose introduction is always risky but promises high profits if the item becomes popular. The firm advertises regularly on Saturday morning television shows for children.

Late last year, just before Christmas, the Johnson Toy Company introduced Jungle Jim the Jogger doll, modeled after a popular television show. Sales skyrocketed, and every retailer's stock of Jungle Jim the Jogger dolls was sold out in mid-December; the Johnson Company could have sold several million more units if they had been available before Christmas. Based on the sales success of this doll, Amy and Lori made commitments to manufacture 10 million Jungle Jim the Jogger dolls this year and to introduce a wide line of accessory items, which they hoped every doll owner would also want to have. Production was well under way, and many retailers were happy to accept dolls in January and February because they were still a fast-selling item, even though the toy business itself was sluggish during these months.

Unfortunately, in the aftermath of a Valentine's Day party in Hollywood, the television actor who portrayed Jungle Jim the Jogger became involved in a widely publicized sexual misadventure, the details of which shocked and disgusted many readers and TV viewers, and we would be embarrassed to describe them. Ratings of the television series plummeted, and within a month it had been dropped from the air. On March 1, the Johnson Company had canceled further production of the Jungle Jim the Jogger dolls, although it had to pay penalties to some of its suppliers because of the cancellation. The company had little choice because it was obvious that sales had stopped.

On April 1, a gloomy group assembled in the Johnson Company conference room. Besides Amy and Lori, those present included Carolyn Coggins, the firm's sales manager; Cheryl Guridi, the logistics manager; Greg Sullivan, the controller; and Kevin Vidal, the plant engineer. Coggins had just reported that she believed there were between 1.5 million and 2 million Jungle Jim the Jogger dolls in retail stores, and Sullivan had indicated there were 2,567,112 complete units in various public warehouses in Biloxi. Vidal said that he was still trying to count all the unassembled component parts, adding that one problem was that they were still being received from suppliers, despite the cancellation.

Amy said, "Let's wait a few weeks to get a complete count of all the dolls and all the unassembled component parts. Lori, I'm naming you to work with Carolyn and Kevin to develop recommendations as to how we can recycle the Jungle Jim item into something we can sell. Given the numbers involved, I'm willing to turn out some innocuous doll and sell it for a little more than the cost of recycling because we can't take a complete loss on all these damned Jungle Jim dolls! Greg says we have nearly 2.6 million of them to play with, so let's think of something."

"Your 2.6-million figure may be low," said Coggins. "Don't forget that there may be nearly 2 million in the hands of the dealers and that they will return them."

"Return them?" questioned Amy. "They're not defective. That's the only reason we accept returns. The retailers made a poor choice. It's the same as if they ordered sleds and then had a winter with no snow. We are no more responsible for Jungle Jim's sex life than they are!"

Cheryl Guridi spoke up: "You may be underestimating the problem, Amy. One of our policies is to accept the dealer's word as to what is defective, and right now there are a lot of dealers out there claiming defects in the Jungle Jim dolls. One reason that Kevin can't get an accurate count is that returned dolls are showing up on our receiving dock and getting mixed up with our in-stock inventory."

"How can that happen?" asked Amy, angrily. "We're not paying the freight, also, are we?"

"So far, no," responded Guridi. "The retailers are paying the freight just to get rid of them."

"We've received several bills in which the retailer has deducted the costs of the Jungle Jim dolls and of the freight for shipping them back from what he owes us," said Sullivan. "That was one item I wanted to raise while we were together."

"We can't allow that!" exclaimed Amy.

"Don't be so sure," responded Sullivan. "The account in question has paid every bill he's owed us on time for 40 years. Do you want *me* to tell him we won't reimburse him?"

"This is worse than I imagined," said Amy. "Just what are our return policies, Lori?"

"Well, until today, I thought we had only two," said Lori. "One for our small accounts involves having our salespeople inspect the merchandise when they make a sales call. They can pick it up and give the retailer credit off the next order."

"Sometimes they pick up more than defective merchandise," added Coggins. "Often, they'll take the slow movers out of the retailer's hands. We have to do that as a sales tool."

"That's not quite right," interjected Vidal. "Sometimes, the returned items are just plain shopworn—scratched, dented, and damaged. That makes it hard for us because we have to inspect every item and decide whether it can be put back into stock. When we think a particular salesperson is accepting too many shopworn items, we tell Carolyn, although it's not clear to me that the message reaches the salespeople in the field."

"I wish I had an easy solution," said Coggins. "We used to let our salespeople give credit for defects and then destroy everything out in the field. Unfortunately, some abused the system and resold the toys to discount stores. At least now we can see everything we're buying back. I agree we are stuck with some shopworn items, but our salespeople are out there to sell, and nothing would ruin a big sale quicker than for our salespeople to start arguing with the retailer, on an item-by-item basis, as to whether something being returned happens to be shopworn."

"Is there a limit to what a salesperson is permitted to allow a retailer to return?" asked Amy.

"Well, not until now," responded Coggins. "But with this Jungle Jim snafu we can expect the issue to occur. In fact, I have several phone queries on my desk concerning this. I thought I'd wait until after this meeting to return them."

"Well, I think we'd better establish limits—right now," said Amy.

"Be careful," said Lori. "When I was out with the salespeople last year, I gathered the impression that some were able to write bigger orders by implying that we'd take the unsold merchandise back, if need be. If we

assume that risk, the retailer is willing to take more of our merchandise."

"Are there no limits to this policy?" asked Amy.

"Informal ones," was Coggins's response. "It depends on the salesperson and the account. I don't think there is much abuse, although there is some."

"How do the goods get back to us under these circumstances?" asked Amy.

"The salespeople either keep them and shuffle them about to other customers or—if it's a real loser—they ask us what to do," replied Coggins.

"Greg," said Amy, "do our records reflect these returns and transfers?"

"Oh, fairly well," was his response. "We lose track of individual items and quantities, but if the salesperson is honest—and I think ours are—we can follow the dollar amount of the return to the salesperson's inventory, to another retailer, or back here to us. We do not have good controls on the actual items that are allowed for returns. Kevin and I have difficulty in reconciling the value of returned items that wind up back here. Carolyn's records say they're okay for resale, and Kevin says they're too badly damaged."

"I insist on the reconciliation before we allow the goods back into our working inventory," said Guridi. "That way I know exactly what I have here, ready to ship."

"You know, I'm finding out more information about inventories and returns than I thought existed," said Amy.

"Too many trips to Paris, dearest," said Lori, and the others all suppressed smiles.

Amy decided to ignore Lori's remark, and she looked at Guridi and asked, "Are you satisfied with your control over inventories, Cheryl?"

"I have no problem with the ones here in Biloxi," was Guridi's response, "but I have an awful time with the inventories of return items that salespeople carry about with them, waiting to place them with another retailer. I'm not always certain they're getting us top dollar, and each salesperson knows only his or her own territory. When Carolyn and I are trying to monitor the sales of some new item, we never know whether it's bombing in some areas and riding around in salespeople's cars as they try to sell it again."

"Have you now described our returns policy, such as it is?" asked Amy, looking at everybody in the room.

"No," was the response murmured by all. Sullivan spoke: "For large accounts we deduct a straight 2 percent off wholesale selling price to cover defectives, and then we never want to hear about the defectives from these accounts at all."

"That sounds like a better policy," said Amy. "How well is it working?"

"Up until Jungle Jim jogged where he shouldn't, it worked fine. Now a number of large accounts are pleading 'special circumstances' or threatening to sue if we don't take back the dolls."

"They have no grounds for suit," declared Amy.

"You're right," said Coggins, "but several of their buyers are refusing to see our sales staff until the matter is resolved. I just heard about this yesterday and meant to bring it up in today's meeting. I consider this very serious."

"Damn it!" shouted Amy, pounding the table with her fist. "I hope that damned jogger dies of jungle rot! We're going to lose money this year, and now you're all telling me how the return policy works, or doesn't work, as the case may be! Why can't we just have a policy of all sales being final and telling retailers that if there is an honest defect they should send the goods back here to us in good old Biloxi?"

"Most of the small accounts know nothing about shipping," responded Vidal. "They don't know how to pack, they don't know how to prepare shipping documents, and they can't choose the right carriers. You ought to see the hodgepodge of shipments we receive from them. In more cases than not, they pay more in shipping charges than the products are worth to us. I'd rather see them destroyed in the field."

Sullivan spoke up. "I'd object to that. We would need some pretty tight controls to make certain the goods were actually destroyed. What if they are truly defective, but improperly disposed of, then fall into the hands of children who play with them and the defect causes an injury? Our name may still be on the product, and the child's parents will no doubt claim the item was purchased from one of our retailers. Will we be liable? Why can't we have everything come back here? We have enough volume of some returned items that we could think in terms of recycling parts."

Vidal responded, "Recycling is a theoretical solution to such a problem, but only in rare instances will it pay. In most instances the volume is too small and the cost of taking toys apart is usually very high. However, the Jungle Jim product involves such a large volume that it is prudent and reasonable to think up another product that utilizes many of the parts. It would even pay to modify some machines for disassembling the Jungle Jim doll."

"As I listen to this discussion," said Lori, "one fact becomes obvious: We will never have very good knowledge about volume or patterns of returns until it's too late. That's their very nature."

Guridi asked, "Could we have field representatives who do nothing but deal with this problem? The retailers would be told to hang onto the defectives until our claims reps arrive."

Coggins replied, "That would be expensive, because most retailers have little storage space for anything and would expect our claims rep to be there immediately. Besides, it might undermine our selling efforts if retailers could no longer use returns to negotiate with as they talked about new orders."

"That may be," interjected Amy, "but we cannot continue having each salesperson tailoring a return policy for each retailer. That's why we're in such a mess with the jogger doll. We have to get our return policy established, made more uniform, and enforced. We cannot go through another fiasco like Jungle Jim the Jogger for a long time. We're going to lose money this year, no matter what, and I have already told Kevin that there will be virtually no money available for retooling for next year's new products."

Questions

1. From the standpoint of an individual concerned with accounting controls, discuss and evaluate Johnson Toy Company's present policies for handling returned items.

2. Answer Question 1, but from the standpoint of an individual interested in marketing.

3. Propose a policy for handling returns that should be adopted by the Johnson Toy Company. Be certain to list circumstances under which exceptions would be allowed. Should it apply to the Jungle Jim dolls?

4. Should this policy, if adopted, be printed and distributed to all of the retailers who handle Johnson Toy Company products? Why or why not? If it should not be distributed to them, who should receive copies?

5. Assume that it is decided to prepare a statement on returns to be distributed to all retailers and that it should be less than a single double-spaced page. Prepare such a statement.

6. On the basis of the policy in your answer to Question 3, develop instructions for the Johnson Toy Company distribution and accounting departments with respect to their roles and procedures in the handling of returns.

7. Assume that you are Cheryl Guridi, the firm's logistics manager. Do you think that the returns policy favored by the logistics manager would differ from what would be best for the firm? Why or why not?

8. Until the policy you recommend in your answer to Question 3 takes effect, how would you handle the immediate problem of retailers wanting to return unsold Jungle Jim the Jogger dolls?

6 | PROCUREMENT

Procurement, which refers to the raw materials, component parts, and supplies bought from outside organizations to support a company's operations, is an important activity and closely related to logistics because acquired goods and services must be entered into the supply chain in the exact quantities and at the precise time they are needed. While procurement has been traditionally viewed as transactional in nature, recent studies indicate that the function's profile is rising due to the increased globalization and complexity of today's supply chains.[1] Procurement is also important because its costs often range between 60 and 80 percent of an organization's revenues.

The magnitude of procurement expenditures meant that procurement's historical focus in many organizations was to achieve the lowest possible cost from potential suppliers; oftentimes these suppliers were pitted against each other in "cutthroat" competition involving three- or six-month arm's-length contracts awarded to the lowest bidder. Once this lowest bidder was chosen, the bidding cycle would almost immediately start again, and another low bidder would get the contract for the next several months. Today, by contrast, procurement has a much more

---

[1]John Hyatt, "The Rise and Rise of Procurement," *CFO* 28, no. 4 (2012): 57–59.

strategic orientation in many organizations, and a contemporary procurement manager might have responsibility for reducing cycle times, playing an integral role in product development, or generating additional revenues by collaborating with the marketing department.[2]

Historically, procurement, **purchasing**, and **supply management** were terms that could be used almost interchangeably, but this is no longer the case. Although "procurement" and "purchasing" are sometimes viewed as synonymous terms, supply management is now viewed as a relational exchange approach involving a limited number of suppliers. You might recall from Chapter 5 that relational exchanges adopt a long-term orientation that can be characterized by attributes such as trust, commitment, dependence, and shared benefits.

Electronic commerce continues to bring many changes to the procurement discipline, such as *electronic procurement* and *reverse auctions*, which were discussed in Chapter 2. Moreover, utilization of **procurement cards** (also referred to as **p-cards**) has also grown dramatically with the evolution of electronic commerce. P-cards are similar to charge cards such as Visa and MasterCard that are typically focused on personal use, with p-cards being used for an organization's buying needs. Organizations generally restrict the number of employees authorized to use procurement cards, and each month, an organization receives a detailed statement listing employees, details of their purchases, and purchase prices. P-cards may require control processes that measure usage and identify procurement trends, limit spending during the appropriate procurement cycle, and block unauthorized expenditures at gaming casinos or massage parlors.[3] However, the incidence of fraud has been found to be low primarily due to investments that the card issuers have made in programs to seek out and eliminate it.[4]

P-cards can benefit organizations in several ways, one of which is a reduction in the number of invoices. Unlike personal credit cards, with p-cards an organization will make one payment for the total amount of purchases during one month, as opposed to making individual payments for each p-card holder. In addition, these cards allow employees to make purchases in a matter of minutes, as opposed to days, and procurement cards generally allow suppliers to be paid in a more timely fashion.

While the benefits of using p-cards increase exponentially as more people within an organization use them, expanding use beyond the domestic market can be a challenge. Issues associated with an expansion of p-cards overseas include currency differences, availability of technology, difference in card acceptance and cultural issues with the program. For example, in some Asian markets, employee turnover is so high that card security is a major concern.[5]

Because entire textbooks are devoted to procurement, it's really not possible for us to cover all aspects of this topic in just one chapter. We'll begin our examination with a brief overview of possible objectives for procurement, and this will be followed by a description of supplier selection and evaluation. We'll also look at global procurement and sustainable procurement.

PROCUREMENT OBJECTIVES[6]

Because procurement has become more strategic in nature, its primary objective is no longer to only achieve the lowest possible cost of supply. Potential procurement objectives include, but are not limited to, (1) supporting organizational goals and objectives, (2) managing the purchasing process effectively and efficiently, (3) managing the supply base, (4) developing strong relationships with other functional groups, and (5) supporting operational requirements. Each objective will be briefly highlighted in the following paragraphs.

---

[2]Carlos Niezen and Wulf Weller, "Procurement as Strategy," *Harvard Business Review* 84, no. 9 (2006): 22–24.
[3]Bob Martinson, "The Power of the P-Card," *Strategic Finance*, February 2002, 30–35.
[4]Pam Miller, "Busting the P-Card Myth," *Managing Accounts Payable* 12, no. 3 (2012): 1–11.
[5]David Hannon, "P-card Program Expansion Is a Global Challenge," *Purchasing* 138, no. 12 (2009): 53–55.
[6]The material in this section is drawn from Robert Monczka, Robert Trent, and Robert Handfield, *Purchasing and Supply Chain Management*, 3rd ed. (Mason, OH: Thomson/South-Western, 2005).

First and foremost, procurement's objectives must *support organizational goals and objectives.* If, for example, minimal inventory is an organizational objective, then procurement probably should not be attempting to minimize total procurement costs. With respect to *managing the purchase process effectively and efficiently,* effectively is concerned with how well procurement keeps its promises, whereas efficiently refers to how well (or poorly) procurement uses company resources in keeping its promises. A third procurement objective, *managing the supply base,* refers to the selection, development, and maintenance of supply sources.

Developing strong relationships with other functional groups recognizes that the interfunctional consequences of procurement decisions require more cooperation and coordination than has traditionally existed between procurement and areas such as logistics, manufacturing, and marketing. The lack of cooperation and coordination between procurement and other functions can result in supply shortages, excess inventory, frequent write-downs, and increased lead times.[7] *Supporting operational requirements* means that procurement's focus is on satisfying internal customers and can be summarized by buying the right products, at the right price, from the right source, at the right specifications, in the right quantity, for delivery at the right time to the right internal customer.

SUPPLIER SELECTION AND EVALUATION

One of procurement's most important responsibilities involves supplier (vendor) selection and evaluation. The selection and evaluation of suppliers is a process that involves stating an organization's needs and then determining how well various potential suppliers can fulfill these needs (see Figure 6.1). The first step in this process, *identify need for supply,* can arise from a number of considerations, such as the end of an existing supply agreement or the development of a new product. *Situation analysis,* the second step, looks at both the internal and external environments within which the supply decision is to be made. Internal considerations include identification of the relevant stakeholders, where the supply is needed, and the appropriate quantity and quality of the supply, as well as applicable supply policies (e.g., minority supplier initiatives). The external environment includes economic considerations, the legal and regulatory frameworks controlling the purchase, and the marketplace within which potential suppliers operate.

Identify and evaluate possible suppliers is the third step. A myriad of sources can be used to *identify possible suppliers,* such as salespeople, trade shows, trade publications, and the Internet. It's important to recognize and understand the potential advantages and disadvantages of each source. For example, although trade shows might highlight offerings from several different supply sources (which could facilitate supplier comparisons), the costs to attend or exhibit at trade shows have skyrocketed in recent years; moreover, trade shows are often held only once a year.

Evaluating suppliers can be facilitated if an organization (1) delineates relevant selection criteria and (2) assigns weights to these criteria. With respect to the latter, if an organization uses four relevant selection criteria, should all four be assigned equal weight (i.e., 25 percent per criteria), or should certain criteria be weighted more heavily than others (e.g., two criteria weighted at 30 percent apiece and two others weighted at 20 percent each)? This weighting technique serves as a foundation for generating a rating (score) for each possible supplier, and these ratings are instrumental in the fourth step of the supplier selection process, *select supplier(s),* which is where an organization chooses one or more companies to supply the relevant product.

Selecting the most appropriate number of suppliers a firm should use has been the subject of continuing debate. Internal considerations, which were mentioned in Step 2, could influence the decision to use a single-source or a multiple-source approach. While the goal

---

[7]Ashutosh Dekhne, Xin Huang, and Apratim Sarkar, "Bridging the Procurement-Supply Chain Divide," *Supply Chain Management Review* 16, no. 5 (2012): 36–42.

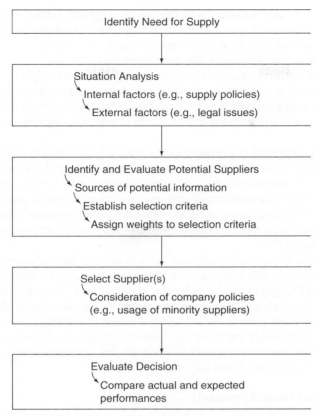

FIGURE 6.1 Supplier Selection Framework

of both approaches is to provide the buying organization with the best value of a supplied part, each offers distinct advantages. **Multiple sourcing** proponents argue that by having more than one supplier increased amounts of competition, greater supply risk mitigation and improved market intelligence can arise. **Single sourcing**, on the other hand, consolidates purchase volume with a single supplier with the hopes of enjoying lower costs per unit and increased cooperation and communication in the supply relationship. However, the achievement of these potential savings is connected to the buyer's relative size in the market. For some smaller buyers, single sourcing might actually reduce their alternatives and ultimately raise the price they pay.[8]

The final step of the supplier selection process, *evaluate decision*, involves a comparison of expected supplier outcomes to actual supplier outcomes. There are two primary approaches for evaluating suppliers: process based and performance based. A process-based evaluation is an assessment of the supplier's service and/or production process (typically involving a **supplier audit**). A supplier audit usually involves an onsite visit to a supplier's facility. The goal of this visit is to gain a deeper knowledge of the supplier. Supplier audits can involve assessments of the supplier's structure (management, people, quality, innovation), resources (technology, processes), health (financials, risk), and responsibility (social, environmental).[9]

[8]Roman Inderst, "Single Sourcing versus Multiple Sourcing," *RAND Journal of Economics* 39, no. 1 (2008): 199–213.
[9]Mike Hales and Raj Arumugam, "The Case for Supplier Development," *Supply Chain Management Review* 16, no.2 (2012): 60–61.

A performance-based evaluation is focused on the supplier's actual performance on a variety of criteria, such as cost and quality. This evaluation can be facilitated if an organization has explicitly defined selection criteria, as mentioned in Step 4. Many companies use **supplier scorecards** to report performance information to their suppliers. Scorecards can be *categorical* (simple check-offs items that reflect supplier performance), *weighted point* (weights assigned to multiple categories with defined performance scales), or cost based (attempts to quantify total cost of doing business with a supplier over time).[10] PolyOne Corp., a producer of latex, compounds, and plastics, has used a scorecard program with their top suppliers to improve on-time delivery and grow sales.[11]

The preceding paragraphs have presented supplier selection and evaluation as a seemingly straightforward and easy-to-follow process, but supplier selection and evaluation can actually be quite complex. First off, supplier selection and evaluation generally involve multiple criteria, and these criteria can vary both in number and importance, depending on the particular situation. As an example, a study involving the procurement of electronic components[12] looked at 10 possible selection criteria, whereas 16 selection criteria were investigated in a study of overseas vendors by Canadian apparel buyers.[13]

Second, because some vendor selection criteria may be contradictory, it is important to understand potential trade-offs between them. For instance, it may be difficult for a supplier to achieve both competitive pricing and high-quality supply. Third, the evolution of business practices and philosophies, such as just-in-time, green purchasing, and supply chain management, may require new selection criteria or the reprioritization of existing criteria. As an example, whereas EDI capabilities might have been an important supplier selection criteria in the early 1990s, in the contemporary environment Internet-related capabilities (e.g., tracking, pricing) have assumed increased relevance and importance.[14]

Procurement Portfolio Approach

As part of the situation analysis mentioned previously, procurement managers must continually be aware of the supply and demand characteristics of the raw materials, component parts, and supplies they purchase. **Kraljic's Portfolio Matrix** (see Figure 6.2) is used by many managers to classify corporate purchases in terms of their importance and supply complexity with a goal of minimizing supply vulnerability and getting the most out of the firm's purchasing power.[15] The matrix delineates four categories: *noncritical* (low importance, low complexity), *leverage* (high importance, low complexity), *strategic* (high importance, high complexity), and *bottleneck* (low importance, high complexity). Each category requires distinct procurement strategies for managing supply. For example, P-cards might be used for noncritical items, leverage items might rely upon reverse auctions, and strategic items would tend to use long-term, cost-based contracts with key suppliers, whereas firms may turn to buying consortiums to address the complexity of bottleneck items. Many researchers and companies have built upon Kraljic's approach by proposing new portfolio dimensions for classifying both products and suppliers.[16] The key will be for procurement to work with other functional areas to identify the most appropriate segmentation dimensions for their firm. This segmentation should also be reviewed and updated on a regular basis.

---

[10]Robert J. Trent, "Creating the Ideal Supplier Scorecard," *Supply Chain Management Review* 14, no. 2 (2010): 24–29.

[11]Frank Esposito, "PolyOne Reports Progress on Supplier Scorecards," *Rubber & Plastic News* 41, no. 5 (2011): 14.

[12]Neeraj Bharadway, "Investigating the Decision Criteria Used in Electronic Components Procurement," *Industrial Marketing Management* 33, no. 4 (2004): 317–323.

[13]Ismat Thaver and Anne Wilcock, "Identification of Overseas Vendor Selection Criteria Used by Canadian Apparel Buyers," *Journal of Fashion Marketing and Management* 10, no. 1 (2006): 56–70.

[14]Birsen Karpak, Rammohan R. Kasuganti, and Erdooan Kumcu, "Are You Using Costly Outmoded Techniques to Purchase Materials?" *Business Forum* 27, no. 1 (2005): 14–19.

[15]Peter Kraljic, "Purchasing Must Become Supply Management," *Harvard Business Review* 61, no. 5 (1983): 109–117.

[16]Sidhartha S. Padhi, Stephan M. Wagner, and Vijay Aggarwal, "Positioning of Commodities Using the Kraljic Portfolio Matrix," *Journal of Purchasing & Supply Management* 18, no. 1 (2012): 1–8.

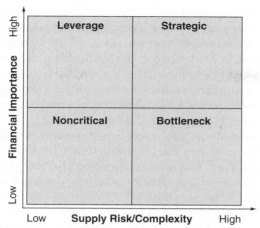

FIGURE 6.2 Kralijic Portfolio Matrix *Source:* Peter Kraljic, "Purchasing Must Become Supply Management." *Harvard Business Review* 61, no. 5 (1983): 109–117.

Supplier Development (Reverse Marketing)

Our description of supplier selection and evaluation has taken a "traditional" approach in the sense that there has been underlying assumptions that (1) suppliers initiate marketing efforts toward purchasers and (2) potential suppliers are available and willing to serve prospective purchasers. However, because it has become increasingly common for potential suppliers to not be available and willing to serve prospective purchasers, some purchasers are taking a more proactive role in the procurement process. To this end, **supplier development (reverse marketing)** refers to aggressive procurement involvement not typically part of supplier selection and can include a purchaser initiating contact with a supplier or a purchaser establishing prices, terms, and conditions, among other behaviors.

There are several key reasons for why purchasers are adopting a more proactive and aggressive role in the procurement process. One is the myriad of inefficiencies associated with suppliers initiating marketing efforts toward purchasers, such as suppliers possessing inadequate, insufficient, or untimely information. A second reason for more proactive and aggressive procurement is that the purchaser may be aware of important benefits, such as reduced inventory and improved forecasting accuracy, which are unknown to the supplier. Yet another reason is that achieving competitive advantage in the supply chain is predicated on purchasers adopting a more aggressive approach so as to compel suppliers to meet the necessary requirements.[17]

GLOBAL PROCUREMENT (SOURCING)[18]

While world trade continues to grow, the pace of this growth has slowed significantly since the 2008/2009 world economic downturn. The continuing growth of globalization means that many organizations, rather than relying on local and domestic suppliers, will continue to cast a wider net in search of supply sources. Indeed, a recent procurement study projected that half of all firms would have a global spend of over 40 percent.[19]

---

[17]Michiel Leenders, P. Fraser Johnson, Anna Flynn, and Harold E. Fearon, *Purchasing & Supply Management*, 13th ed. (Boston: McGraw-Hill/Irwin, 2006), Chapter 11.
[18]This material in this section is drawn from Donald F. Wood, Anthony Barone, Paul R. Murphy, and Daniel L. Wardlow, *International Logistics*, 2nd ed. (New York: Amacom, 2002), Chapter 14.
[19]William Atkinson, "The Big Trends in Sourcing and Procurement," *Supply Chain Management Review*, May/June 2008, S48–S50.

Global procurement (sourcing), which refers to buying components and inputs anywhere in the world, is driven by two primary reasons, namely, the factor-input strategy and the market-access strategy. With the factor-input strategy, an organization is seeking low-cost or high-quality sources of supply, whereas the market-access strategy involves sourcing in markets where an organizations plans to do significant business.

A global sourcing development model would include the following components: planning, specification, evaluation, relationship management, transportation and holding costs, implementation, and monitoring and improving. Each of these will be briefly detailed next. *Planning* is the first step in global procurement and involves an honest assessment of global sourcing opportunities and challenges. The outcome of this stage should be a set of global procurement policies and procedures that are consistent with an organization's overall objectives. *Specification* involves quantifying and qualifying current sources across a variety of dimensions such as quality, costs, reliability, and standardization, among others.

An earlier section in this chapter discussed supplier selection and evaluation, and although the *evaluation* process associated with global procurement has similarities, there are potential differences as well. For example, should an organization use the same standards to evaluate international sources as are used to evaluate domestic sources? Another component in a global sourcing development framework, *relationship management*, has been discussed in previous chapters. Relationship management in global procurement is exacerbated by potential difficulties in cross-cultural communication such as language and time considerations.

Because global sourcing increases the distance that components and inputs must be moved, managers must consider trade-offs between *transportation and holding costs*. The choice of a faster transportation alternative (e.g., air) will likely create higher transportation costs and lower inventory holding costs; alternatively, a slower transportation alternative (e.g., water) will create lower transportation costs and higher inventory holding costs. *Implementation,* or carrying out, is often a major shortcoming to many global procurement plans; indeed, some organizations fail to specify an implementation plan. Moreover, the greater uncertainty associated with global sourcing means that implementation plans must be flexible and provide guidance for decision making when confronted with the unexpected.

Finally, *monitoring and improving* means that performance measures must be established for global procurement systems and that these measures should be reviewed on a regular basis. Comparisons can be made between actual and expected performance, and the results of these comparisons can be used to improve the global sourcing process. Commonly used performance measures for monitoring global sourcing systems include the percentage of shipments that arrive early or late, completeness of orders, and percentage of orders accepted or rejected on delivery.

Establishing a successful global sourcing strategy can be one of the most difficult assignments for the procurement function. As organizations continue to expand their supply bases, many are realizing hidden cost factors are affecting the level of benefits that were projected to be achieved through this approach. Some of these hidden costs include increased costs of dealing with suppliers outside the domestic market, duty and tariff changes that occur over the life of a supply agreement, increased inventory-related costs associated with global supply chains, and rising levels of logistics cost volatility (e.g., ocean freight rates) that can occur unexpectedly.[20] Thus, when assessing the costs of global sourcing, it is important to examine all cost implications of this strategy. The need to fully evaluate the implications of global sourcing has motivated an increased examination of the **total cost of ownership (TCO)** when procuring items from outside countries. When taking a TCO approach, firms consider all the costs that can be assigned to the acquisition, use, and maintenance of a purchase.[21] While these additional costs can take many forms, logistics

---

[20]David Hannon, "The 9 Hidden Costs of Global Sourcing," *Purchasing*, March 12, 2009, 38–41.
[21]Lisa M. Ellram and Sue Perrott Siferd, "Purchasing: The Cornerstone of the Total Cost of Ownership Concept," *Journal of Business Logistics* 14, no. 1, (1993): 163–184.

costs related to the typically longer delivery lead times associated with global shipments are a key consideration. Ideally, firms should create their own TCO models that provide a more realistic view of the costs of global sourcing.[22]

Recently, rising transportation and energy costs, growing desires to be able to quickly adapt to changing market trends, along with risk and sustainability concerns have all influenced an examination of **near-sourcing** (procuring products from suppliers closer to one's own facilities) by many firms.[23] Given that procurement strategies and logistics strategies are intertwined, managers considering when to source globally and when to source close to their home markets must carefully consider the inbound and outbound logistics implications of these decisions. Decisions that made sense a few years ago in terms of labor cost savings may not be as clear-cut in today's environment.

SUSTAINABLE PROCUREMENT

As previously mentioned in Chapter 4, the sustainability concept suggests that an organization's responsibilities transcend economic considerations, such as the maximization of shareholder's wealth, and should incorporate societal and environmental objectives and values. There are sustainability concerns at the corporate level (e.g., what are the behaviors of a socially and environmentally responsible organization?), as well as sustainability issues associated with organizational functions such as procurement. For purposes of this discussion, **sustainable procurement** refers to the integration of social and environmental considerations into all stages of the purchasing process with the goal of minimizing the impact of procurement activities on human health and the environment.

Social Responsibility

Research suggests that socially responsible procurement consists of five dimensions, namely, *diversity, the environment, human rights, philanthropy*, and *safety*. Diversity is concerned with procurement activities associated with minority or women-owned organizations, whereas the environment includes considerations such as waste reduction and the design of products for reuse or recycling. Human rights issues include child labor laws as well as sweatshop labor. Philanthropy focuses on employee volunteer efforts and philanthropic contributions, and safety is concerned with the safe transportation of purchased products, as well as the safe operation of relevant facilities.[24]

Many believe that ethical considerations (i.e., standards of conduct and moral principles) are also a part of socially responsible procurement. Indeed, research on procurement ethics dates back to the mid-1960s, and the competitiveness of the contemporary business environment creates—for some companies—a "win at all costs" philosophy that can exacerbate unethical behavior. Areas of ethical concern in procurement include gift giving and gift receiving; **bribes** (money paid before an exchange) and **kickbacks** (money paid after an exchange); misuse of information; improper methods of knowledge acquisition; lying or misrepresentation of the truth; product quality (lack thereof); misuse of company assets, to include abuse of expense accounts; and conflicts of interest, or activity that creates a potential conflict between one's personal interests and the employer's interests.

The topic of socially responsible procurement is much broader than the space devoted to it in this chapter indicates. Moreover, it's important to understand that the relevance, importance, and challenges associated with socially responsible procurement are likely to increase in

---

[22]Yash Sutarlya, "TCO: From Buzzword to Reality," *SMT Magazine* 27, no. 8, (2012): 66–75.
[23]Brad Mitchell, "The Sourcing Dilemma: Should You Go Near or Far?" *World Trade* 22, no. 4 (2009): 19.
[24]Ibid.

the coming years. As an example, BMW is now requiring potential vendors to answer 29 questions on their social and environmental standards, and the results are an integral part of BMW's vendor selection process.[25]

Investment Recovery[26]

Investment recovery, which identifies opportunities to recover revenues or reduce costs associated with scrap, surplus, obsolete, and waste materials, is often the responsibility of the procurement manager. Investment recovery can provide an organization with the opportunity to simultaneously do well and do good in the sense that investment recovery increases a seller's revenues (reduces a seller's costs) while addressing selected environmental considerations. For example, although aluminum recycling can provide revenues to an organization, the recycling conserves raw materials, uses less energy, and reduces various types of pollution. Figure 6.3 shows an example of how aluminum cans might be recycled.

Because even the best managed organizations will generate excess, obsolete, scrap, and waste materials, it's important to distinguish among these different categories of material. **Excess (surplus) materials** refer to stock that exceeds the reasonable requirements of an organization, perhaps because of an overly optimistic demand forecast. If an organization has several production facilities, excess materials might be transferred to the other facilities. Unlike excess materials, **obsolete materials** are not likely to ever be used by the organization that purchased it. Having said this, materials that are obsolete to one organization might not be obsolete to other users; as such, it might be possible to sell obsolete materials to other organizations.

FIGURE 6.3 The Recycling of Aluminum Cans   *Source:* Courtesy of Aluminum Company of America.

---

[25]"BMW Broadens Its Supply Standards." *Supply Management* 14, no 21 (2009): 11.
[26]Much of the material in this section is drawn from Leenders et al., *Purchasing & Supply Management.*

Scrap materials refer to materials that are no longer serviceable, have been discarded, or are a by-product of the production process (e.g., scrap steel when producing an automobile or washing machine). Certain scrap materials, such as copper and nickel, have such economic value that procurement contracts sometimes include a price at which the scrap will be repurchased by the supplier. **Waste materials** refer to those that have been spoiled, broken, or otherwise rendered unfit for further use or reclamation. Unlike scrap materials, waste materials have no economic value.

The ways that organizations manage the investment recovery of excess, obsolete, scrap, and waste materials should be influenced by the materials' classification. Waste materials have limited investment recovery options because they are unfit for further use and have no economic value. As a result, it wouldn't be realistic to search for ways to reuse waste materials elsewhere in an organization or to find prospective buyers for the waste products. On the other hand, there are more expansive investment recovery options for excess materials, to include using them elsewhere within an organization, selling to another organization, returning to the supplier, and selling through a surplus dealer.

Summary

Procurement is closely related to logistics because nearly anything purchased must be moved to wherever it is needed—in the right quantity and at the precise time. Logistics services may also be an important focus of procurement activities within an organization. Procurement, an important activity because its costs often range between 60 and 80 percent of an organization's revenues, has assumed greater strategic orientation in many contemporary firms.

The chapter began with a discussion of procurement objectives and the importance for these objectives to be aligned with, and supportive of, those of the organization. One of procurement's most important responsibilities is supplier selection and evaluation, and this can be quite challenging, in part because of the multiple, and sometime conflicting, selection and evaluation criteria. Kraljic's Portfolio Matrix was introduced as a way to segment procured items in order to more effectively align sourcing strategies. Supplier development (reverse marketing) was also introduced as being a more important part of the procurement process.

Global sourcing, which refers to buying components and inputs anywhere in the world, continues to grow in scope. Because of the tremendous distances that can be involved in global sourcing, managers must understand the trade-offs between transportation and holding costs.

The chapter also described sustainable procurement, with an emphasis on socially responsible procurement. We learned that a number of ethical issues are associated with procurement. In addition, the environmental implications of investment recovery (managing excess, obsolete, scrap, and waste materials) were detailed.

Questions for Discussion and Review

6.1 What is procurement? What is its relevance to logistics?

6.2 Contrast procurement's historical focus to its more strategic orientation today.

6.3 Discuss the benefits and potential challenges of using electronic procurement cards.

6.4 Discuss three potential procurement objectives.

6.5 Name and describe the steps in the supplier selection and evaluation process.

6.6 Distinguish between a single sourcing approach and a multiple sourcing approach.

6.7 What are the two primary approaches for evaluating suppliers? How do they differ?

6.8 Discuss the factors that make supplier selection and evaluation difficult.

6.9 Distinguish between supplier audits and supplier scorecards. When should each be used?

6.10 Describe Kraljic's Portfolio Matrix. What are the four categories of this segmentation approach?

6.11 Define supplier development, and explain why it is becoming more prominent in some organizations.

6.12 What are the components of the global sourcing development model presented in this chapter?

6.13 What are some of the challenges of implementing a global sourcing strategy?

6.14 Pick, and discuss, two components of the global sourcing development model presented in this chapter.

6.15 What is total cost of ownership and why is it important to consider?

6.16 Why are some firms considering near-sourcing?

6.17 Name, and give an example of, the five dimensions of socially responsible purchasing.

6.18 Discuss some of the ethical issues that are associated with procurement.

6.19 Distinguish between excess, obsolete, scrap, and waste materials.

6.20 Should investment recovery be the responsibility of the procurement manager? If yes, why? If not, which party (parties) should be responsible for investment recovery?

Suggested Readings

Cheraghi, S. Hossein, Mohammed Dadashzadeh, and Mutho Subramanian. "Critical Success Factors for Supplier Selection: An Update." *Journal of Applied Business Research* 20, no. 2 (2004): 91–108.

Choi, Thomas and Tom Linton. "Don't Let Your Supply Chain Control Your Business." *Harvard Business Review* 89, no. 12 (2011): 112–117.

Christensen, John, Christopher Park, Earl Sun, Max Gorainick, and Jayanth Iyengar. "A Practical Guide to Green Sourcing." *Supply Chain Management Review* 12, no. 8 (2008): 14–21.

Handfield, Robert B. and David L. Baumer. "Managing Conflict of Interest Issues in Purchasing," *Journal of Supply Chain Management* 42, no. 3 (2006): 41–50.

Ho, William, Xiaowei Xu, and Prasanta K. Dey, "Multi-criteria Decision Making Approaches for Supplier Evaluation and Selection: A Literature Review." *European Journal of Operational Research* 202, no. 1 (2010): 16–24.

Johnson, P. Frazier, Michiel R. Leenders, and Harold E. Fearon. "Supply's Growing Status and Influence: A Sixteen-Year Perspective." *Journal of Supply Chain Management* 42, no. 2 (2006): 33–43.

Martinson, Bob. "The Power of the P-Card." *Strategic Finance* 83, no. 8 (2002): 30–36.

Minahan, Tim A. "Strategies for High-Performance Procurement." *Supply Chain Management Review* 9, no. 6 (2005): 46–54.

Monczka, Robert M. and Kenneth J. Petersen. "The Competitive Potential of Supply Management." *Supply Chain Management Review* 16, no. 3 (2012): 10–18.

Sanchez-Rodriguez, Christobal and Angel R. Martinez-Lorente. "Quality Management Practices in the Purchasing Function: An Empirical Study." *International Journal of Operations & Production Management* 24, no. 7 (2004): 666–687.

Schneider, Lena and Carl Marcus Wallenburg. "Implementing Sustainable Sourcing—Does Purchasing Need to Change?" *Journal of Purchasing & Supply Management* 18, no. 4 (2012): 243–257.

Spray, Gregory. "The Art of Procurement Mastery." *Supply Chain Management Review* 13, no. 1 (2009): 36–43.

Teo, Thompson S.H. and Kee-hung Lai. "Usage and Performance Impact of Electronic Procurement." *Journal of Business Logistics* 20, no. 2 (2009): 125–139.

Trent, Robert J. and Robert M. Monczka. "Achieving Excellence in Global Sourcing." *MIT Sloan Management Review* 47, no. 1 (2005): 24–32.

Turner, Martha and Pat Houston. "Going Green? Start with Sourcing." *Supply Chain Management Review* 13, no. 2 (2009): 14–21.

Wagner, Stepan M. and Daniel R. Krause. "Supplier Development: Communication Approaches, Activities and Goals." *International Journal of Production Research* 47, no. 12 (2009): 3161–3177.

CASE

CASE 6.1 Tempo Ltd.

Fatih Terim was in his small office in Antalya, a Mediterranean port in southwestern Turkey. He looked at the clock on the wall and realized he had spent the entire afternoon thinking about one thing and one thing only—the most recent meeting with his Romanian business "connection." Terim had just completed a trip to the Balkans and was in his office evaluating his firm's progress in the region. This was necessary because he was thinking of going to Syria for the same reasons that had taken him to the Balkans: finding goods at cheap prices and selling them with handsome markups at home in Turkey or in other neighboring countries.

Terim had established Tempo Ltd. in 1989 in Antalya. Terim, then fresh out of Akdeniz University, quickly became an entrepreneur. The focus of his business was to buy goods from nearby foreign sources and then find buyers for those products in the domestic Turkish market. The first couple of years were easy for Terim because he was working very hard, and the Turkish economy was soaring. With the fall of communism, Terim saw even more opportunities. He started marketing Turkish-made goods to former communist countries around Turkey and in central Asia.

However, the Turkish economy took a major hit in April 1994. The sudden death of the country's president added to the nation's political instability. The value of Turkish lira (TL) plummeted against the U.S. dollar ($US). In the following years, the Turkish economy took many more hits, including the financial crisis in the Asian markets, the Russian market crash, and most recently, the Argentinean crisis. In 1999, two major earthquakes hit the northwestern part of Turkey, where one-third of the nation's 67 million persons reside and which is the heartland of Turkish industry. Although Turkey recovered quickly from the earthquakes, political instability continued and pushed the entire economy into a slowdown. In 1993, one U.S. dollar could buy 7,000 Turkish liras. In 2003, that same one U.S. dollar could buy 1,567,000 TL. Despite these discouraging events, the Turkish economy still has opportunities for growth. One reason such a major potential still exists is the simple fact that hard-working, sharp-trading people like Fatih Terim never stood still and kept putting together the best deals they could.

Today Terim's company has some connections in almost every European country and is working very hard to maintain these connections by generating steady flows of commerce. Terim's latest trip was to the Balkan nations of Bulgaria, Romania, and Greece. Terim held meetings with key businesspeople in all three nations. In both Bulgaria and Greece, Terim had entered into modest sales agreements that extend into the middle of next year.

In Romania, matters did not move as quickly. Terim's Romanian connection, George Hagi, was not interested in any of the small transactions that Terim was suggesting. Hagi, in an almost mysterious manner, did tell Terim that he looking for a Turkish partner willing to participate in a substantial, although not exactly legitimate, deal. The first aspect was that the customer wanted to buy Turkish chemicals to be used for fertilizers in agriculture. However, the terms of payment from the prospective customers would be in the form of barter rather than cash, and the goods bartered

for the chemicals would be *kereste* (lumber). Although "barter" was a term and practice with which Terim was familiar, he had no idea what to do with *kereste*. Over the years, Tempo Ltd. had concentrated its business on small consumer products. However, he wasn't going to let a detail like this get in the way of new markets. He knew he could find a market in Turkey for lumber because little was produced domestically, and both new construction and earthquake reconstruction were underway.

What worried Terim were his new customers. He learned from Hagi that these new customers were either a large state-owned company in North Korea or the North Korean government itself, which is why Terim spent that entire afternoon thinking about just one thing. All day he tried to justify his possible decisions to himself. The problem was that North Korea was a communist regime, and beyond that, North Korea, according to NATO and the United Nations, was a country that provided support to certain terrorist activities all over the world. In early 2002, U.S. President George W. Bush had described Iran, Iraq, and North Korea as an "axis of evil." North Korea and those with whom it traded were under tight scrutiny from both the United Nations and the United States (which still stationed troops in South Korea).

Terim came up with the excuse that if he didn't sell to the North Koreans, someone else would eventually, so why should he give up this money? However, the solution was not that easy. Hagi said in his e-mail to Terim that if the negotiations went well, a party of North Korean bureaucrats would wish to visit Antalya for "inspection" purposes and that Terim would have to cover the costs of entertainment and accommodations. Those accommodations would range from luxurious hotel rooms to young attractive companions, of both sexes, for business-related dinners and receptions. Terim knew exactly what those inspection purposes were. They were pleasure trips for certain bureaucrats in North Korea. Unfortunately, he was also aware that this was the way things worked in Third World governments. Over the years, he had learned the tricks of the trade, and one thing he knew well was that without the *rusvet* (bribe: the grease money or large amounts of payments specifically for one-time transactions), such risky situations would end up as a "no sale." He wondered whether he should ask the Turkish agricultural chemical manufacturers to help with the entertainment costs. Also, should he and the chemical manufacturers touch base with each other with respect to the *rusvet* that would undoubtedly be expected by the North Koreans? Terim's position regarding *rusvet* was unclear. Indeed, the chemical manufactures should be expected to give him, or Hagi, a kickback for facilitating the sale of chemicals.

"Talk about core competency," Terim mumbled to himself. To get his mind off these sticky issues, he looked into the logistics costs to move the bartered lumber from North Korea. He would need to know those costs before proceeding. He had a couple of options.

The first option would be to ship the lumber by sea from Wonsan, North Korea, through the Sea of Japan, across the Indian Ocean, through the Suez Canal, and into the Liman (port) of Antalya, Turkey. (See Exhibits 6.A and 6.B.) This would be the perfect solution, except, he suddenly realized, he would not be able to bring the lumber into Turkey legally because of trade sanctions against North Korea. Hence, this option was dropped.

His second option would be to send the lumber to a country where its entry would be legal. The country

EXHIBIT 6.A Korean Peninsula

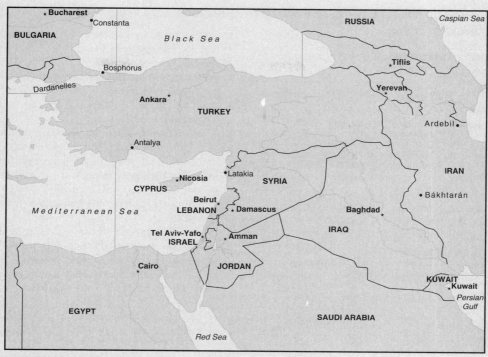

EXHIBIT 6.B Mediterranean Sea

to which the *kereste* could be shipped legally was none other than Romania, one of Turkey's neighbors on the Black Sea. The reason was hidden in history. Since their communist years, Romania and North Korea had had strong ties that remained nearly intact after the fall of communism in Romania. So lumber could be loaded on to a *gemi* (ship) and could be shipped to Romania via the Dardanelles and the Bosphorus (the two straits that make up the gateway to the Black Sea) and finally to the port of Constantza, Romania, in the Black Sea. Once there, the lumber could be covered by new documents, and eventually the origin of the goods could be stated as "Romania," not "North Korea." The lumber could then move by *tir* (truck) to Turkey. This sounded like a feasible solution, but how much would such an operation cost? Terim recalled that Hagi had said that redoing documents in situations like this cost about 16,000,000,000 TL, including *rusvets*.

Terim's mind then shifted to a third option. From Wonsan, the lumber could be shipped to a port in Syria, in this case Latakia. From there, *tirs* could haul the lumber to Iskenderun at the southeastern border of Turkey. Because the border at Iskenderun is the most laxly guarded border in Turkey, small *rusvets* to low-ranking officers at the gates would allow the *kereste* to enter Turkey without any problems. The *rusvets* would be about 10 percent of the *kereste* shipment's value.

The same could be done at the Liman of Antalya. However, the chances of getting caught were much higher. If Tempo Ltd. were caught red-handed, it would be fined a sum of double the total value of goods entering the country. Thus, this was a fourth, but discarded, option.

Only two options were feasible, and each came with certain risks. One was to ship the *kereste* to Romania, have new documents drawn, falsify the shipment's origin, and then send it to Turkey by *tir*. The other was to send the *kereste* by ship to Syria, truck it to Turkey, and bribe customs inspectors at the Turkish border. Terim was initially concerned with the logistics costs of getting the *kereste* inside the Turkish border. The *kereste* would be of various dimensions, bound together by metal straps into bundles measuring 1 meter by 1 meter by 5 meters, and the North Koreans would deliver and load the *kereste* aboard a break-bulk vessel in a North Korean port.

If Terim could get the *kereste* inside Turkey, it should sell for 783,500,000,000 TL. The Turkish chemical manufacturers expect to be paid 60 days after the chemicals leave the Turkish port, which will be same date as the *kereste* leaves North Korea.

Terim gazed at his notes, which were full of numbers and currency exchange rates.

Ocean transportation costs for Gemi (Shipping lines require payment in U.S. dollars):

Wonsan to Constantza	$US42,000
Wonsan to Latakia	$US33,000
Suez Canal charges	$US3,100
Tir:	
Constantza into Turkey	$US15,000
Latakia into Turkey	$US12,000
Handling fees at the Liman (Syria or Romania)	1.25 percent of the total value of goods
Generating false Romania-origin Documents	16,000,000,000 TL
Projected amount *rusvet* at Syrian–Turkish border	10 percent of shipment's value
Currency exchange rates	$US1 = 1,567,000 TL
Option 1: Wonsan/ Constantza/Turkey would take 43 days	Option 2: Wonsan/ Latakia/Turkey would take 22 days

Questions

1. Should Terim let somebody else complete the transaction because he knows that if he doesn't sell to the North Koreans, someone else will?
2. What are the total costs given in the case for the option of moving via Romania?
3. What are the total costs given in the case for the option of moving via Syria?
4. Which option should Terim recommend? Why?
5. What other costs and risks are involved in these proposed transactions, including some not mentioned in the case?
6. Regarding the supply chain, how—if at all—should bribes be included? What functions do they serve?
7. If Terim puts together this transaction, is he acting ethically? Discuss.
8. What do you suggest should be done to bring moral values into the situation so that the developing countries are somewhat in accordance with Western standards? Keep in mind that the risks involved in such environments are much higher than the risks of conducting business in Western markets. Also note that some cultures see bribery as a way to better distribute the wealth among their citizens.

ELEMENTS OF LOGISTICS SYSTEMS

Part III presents a detailed examination of some of the more prominent elements of logistics systems. Chapter 7 looks at demand management, order management, and customer service. Demand management involves managing customer demand through the supply chain, whereas order management deals with incoming orders, and customer service deals with keeping existing customers happy. Chapter 8 discusses inventory management and you will learn about inventory classifications as well as inventory-related costs. This chapter also examines how much inventory to order, when to order inventory, and special concerns with inventory.

The topic of Chapter 9 is facility location, which has moved from a tactical to a strategic consideration in many companies in part because of globalization. You will learn about general and specific factors in facility location in this chapter. Chapter 10 focuses on warehousing management and you will be introduced to the various types of warehousing, warehousing's role in a logistics system, and design considerations in warehousing. The effectiveness and efficiency of warehousing operations can be greatly influenced by packaging and materials handling considerations, and Chapter 11 looks at these two topics.

Two chapters are devoted to transportation because it often represents the highest cost logistics activity in a company. Chapter 12, "Transportation," discusses the five modes of transportation, intermodal transportation, and select transportation specialists. Chapter 13, "Transportation Management," focuses on some of the primary responsibilities of a transportation manager which include rate considerations, modal and carrier selection, and domestic documentation. Chapter 14, the last chapter in this section, deals with international logistics, which tends to be more challenging and more costly than domestic logistics. Among the topics covered in Chapter 14 are macroenvironmental influences on international logistics, international documentation, terms of sale, and international trade specialists.

7

DEMAND MANAGEMENT, ORDER MANAGEMENT, AND CUSTOMER SERVICE

KEY TERMS

- Activity-based costing (ABC)
- Benchmarking
- Cause-and-effect (associative) forecasting
- Collaborative planning, forecasting, and replenishment (CPFR)
- Customer profitability analysis (CPA)
- Customer service
- Demand management

- Judgmental forecasting
- Make-to-order
- Make-to-stock
- Multichannel marketing systems
- Order cycle
- Order delivery
- Order fill rate
- Order management
- Order picking and assembly

- Order processing
- Order to cash cycle
- Order transmittal
- Order triage
- Pick-to-light technology
- Service recovery
- Time series forecasting
- Voice-based order picking

LEARNING OBJECTIVES

- To understand the linkages between demand management, order management, and customer service
- To introduce you to demand forecasting models
- To examine the order cycle and its four components

- To understand the four dimensions of customer service as they pertain to logistics
- To familiarize you with select managerial issues associated with customer service

This chapter discusses two key issues: (1) how an organization determines what the customer wants and (2) how an organization facilitates the customer getting what is wanted. We will analyze these issues in terms of demand management (how an organization determines what the customer wants) along with order management and customer service (how an organization facilitates the customer getting what is wanted). Demand management is important because effective and efficient supply chains have learned to match both supply and demand; failure to do so can result in oversupply (more supply than demand) or undersupply (less supply than demand) of products. Oversupply likely means higher-than-desired inventory costs, whereas undersupply can mean a dissatisfied—or even lost—customer.

Order management and customer service begin where demand management ends. The ability to determine that the customer wants, say, a black shovel, is nice, but is the customer able to communicate this desire to an organization? Once the customer's desire for a black shovel is communicated to an organization, is the organization able to fulfill this desire? Although these might seem like basic, commonsense questions, reality may be quite different. Indeed, one lesson learned in the early years of online retailing was that many companies were quite good at understanding and stimulating customer demand as well as receiving orders associated with the demand. Unfortunately, some of these companies were far less adept at processing these orders; orders arrived late (if they arrived at all), arrived incomplete, and arrived with incorrect product(s). Not surprisingly, these fulfillment shortcomings caused a great deal of customer dissatisfaction, which explains why some early online retailers (e.g., etoys.com) are no longer in business.

DEMAND MANAGEMENT

Demand management can be defined as "the creation across the supply chain and its markets of a coordinated flow of demand."[1] A key component in demand management is demand (sales) forecasting, which refers to an effort to project future demand. Without question demand forecasting is helpful in **make-to-stock** situations (when finished goods are produced prior to receiving a customer order). However, demand forecasting can also be helpful in **make-to-order** situations (when finished goods are produced after receiving a customer order). Make-to-order situations generally involve some combination of standard and custom components, and forecasting could be quite helpful in projecting the standard components needed. For example, although a computer manufacturer might not be able to forecast the exact configuration of each order for computers that it receives, the manufacturer might be able to forecast the percentage of orders for desktop and laptop computers (i.e., standard components).

Entire books are devoted to demand forecasting, and space limitations prevent a comprehensive discussion of the topic in this text. Rather, we will offer an overview of demand forecasting so the reader can understand forecasting's role in determining what the customer wants.

Demand Forecasting Models[2]

The three basic types of forecasting models are (1) judgmental, (2) time series, and (3) cause and effect. **Judgmental forecasting** involves using judgment or intuition and is preferred in situations where there is limited or no historical data, such as with a new product introduction. Judgment forecasting techniques include surveys and the analog technique, among others. With survey forecasting, questionnaires (surveys) are used to learn about customer preferences and intentions. A strong understanding of survey design and population sampling methodologies is necessary in survey forecasting, and you should recognize that customer intentions don't always translate into actual behavior. Analog forecasting involves determining an analog (similar item) to the item being forecast and then using the analog's demand history as a basis for the relevant forecast. A key challenge is selecting the appropriate analog to use.

An underlying assumption of **time series forecasting** is that future demand is solely dependent on past demand. For example, if this year's sales were 7 percent higher than last year's sales, a time series forecast for next year's sales would be this year's sales plus 7 percent. Time series forecasting techniques include, but are not limited to, simple moving averages and weighted moving averages. The simple moving average is calculated by summing the demand across different time periods and then dividing by the number of time periods. Because each time period is assigned the same importance (weight), the simple moving average may not adequately reflect recent upturns or downturns in demand. To address this shortcoming, the weighted moving average technique assigns greater importance (weight) to the more recent data. The differences in forecasted demand between the simple and weighted moving averages can be seen in the example in Table 7.1.

---

[1]John T. Mentzer, "A Telling Fortune," *Industrial Engineer*, April 2006, 42–47.

[2]The discussion of demand forecasting models is drawn from Chaman L. Jain, "Benchmarking Forecasting Models," *Journal of Business Forecasting* 24, no. 4 (2005/2006): 9–10, 12 as well as Joel D. Wisner, G. Keong Leong, and Keah-Choon Tan, *Principles of Supply Chain Management: A Balanced Approach*, 3rd ed. (Mason, OH: South-Western Publishing, 2012), Chapter 5.

				Weighted	
		Simple Moving		Moving	
		Average	Projected	Average	Projected
	Demand	Weighting	Demand	Weighting	Demand
Time Period (1)	(2)	Factor (3)	(4; = 2 × 3)	Factor (5)	(6; = 2 × 5)
Last month	250	.25	62.5	.40	100
Two months ago	230	.25	57.5	.30	69
Three months ago	200	.25	50	.20	40
Four months ago	180	.25	45	.10	18
Forecast			**215**		**227**

TABLE 7.1 Forecast Example Using the Simple and Weighted Moving Average Techniques

Cause-and-effect (also referred to as associative) forecasting assumes that one or more factors are related to demand and that the relationship between cause and effect can be used to estimate future demand. In many western countries, for example, there tends to be an inverse relationship between the level of interest rates and the consumers' ability to buy a house (e.g., as interest rates increase, housing sales tend to decrease). Examples of cause-and-effect forecasting include simple and multiple regression; in simple regression, demand is dependent on only one variable, whereas in multiple regression demand is dependent on two or more variables.

Demand Forecasting Issues

It is important to recognize that the selection of a forecasting technique (or techniques) depends on a variety of factors, such as the situation at hand, forecasting costs in terms of time and money, and the accuracy of various forecasting techniques. With respect to the situation at hand, as pointed out earlier, judgmental forecasting is appropriate where there is little or no historical data available. For instance, Apple Corporation's initial sales estimates for the iPod, which was introduced in 2001, were based on judgment and intuition—the iPod was not only a new product, but a somewhat revolutionary product as well.

Managers should also understand the time and monetary costs associated with each particular forecasting technique. Survey research, for example, can require quite a bit of both money and time, depending on the media (i.e., mail, telephone, electronic, in-person) used to collect and analyze the data. For example, in-person surveys can take a great of time to complete and can be quite expensive (e.g., compensation costs of the researcher who conducts in-person surveys).

Forecasting accuracy refers to the relationship between actual and forecasted demand, and accuracy can be affected by various considerations. One of the challenges with the analog technique is selecting the appropriate analog, because an inappropriate selection will reduce forecast accuracy. For instance, when a movie studio releases a sequel to a previously successful motion picture, a forecasting analog based on the initial release will likely generate a different revenue estimate than a forecasting analog based on the performance patterns of sequels to other movies—and one analog will be more accurate than the other.

Forecast accuracy can have important logistical implications, as illustrated at Lighthouse Foods, where improved forecasting resulted in substantial reductions in the amount of finished goods inventory. More specifically, Lighthouse used to carry nearly twice as much inventory as actually needed for certain stockkeeping units (SKUs) because of inaccurate demand forecasts for those items.[3]

---

[3]Carol Casper, "Demand Planning Comes of Age," *Food Logistics*, January/February 2008, 19–24.

Up to this point, we have treated demand forecasting as a discrete entity in the sense that each supply chain member generates its own demand forecasts. You may recall that Chapter 1 briefly mentioned the **CPFR (collaborative planning, forecasting, and replenishment)** concept, where supply chain partners share planning and forecasting data to better match up supply and demand. Conceptually, CPFR suggests that supply chain partners will be working from a collectively agreed-to single forecast number as opposed to each member working off its own forecast projection. Successful CPFR implementations have yielded smoother ordering patterns, increased sales revenues, decreased safety stock, higher order fill rates and improved forecasting accuracy.[4] Despite these potential benefits, you should recognize that (1) not all CPFR initiatives have been successful and (2) there can be significant challenges associated with getting supply chain partners to share the relevant data needed to develop the forecast(s).

We'll conclude our discussion of demand forecasting with a brief look at forecasting that is done via computer software. Computer software forecasting dates back over 30 years and there has been tremendous advancement in its breadth and computational power—forecasts that might have taken hours or days can now be generated in a matter of minutes or hours. And although it would seem as if this advancement would contribute to improved forecasts, software packages should not be viewed as a forecasting panacea. For example, enterprise resource planning (ERP) systems conceptually should lead to much lower forecasting errors. However, the Grocery Manufacturers Association found forecasting errors that averaged more than 20 percent among companies that had implemented ERP-based forecasts.[5] It's important to keep in mind that no software package—regardless of its sophistication and cost—is capable of totally eliminating forecast errors.

ORDER MANAGEMENT

Order management refers to management of the various activities associated with the **order cycle**; the order cycle (which can also be referred to as replenishment cycle or lead time) refers to the time from when a customer places an order to when the order is received. In recent years some organizations have expanded the order management concept to include the length of time it takes an organization to receive payment for an order, or what is called the **order to cash cycle**.

There is a key link between order management and demand forecasting, in that a firm does not simply wait for orders to arrive to learn what's happening with respect to demand. Forecasts are made of sales and of the inventories that must be stocked so that the firm can fill orders in a satisfactory manner. There is also a key link between order management and customer service because many organizations analyze customer service in terms of order cycle performance.

Before proceeding to a discussion of the four order cycle stages, several points should be made. First, the order cycle should be analyzed not only in terms of total cycle time but in cycle time variability (reliability) as well. Just as longer order cycles necessitate increased levels of inventory, so too does greater cycle time variability require additional levels of inventory (regardless of cycle time length). Consider the U.S. railroad that analyzed transit times on one of its origin–destination pairs located approximately 400 miles apart. The railroad discovered an average transit time of eight days, with a minimum of three days and a maximum of 28 days, and the railroad's customers coped with the erratic transit times by holding additional inventory to avoid out-of-stock situations.[6]

A second point is that order management has been profoundly affected by advances in information systems. For example, one of this book's authors worked in the U.S. trucking

[4]Jerry Andrews, "CPFR: Considering the Options, Advantages, and Pitfalls," *Supply and Demand Chain Executive*, April/May 2008, 8–12.
[5]Kevin T. Higgins, "Forecasting to Believing," *Food Engineering*, October 2009, 57–64.
[6]Judy A. Perry, "Who's Watching the Numbers That Count?" *Railway Age*, May 2005, 10.

industry in the early 1980s, and if a customer telephoned to learn about a shipment's status, a very manual—and, unfortunately, a time-consuming (at a minimum, the phone call had to be answered) and not always successful—shipment tracking process was initiated. Today, by contrast, that same customer doesn't have to place a phone call; in many cases, she/he can simply log on to a particular carrier's website to learn about a shipment's status.

You should also recognize that the various activities associated with an order cycle are not uniformly agreed upon. For example, the Supply Chain Council lists over 25 distinct activities as part of the order cycle.[7] By contrast, we view the order cycle as consisting of four components or stages: order transmittal, order processing, order picking and assembly, and order delivery. Each of the four components will be discussed below.

Order Transmittal

Order transmittal refers to the time from when the customer places an order until the seller receives the order. In general, there are five possible ways to transmit orders: in person, by mail, by telephone, by facsimile (fax) machine, and electronically. Each method of order transmittal has advantages and disadvantages, and each performs differently with respect to the cost of ordering, the time to order, the potential for order errors, and ordering convenience. For example, in-person orders greatly reduce the potential for order errors, if for no other reason that the order can be physically inspected prior to being accepted. However, in-person ordering isn't always convenient (or practical) in situations where the supplier is geographically distant.

Although ordering by mail might be more convenient than in-person ordering, mail is considered to be a relatively slow form of order transmittal, and there are occasions when the order never reaches the intended destination (lost in the mail). Ordering by telephone can be relatively fast and convenient, but order errors may not be detected until the order is delivered. You may have placed a telephone order for home delivery of a large, pepperoni pizza, only to be delivered a small, mushroom pizza!

Both facsimile and electronic ordering are techniques that have emerged over the past 30 years, and both have had immense impacts on the order transmittal process. The fax can be fast and convenient, and, unlike the telephone, it provides hard copy documentation of an order. However, the seller's fax machine can be cluttered with junk (unwanted) faxes, and the quality of the fax transmission can result in hard-to-read orders—which increases the chances of order errors in the form of incorrect product or incorrect quantity. Electronic ordering, which includes EDI and the Internet, can be fast, convenient, and accurate, particularly those orders involving scanners and bar codes. Concerns with ordering via the Internet include the security of the information being transmitted and the potential loss of privacy (due to cookies and tracking software).

Order Processing

Order processing refers to the time from when the seller receives an order until an appropriate location (such as a warehouse) is authorized to fill the order. Advances in technology have allowed most firms to computerize many aspects of their order processing systems. For instance, order forms, whether printed or in computer format, are designed so that the use of computers by both the customer and the vendor is facilitated. Similarly, the billing of customers is increasingly done through computerized and electronic networks.

Figure 7.1, which presents an order processing flowchart, highlights that there are many distinct order processing activities. Typical order processing activities include checking an order for completeness and accuracy, checking the buyer's ability to purchase, entering the order into

---

[7]http://supply-chain.org/.

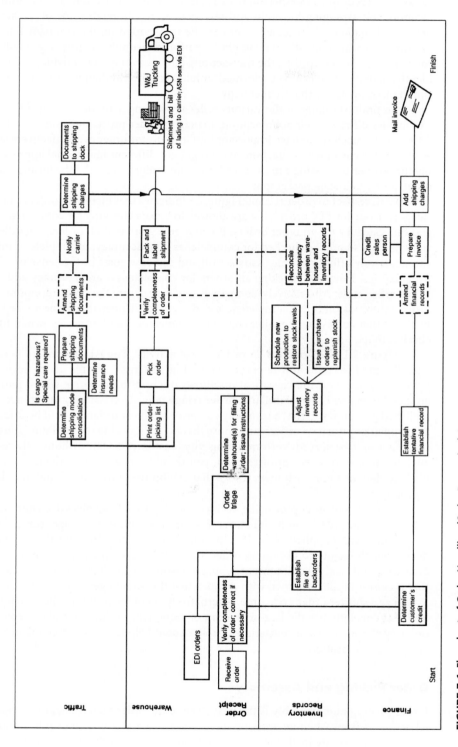

FIGURE 7.1 Flowchart of Order Handling (Order Processing) System

115

the system, crediting a salesperson with a sale, recording the transaction, determining inventory location, and arranging for outbound transportation. Although some of the activities must be performed sequentially (e.g., an order can't be transported until a company knows from which location(s) it will be filled), some might be performed simultaneously (e.g., crediting a salesperson with a sale and recording the transaction). Note that one way to reduce order cycle time is to identify activities that can be performed simultaneously and then perform the relevant activities simultaneously, rather than sequentially.

An understanding of the various order processing activities is only a first step, however. Companies differ in their approaches to managing order processing and its activities, and these different approaches can have important implications for order cycle effectiveness and efficiency as well for customer satisfaction. We'll highlight different managerial approaches by discussing three order processing activities, order receipt, order triage, and the location(s) used to fill an order, in the following paragraphs.

With respect to order receipt, Figure 7.1 indicates that incoming orders can be divided into categories, one for EDI orders that are allowed to bypass checking for completeness and accuracy and one category for all other orders. It could be argued that all orders, regardless of transmission method, should be checked for completeness and accuracy; incomplete or inaccurate orders can negatively affect customer satisfaction and increase costs in the sense of addressing order irregularities. However, checking all orders for completeness and accuracy adds costs and time to the order cycle. Alternatively, companies might structure the order receipt function to reflect historical trends on order completeness and accuracy. Under this scenario, order transmission methods that consistently exhibit superior completeness and accuracy would bypass the order check activity.

Figure 7.1 also contains an order triage activity. The triage concept is often associated with the medical field and refers to classifying patients in terms of the severity of their illness or malady, and the classification allows doctors to prioritize which patients should be attended to before others. Similarly, **order triage** refers to classifying orders according to preestablished guidelines so that a company can prioritize how orders should be filled. However, not all companies prioritize orders, and those that do must decide the attribute(s) used to prioritize (e.g., first in, first served; customer longevity; customer sales). Although there is no one right attribute to use for order prioritization, you should recognize that the chosen attribute(s) are likely to delight some customers (those that exhibit the chosen attribute) and disappoint other customers.

Another key order processing decision (see Figure 7.1) involves determining the location(s) from which an order is to be filled. As was the case with order triage, companies should have clear, consistently applied rules to help in making this decision, but there are companies that decide which facility to use on an order-by-order basis—which can lead to inconsistent order cycle time and cost. A commonsense approach would be to fill an order from the facility location that is closest to the customer, with the idea that this should generate lower transportation costs as well as a shorter order cycle time. Alternatively, an order could be filled from the facility location that currently has the largest amount of requested product; this likely would increase both order cycle time and transportation cost, but could help the seller by reducing excess inventory at a particular location.

Order Picking and Assembly

Order picking and assembly is the next stage of the order management process, and it includes all activities from when an appropriate location (such as a warehouse) is authorized to fill the order until goods are loaded aboard an outbound carrier. Although order picking and assembly is sometimes overlooked because neither activity is very glamorous, order picking and assembly often represents the best opportunity to improve the effectiveness and efficiency of an order cycle; order picking and assembly can account for up to two-thirds of a facility's operating cost and time.

Importantly, the effectiveness and efficiency of order picking and assembly can often be improved without large expenditures. One low-cost method to improve effectiveness and efficiency is to analyze order pickers' travel time, in part because travel time accounts for between 60 and 80 percent of total pick time. Moreover, travel time can be reduced through better slotting (placement) of products in the relevant facility.[8] To this end, a company might place its most heavily demanded items in a fairly central and easily accessible location as opposed to a more remote and less-accessible location. Another low-cost suggestion for improving the effectiveness and efficiency of the pick process is to match the picker to the order being picked. For example, an order consisting of fragile items might be assigned to a picker who exhibits a low percentage of damaged picks.[9]

Order picking and assembly has been greatly affected by advances in technology such as handheld scanners, radio-frequency identification (RFID), and voice-based order picking. **Voice-based order picking** refers to the use of speech to guide order picking activities. Early voice-based picking systems were characterized by high adoption costs, poor voice quality, and systems that were easily disrupted by other noises. Contemporary voice-based systems, by contrast, are less costly, are more powerful, have better voice quality, and are less cumbersome for workers to use. Companies that have adopted newer-generation voice-based technology have reported increased productivity and higher pick accuracy. The implementation of voice-based order picking at one company resulted in 99.66 percent pick accuracy, which also saved the company nearly $100,000 through the elimination of four order checkers' positions.[10]

Another order picking technique that has grown in popularity in recent years is **pick-to-light technology**, in which orders to be picked are identified by lights placed on shelves or racks. Pick-to-light systems simplify the pick process because the worker simply follows the lights from pick to pick, as opposed to the worker having to figure out an optimal picking path. Pick to light can yield impressive operational improvements; for example, a candle company that implemented pick-to-light technology reported a 50 percent improvement in pick efficiency (measured by lines picked per hour), a 50 percent decrease in picking errors, and a 40 percent increase in shipping volumes.[11]

Order Delivery

The final phase of the order cycle is **order delivery**, which refers to the time from when a transportation carrier picks up the shipment until it is received by the customer. You will learn more about transportation in Chapters 12 and 13, so our discussion here will look at several key issues that can impact the effectiveness or efficiency of order delivery.

When the first edition of this book was published in the 1970s, transportation carriers provided a limited number of options in terms of transit times, and shippers thus had to incorporate the rather inflexible transit times into calculations of the length of an order cycle. For example, in the late 1970s, "next-day delivery" meant that a shipment would arrive sometime during the next business day—the customer could not request a specific delivery time. Today, by contrast, a customer can choose several next-day delivery options, such as delivery by 12 noon and delivery by 4:30 P.M.

Another key order delivery issue is that a number of shippers are emphasizing both elapsed transit time as well as transit time reliability (variability), which is important because increases in order cycle variability translate into higher inventory levels. To this end, more buyers are utilizing delivery appointments that contain delivery windows, or the time span within which an order

---

[8]Susan Lacefield, "Ten Tips for Faster Picking," *Logistics Management*, July 2005, 71–76.

[9]Andre Siepenkort, Matthew Stinson, and Stefan Gerlach, "Match Order to Picker for Better Efficiency," *Material Handling and Logistics*, May 2012, 30–32.

[10]Joe Ryan, "Speech is Right for the Warehouse," *Speech Technology Magazine*, March 2008, 36–37.

[11]No author, "Candle Maker Opts for Pick to Light," *Logistics Manager*, May 2010, 15.

must arrive. Although some delivery windows are one hour in length, other windows are as narrow as 15 minutes. So, if a carrier has a 9:00 A.M. appointment with a 15-minute delivery window, it must arrive no later than 9:15 A.M. Oftentimes, failure to meet the relevant delivery window means that the carrier must wait for the next open delivery time—which might not be until the end of the day.

A third key order delivery issue involves transportation carriers revamping their operations to provide faster transit times to customers. For example, 500 miles traditionally served as the maximum range for overnight service in the trucking industry. In recent years, by contrast, the maximum range for overnight service by truck has been pushed to between 600 and 700 miles. This expanded coverage allows customers to shift shipments from air to truck—an important consideration because truck transportation is less costly than air transportation.

CUSTOMER SERVICE

Customers are important to organizations, and organizations that view customers as a "nuisance" may not last very long in today's highly competitive business environment. Consider several metrics associated with unhappy customers; a frequently cited metric is that it costs approximately five times as much to develop a new customer as it does to retain an existing one. In addition, approximately 95 percent of unhappy customers do not communicate their unhappiness to the responsible organization and they won't return as customers—but will tell nine people about their unhappiness.[12] Quite simply, it's easier for an organization to keep an existing customer than it is to acquire new customers. To this end, customer service strives to keep customers happy and creates in the customer's mind the perception of an organization that is easy to do business with.

Customer service can be an excellent competitive weapon and is more difficult for competitors to imitate than other marketing mix variables such as price and promotion. Nordstrom's (a high-end retailer) has a long-standing reputation for excellent customer service, and this customer focus often leads Nordstrom's to do things that competitors cannot or will not match. For example, one of the authors was shopping at a Nordstrom's and found a belt that he liked, but the store didn't have the correct size in stock. Several days later, the author received a telephone call from a Nordstrom's salesperson indicating that the desired belt was available for purchase at the local store. The salesperson had located the belt at another Nordstrom's and had the belt expedited—via *air freight*—to the local store. With a retail value of approximately $45, it's likely that the particular Nordstrom's lost money on this purchase. It's a reasonable assumption, however, that few other retailers would copy Nordstrom's behavior in servicing the customer.

Macroenvironmental changes, such as globalization and advances in technology, are causing organizations and individuals to demand higher levels of customer service. As was pointed out in an earlier chapter, customer expectations continue to increase over time; if the associated performance (service) levels fail to keep up, then customer dissatisfaction is a likely outcome. In addition, as emphasized in this chapter, reliable service enables a firm to maintain a lower level of inventory, especially of safety stocks, which produces lower inventory holding costs. Third, in an increasingly automated and computerized world, the relationships between customers and vendors can become dehumanized. This situation is both frustrating and inefficient from the customer's viewpoint. The firm that can offer a high level of customer service, especially on a personal basis, should find that it has a powerful sales advantage in the marketplace.

Furthermore, the increased use of vendor quality-control programs necessitates higher levels of customer service. In recent years, many firms, especially retailers and wholesalers, have become more inventory conscious. This emphasis has resulted in computer-assisted analysis to identify vendors that consistently give either good or bad levels of service. In the past, with manual systems, repeated and serious customer service errors occurred before a vendor's activities

---

[12]Jessica Tremayne, "The Science of Service," *Smart Business Cleveland*, March 2009, 61–66.

were singled out for corrective action. Today, these factors are automatically programmed into computers, and companies are able to closely monitor the quality of service they receive from each vendor.

We've talked at some length about customer service, but we've yet to offer a formal definition of it. Keeping in mind that there are myriad customer service definitions, for our purposes **customer service** will be defined as "the ability of logistics management to satisfy users in terms of time, dependability, communication, and convenience."[13] Let's take a closer look at each of these four dimensions of customer service.

Time

Time refers to the period between successive events, and clearly the order cycle is an excellent example of the time dimension of customer service. At the risk of sounding redundant, many businesses today are looking to reduce order cycle times—longer cycle times translate into higher inventory requirements.

Dependability

Dependability refers to the reliability of the service encounter and consists of three elements, namely, consistent order cycles, safe delivery, and complete delivery.[14] Our earlier discussion of the order cycle highlighted the importance of consistency (reliability/dependability)—inconsistent order cycles necessitate higher inventory requirements. And although order cycle time is important, an increasing number of companies are trading off order cycle speed for order cycle consistency. More specifically, these companies are willing to accept a slower order cycle so long as it exhibits a high level of consistency.

Safe delivery brings loss and damage considerations into play. Product can be lost or damaged for a multitude of reasons, but the reasons are rather immaterial to a customer—a lost or damaged product can cause a variety of negative ramifications for a customer, such as out-of-stock situations. **Order fill rate**, or the percentage of orders that can be completely and immediately filled from existing stock, is one way of measuring the completeness of delivery. As is the case with loss and damage, incomplete deliveries result in negative customer ramifications, such as out-of-stock situations.

It is unlikely that loss and damage can ever be totally eliminated; because orders are picked and assembled, they are handled—and every time product is handled it provides opportunities for loss or damage. However, the seller may be able to minimize the number of times an order is handled, perhaps by redesigning the order pick process. And, even if an organization has highly accurate demand forecasting, it's also unlikely that it will be able to achieve a 100 percent fill rate (i.e., all incoming orders are filled completely). Consider the situation of the McDonald's restaurant where two people walked in and *placed a take-out order for 142 Egg McMuffins*! Although the restaurant was successfully able to fill this order (but not before ensuring that the two customers could pay for it), the inventory needed to fill it meant that a lot of other orders for Egg McMuffins went unfilled, at least until the next scheduled delivery of foodstuffs.

Communication

Effective communication should be a two-way exchange between seller and customer, with the goal of keeping both parties informed. Moreover, effective communication requires that the correct parties be involved in the process; if a customer has a logistics-related question, then the customer should be communicating with someone with logistics expertise. Moreover, customer

---

[13]Roger A. Kerin, Steven W. Hartley, and William Rudelius, *Marketing*, 10th ed. (Boston: McGraw-Hill/Irwin, 2011), Chapter 16.
[14]Ibid.

service can be enhanced if *complete information* is exchanged between the participants; a delivery address can be helpful, but detailed characteristics of the delivery address would be even more helpful, as illustrated by the case of the transportation company that was responsible for delivering a $750,000 shipment of computer racks. What the transportation company didn't find out—until it actually made the delivery—was that the customer was located on the 17th floor of an office building in the central business district of a major city. Because neither the transportation company nor the office building had the appropriate equipment to facilitate the shipment's handling, the delivery had to be delayed until the proper equipment could be located and brought to the building.[15]

Two-way communication between seller and customer has certainly benefited from technological advances such as cell phones, smart phones, and the Internet. These technological advances allow for less costly and more frequent contacts between the two parties. However, technology such as text messaging and the Internet can depersonalize the communication process, which is why periodic telephone interaction and even face-to-face contact between seller and customer are recommended.[16] You should recognize that face-to-face personal communication is an essential part of conducting business in some cultures.

Convenience

The convenience component of customer service focuses on the ease of doing business with a seller. Having said this, different customers may have different perceptions of the "ease of doing business" concept. For example, for a college student the "ease of doing business" with a bank might mean access to automatic teller machines, whereas for a small business owner it might mean bank tellers who specifically focus on commercial deposits and withdrawals. As such, sellers should have an understanding of their customer segments and how each segment views the "ease of doing business."

Moreover, from the seller's perspective, certain costs may be associated with convenience; for example, there may be a charge for pizza that's delivered to your residence or workplace (or "free delivery areas" might be very small in geographic coverage). As a result, sellers must assess the extent to which their customers are willing to pay for convenience. In recent years, many airlines have discovered that allowing customers to arrange their own travel via the Internet is quite cost effective for the airlines in that the costs of processing an electronic ticket are approximately $1 compared to $10 for processing a paper ticket. As a result, customers who arrange their travel by telephoning an airline's customer service agent may be charged a fee for talking to the service agent (a service that for many years was "free" to the customer).

The convenience dimension also plays a key role in a consumer's purchasing decision. Today's consumer likes to have multiple purchasing options at her/his disposal, and organizations have responded by developing **multichannel marketing systems**, that is, separate marketing channels to serve customers. A retailer, for example, can facilitate customer purchasing with brick-and-mortar stores (one channel) as well with a website (another channel). The convenience dimension in multichannel marketing systems is increasingly manifested through customer orders in one channel (e.g., online) and customer delivery in another channel (e.g., in store).[17]

MANAGING CUSTOMER SERVICE

In addition to understanding what customer service is, the logistician faces multiple managerial considerations with customer service. The remainder of this chapter will discuss four specific consideration: establishing customer service objectives, measuring customer service, customer profitability analysis, and service failure and recovery.

---

[15]John Paul Quinn, "How to Avoid Communication Breakdowns," *Logistics Management*, April 2006, 37–41.
[16]Ibid.
[17]Paul Brooks, "The Multichannel Challenge," *Logistics Manager*, October 2008, 50.

Establishing Customer Service Objectives

Because customer service standards can significantly affect a firm's overall sales success, establishing goals and objectives is an important management decision. Goals tend to be broad, generalized statements regarding the overall results that the firm is attempting to achieve. Unfortunately, some firms' statements of customer service goals are couched in platitudes lacking specific objectives specifying how the goals are to be achieved. This is a serious problem because if the customer service objectives or standards are not stated in specific terms, they may be ignored or be too vague to provide any real guidance to operating personnel.

Objectives, the means by which goals are to be achieved, state certain minimum requirements and are more specific than goals. Objectives should be *specific, measurable, achievable*, and *cost effective*; the latter two are extremely important because relatively small increases in the overall level of customer service objectives can substantially increase the costs of maintaining the increased level of customer service. In other words, although it might be possible to achieve a particular objective, to do so might be cost prohibitive. Consider, for example, an objective to reduce order picking errors from 5 to 2 percent within a 12-month time period; let's assume that this objective is *specific* and *measurable*. Although 12 months might be a *reasonable* time period in which to achieve the 3 percent reduction in order pick errors, what will it *cost* to achieve this reduction? Will the company be forced to hire additional personnel to check the picked orders? Will the current order picking process need to be restructured, perhaps through the addition of new technology? Can the company afford new people or new technology? If so, is the improvement in customer service (i.e., from 5 percent order picking errors to 2 percent order picking errors) worth the additional costs?

A central element in establishing customer service goals and objectives is determining the customer's viewpoint and this means asking customers for their insights about customer service. For example, what services would the customer like to receive that presently aren't available from the seller? What services do customers view as the most important? How well does the seller currently provide what the customer wants? What could be improved?

Because customer service is a competitive tool, it's also important to learn how the customer evaluates the service levels of competing sellers. Many companies evaluate their service performance through **benchmarking**, which refers to a process that continuously identifies, understands, and adapts outstanding processes found inside and outside an organization. Well-run organizations benchmark not only against competitors (where possible) but against best-in-class organizations as well.

For maximum results, organizations should engage in *performance benchmarking*, which compares quantitative performance (e.g., fill rate performance), as well as *process benchmarking*, which is qualitative in nature and compares specific processes (e.g., how organizations achieve their fill rates). From a managerial perspective, performance benchmarking identifies gaps in a desired result while process benchmarking provides information as to why the gaps exist.

The nature of the product also affects the level of the customer service that should be offered. Substitutability, which refers to the number of products from which a firm's customers can choose to meet their needs, is one aspect. If a firm has a near monopoly on an important product (i.e., few substitutes are available), a high level of customer service is not required because a customer who needs the product will buy it under any reasonable customer service standard. However, if many products can perform the same task, then customer service standards become important from a competitive marketing point of view.

Another product-related consideration when establishing customer service goals and objectives is where the product is in its product life cycle. A product just being introduced needs a different kind of service support than one that is in a mature or declining market stage. When introducing a new product, companies want to make sure that there is sufficient supply of it to meet potential customer demand, and so companies might use expedited transportation to protect against out-of-stock situations. It is far less likely that the same company would use expedited transportation to guard against an out-of-stock situation with a product in the decline phase of the product life cycle.

Establishing minimum acceptable order sizes is an ever-present customer service problem because many customers want to order smaller quantities at more frequent intervals. Orders of decreasing size make diminishing (and eventually negative) contributions to profits. In any particular marketing situation, detailed analysis is needed regarding both why small orders are placed and the possible reactions of existing customers to a new policy that requires either a larger minimum order size or a surcharge on small orders to offset losses. A number of retail stores, for example, require a specified level of spending before customers are allowed to pay with credit cards.

Measuring Customer Service

Grandiose statements and platitudes regarding a firm's level of customer service represent little more than rhetoric unless the customer service standards to support them are actually implemented. To accomplish this, a systematic program of measurement and control is required, because *you can't manage what you can't measure*. Control is the process of taking corrective action when measurements indicate that the goals and objectives of customer service are not being achieved. Measurement by itself is merely wasted time and effort if no action is taken based on the feedback received. The actions taken after deficiencies have been identified can lead to an effective and efficient customer service program.

Several key issues are associated with measuring customer service, one of which involves determining the data sources to be used. Ideally, an organization might want to collect measurement data from both internal and external sources. With respect to internal sources, an organization might audit credit memos, which are the documents that must be issued to correct errors in shipping and billing. Comparing them with the volume of error-free activity gives a measure of relative activity accuracy in performance. External measurement data can be collected from actual customers, as illustrated in Figures 7.2 and 7.3. Figure 7.2

⊘ temper

CONTROL DEL TIEMPO DE TRANSPORTE

*Estimado cliente: estamos intentado reducir al mínimo el tiempo de transporte de nuestro almacén al suyo. Le agradeceríamos mucho si nos indica el día y la hora aproximada en que recibió este material y **nos pasa este documento por fax.***

Albarán n° [   ]

RECIBIDO EL DIA [/ /]   **HORA APROXIMADA** [:]

COMENTARIOS _____

_____

_____

_____

Número de fax GRATUITO: 900 121 875

¡ MUCHAS GRACIAS POR SU AYUDA !

FIGURE 7.2 Form Used by a Spanish Firm for Surveying the Time Element of Delivery Service
The customer is asked to provide the invoice number, note the date that the order was received, and fax it (toll-free) to the shipper.   *Source:* SFT Group.

CALIDAD DEL SERVICIO DE ALMACÉN

Estimado cliente,

Con objeto de seguir mejorando nuestro servicio, le rogamos conteste a este breve cuestionario y nos lo envíe a nuestro **fax GRATUITO 900 121 875**, *o por correo, a la atención de la Srta. Rosa Pereda, si desea asegurar la confidencialidad (en algunos envíos por fax consta el nombre de la empresa).*

- ¿ Hay equivocaciones en las cantidades de los materiales que les suministramos ?

Muchas veces	☐
A menudo	☐
Algunas veces	☐
Casi nunca	☐
Nunca lo tuvimos	☐

OBSERVACIONES Y CONSEJOS:

_____
_____
_____

- ¿ Hay equivocaciones en las referencias de los materiales (servir un tipo por otro)?

Muchas veces	☐
A menudo	☐
Algunas veces	☐
Casi nunca	☐
Nunca lo tuvimos	☐

OBSERVACIONES Y CONSEJOS:

_____
_____
_____

- El embalaje, ¿ es el correcto y los materiales llegan bien o no es correcto y los productos llegan dañados ?

Mal muchas veces	☐
Mal a veces	☐
Normal	☐
Bueno (mejor que la media)	☐
Muy bueno	☐

OBSERVACIONES Y CONSEJOS:

_____
_____
_____

- El paquete exteriormente y el albarán interior, ¿ recogen toda la información que Vd. necesita ?

Información mala	☐
Información normal	☐
Información buena	☐

OBSERVACIONES Y CONSEJOS:

_____
_____
_____

FIGURE 7.3 Form Used by a Firm Located in Northern Spain to Query Customers about Several Service Elements

Question 1 asks about mistakes in quantities shipped. Question 2 asks whether correct goods were shipped. Question 3 asks about the adequacy of packaging, and question 4 is about labeling. The completed form can be returned by toll-free fax.   *Source:* SFT Group.

shows a relatively short form used by a company located in Northern Spain to learn the data and time of product delivery. The form in Figure 7.3 is a bit more detailed and asks customers about mistakes in quantities received as well as whether the correct product was shipped, along with other issues.

TABLE 7.2 Select Customer Service Measures	
Customer Service Dimension	**Measure**
Time	Order cycle time
	Inquiry response time
Dependability	Perfect order
	On-time delivery
Communication	Customer complaints
	Order status information
Convenience	Returns process
	Response to emergency situations

A second key issue associated with customer service measurement is determining what factors to measure. Some firms choose those aspects of customer service that are the easiest to measure, which isn't necessarily a good idea because aspects that are difficult to measure may provide better insights into customer likes and dislikes. Some firms choose those aspects of customer service that they believe are most important, which isn't necessarily a good idea either because these aspects might be relatively unimportant from the customer's perspective.

Because so many potential customer service measurements exist, it's not possible to provide a simple list that would be applicable across the board. At a minimum, the measures should be consistent with the four dimensions of customer service—time, dependability, communication, and convenience—discussed earlier in this chapter. Table 7.2 provides representative customer service measures for each of these four dimensions.

In addition, the metrics that are chosen should be relevant and important from the customer's perspective. While the following example might seem like the proverbial "no brainer," consider the call center that measured customer service in terms of the length of customer calls, with shorter call lengths preferred to longer call lengths. As such, the call center singled out a particular employee for "improvement" because her call times were much longer than those of other call center employees. Additional research indicated that this "laggard" employee was actually *the most effective employee* when measured in terms of the number of customer problems solved per day. In short, the call center's primary customer service metric—the time length of customer calls—was different than the customer's primary customer service metric—solving the problem at hand.[18]

Although customer service must be measured if it is to be managed, organizations should resist the tendency to "measure everything that moves." Excessive measurement can strain an organization because it requires the collection of tremendous amounts of data, and once collected, the data must be analyzed. This can result in "analysis paralysis," or the idea that so much time is required for analysis that there's little if any time left to make decisions based on the data. Rather, organizations should utilize a limited number of meaningful and relevant metrics and it's possible for organizations to use only *one* customer service metric as illustrated in the previous paragraph's call center anecdote.

Customer Profitability Analysis

Customer profitability analysis (CPA) refers to the allocation of revenues and costs to customer segments or individual customers to calculate the profitability of the segments or customers. Customer profitability analysis suggests that different customers (segments) consume differing amounts and types of resources; for example, some customers might require telephone-based communication with an organization, whereas other customers are able to communicate electronically with an organization.

---

[18]No author, "Mistaken Metrics," *T&D*, February 2009, 88.

Customer profitability analysis explicitly recognizes that all customers are not the same, and some customers are more valuable than others to an organization. CPA can be used to identify different groups of customers from a profitability perspective, and such a grouping can better help in allocating an organization's resources. One suggested classification, for example, divides customers into four groups (high revenues/high costs; high revenues/low costs; low revenues/high costs; low revenues/low costs); "high revenues/low costs" represents the most attractive customers, while "low revenues/high costs" represents the least attractive customers.[19] From a resource allocation perspective, an organization should pursue different logistical approaches for different customer groups. With respect to product selection, for example, an organization might provide a substantial number of product offerings for "high revenues/high costs" customers (sometimes referred to as "demanding customers"[20]), whereas limited product offerings might be provided to "low revenues/low costs" customers.

Thorough customer profitability analysis only works if it is grounded in activity-based costing in the sense that activity-based costing suggests that different products are characterized by differences in the amount and types of resources consumed. (Appendix 7 provides a closer look at activity-based costing.) Consider the experience of a specialty distributor of fluid-related products that established activity-based costing as the foundation of its customer profitability analysis program. The distributor, which served approximately 2,000 customers prior to initiating customer profitability analysis, learned that 150 customers accounted for 90 percent of company profits. In addition, the customer profitability analysis identified over 1,000 unprofitable customers and the distributor no longer does business with them.[21]

Service Failure and Service Recovery

Regardless of how well run an organization is, some situations will occur where its actual performance does not meet the customer's expected performance (i.e., a service failure). Service failure has emerged as a prominent business issue in recent years, in part because organizations have learned that customers can easily become disaffected. For example, it has been suggested that nearly two-thirds of customers who experience a problem with *purchases of less than $5* won't do business with that company again.[22] Service failure is particularly relevant to the order cycle; examples of order-related service failures include lost delivery, late delivery, early delivery, damaged delivery, and incorrect delivery quantity, among others.

Given that service failures are inevitable, organizations will be faced with service recovery decisions. For our purposes, **service recovery** will refer to a process for returning a customer to a state of satisfaction after a service or product has failed to live up to expectations. Although service recovery often generates significant out-of-pocket costs, good (or excellent) service recovery may actually result in *increased* customer loyalty. In addition, service recovery can also result in a better performing organization in the sense that an organization can learn from failure and then implement processes and policies to lessen the occurrence of future service failures.[23]

There is no set formula for service recovery, in part because each service failure is unique in its impact on a particular customer. Having said this, there are general guidelines for dealing with service recovery, and it's important to recognize that these guidelines may not only assuage the customer but also result in an organization improving its operations.[24] For example, one recovery guideline is fair treatment for customers. In the logistics discipline, one example of fair treatment involves service guarantees by transportation companies; if a shipment misses various

[19]Lynette Ryals, "Managing Customers Profitably," *Credit Control* 32, no. 3&4 (2011): 37–42.
[20]Ibid.
[21]Victoria F. Kickham, "Staying Focused on Hose," *Industrial Distribution*, October 2008, 22–25.
[22]John Tschohl, "Turning Service into Opportunities," *TWICE: This Week in Consumer Electronics*, March 27, 2006, 78.
[23]Robert Johnston and Stefan Michel, "Three Outcomes of Service Recovery," *International Journal of Production and Operations Management* 28, no. 1 (2008): 79–99.
[24]Gail Scott, "Service Recovery," *Healthcare Executive*, January/February 2009, 44–47.

delivery parameters (e.g., on time, undamaged), then customers might receive a full refund (or aren't billed for the transportation). Besides reducing customer risk, many transportation companies that have implemented service guarantees have improved relevant aspects of their performance such as on-time delivery, which has meant a decrease in the amount of payouts for deficient service.

Summary

Demand management deals with determining what customers want, and a key component involves demand forecasting. The chapter discussed basic demand forecasting models along with select forecasting issues such as cost and accuracy.

The chapter also looked at order management and the order cycle, which refers to the period of time from when the order is placed until it is received. Four components of an order cycle—order transmittal, order processing, order picking and assembly, and order delivery—were identified and discussed in some detail.

Customer service was the third major topic addressed in this chapter and the four dimensions of customer service—time, dependability, communication, and convenience—were discussed. The chapter also looked at managing customer service, with a specific focus on establishing customer service objectives, measuring customer service, customer profitability analysis, and service failure and service recovery.

Questions for Discussion and Review

7.1 What is the relationship between demand management, order management, and customer service?

7.2 Discuss the three basic demand forecasting models.

7.3 Discuss several demand forecasting issues.

7.4 Define and describe the order cycle. Why is it considered an important aspect of customer service?

7.5 What are some causes of order cycle variability? What are the consequences of order cycle variability?

7.6 List the various methods of order transmittal and discuss relevant characteristics of each.

7.7 What are some advantages and disadvantages to checking all orders for completeness and accuracy?

7.8 Define order triage and explain how it can affect order processing.

7.9 Discuss how the effectiveness and efficiency of order processing can be improved without large expenditures.

7.10 What is pick-to-light technology, and how can it improve order picking?

7.11 Discuss the order delivery stage of the order cycle.

7.12 How can customer service act as a competitive weapon?

7.13 How are macroenvironmental factors causing organizations and individuals to demand higher levels of customer service?

7.14 List and discuss the three elements of the dependability dimension of customer service.

7.15 What are some advantages and disadvantages to technological advances designed to facilitate buyer–seller communications?

7.16 What is customer profitability analysis and how might it be used in logistics?

7.17 Define and explain how organizations might engage in benchmarking.

7.18 How do characteristics such as substitutability and product life cycle stage influence the development of customer service goals and objectives?

7.19 Describe some of the key issues associated with measuring customer service.

7.20 What is meant by service recovery? How is it relevant to logistics?

Suggested Readings

Cederlund, Jerold P., Rajiv Kohli, Susan A. Sherer, and Yao Yuliang. "How Motorola Put CPFR into Action." *Supply Chain Management Review* 11, no. 7 (2007): 28–35.

Diaz, Angel, Bjorn Claes, and Luis Solis. "Benchmarking Logistics and Supply Chain Practices in Spain." *Supply Chain Forum: An International Journal* 12, no. 2 (2011): 82–90.

Eroglu, Cuneyt and A. Michael Knemeyer. "Exploring the Potential Effects of Forecaster Motivational Orientation and Gender on Judgmental Adjustments of Statistical Forecasts." *Journal of Business Logistics* 31, no. 1 (2010): 179–195.

Forslund, Helena. "The Size of a Logistics Performance Measurement System." *Facilities* 29, no. 3 & 4 (2011): 133–148.

Guerreiro, Reinaldo, Sergio Rodrigues Bio, Elvira Vazquez, and Villamor Merschmann. "Cost-to-Serve Measurement and Customer Profitability Analysis." *International Journal of Logistics Management* 19, no. 3 (2008): 389–407.

Gustavsson, Mattias and Patrik Jonsson. "Perceived Quality Deficiencies of Demand Information and Their Consequences." *International Journal of Logistics: Research & Applications* 11, no. 4 (2008): 295–312.

Jain, Chaman L. and Mark Covas. "Six Rules for Effective Demand Planning in a Volatile Economy." *Journal of Business Forecasting* 29, no. 2 (2010): 4–13.

Johnson, Carol J., Curtis M. Grimm, and Valdis Blome. "Customer Service in the Baltic Region: An Exploratory Study." *International Journal of Logistics Management* 18, no. 2 (2007): 157–173.

Neslin, Scott A. and Venkatesh Shankar. "Key Issues in Multichannel Customer Management: Current Knowledge and Future Directions." *Journal of Interactive Marketing* 23, no. 1 (2009): 70–81.

Ramanathan, Usha, Angappa Gunasekaran, and Nachiappan Subramanian. "Supply Chain Collaboration Performance Metrics: A Conceptual Framework." *Benchmarking: An International Journal* 18, no. 6 (2011): 856–872.

Syntetos, A.A., M. Keyes, and M.Z. Babai. "Demand Categorisation in a European Spare Parts Logistics Network." *International Journal of Operations & Production Management* 29, no. 3 (2009): 292–316.

Thomas, Rodney W., Terry L. Esper, and Theodore P. Stank. "Coping with Time Pressure in Interfirm Supply Chain Relationships." *Industrial Marketing Management* 40, no. 3 (2011): 414–423.

CASE

CASE 7.1   Handy Andy, Inc.

Handy Andy, Inc., produced residential trash compactors at a factory in St. Louis, Missouri, and sold them throughout the United States. Over 90 percent of Handy Andy's sales were in large urban areas where trash-collection costs were high.

The standard model compactor was about 3 feet high, 2 feet deep, and 1 1/3 feet wide, and the deluxe model had the same dimensions but contained better features such as greater capacity and greater horsepower. Because most of the compactors would be placed in home kitchens, a wide variety of colors and trims were manufactured, providing an exterior that would match many kitchen decors. The standard model came in five colors with three different trims for a total of 15 different combinations, while the deluxe model came in eight colors and four different trims for a total of 32 different combinations. Retail prices were set by the dealer, with prices for the standard model ranging between $600 and $725 and for the deluxe model between $950 and $1,100. Sales in an area were usually slow until trash collectors, faced with rising landfill costs, raised their rates per can of refuse picked up.

There was one authorized Handy Andy factory distributor in each large urban area and the distributor was responsible for filling orders from licensed Handy Andy retailers. The factory distributors were also allowed to sell compactors to the final consumer. Each factory distributor maintained a complete stock of all styles and trims of the Handy Andy compactors, and these distributors were required to stock at least five units each of the 47 different styles available.

Because of the sporadic sales patterns and the wide number of colors and trims available, the licensed retailers usually stocked only a display unit or two. Each retailer carried a "design your dream compactor" software package that allowed prospective buyers to design the model, color, and trim they wanted. When the retailer completed the sale, the order would be transmitted to the nearest Handy Andy factory distributor.

The general agreement between the factory distributors and Handy Andy was that the distributors would deliver and install the compactor within five days after receiving an order from a licensed retailer. For the delivery and installation, the factory distributor received 9 percent of the unit's wholesale price, half paid by the licensed retailer that had made the sale and half paid by Handy Andy.

José Ortega worked in Handy Andy's distribution department in the St. Louis headquarters. He currently was working on a project to determine whether the compactor's warranty should be extended from one year to two years. The units were well built, and there had been almost no warranty work requested in the first year of each model's life. Because Handy Andy would have no records of repair work performed after the one-year period had expired, Ortega was randomly contacting buyers via their mobile phones to learn about their experience to date. Handy Andy's buyer database, which included customer names and mobile phone numbers, was generated when buyers activated their product warranty online (see Exhibit 7.A).

BUYER DETAILS

First Name*

Last Name*

Email*

Mobile Phone*

Mailing Address

City

State

Zip Code

PRODUCT DETAILS

Product Name*

Unit Number*

Transaction Number*

ADDITIONAL DETAILS

Retailer Name*

Purchase Date*

Installation Date*

☐ I wish to be informed of new Handy Andy products

*Mandatory Field

SEND

EXHIBIT 7.A Warranty Activation Form

Ortega was in the process of contacting 500 purchasers who had owned the compactors for between one year and four years (when they had first been introduced) to determine whether the compactors had required repairs and, if so, the extent and cost of the repairs. In talking to purchasers, Ortega was impressed by the fact that there were remarkably few complaints involving the durability of the compactors.

Another type of complaint did arise, however, one that Ortega had difficulty understanding until he heard many buyers, usually from the same few cities, tell an almost identical story. It appeared that in these cities the factory distributor would contact individuals who had purchased a standard model compactor from licensed retailers. The factory distributor would tell these buyers that the model originally requested was out of stock but that they could purchase a deluxe model for only $100 more than they originally paid for the standard model. The factory distributors also indicated that buyers would receive better after-sale service because higher-priced purchases would receive priority over lower-priced purchases if something malfunctioned. In addition, the factory distributors in these few cities indicated that they, not Handy Andy, Inc., stood behind the one-year warranty.

Ortega realized that he was uncovering a much larger—and more serious—problem than he had been assigned to explore. He chatted briefly with his supervisor, Sheryl Booher, who told Ortega to revise the format of his interview to include several questions concerning the installation. Booher also told Ortega to begin calling individuals who had owned compactors for less than a year. Ortega did this, and he discovered marked differences in the installation process based upon whether the customer purchased from a factory distributor or from a licensed retailer.

As a general rule, compactors purchased from factory distributors exhibited fast delivery in terms of elapsed time since sale. Importantly, over 90 percent of the deliveries occurred within the two-hour delivery windows that buyers were promised. Moreover, the installation personnel carefully explained how the compactor worked, and follow-up contacts were made to the customer three days and 10 days after installation to make certain that the customer had no additional questions concerning the compactor's operation.

On the other hand, Ortega learned of troubling inconsistencies in the delivery times of compactors purchased from licensed retailers. More specifically, fewer than 20 percent of the deliveries occurred within the two-hour delivery windows that buyers were promised. Even more disturbing was that in some cases the compactor was left in the middle of the kitchen floor in its shipping container—that is, uninstalled! Customers of the licensed retailers also indicated that installation personnel would not explain how the compactor worked and that some installers were rude and disrespectful. As an example, in response to one customer's question an installer stated, "Assuming you can read, the answer can be found in the owner's manual."

Ortega had another meeting scheduled with his supervisor. As Ortega entered Booher's office, he was surprised to see Handy Andy's vice president of marketing, Bob Bixby, also sitting in the office. Booher asked Ortega to tell Bixby the results of his interviews. After listening to Ortega, Bixby asked, "Do you think this pattern exists in all markets?"

"No," was Ortega's reply. "I'd say it is a problem in Jacksonville, Baltimore, Cleveland, Louisville, Denver, and San Diego. It may be a problem in Dallas and New Orleans. My sample wasn't very well structured in a metropolitan market sense; you will recall that it was a nationwide sample that was trying to look at repairs."

Questions

1. Is this a customer service problem? Why or why not?
2. It appears that the factory distributors are exploiting the licensed retailers. Yet from what we can tell, Handy Andy in St. Louis has heard no complaints from the licensed retailers. Why wouldn't they complain?
3. What should Handy Andy's marketing vice president do? Why?
4. In the case is the statement, "The factory distributors in these few cities indicated that they, not Handy Andy, Inc., stood behind the one-year warranty." Is this a problem for Handy Andy? Why or why not?
5. Bixby, Booher, and Ortega recognize that Handy Andy needs a better way to learn about the buyer's installation experience. One alternative is to add an open-ended question, dealing with the installation experience, to the warranty activation form. Another alternative is to e-mail a brief survey about the installation experience within three to five days of receiving a warranty activation form. Which of these alternatives should Handy Andy choose? Why?
6. Discuss the pros and cons to allowing Handy Andy trash compactors to be sold only through licensed retailers (i.e., factory distributors would no longer be able to sell to consumers).
7. Is it too late for Handy Andy to attempt service recovery with customers who reported a less-than-satisfactory installation experience? Why or why not?

APPENDIX 7

Activity-based costing is focused on better understanding the cost of a product by identifying what activities drive particular costs. Unlike traditional accounting techniques, activity-based costing attempts to trace an expense category to a particular cost object. With activity-based costing, cost objects consume activities, and activities consume resources.[25]

Activity-based costing consists of five steps:

- Identify activities
- Determine cost for each activity

---

[25]www.pitt.edu/~roztocki

TABLE 7A.1	Cost for Each Activity
Activity	**Cost**
Order transmittal	$1,000
Order processing	$3,000
Order picking and assembly	$12,000
Order delivery	$6,000

- Determine cost drivers
- Collect activity data
- Calculate product cost[26]

This five-step activity-based costing process will be illustrated by the following hypothetical example. Suppose that a company is interested in applying the activity-based costing process to its order cycle process for two products that it sells. So, we've identified the relevant activities (step 1); next comes a determination of cost for each activity, as shown in Table 7A.1. Step 3 requires us to determine cost drivers, and in this example they are order transmittal → number of orders; order processing → number of processing activities; order picking and assembly → number of boxes; order delivery → number of delivery locations.

The two remaining steps, activity data and product cost calculation, appear in Table 7A.2. With respect to order transmittal, 3 orders were received for Product 1 and 7 orders for Product 2, for a total of 10 orders. Because Product 1 accounts for 30 percent of the total orders (3/10), the relevant transmittal cost is $300, which represents 30 percent of the $1,000 total order transmittal cost. Likewise, because Product 2 accounts for 70 percent (7/10) of the total orders, its relevant transmittal costs are $700. The product costs for the three other activities are calculated in a similar fashion. Note that the data in Table 7A.2 indicate that the total order cycle cost is $22,000; according to the activity-based costing process, Product 1 is responsible for $12,600 in costs, and Product 2 is responsible for $9,400.

Before concluding this brief discussion of activity-based costing, it's important to recognize that the cost drivers can vary from organization to organization and should be driven by company-specific considerations such as organizational structure, operational structure, and products.[27] For example, in our hypothetical example the number of delivery locations was the cost driver associated with order delivery. Another potential cost driver for order delivery could be the number of customers receiving deliveries.

TABLE 7A.2	Activity Data and Product Cost Calculation				
Activity	**Cost**	**Product 1 Data**	**Product 1 Cost**	**Product 2 Data**	**Product 2 Cost**
Order transmittal	$1,000	3 orders	$300	7 orders	$700
Order processing	$3,000	4 activities	$1,200	6 activities	$1,800
Order picking and assembly	$12,000	110 boxes	$6,600	90 boxes	$5,400
Order delivery	$6,000	30 locations	$4,500	10 locations	$1,500
Total	**$22,000**		**$12,600**		**$9,400**

[26]Ibid.
[27]John Karolefski, "Time is Money," *Food Logistics*, June 2004, 18–22.

8 INVENTORY MANAGEMENT

KEY TERMS

- ABC analysis of inventory
- Back order
- Complementary products
- Cycle (base) stock
- Dead inventory (dead stock)
- Economic order quantity (EOQ)
- Fixed order interval system
- Fixed order quantity system
- Inventory
- Inventory carrying (holding) costs
- Inventory shrinkage
- Inventory turnover
- Just-in-time (JIT) approach
- Lean manufacturing (lean)
- Ordering costs
- Pipeline (in-transit) stock
- Psychic stock
- Reorder (trigger) point (ROP)
- Safety (buffer) stock
- Service parts logistics
- Speculative stock
- Stockout costs
- Substitute products
- Vendor-managed inventory (VMI)

LEARNING OBJECTIVES

- To learn about the ways that inventory can be classified
- To discuss inventory costs and the trade-offs that exist among them
- To identify when to order and how much to order, with a particular emphasis on the economic order quantity
- To differentiate the various inventory flow patterns
- To discuss special concerns with inventory management
- To identify several contemporary approaches to managing inventory

Inventory refers to stocks of goods and materials that are maintained for many purposes, the most common being to satisfy normal demand patterns. In production and selling processes, inventories serve as cushions to accommodate the fact that items arrive in one pattern and are used in another pattern. For example, if you eat one egg a day and buy eggs by the dozen, every 12 days you would buy a new container of eggs, and the inventory of eggs remaining in your refrigerator would decline at the rate of one egg per day.

Inventory management is a key component in logistics and supply chain management, in part because inventory decisions are often a starting point, or driver, for other business activities, such as warehousing, transportation, and materials handling. Moreover, different organizational functions can have different inventory management objectives. Marketing, for example, tends to want to ensure that sufficient inventory is available for customer demand to avoid potential stockout situations—which translate into higher inventory levels. Alternatively, the finance group generally seeks to minimize the costs associated with holding inventory, which translates into lower inventory levels. As if managing these seemingly conflicting objectives within one organization isn't challenging enough, supply chains are made up of multiple organizations—each of which may have its own distinct inventory management philosophy. Indeed, each link in the supply chain may prefer having other links maintain the inventory.

Organizations strive for the proper balance (i.e., right amount) of inventory, but achieving the proper balance can be quite difficult because of the trade-offs between inventory carrying cost and stockout cost, both of which will be discussed in greater detail later in the chapter. More specifically, holding high levels of inventory (overstock) results in high inventory carrying costs and low (or no) stockout costs. Alternatively, holding low levels of inventory results in low inventory carrying costs and some (high) stockout costs.

It is important to note here that inventory carries its greatest cost after value has been added through manufacturing and processing. Finished goods inventories are, therefore, much more expensive to hold than raw materials or work in progress. Carrying costs for inventories can be significant, and the return on investment to a firm for the funds it has tied up in inventory should be as high as the return it can obtain from other, equally risky uses of the same funds.

This chapter begins with a brief look at various classifications of inventory, followed by a discussion of inventory costs. Next is an examination of when to order inventory and how much inventory to order. This chapter also looks at inventory flows and special concerns with inventory and concludes by discussing several contemporary issues with managing inventory.

INVENTORY CLASSIFICATIONS

It's important to understand the various classifications of inventory because the classification can influence the way that inventory is managed. Inventory generally exists to satisfy demand and can be classified as cycle (base) stock, safety (buffer) stock, pipeline (in-transit) stock, or speculative stock. Each type is explained in the following paragraphs.

Cycle, *or base,* **stock** refers to inventory that is needed to satisfy normal demand during the course of an order cycle. With respect to the egg example at the beginning of this chapter, one dozen (12) eggs represents the cycle stock—we use one egg per day, and we buy eggs every 12 days. Recall from Chapter 7 that order cycle times continue to decrease in length, meaning that the associated levels of cycle stock continue to decrease as well.

Safety, *or buffer,* **stock** refers to inventory that is held in addition to cycle stock to guard against uncertainty in demand or lead time. For example, uncertainty in demand could come from the fact that you occasionally decide to make a three-egg omelet as opposed to eating one egg per day. As an example of lead time uncertainty, you may sometimes buy eggs every 14 days, rather than every 12 days. In both cases, a few extra eggs would ensure that you won't run out of eggs. As pointed out in Chapter 7, higher levels of uncertainty lead to higher levels of safety stock.

Pipeline, *or in-transit,* **stock** is inventory that is en route between various fixed facilities in a logistics system such as a plant, warehouse, or store. Pipeline inventory is represented here by eggs that are in transit between a chicken farm and, say, a food wholesaler's distribution center or between the retail store and your kitchen.

Speculative stock refers to inventory that is held for several reasons, including seasonal demand, projected price increases, and potential shortages of product. For example, the fact that eggs are associated with Easter (e.g., Easter egg rolls, colored eggs) tends to cause an increase in demand for them prior to the Easter holiday.

Although inventory generally exists to satisfy demand, in some situations inventory is carried to stimulate demand, also known as **psychic stock**. This type of inventory is associated with retail stores, and the general idea is that customer purchases are stimulated by inventory that they can see.[1] This concept helps to explain, in part, why some retailers stock huge amounts of certain merchandise.

---

[1]Paul D. Larson and Robert A. DeMaris, "Psychic Stock: An Independent Variable Category of Inventory," *International Journal of Physical Distribution & Logistics Management* 20, no. 7 (1990): 27–37.

INVENTORY COSTS

You might remember the basic accounting equation that assets are equal to liabilities plus stock-holder's equity. The managerial significance of the accounting equation is that assets must be paid for in some manner; quite simply, *assets cost money*, which means that inventory costs money. Not only does inventory appear as an asset on company balance sheets, but inventory tends to be one of the largest assets (in terms of dollar value) on the balance sheets. As such, it's important for logisticians to have an understanding of inventory costs.

The data in Table 8.1 offer insights about the absolute and relative magnitude of inventory costs in the United States between 2006 and 2012; note how Table 8.1 highlights the impacts of the economic recession in 2008 and 2009. From an absolute perspective, Table 8.1 indicates that the value of business inventory ranged between $1.86 trillion and $2.27 trillion between 2006 and 2012. In relative terms, inventory costs in the twenty-first century represent approximately one-third of total logistics costs.

We will take a closer look at three inventory costs—carrying cost, ordering cost, stockout cost—that should factor into an organization's inventory management policy. The logistics man-ager must understand both the nature of each of these costs as well the trade-offs among them.

Inventory Carrying Costs

A prominent concern involves the costs associated with holding inventory, which are referred to as **inventory carrying (holding) costs**. In general, inventory carrying costs are expressed in per-centage terms, and this percentage is multiplied by the inventory's value. The resulting number represents the dollar value associated with holding the particular inventory. As an example, refer-ring to Table 8.1, when the value of business inventory in 2006, $1859 billion, is multiplied by the carrying cost in 2006, 24.0 percent, the relevant carrying costs are $446 billion.

Not surprisingly, an increase or decrease in the carrying cost percentage will affect the relevant inventory expense. Generally speaking, companies prefer to carry lower inventory as the carrying cost percentage increases, in part because there is greater risk (e.g., obsolescence) to holding the inventory. As a result, the determination of a carrying cost percentage should be quite important for many companies. However, the reality is that many companies don't know their actual inventory car-rying costs. Rather, many companies simply assign carrying costs as 25 percent of the value of their inventory—and this 25 percent figure has been used since the mid-1950s![2] Table 8.1 suggests that the range of U.S. inventory carrying costs since 2006 has been between 19 percent and 24 percent.

Table 8.1	Magnitude of Inventory Costs				
Year	Value of Business Inventory ($ billion)	Inventory Carrying Cost (%)	Inventory Carrying Cost ($ billion)	Total Logistics Cost ($ billion)	Inventory as a Percentage of Total Logistics Cost
2006	1,859	24.0	446	1,305	34.2
2007	2,015	24.1	485	1,394	34.8
2008	1,963	21.4	420	1,344	31.3
2009	1,833	19.3	353	1,101	32.1
2010	2,018	19.2	387	1,204	32.1
2011	2,182	19.1	478	1,287	32.1
2012	2,269	19.1	434	1,331	32.6

Source: 24th Annual State of Logistics Report, 2013, prepared by Rosalyn Wilson for the Council of Supply Chain Management Professionals (www.cscmp.org).

---

[2]See L. P. Alford and John R. Bangs (eds.), *Production Handbook* (New York: Ronald, 1955).

Table 8.2   Components of Inventory Carrying Cost
Obsolescence costs
Inventory shrinkage
Storage costs
Handling costs
Insurance costs
Taxes
Interest costs

Inventory carrying costs consist of a number of different components (see Table 8.2), and the importance of these factors can vary from product to product. For example, perishable items such as dairy products, meat, and poultry are often sold with expiration dates, causing them to have little or no value after a certain date. By contrast, a box of lead pencils loses its value much more slowly through time. These two examples illustrate the *obsolescence* category of inventory carrying costs and refer to the fact that products lose value through time. Note that some products (e.g., perishables) lose their value much more quickly than others (e.g., pencils).

Inventory shrinkage is another component of inventory carrying cost and refers to the fact that more items are recorded entering than leaving warehousing facilities. Shrinkage is generally caused by damage, loss, or theft, and although shrinkage costs can be reduced, such efforts often generate other costs. For example, although better packaging may reduce damage, loss, or theft costs, better packaging likely translates into increased packaging costs.

Another component of inventory carrying costs, *storage* costs, refers to those costs associated with occupying space in a plant, storeroom, or warehousing facility. Some products have very specialized storage requirements; ice cream, for example, must be stored at a temperature below –20 degrees Fahrenheit. You should recognize that specialized storage requirements, such as refrigeration, result in higher storage costs. *Handling* costs, another component of inventory carrying costs, involve the costs of employing staff to receive, store, retrieve, and move inventory. Note that specialized storage requirements may also increase handling costs; a refrigerated warehouse requires workers to wear gloves, head coverings, and coats to protect them from the cold temperatures.

Insurance costs, which insure inventory against fire, flood, theft, and other perils, are another component of inventory carrying costs. Insurance costs are not uniform across products; diamonds, for example, are more costly to insure than shampoo. *Taxes* represent yet another component of inventory carrying costs, and they are calculated on the basis of the inventory on hand on a particular date; considerable effort is made to have that day's inventory be as low as possible. Finally, *interest costs* take into account the money that is required to maintain the investment in inventory. In the United States, the prime rate of interest has traditionally provided a convenient starting point when estimating the interest charges associated with maintaining inventory.

Some inventory items have other types of carrying costs because of their specialized nature. Pets and livestock, for example, must be watered and fed. Tropical fish must be fed and have oxygen added to the water in which they are kept. Another cost, although it is generally excluded from carrying cost, is opportunity cost—the cost of taking a position in the wrong materials. This can be an issue for those companies that engage in speculative inventory. Opportunity costs are also incurred by firms that hold too much inventory in reserve for customer demand.

Ordering Costs

Ordering costs refer to those costs associated with ordering inventory, such as order costs and setup costs. Order costs include, but are not limited to, the costs of receiving an order (e.g., the wages of a person who takes orders by telephone), conducting a credit check, verifying inventory availability, entering orders into the system, preparing invoices, and receiving payment. Note that a number of the ordering costs involve the order transmittal and order processing components of the order cycle. Setup costs are those necessary to modify production processes to make the products necessary to satisfy particular orders.

Trade-Off Between Carrying and Ordering Costs

The trade-off that exists between carrying and ordering costs is that they respond in opposite ways to the number of orders or size of orders. That is, an increase in the number of orders leads to higher order costs and lower carrying costs. We'll illustrate this trade-off with a mathematical example, but before doing so it's necessary to understand how to calculate ordering costs and carrying costs.

Ordering cost can be calculated by multiplying the number of orders per year times the ordering cost per order. Because of the assumption of even outward flow of goods, inventory carrying costs are applied to one-half of the order size, a figure that represents the average inventory. Average inventory is multiplied by the carrying costs of the inventory (expressed as a percentage of the dollar value).

Suppose weekly demand is 100 units, order cost per order is $80, the value of an item is $50 and carrying cost is 20 percent of the value of an item. If we place one order per year for the product,

Ordering cost = number of orders per year (1) × ordering cost per order ($80),

or

Ordering cost = 1 × $80 = $80

Carrying cost = average inventory [(100 × 52)/2] × carrying costs
[value of the product ($50) × carrying cost (.20)],

or

Carrying cost = 2,600 × $10 = $26,000

Alternatively, look what happens to ordering and carrying costs if we place one order per week:

Ordering cost = 52 orders × $80 per order, or $4,160

Carrying cost = average inventory (50) × carrying cost ($10), or $500.

Stockout Costs

If avoiding oversupply were the only problem associated with inventories, the solution would be relatively simple: Store fewer items. However, not having enough items can be as bad as, and sometimes worse than, having too many items. Such costs can accrue during stockouts, when customers demand items that aren't immediately available.

Although calculation of stockout costs can be difficult and inexact, it is important for organizations to do so because such knowledge can be beneficial when determining how much inventory to hold, keeping in mind that a trade-off must be balanced between inventory carrying costs and stockout costs. **Stockout costs**, or estimating the costs or penalties for a stockout, involve an understanding of a customer's reaction to a company being out of stock when a customer wants to buy an item.

Consider the following customer responses to a particular stockout situation. How should they be evaluated?

1. The customer says, "I'll be back," and this proves to be so.
2. The customer says, "Call me when it's in."
3. The customer buys a substitute product that yields a higher profit for the seller.
4. The customer buys a substitute product that yields a lower profit for the seller.
5. The customer places an order for the item that is out of stock (a **back order**) and asks to have the item delivered when it arrives.
6. The customer goes to a competitor only for this purchase.
7. The customer goes to a competitor for this and all future purchases.

Clearly, each of these situations has a different cost to the company experiencing a stockout. For example, the loss in situation 1 is negligible because the sale is only slightly delayed. The outcome from situation 2 is more problematic in that the company doesn't know whether the customer will, in fact, return. Situation 7 is clearly the most damaging, because the customer has been lost for good, and it's necessary to know the cost of developing a new customer to replace the lost customer. As pointed out in Chapter 7, a commonly used guideline is that it costs five times as much to acquire a new customer as it does to retain an existing one.

To illustrate the calculation of stockout costs, assume for simplicity's sake that customer responses to a stockout can be placed into three categories: delayed sale (brand loyalty), lost sale (switches and comes back), and lost customer. Assume further that, over time, of 300 customers who experienced a stockout, 10 percent delayed the sale, 25 percent switched and came back, but the remaining 65 percent were lost for good (see Table 8.3).

The probability of each event taking place can be used to determine the average cost of a stockout. More specifically, as illustrated in Table 8.3, each probability is multiplied by the respective loss to yield an average cost per event. These average costs are then summed, and the result is the average cost per stockout. A delayed sale is virtually costless because the customer is brand loyal and will purchase the product when it becomes available. The lost sale alternative results in a loss of the profit that would have been made on the customer's purchase. In the lost customer situation, the customer buys a competitor's product and decides to make all future purchases from that competitor; the relevant cost involved is that of developing a new customer.

Having an understanding of how to calculate stockout costs highlights several key managerial issues. As a general rule, the higher the average cost of a stockout, the better it is for the company to hold some amount of inventory (safety stock) to protect against stockouts. In addition, the higher the probability of a delayed sale, the lower the average stockout costs— and the lower the inventory that needs to be held by a company. For example, if we switch the probabilities in Table 8.3 for brand loyalty and lost customer (i.e., brand loyal probability is .65, lost customer probability is .10), then the average cost of a stockout becomes $129.25 (as opposed to Table 8.3's $789.25).

Table 8.3	Determination of the Average Cost of a Stockout		
Alternative	**Loss**	**Probability**	**Average Cost**
1. Brand-loyal customer	$00.00	.10	$00.00
2. Switches and comes back	37.00	.25	9.25
3. Lost customer	1,200.00	.65	780.00
Average cost of a stockout		1.00	$789.25

Note: These are hypothetical figures for illustration.

Table 8.4 Determination of Safety Stock Level					
Number of Units of Safety Stock	**Additional Safety Stock ($480 per Unit)**	**25% Annual Carrying Cost**	**Total Value of Incremental Safety Stock**	**Additional Orders Filled**	**Stockout Costs Avoided**
10	$4,800	$1,200	$1,200	20	$8,000.00
20	9,600	2,400	1,200	16	6,400.00
30	14,400	3,600	1,200	12	4,800.00
40	19,200	4,800	1,200	8	3,200.00
50	24,000	6,000	1,200	6	2,400.00
60	28,800	7,200	1,200	4	1,600.00
70	33,600	8,400	1,200	3	1,200.00

Trade-Off Between Carrying and Stockout Costs

The trade-off between carrying and stockout costs is that both move in opposite directions—higher inventory levels (hence higher inventory carrying costs) result in lower chances of a stockout (hence lower stockout costs). One way to illustrate this relationship is to look at the trade-offs between levels of safety stock and the number of stockouts prevented, as illustrated in Table 8.4. In this example, we assume that inventory can only be ordered in multiples of 10 and that each unit of inventory is valued at $480 with carrying costs of 25 percent. As a result, the incremental carrying costs of moving from 0 units of safety stock to 10 units of safety stock are $(10 \times \$480) \times .25$, or $1,200. Likewise, the incremental carrying costs of moving from 10 to 20 units of safety stock are $1,200.

This example also assumes that the various levels of safety stock prevent a certain number of stockouts. For example, holding 10 units of safety stock for an entire year allows the firm to prevent 20 stockouts; moving from 10 units to 20 units of safety stock allows 16 additional orders to be filled. Using an average cost per stockout of $400, a safety stock of 10 units allows the firm to prevent 20 stockouts, which saves the firm $8,000 ($400 \times 20$). The savings of $8,000 is much greater than the additional carrying costs of $1,200, so the firm wants to hold at least 10 units of safety stock. Twenty units of safety stock result in $1,200 of additional carrying costs, whereas the additional stockout costs avoided are $6,400 ($16 \times \$400$). According to the data in Table 8.4, the optimum quantity of safety stock is 70 units. At this point, the cost of 10 additional units of inventory is $1,200, and $1,200 is saved in stockout costs.

WHEN TO ORDER

A key issue with respect to inventory management involves when product should be ordered; one could order a fixed amount of inventory (**fixed order quantity system**), or orders can be placed at fixed time intervals (**fixed order interval system**). In a fixed order quantity system, the time interval may fluctuate while the order size stays constant; for example, a store might always order 200 cases of soft drinks. Its first order may be placed on January 3, a second order on January 6 (three-day interval), with a third order on January 11 (five-day interval). By contrast, in a fixed order interval system, the time interval is constant, but the order size may fluctuate. For example, a man goes grocery shopping with his wife every Sunday. Although the time interval for shopping is constant at seven days, the shopping list (inventory requirements) differs from week to week.

There needs to be a **reorder (trigger) point** (i.e., the level of inventory at which a replenishment order is placed) for there to be an efficient fixed order quantity system. Reorder points

(ROPs) are relatively easy to calculate, particularly under conditions of certainty; a reorder point is equal to the average daily demand (DD) in units times the length of the replenishment cycle (RC):

$$ROP = DD \times RC$$

Suppose, for example, that average daily demand is 40 units and the replenishment cycle is 4 days. The reorder point in this example is 40×4, or 160 units; in other words, when the inventory level reaches 160 units, a reorder is placed.

The reorder point under conditions of uncertainty can be calculated in a similar manner; the only modification involves including a safety stock (SS) factor:

$$ROP = (DD \times RC) + SS$$

Continuing with the previous example, suppose that the company decides to hold 40 units of safety stock. The reorder point becomes $(40 \times 4) + 40$, or 200 units.

The fact that a fixed order quantity system works best when there is a predetermined reorder point indicates that this system requires relatively frequent, if not constant, monitoring of inventory levels. Under a fixed order quantity system, if sales start to increase, the reorder point will be reached more quickly, and a new order will automatically be placed. In most fixed order interval systems, by contrast, inventory levels are monitored much less frequently—often just before the scheduled order time. The infrequency of inventory monitoring makes the fixed interval system much more susceptible to stockout situations, and one is more likely to see higher levels of safety stock in a fixed interval system. It's entirely possible that a company could have some of its inventory under a fixed order quantity system, whereas other inventory uses a fixed order interval system.

HOW MUCH TO ORDER

Economic Order Quantity

A long-standing issue in inventory management concerns how much inventory should be ordered at a particular time. The typical inventory order size problem, referred to as the **economic order quantity (EOQ)**, deals with calculating the proper order size with respect to two costs: the costs of carrying the inventory and the costs of ordering the inventory. The EOQ determines the point at which the sum of carrying costs and ordering costs is minimized, or the point at which carrying costs equal ordering costs. The nature of carrying costs and ordering costs is presented in Figure 8.1.

The basic EOQ model is grounded in the following assumptions:

1. A continuous, constant, and known rate of demand
2. A constant and known replenishment or lead time
3. A constant purchase price that is independent of the order quantity
4. All demand is satisfied (no stockouts are allowed)
5. No inventory in transit
6. Only one item in inventory or no interaction between inventory items
7. An infinite planning horizon
8. Unlimited capital availability.

Mathematically, the EOQ can be calculated in two ways; one presents the answer in dollars, the other in units. In terms of dollars, suppose that $1,000 of a particular item is used each year, the order costs are $25 per order submitted, and inventory carrying costs are 20 percent. The EOQ can be calculated using this formula:

$$EOQ = \sqrt{2AB/C}$$

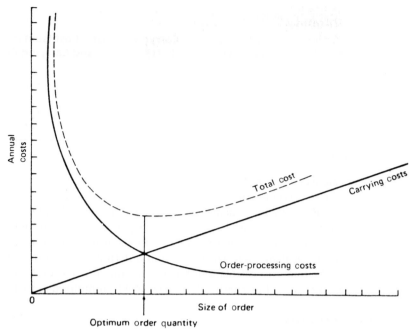

FIGURE 8.1 Determining EOQ by Use of a Graph

Where

EOQ = the most economic order size, in dollars

A = annual usage, in dollars

B = administrative costs per order of placing the order

C = carrying costs of the inventory (expressed as an annual percentage of the inventory dollar value)

Thus,

$$EOQ = \sqrt{2 \times 1{,}000 \times 25/.20} = \sqrt{250{,}000} = \$500 \text{ order size}$$

Alternatively, the EOQ can be calculated in terms of the number of units that should be ordered. Using the same information as in the previous example, and assuming that the product has a cost of $5 per unit, the relevant formula is as follows:

$$EOQ = \sqrt{2DB/IC}$$

Where

EOQ = the most economic order size, in units

D = annual demand, in units (200 units; $1,000 value of inventory/$5 value per unit)

B = administrative costs per order of placing the order

C = carrying costs of the inventory (expressed as an annual percentage of the inventory's dollar value)

I = dollar value of the inventory, per unit

Thus,

$$EOQ = \sqrt{2 \times 200 \times 25/.20 \times 5} = \sqrt{10{,}000/1} = 100 \text{ units}$$

By contrast, high turnover may signal a low level of inventories, which can increase the chance of product stockouts. Despite this, most organizations today strive to increase their inventory turnover and one way to do this is by reducing average inventory. Although reducing average inventory is easier said than done, you should recognize that an understanding of two concepts discussed earlier in this section, ABC analysis and dead inventory, can help to reduce average inventory. For example, eliminating some or all of a company's dead inventory automatically reduces both beginning and ending inventory—hence average inventory is also reduced.

The inventory turnover concept provides an excellent example of trade-offs involving multiple organizational functions such as finance, logistics, and marketing. One illustration of these trade-offs is provided by used-car dealers, who must balance price (marketing), profit (finance), and inventory turnover (logistics). As an example, the used-car dealer that decides to maximize average profit per vehicle will likely charge a higher price for each vehicle, and the higher price might result in a longer selling time, hence slower inventory turnover, for each vehicle.[9]

Complementary and Substitute Products

This book takes a rather narrow view of **complementary products** and defines them as inventories that can be used or distributed together, such as razor blades and razors. These products may only intensify the pressures on retailers or wholesalers concerned with inventory maintenance. For example, consider the following dilemma: "So many complementary items exist for cooking meat and fish that you'll never be able to display them in the same section (of the store)." Possible complementary products for the meat and fish section include cheeses, seasonings, skewers, skillets, and wines, among others.[10]

Another issue associated with complementary products involves the amount of inventory to be carried. Purchasing a canister vacuum cleaner, for example, generally means that a customer will periodically need to buy replacement bags for the canister. As such, the canister bags might be slow sellers, and some might argue that the bags should be dropped in favor of faster-moving products. Others, however, would point out that the sale and display of these bags is necessary to support the sale of canister vacuums.

Substitute products refer to products that can fill the same need or want as another product. The substitutability can occur at a specific product level (e.g., one brand of cola is viewed as a substitute for another brand of cola), or it can occur across product classes (e.g., potatoes may be viewed as a substitute for rice). As pointed out earlier, knowledge of substitutability has important implications with respect to stockout costs and the sizes of safety stocks to be maintained. Thus, if a consumer has little hesitation in making substitutions, there would appear to be minimal penalties for a stockout. However, a point may be reached where customers become sufficiently annoyed at having to make substitutions that they decide to take their business elsewhere. Because of the many possibilities for substitutability, many grocery chains target in-stock rates of 95 percent for individual stores so that sufficient substitutes exist for a customer to purchase a substitute item rather than go to a competing store.

Moreover, some substitute product decisions are much more challenging than others. Consider, for example, some of the issues that hospitals confront with respect to substitute products:

- What safety risks does a substitute product pose for patients and hospital staff?
- Is the substitute product compatible with current equipment?
- How will information about the substitute product be communicated to hospital staff?
- How do a patient's insurance requirements impact the ability to use a substitute product?[11]

---

[9]David Ruggles, "Turn, Baby, Turn," *Ward's Dealer Business*, November 1, 2011, 23–24.
[10]James Mellgren, "Category Complements: Increasing Specialty Food Sales," *Gourmet Retailer*, June 2006, 38–44.
[11]Colleen Cusick, "Successful Substitutions Are a Product of Good Communication," *Material Management in Health Care*, March 2008, 28–31.

It's also important that companies have a thorough understanding of substitution patterns. For example, in many cases, substitutions are two-way, meaning that if brand A is substitutable for brand B, then brand B is substitutable for brand A. In some situations, however, one-way relationships exist; a bolt 7/16 inch in diameter could be used in place of a bolt that is 1/2 inch in diameter, but the reverse may not hold.

CONTEMPORARY ISSUES WITH MANAGING INVENTORY

Much of what has been discussed to this point represents traditional thinking about inventory management. Although traditional thinking about inventory continues to be relevant, this chapter concludes with a look at three contemporary issues with managing inventory—lean manufacturing, service parts logistics, and vendor-managed inventory.

Lean Manufacturing (Lean)

Broadly speaking, **lean manufacturing** (also referred to as **lean**) focuses on the elimination of waste and the increase of speed and flow. The lean manufacturing approach identifies seven major sources of waste, one of which is inventory. Just-in-time (JIT) is one of the best known lean inventory practices, and we'll take a closer look at JIT in the paragraphs that follow.

From an inventory perspective, the **JIT approach** seeks to minimize inventory by reducing (if not eliminating) safety stock, as well as by having the required amount of materials arrive at the production location at the exact time that they are needed. Although the just-in-time approach is generally associated with inventory management because of its focus on minimizing inventory, the consequences of JIT actually go far beyond inventory management. The JIT approach has a number of important implications for logistical efficiency, one of which is that suppliers must deliver high-quality materials to the production line; because of JIT's emphasis on low (no) safety stock, defective materials result in a production line shutdown. Improved product quality from suppliers can be facilitated by looking at suppliers as partners, as opposed to adversaries, in the production process.

JIT emphasizes minimal inventory levels, and as a result customers tend to place smaller, more frequent orders. As such, it is imperative that suppliers' order systems be capable of handling an increased number of orders in an error-free fashion. In addition, because the transit-time reliability tends to decrease with distance, suppliers need to be located relatively close to their customers.

The combination of smaller, more frequent shipments and close supplier location means that trucking is an important mode of transportation in the JIT approach. As such, production and distribution facilities should be designed to support truck shipments—that is, there should be truck docks to facilitate product loading and unloading. Although this may appear to be the proverbial "no-brainer," consider the case of a U.S. manufacturer that designed a state-of-the-art distribution facility to be served by rail, only to switch to a JIT approach, thus making the new facility totally worthless. In fact, some companies involved in JIT have designed their production facilities so that trucks can drive inside them, thus bringing the product that much closer to the actual production point. Figure 8.3 shows a truck trailer that opens on its side for rapid discharge of parts for JIT inventory management.

Other examples of lean inventory include efficient consumer response (ECR), which is associated with the grocery and beverage industries, and quick response (QR), which is associated with the apparel industry. Where JIT tends to encompass movement of materials and component parts from supplier to producer, ECR and QR tend to focus on product movement from manufacturer to retailer.

Although lean is an important concept in contemporary logistics, a confluence of events suggests that organizations should carefully consider the potential trade-offs before adopting a lean philosophy. More specifically, the lean philosophy was conceived and nurtured in an

FIGURE 8.3 Trailer That Opens on the Side and Is Used for Rapid Discharge of Parts   *Source:* Photo Courtesy of fotolia.

environment—low fuel prices, local or regional sourcing, fewer human-made or natural disasters—far different than today's environment. For example, today's high fuel prices (by historical standards) cause transportation companies to focus on lower costs through moving larger freight volumes—a practice that doesn't align very well with lean's emphasis on smaller shipments. In a similar fashion, today's emphasis on global sourcing translates into longer and more erratic transit times—and longer and more erratic transit times don't align very well with lean's emphasis on shipments that arrive exactly when needed. Furthermore, the 2011 Japan earthquake as well as the severe 2011 flooding in Thailand caused tremendous supply disruptions that are antithetical to the lean philosophy.

Service Parts Logistics

Service parts logistics involves designing a network of facilities to stock service parts, deciding upon inventory ordering policies, stocking the required parts, and transporting parts from stocking facilities to customers.[12] Long viewed as an afterthought or—even worse—as a nuisance, service parts logistics has gained greater attention and appreciation in recent years. One reason for this is that the customer expectations associated with service parts logistics continue to increase, particularly in the automotive industry where the *maximum* customer wait time for repair or replacement parts is one day.[13] Another reason for increased emphasis on service parts logistics

---

[12]Mehmet Ferhat Candas and Erhat Kutanoglu, "Benefits of Considering Inventory in Service Parts Logistics Network Design Problems with Time-Based Service Constraints," *IIE Transactions* 39, no. 2 (2007): 159–176.
[13]Anthony Coia, "The Replacement Fillers," *Automotive Logistics*, September–October 2008, 28–32.

is that the worldwide economic slowdown of 2008 and 2009 caused many organizations to repair, rather than replace, aging or defective equipment. This "repair, rather than replace" ethos, continues to be prevalent in today's marketplace.

Service parts logistics creates a variety of potential challenges for logisticians; one challenge is it can be extremely difficult to forecast the demand for the necessary parts. For example, although companies might have some knowledge about the repair parts needed for routine or preventive maintenance of products, it is virtually impossible to forecast when the product might break down or fail. The difficulties in forecasting demand lead to challenges with respect to which parts to carry, the appropriate stocking levels for the parts that are carried, and higher inventory levels, among others.[14]

Another challenge involves the number of warehousing facilities that should be used in service parts logistics. One possibility is to locate the parts at numerous warehousing facilities in that this allows the parts to be fairly close to potential customers, and in emergency situations, where time is of the essence, this can be critical to customer satisfaction. Alternatively, the parts could be located at one centralized facility; although this would require use of premium transportation for some shipments, this cost can be offset by the inventory cost savings that result from inventory being held in only one facility.

These and other challenges have led some organizations to outsource their service parts logistics to companies that specialize in this area (see Figure 8.4). For example, Choice Logistics has developed expertise in managing service parts logistics for technology and telecommunications companies. Choice Logistics offers prospective customers approximately 400 stocking facilities, ranging in size from 100 to 10,000 square feet, in over 90 countries. Importantly, superior inventory control is cited as the most prominent reason for using service parts logistics specialists such as Choice Logistics.[15]

This discussion of service parts logistics offers an opportunity to point out the importance of informal considerations when managing inventories and making logistics-related decisions. Some years ago, the owner of an automotive parts distributor became concerned with the amount of inventory his company was holding. A visit to the distributor's storage facility revealed that it was literally overrun with oil filters from one particular manufacturer; this one brand of oil filters accounted for approximately 20 percent of the facility's total inventory, a figure far higher than its actual demand.

At first glance, the solution seemed clear: Reduce the inventory of oil filters to a level more in line with demand. However, there was a reason for the high inventory of oil filters: The oil filter manufacturer sponsored annual contests that offered all-expenses-paid trips for two to attractive vacation locations such as Hawaii, and the trips were awarded based on the amount of oil filters purchased in a particular time frame. Because the distributor's spouse had become quite fond of these annual trips, each year the owner placed very large orders for the particular brand of oil filters, despite the fact that they weren't needed. As a result, the "obvious" solution to the problem—reducing the inventory of oil filters—wasn't feasible because the owner wanted to please his spouse. In this situation, personal considerations were more important than professional ones, and you should recognize that personal considerations often play a very important role when making decisions in family-run businesses.

Vendor-Managed Inventory (VMI)

In traditional inventory management, the size and timing of replenishment orders are the responsibility of the party using the inventory, such as a distributor or a retailer. Under **vendor-managed inventory (VMI)**, by contrast, the size and timing of replenishment orders

[14]Lisa Harrington, "Getting Service Parts Logistics Up to Speed," *Inbound Logistics,* November 2006, 72–79.
[15]William Hoffman, "A Bigger Part," *Traffic World,* January 19, 2009, 17.

FIGURE 8.4 Advertisement from a Parts Bank Service *Source:* Courtesy of Associated Distribution Logistics (ADL).

are the responsibility of the *manufacturer*. Operationally, VMI allows manufacturers to have access to a distributor's or retailer's sales and inventory data, and this access is accomplished electronically by electronic data interchange (EDI) or the Internet. Although VMI is often associated with consumer products, it also has been applied to industrial products such as airplanes, construction equipment, fasteners (e.g., bolts, screws), and heating and cooling systems, among others.

VMI represents a huge philosophical shift for some organizations in the sense that they are allowing another party to have control over their inventories. This is a situation that necessitates tremendous trust on the part of distributors and retailers because of the potential for unscrupulous manufacturers to abuse the system by pushing unneeded inventories onto downstream parties.

VMI's benefits include reduced inventories, fewer stockouts, and improved customer retention because it can be difficult and costly for customers to switch suppliers. In addition, since VMI is based on actual point-of-sale data, there is reduced reliance on demand forecasting—and we learned in Chapter 7 that demand forecasts always contain errors. Alternatively, one drawback to VMI is inadequate data sharing between the relevant parties, in part because of trust and control concerns. Another VMI drawback is that some employees may resist the change to a new and different system. In addition, organizations that adopt VMI must recognize that the process will not produce immediate benefits, and that its adoption will likely produce some errors in the short run.[16]

Summary

Inventory is a key component in logistics because inventory decisions are often a starting point for other business activities. The chapter began with a look at the various classifications of inventory, and this was followed by a discussion of inventory costs. When deciding what levels of inventories to maintain, companies try to minimize the costs associated with both too much and too little inventory. Too much inventory leads to high inventory carrying costs; too little inventory can lead to stockouts and the associated stockout costs. The worst outcome of a stockout is to lose both a sale and all future business from the customer.

The chapter also addressed when to order inventory, as well as how much inventory to order, and we learned that reorder points signify stock levels at which a new order should be placed. With respect to how much to order, the economic order quantity (EOQ) minimizes ordering costs and inventory carrying costs.

The chapter looked at special concerns associated with inventory management including ABC analysis and inventory turnover and we learned that an understanding of ABC analysis can help organizations increase their inventory turnover. The chapter concluded with a discussion of several contemporary issues with managing inventory.

Questions for Discussion and Review

8.1 How might different organizational functions have different inventory management objectives?

8.2 What makes it difficult for managers to achieve the proper balance of inventory?

8.3 Distinguish among cycle, safety, pipeline, and speculative stock.

8.4 Define what is meant by inventory carrying costs and list its primary components.

8.5 What are ordering costs and what is the trade-off between inventory carrying costs and ordering costs?

8.6 Discuss the concept of stockout costs. How can stockout costs be calculated?

---

[16]Paul Evanko, "Vendor-Managed Inventory," *HVACR Distribution Business*, December 2010, 32, 34–35.

8.7 Distinguish between a fixed order quantity and fixed order interval system. Which one generally requires more safety stock? Why?

8.8 Explain the logic of the EOQ model.

8.9 What assumptions are associated with the EOQ model?

8.10 How can inventory flow diagrams be useful to a logistics manager?

8.11 Discuss what is meant by ABC analysis of inventory. What are several measures that can determine ABC status?

8.12 Define what is meant by dead inventory. What are several ways to manage it?

8.13 In what ways can inventory turnover provide important insights about an organization's competitiveness and efficiency?

8.14 Discuss some of the managerial challenges that complementary products present.

8.15 What are substitute items and how might they affect safety stock policies?

8.16 How might a hospital's decisions with respect to substitute products differ from a supermarket's decisions with substitute products?

8.17 How do the consequences of JIT go far beyond inventory management?

8.18 Why should organizations carefully consider potential trade-offs before adopting a lean philosophy?

8.19 Discuss some challenges that service parts logistics creates for logistics managers.

8.20 How does vendor-managed inventory differ from traditional inventory management?

Suggested Readings

Ettouzani, Youmas, Nicola Yates, and Carlos Mena. "Examining Retail on Shelf Availability: Promotional Impact and Call for Research." *International Journal of Physical Distribution & Logistics Management* 42, no. 3 (2012): 213–243.

Farooquia, Parveen and M. Nasir Khan. "Returning to Roots for Reducing Inventory Costs in SMEs: A Case of Indian Lock Industry." *Journal of Enterprising Culture* 18, no. 3 (2010): 315–330.

Gebauer, Heiko, Gunther Kuzca, and Chenzi Wang. "Spare Parts Logistics for the Chinese Market." *Benchmarking: An International Journal* 18, no. 6 (2011): 748–768.

Lee, Hau L. and Seungjin Whang. "The Whose, Where, and How of Inventory Control Design." *Supply Chain Management Review* 12, no. 8 (2008): 22–29.

Leeuw, Sander de, Matthias Holweg, and Geoff Williams. "The Impact of Decentralized Control on Firm-level Inventory: Evidence from the Automobile Industry." *International Journal of Physical Distribution & Logistics Management* 41, no. 5 (2011): 435–456.

Stanger, Sebastian H.W., Richard Wilding, Nicky Yates, and Sue Cotton. "What Drives Perishable Inventory Management Performance? Lessons Learnt from the UK Blood Supply Chain." *Supply Chain Management: An International Journal* 17, no. 2 (2012): 107–123.

Willems, Sean. "Inventory Optimization: Evolving from Fad to Necessity." *Supply Chain Management Review* 17, no. 2 (2013): 10–17.

Williams, Brent D. and Travis Tokar. "A Review of Inventory Management Research in Major Logistics Journals." *International Journal of Logistics Management* 19, no. 2 (2008): 212–232.

Woensel, Tom van, Karel van Donselaar, Rob Broekmeulen, and Jan Fransoo. "Consumer Responses to Shelf Out-of-Stocks of Perishable Products." *International Journal of Physical Distribution & Logistics Management* 37, no. 9 (2007): 704–718.

Yu-Lee, Reginald T. "Proper Lean Accounting: Eliminating Waste Isn't Enough; You Have to Reduce Inputs to Save Money." *Industrial Engineer* 43, no. 10 (2011): 39–43.

CASE

CASE 8.1   Low Nail Company

After making some wise short-term investments at a race track, Chris Low had some additional cash to invest in a business. The most promising opportunity at the time was in building supplies, so Low bought a business that specialized in sales of one size of nail. The annual volume of nails was 2,000 kegs, and they were sold to retail customers in an even flow. Low was uncertain how many nails to order at any time. Initially, only two costs concerned him: order-processing costs, which were $60 per order without regard to size, and warehousing costs, which were $1 per year per keg space. This meant that Low had to rent a constant amount of warehouse space for the year, and it had to be large enough to accommodate an entire order when it arrived. Low was not worried about maintaining safety stocks, mainly because the outward flow of goods was so even. Low bought his nails on a delivered basis.

Questions

1. Using the EOQ methods outlined in the chapter, how many kegs of nails should Low order at one time?
2. Assume all conditions in Question 1 hold, except that Low's supplier now offers a quantity discount in the form of absorbing all or part of Low's order-processing costs. For orders of 750 or more kegs of nails, the supplier will absorb all the order-processing costs; for orders between 249 and 749 kegs, the supplier will absorb half. What is Low's new EOQ? (It might be useful to lay out all costs in tabular form for this and later questions.)
3. Temporarily, ignore your work on Question 2. Assume that Low's warehouse offers to rent Low space on the basis of the *average* number of kegs Low will have in stock, rather than on the maximum number of kegs Low would need room for whenever a new shipment arrived. The storage charge per keg remains the same. Does this change the answer to Question 1? If so, what is the new answer?
4. Take into account the answer to Question 1 *and* the supplier's new policy outlined in Question 2 *and* the warehouse's new policy in Question 3. Then determine Low's new EOQ.
5. Temporarily, ignore your work on Questions 2, 3, and 4. Low's luck at the race track is over; he now must borrow money to finance his inventory of nails. Looking at the situation outlined in Question 1, assume that the wholesale cost of nails is $40 per keg and that Low must pay interest at the rate of 1.5 percent per month on unsold inventory. What is his new EOQ?
6. Taking into account all the factors listed in Questions 1, 2, 3, and 5, calculate Low's EOQ for kegs of nails.

9 | FACILITY LOCATION

Facility location is a logistics/supply chain activity that has evolved from a tactical decision to one of tremendous strategic importance in numerous organizations. In particular, this chapter discusses **facility location**, which refers to choosing the locations for distribution centers, warehouses, and production facilities to facilitate logistical effectiveness and efficiency. The chapter begins with an overview of the location process, followed by a discussion of the strategic importance of facility location. Next is a discussion of how to determine the optimum number of facilities, which is followed by a look at general and specific influences on facility location. The chapter next describes several basic techniques for choosing general locations and concludes with a discussion of facility relocation and facility closing.

The location decision process involves several layers of screening or focus, with each step becoming a more detailed analysis of a smaller number of areas or sites. The initial focus is on the region, the delineation of which can vary depending on whether a company has a multinational or domestic focus. Thus, a multinational company might initially focus on a region of the world, such as Western Europe, the Pacific Rim, or North America. By contrast, a domestic focus might target a state (province/territory) or group of states (provinces/territories).

The next focus is more precise; it usually involves a selection of the area(s) in which the facility will be located; once this has been determined, a detailed examination of various locations within the selected area is appropriate. This detailed examination should include a physical inspection of the location as well as a thorough analysis of relevant zoning and regulatory considerations. Failure to do so can result in costly—and potentially embarrassing—mistakes, as illustrated by the unfortunate experience of a supermarket chain.

The company picked a site for a new grocery store, received the appropriate construction permits, built the store, hired relevant personnel, and stocked the store with products. Several days before the store's grand opening, the parent company was threatened with legal action by a competing supermarket that had a store located across the street from the new store. The legal action referred to the relevant zoning laws—*which had not been checked prior to beginning construction*—that prohibited any new grocery store from being built within a one-mile radius of the existing grocery store! As a result, the supermarket chain had to cancel its grand opening, close the brand-new store, transfer the products to other stores, and lay off many of the newly hired personnel.[1]

THE STRATEGIC IMPORTANCE OF FACILITY LOCATION[2]

Logistics managers face a marketplace that is dynamic and ever-changing, and this dynamism and change are two reasons why facility location has evolved from a tactical to a strategic consideration. Facilities such as manufacturing plants and warehousing represent fixed points where goods are produced, processed, assembled, or stored. Because these facilities can be very expensive to lease or build, companies are often hesitant to close them. However, poorly located facilities can negatively impact logistical effectiveness (e.g., due to longer and less reliable delivery times) and efficiency (e.g., due to increased delivery costs). This section discusses several overarching factors that can influence facility location decisions.

Cost Considerations

Cost considerations are hardly new to logistics managers. Recall from Chapter 1 that the systems approach to logistics is predicated on the total costs of various logistics activities. Today's cost considerations arise because many consumers have become sensitized to buy products only when prices are low, due in part to lingering effects of the 2007–2009 recession. Businesses have also contributed to consumer fixation with low prices, and businesses have conditioned many customers to only purchase if products are deeply discounted.[3] If retailers offer consistently low prices, then their costs must also be consistently low in order for organizations to be profitable.

For many years, this low price/low cost framework led many companies to manufacture in countries characterized by plentiful and low-cost labor. However, this paradigm has begun to shift in recent years in part because a tremendous surge in oil prices (which culminated in 2008 with a peak price of approximately $147 per barrel) forced some companies to reconsider their manufacturing locations because of soaring transportation costs. In addition, the People's Republic of China, long characterized by plentiful, low-cost labor, recorded labor cost increases of 20 percent per year between 2006 and 2010, with similar annual increases expected through 2015.[4] As a result, some organizations have adopted near-sourcing, in which companies reconfigure their logistics networks to bring some production facilities closer to key consumer markets. For example, Mexico is the most popular location for near-sourcing among companies that do business in North America.[5]

[1]Example drawn from one author's personal experience.
[2]The discussion in this section is based on factors identified in John J. Coyle, C. John Langley, Brian J. Gibson, Robert A. Novack, and Edward J. Bardi, *Supply Chain Management: A Logistics Perspective*, 8th ed. (Mason, OH: South-Western Cengage Learning, 2009), Chapter 12.
[3]Cecile Rohwedder, "U.K. Grocers Wage Price War, Yet Most Can Declare Victory," *The Wall Street Journal*, August 10, 2009, A1, A8.
[4]Mike King, "Rising Labor Costs, Land Prices Challenge China's Competitiveness," *JoC Online*, May 4, 2012, 1–5.
[5]Peter T. Leach, "Closer to Near-Sourcing," *Journal of Commerce*, January 16, 2012, 8–11.

Customer Service Expectations

One point that has been repeatedly emphasized in this text is that customer service expectations continue to increase over time. We know, for example, that today's customers are looking for faster and more reliable order cycles, but how are faster and more reliable order cycles operationalized from a facility location perspective? Should an organization rely on one or two facilities to serve its customers, or should it rely on multiple facilities to serve them? The former alternative leads to fewer facilities and lower inventory costs, but higher transportation costs; the latter leads to more facilities and higher inventory costs, but lower transportation costs.

Location of Customer or Supply Markets

Improvements in transportation (e.g., high-speed highways) and technology (e.g., air conditioning) allow consumers to migrate relatively easily from one region or country to another. An example of such migration can be seen in Table 9.1, which lists the five most populous states in the United States in 1950, 1980, and 2010. Note that in 1950, four of the five most populated states were located in the Northeast and Midwest, and thus in relatively close geographic proximity. Alternatively in 2010, the most populous states were located in the West, Southwest, Northeast, Southeast, and Midwest, respectively—and thus are much more geographically diverse than in 1950. This population shift necessitates different production and distribution facility locations than in the 1950s and cities like Atlanta, Dallas, and Reno (Nevada) are today important distribution hubs in the United States.

Economic growth is another variable that influences the location of customer markets in the sense that organizations sometimes expand their geographic scope to serve new customers. From purely a population perspective, China and India have been potentially attractive markets because the two countries account for approximately one-third of the world's population. What makes China and India even more attractive today is that both are experiencing tremendous growth in the number of middle-class families—families that often prefer name-brand Western goods and services.

By the end of 2013, for example, McDonald's is projected to have approximately 2,000 restaurant locations in China, up from 1,000 at the end of 2008. In addition to selecting the new store locations, the new stores will need to be supplied with foodstuffs and the like, which will likely necessitate additional distribution facilities to be located in China. This expansion also highlights supply location issues, such as will McDonald's use current, or new, suppliers for the new restaurants? The use of current suppliers might lead to lengthy supply lines—and possibly longer and more erratic transit times—but would allow McDonald's to work with familiar companies. Alternatively, new suppliers might be located in closer proximity to the new restaurants and distribution facilities but McDonald's will need to learn how to work with the new suppliers.

The sustainability concept is another strategic consideration that can potentially impact the location of supply markets. You might recall from Chapter 1 that sustainability refers to products that meet present needs without compromising the ability of future generations to meet their needs. A key sustainability issue involves the sourcing of products and an emerging trend

Table 9.1	Five Most Populous States in the United States—1950, 1980, and 2010		
Rank	**1950**	**1980**	**2010**
1	New York	California	California
2	California	New York	Texas
3	Pennsylvania	Texas	New York
4	Illinois	Pennsylvania	Florida
5	Ohio	Illinois	Illinois

Source: Derived from data at www.census.gov.

involves companies that pursue a **locavore strategy**, that is, purchasing locally grown or produced foods. Locavore foods are desirable from a sustainability perspective because they reduce carbon footprints related to production and transportation.[6]

DETERMINING THE NUMBER OF FACILITIES

An early, albeit overlooked, step in the facility location decision should involve determining the total number of facilities that a firm should operate. That is, rather than asking the question, "Where should we locate a new facility?" organizations should be thinking about the optimal number of facilities in their system. Although an additional facility may indeed be required, the general trend in recent years has been for companies to reduce the number of facilities in their distribution networks.

Few firms start business on one day and have a need for large-scale production and distribution the next day. Rather, distribution and production facilities tend to be added one at a time, as needed. The need for additional distribution and production facilities often arises when an organization's service performance from existing facilities drops below "acceptable" levels. Retailers, for example, might add a distribution center when some of its stores can no longer consistently be supplied within two days by existing facilities.

Most analytical procedures for determining the number of facilities are computerized because of the vast number of permutations involved, as well as the complementary relationships between current facilities in a distribution network. Analyzing, for example, whether an organization with 250 stores and five distribution centers should add or remove one distribution center is challenging enough in and of itself. Factoring in that each distribution center is designed to serve a specific number of retail locations—and serve as a backup to one or more of the other distribution centers—makes the decision even more complex. Furthermore, conducting sensitivity analysis on varying levels of customer service could result in an entirely different series of ideal facility locations, depending on the level of customer service that is expected.

Fortunately, a number of software packages exist to help organizations determine both the number and location of facilities in their logistics networks. Chicago Consulting, for example, annually develops a list entitled, "The 10 Best Warehouse Networks," which lists those available for serving the U.S. population, and in 2006 Chicago Consulting debuted a list of "The 10 Best Chinese Warehouse Networks" for serving mainland China (see Figure 9.1). Although these lists are limited in the sense that they only look at one component in location (how long it takes to get from a particular city—or cities—to the majority of the country's population), the network is valuable in showing how altering the number of facilities affects transit time to the particular population. With respect to China, for example, going from two to five warehouses allows a company to save nearly one day of lead time to the Chinese population. By contrast, moving from five to ten warehouses saves a bit less than one-half day in lead time.[7]

GENERAL FACTORS INFLUENCING FACILITY LOCATION

Tangible products are the combination of raw materials, component parts, and labor—with the mixture varying from product to product—made for sale in various markets. Thus, raw materials, component parts, labor, and markets all influence where to locate a manufacturing, processing, or assembly facility. Warehouses, distribution centers, and cross-docking facilities exist to facilitate the distribution of products. Their locations are in turn influenced by the locations of plants whose products they handle and the markets they serve.

---

[6]Kate Leahy, "The Era of Sustainability," *Restaurants and Institutions*, October 2008, 38–46.
[7]www.chicago-consulting.com

THE 10 BEST CHINESE WAREHOUSE NETWORKS
Networks with the Lowest Possible "Time-to-the-Chinese Population"

Number of Warehouses	Average Distance to the Chinese Population (Miles)	Average Transit Lead-Time to the Chinese Population (Days)	Best Warehouse Locations		
ONE	504	3.38	XINYANG		
TWO	377	2.55	LIANYUAN	FEICHENG	
THREE	309	2.15	PINGXIANG	JINAN	ZIYANG
FOUR	265	1.87	PINGXIANG CHANGCHUN	JINING	ZIYANG
FIVE	228	1.65	SHAOGUAN CHANGCHUN	HANDAN NANJING	ZIYANG
SIX	207	1.53	SHAOGUAN CHANGCHUN	HANDAN NANJING	NEIJIANG URUMQI
SEVEN	184	1.42	GUANGZHOU CHANGCHUN HONGHU	HANDAN JINGJIANG	NEIJIANG URUMQI
EIGHT	168	1.31	GUANGZHOU CHANGCHUN HONGHU	LIAOCHENG YIXING BAOJI	YIBIN URUMQI
NINE	154	1.24	BEILIU CHANGCHUN YUEYANG	LIAOCHENG LIYANG BAOJI	YIBIN URUMQI ZHANGZHOU
TEN	141	1.20	BEILIU CHANGCHUN YUEYANG TIANJIN	KAIFENG YIXING BAOJI	YIBIN URUMQI ZHANGZHOU

The 10 Best Chinese Warehouse Networks have been developed based on the lowest possible transit lead-times to "customers" represented by the Chinese population. For example, Xinyang provides the lowest possible lead-time for one warehouse. Any other place will increase transit lead-time to the Chinese population. Similarly putting any three warehouses in any locations other than Pingxiang, Jinan or Ziyang will cause the transit lead-time to be higher than 2.15 days.

© Chicago Consulting
8 South Michigan Avenue, Chicago, IL 60603
(312) 346-5080, www.chicago-consulting.com

Chicago Consulting ❬❭

FIGURE 9.1 Chicago Consulting's 10 Best Chinese Warehouse Networks *Source:* Courtesy of Terry Harris, Managing Partner of Chicago Consulting.

The discussion that follows covers the location of manufacturing, processing, assembly, and distribution facilities along the supply chain. The relative importance of each factor varies with the type of facility, the product being handled, its volume, and the geographic locations being considered. Although much of the discussion deals with single facilities, the decision process often involves a combination of facilities, in which case one must take into account the relationships among them.

Natural Resources

The materials used to make a product must be extracted directly from the ground or sea (as in the case of mining or fishing) or indirectly (as in the case of farm products). In some instances, these resources may be located great distances from the point where the materials or their products will be consumed. For materials that lose no weight in processing, known as **pure materials**, the processing point can be anywhere near the raw material source and the market.

However, if the materials must be processed at some point between where they are gathered and where they are needed, their weight-losing or weight-gaining characteristics become important for facility location. If the materials lose considerable weight in processing, known as **weight-losing products**, then the processing point should be near the point where they are mined or harvested, largely to avoid the payment of unnecessary transportation charges. If the raw materials gain weight in processing, known as **weight-gaining products**, then the processing point should be close to the market. Sugar derived from sugar beets provides an example of a weight-losing product (a yield of roughly 1 pound of sugar from 6 pounds of sugar beets), whereas bottled soft drinks are an example of a weight-gaining product.

In addition to its use for bottling, water (of one type or another) is a requirement for the location of many facilities. For some industrial processes, water is used for cooling, and in some climates it is possible to use naturally flowing water for air conditioning during warm months. Some processing operations require water both for cleaning purposes and as a medium for carrying away waste. Water is also necessary for fire protection, and the fire insurance premiums charged depend on the availability of some type of water supply.

Land requirements are another natural resource consideration in facility location, and distribution and production facilities may require large parcels of land to facilitate effective and efficient operations. An example of land requirements for a particular type of facility is a 250,000-square-foot distribution center that could require at least 50 acres of land. In general, real estate tends to be more plentiful and less costly in more rural locations—locations that might not have adequate transportation or labor resources.

Historically, the relationship between natural resources and facility location revolved around how the natural resources would be incorporated into products making their way toward consumers. Over the past quarter century, however, discussion of natural resources and facility location has increasingly factored in environmental and sustainability considerations. One set of considerations involves the various types of pollution, namely, air, noise, and water, while another environmental consideration involves the conservation of natural resources.

Population Characteristics—Market for Goods

Population can be viewed as both a market for goods and a potential source of labor. Customer considerations, particularly as they affect customer service, play a key role in where consumer goods companies tend to locate their distribution facilities. In fact, the popular press is replete with stories involving distribution facilities being located in a particular area so that companies can better serve their current and potential customers.

Planners for consumer products pay extremely close attention to various attributes of current and potential consumers. Not only are changes in population size of interest to planners, but so are changes in the characteristics of the population—particularly as those characteristics influence purchasing habits. With respect to population characteristics, longer life spans can increase the demand for health-related products such as prescription medications.

In an effort to learn more about population size and characteristics, many countries conduct a detailed study, or census, typically once every 10 years or so. Although census methodologies and the type of information collected often vary across countries, the resulting data can provide valuable insights for distribution planners in terms of where populations are growing and at what rates. For instance, although population in the United States is projected to increase by approximately 9 percent between 2010 and 2020, the population growth is unlikely to be uniform across the various states. For example, Michigan's population is expected to *decline* by approximately 3.75 percent between 2010 and 2020, whereas Utah's population is expected to increase by over 22 percent during this time period.

Population Characteristics—Labor

Labor is a primary concern in selecting a site for manufacturing, processing, assembly, and distribution. Organizations can be concerned with a number of labor-related characteristics: the size of the available workforce, the unemployment rate of the workforce, the age profile of the workforce, its skills and education, the prevailing wage rates, and the extent to which the workforce is, or might be, unionized. These and other labor characteristics should be viewed as interrelated rather than as distinct attributes. For example, there may be a positive relationship between the age of the workforce and the prevailing wage rates (i.e., higher wage rates may be associated with an older workforce). Alternatively, there may be an inverse relationship between unemployment and wages (i.e., higher unemployment rates may be associated with lower relative wage rates).

Labor wage rates are a key locational determinant as supply chains become more global in nature. For example, hourly compensation data (including benefits) among manufacturing firms in 2011 indicate average compensation of $47.38 in Germany and $35.53 in the United States. By contrast, hourly compensation rates were $9.34 in Taiwan and $6.48 in Mexico.[8]

Thus, in relative terms, a company could have approximately similar compensation costs by hiring either six Mexican workers or one U.S. worker. This wage differential at least partly explains the popularity of the **maquiladora** assembly plants located just south of the U.S.–Mexican border. These plants, which began in the mid-1960s, provided much needed jobs to Mexican workers and allowed for low-cost, duty-free production so long as all the goods were exported from Mexico. In the first few years of the twenty-first century, many maquiladoras went out of business, in part because companies established production plants in even lower-wage countries such as China and Guatemala. More recently, however, there has been a resurgence of maquiladoras in part by focusing on high-value goods that depend on fast time to market, such as high-tech products. Other reasons for the maquiladora resurgence include Mexico's close proximity to the United States, higher fuel prices, and a narrowing of the wage gap between Mexico and the People's Republic of China.[9]

Companies interested in locating in countries with low-cost labor should recognize that there are sometimes limits to the number of supervisory personnel that can be brought in from other countries. The host-country's government may also insist that its own nationals be trained for and employed in many supervisory posts. In addition, countries with low-cost labor may house a multitude of **sweatshops**, which can be viewed as organizations that exploit workers and that do not comply with fiscal and legal obligations toward employees. Although sweatshops have often been associated with the toy, textiles, and apparel industries, the electronics industry is a prominent sweatshop industry in the twenty-first century. Key shortcomings in the electronics industry include violations of working hours and days of rest provisions, violations of wage and benefits agreements, and discriminatory practices based on sex or age.[10]

A workforce's union status is also a key locational determinant for some organizations. From management's perspective, unions tend to result in increased labor costs, due to higher wages, and less flexibility in terms of job assignments, which often forces companies to hire additional workers. As a result, some organizations prefer geographic areas in which unions are not strong; in the United States, for example, some states have **right-to-work laws**, which mean that an individual cannot be compelled to join a union as a condition of employment. Indeed, since

---

[8]http://www.bls.gov/fls/#compensation

[9]Lara Sowinski, "Mexico Making a Comeback," *World Trade*, March 2011, 44.

[10]Garrett Brown, "Global Electronics Industry: Poster Child of 21st Century Sweatshops and Despoiler of the Environment?" *EHS Today*, September 2009, 45–48.

2000 non–U.S. automakers have chosen to locate new production plants in right-to-work states such as Alabama (Hyundai), Georgia (Kia), Mississippi (Nissan), and Texas (Toyota).

However, the mere presence of a union doesn't necessarily mean that the union is a strong advocate for workers. Consider that the All China Federation of Trade Unions (ACFTU), which represents over 225 million Chinese workers, is controlled by the Chinese government. As such, the ACFTU sometimes faces conflicting objectives in the sense of deciding what's good for the government versus what's good for the workers—and the workers' concerns aren't always the top priority.[11]

Racial, ethnic, and cultural considerations may also be important population characteristics. Many organizations, particularly those with a national or international presence, have workforces comprising different races, ethnicities, and cultures. There may be a hesitancy to establish facilities in areas that are not racially, ethnically, or culturally diverse because it may be difficult to transfer workers to such locations. Moreover, an emerging issue involves managing so-called **expatriate workers**, or those employees who are sent to other countries for extended periods of time. Expatriate assignments can be costly, ranging up to $1 million per assignment, and turnover rates currently run between 20 and 40 percent. What makes the expatriate situation relevant to the current discussion is that the turnover tends to be caused by socialization, rather than technical (i.e., employee knowledge and skills), factors. Indeed, a leading cause of expatriate turnover involves health-related issues of family members that cannot be addressed in the country of assignment.[12]

Taxes and Incentives

Although labor considerations are important for location decisions, taxes can also be important, particularly with respect to warehousing facilities. Warehousing facilities, and the inventories they contain, can be a prime source of tax revenues by the relevant taxing organizations. From a community's standpoint, warehousing facilities are desirable operations to attract because they add to the tax base while requiring relatively little in the way of municipal services. No list of taxes is complete; a partial list includes sales taxes, real estate taxes, corporate income taxes, corporate franchising taxes, fuel taxes, unemployment compensation taxes, social security taxes, and severance taxes (for the removal of natural resources).

Of particular interest to logisticians and supply chain managers is the **inventory tax**, analogous to personal property taxes paid by individuals. As a general rule, the inventory tax is based on the value of inventory that is held on the assessment date(s). Not surprisingly, many logistics managers attempt to have their inventories as low as possible on the assessment date(s), and businesses may offer sales to reduce their inventory prior to the assessment date.

Fewer than 15 U.S. states currently assess inventory taxes, and they have become increasingly difficult to collect, in part because of valuation considerations (e.g., valuation on the basis of first in first out vs. last in first out) as well as a lack of agreement on what is meant by inventory. Some states, for example, classify intellectual property as inventory.[13] In addition, although a state may offer various exemptions from inventory taxes, not all counties within that state will take advantage of the exemptions. Other inventory exemptions deal more explicitly with distribution activities or functions. Some states exempt goods that are stored in public warehouses; some states exempt goods passing through the state on a storage-in-transit bill of lading.

As if business taxes are not difficult enough to understand, they represent only one side of the coin; the other side is to know the value of services being received in exchange for the taxes.

[11]Rudolf Traub-Merz, *All China Federation of Trade Unions: Structure, Functions and the Challenge of Collective Bargaining* (Geneva: Global Labor University, 2011).

[12]Michelle Shelton, "Seven Tips for Employers with Traveling or Expatriate Employees," *OnCall International*, January 31, 2012.

[13]Kathleen Hickey, "Taxing Logistics," *Traffic World*, May 10, 2004, 15–16.

A general rule of thumb is that the services received represent only about 50 percent of the taxes paid, and this imbalance may cause businesses to invest more money to receive the required level of service. For example, inadequate police services might cause a warehousing facility to hire its own security force.

To further complicate matters, governments may offer incentive packages as an inducement for firms to locate facilities in a particular area. To give you an example of the potential magnitude of incentive packages, the state of North Carolina provided Google approximately $210 million in incentives—including over $180 million in tax benefits—over a 30-year period in return for locating a series of computer warehouses in Lenoir, North Carolina. In addition to tax credits, North Carolina also provided Google with job development grants, road widening, and railroad rerouting, among other benefits.[14]

Transportation Considerations

Transportation considerations in the form of transportation *availability* and *costs* are a key aspect of facility location decisions because transportation often represents such a large portion of total logistics costs. Indeed, the accessibility of highway transportation often ranks as one of the most important criteria in facility location and its importance has increased as more and more companies strive to reduce product delivery times.[15]

Transportation availability refers to the number of transportation modes (**intermodal competition**) as well as the number of carriers within each mode (**intramodal competition**) that could serve a proposed facility. The evaluation of transportation availability is likely to depend on the type of facility that is being looked at. For instance, a manufacturing plant might need both rail service (to bring in raw materials) and truck service (to carry the finished goods), whereas a distribution center might need just truck service.

As a general rule, the existence of competition, whether intermodal, intramodal, or both, tends to have both cost and service benefits for potential users. Limited competition generally leads to higher transportation costs and means that users have to accept whatever service they receive. Thus, a poor location can significantly increase transportation costs as well as negatively affect customer service.

Geographically central facility locations are often the result of transportation costs and service considerations. With respect to transportation costs, centralized facilities tend to minimize the total transit distances, which likely results in minimum transportation costs. A centralized location can also maximize a facility's service area, as shown in Figure 9.2, which illustrates truck distances from the state of Nebraska. Note how many states are located within 1,000 miles (generally considered two-day service by truck) of Nebraska.

Proximity to Industry Clusters

When looking at facility location considerations, early business logistics textbooks discussed the **agglomeration** concept, which "refers to the net advantages which can be gained by a sharing of common locations by various enterprises."[16] Although agglomeration continues be a key factor in facility location, it is better known today as the **industry cluster** concept. Silicon Valley, a collection of high-technology firms located in the southern part of San Francisco, California, is a well-known industry cluster.

Industry clusters come in a number of different sizes and shapes, and one type of cluster offers organizations *proximity to key suppliers*. For example, Honda's most recent U.S. assembly

[14]Nanette Byrnes and Coleman Cowen, "The High Cost of Wooing Google," *Business Week*, July 23, 2007, 50–56.
[15]Beth Mattson-Teig, "Top Site Selection Factors: Highway Accessibility—the Need for Speed," *Area Development Online*, November 2011.
[16]James L. Heskett, Nicholas A. Glaskowsky, Jr., and Robert M. Ivie, *Business Logistics*, 2nd ed. (New York: Ronald Press), 1973, Chapter 12.

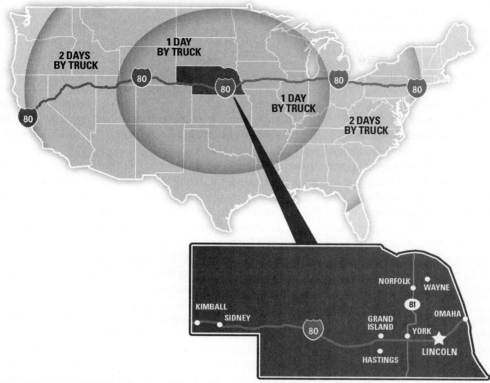

FIGURE 9.2 Truck Distances from Nebraska *Source:* Reprinted with permission from *Inbound Logistics* magazine (September 2011). www.inboundlogistics.com/subscribe. Copyright *Inbound Logistics* 2014.

plant, which opened in 2008, is located in Greensburg, Indiana, in large part because many of Honda's existing automotive suppliers are located within one-half day's transit time from the new facility. Proximity to key suppliers has been the catalyst in the development of **supplier parks**, a concept that developed around automakers and their suppliers in Europe and has spread to other continents, including North America. With supplier parks, key suppliers locate on, or adjacent to, automobile assembly plants, which helps to reduce shipping costs and inventory carrying costs.

Industry clusters can provide potential advantages to prospective participants in terms of facility and transportation considerations. With respect to facilities, the relative proximity of manufacturers in a particular cluster could allow for capacity pooling in the sense that a manufacturer with excess capacity could produce goods for a manufacturer with an excess of orders. From a transportation perspective, industry clusters could allow for faster and more consistent delivery, particularly with supplier parks where many suppliers are located a short distance from their customer(s). Inbound and outbound transportation costs could also be lower in industrial clusters; lower inbound transportation costs result from volume purchases of inbound goods while lower outbound transportation costs result from volume shipments of finished goods.[17]

Trade Patterns

As pointed out earlier in the chapter, firms producing consumer goods follow changes in population to better orient their distribution systems, and there are shifts in the markets for industrial

[17]Lifang Wu, Xiaohan Yue, and Thaddeus Sim, "Supply Clusters: A Key to China's Success," *Supply Chain Management Review* 10, no. 2 (2006): 46–51.

goods as well. General sources of data regarding *commodity flows* can be studied, much like population figures, to determine changes occurring in the movement of raw materials and semiprocessed goods. The availability and quality of such data often vary from country to country, and it may be difficult to compare data across countries because of different methodologies used to collect the data.

With respect to commodity flows, logisticians are especially interested in (1) how much is being produced and (2) where it is being shipped. If a firm is concerned with a distribution system for its industrial products, this information would tell how the market is functioning and, in many instances, how to identify both the manufacturers and their major customers. At this point, the researcher would understand the existing situation and would try to find a lower-cost production–distribution arrangement.

The development and implementation of multicountry trade agreements have generated profound impacts on trade patterns. For example, the United States, Canada, and Mexico are part of the North American Free Trade Agreement (NAFTA). Although Canada has long been the largest trading partner of the United States, since NAFTA's passage, Mexico has become the United States' third-largest trading partner. From a logistics perspective, this has increased the north–south movement of product, and the Interstate 35 corridor (which runs north–south between Mexico and Canada) has become a hotbed for distribution activity. Oklahoma City, Oklahoma, and Dallas, Texas, are two locations along Interstate 35 that have seen a dramatic increase in the construction of distribution facilities in recent years.

Trade patterns have also been influenced among those countries that are members of the European Union (EU). When the EU consisted of 15 countries, the central location and strong transportation infrastructures of the so-called Benelux countries (Belgium, the Netherlands, and Luxembourg) were a favored location for distribution facilities to serve EU countries, and many companies operated only one distribution facility to serve their EU customers. However, the EU's expansion into Central and Eastern European countries has substantially increased the EU's geographic footprint. The vast geographic territory of the expanded EU has caused many companies to operate one major distribution facility and several regional facilities to serve their EU customer base. In addition, as EU expansion has pushed eastward, Poland and the Czech Republic have become favorite distribution sites because of their relatively central geographic location.[18]

Quality-of-Life Considerations

An increasingly important locational factor is what can broadly be called **quality-of-life considerations.** Although it may be difficult to develop a standardized list of quality-of-life factors, their intent is to incorporate nonbusiness factors into the business decision of where to locate a plant or distribution facility. Examples of quality-of-life factors include cost of living, educational opportunities, crime rates, employment opportunities, the weather, and cultural amenities, among others.

There are a number of reasons for including quality-of-life considerations as a factor in facility location. For one, employees who are able to live a reasonable lifestyle tend to be happier and more loyal; happy and loyal employees are less likely to leave their jobs and less likely to offend prospective customers. Second, because many organizations now compete nationally and internationally for talent, less-than-desirable geographic locations might hinder the recruiting process. Quite simply, the quality of life in a region—is it a nice place to live?—impacts both employee retention and the ability to attract new employees.[19]

Locating in Other Countries

Quality-of-life considerations can be especially important when companies are thinking of facility locations in nondomestic countries, and one study indicated quality of life to be the most

---

[18]John W. McCurry, "Heading East," *Site Selection*, September–October 2008, 708–719.

[19]Dan Olson, "Six Keys to Plant Site Selection," *Industry Week*, September 2010, 22.

important factor that executives consider when asked to relocate outside their home country.[20] Besides quality-of-life considerations, many other factors are to be considered if a firm is looking for a plant, office, or distribution site outside its home country. Many of these considerations are governmental in nature and deal with the relevant legal system, political stability, bureaucratic red tape, corruption, protectionism, nationalism, privatization, and expropriation (confiscation), as well as treaties and trade agreements.

For example, the Middle East has been a hotbed of widespread political instability since late 2010; a short list of Middle Eastern countries impacted by political turmoil in recent years includes Egypt, Libya, Saudi Arabia, and Syria. One challenge of this political instability is that alternative systems of governance have been slow to emerge and this uncertainty is causing many organizations to delay, or even cancel, expansion into this region.

SPECIALIZED LOCATION CHARACTERISTICS

The preceding discussion focused on some of the more common general considerations in selecting the site of a manufacturing, distributing, or assembling facility. This section deals with more specialized, or site-specific, considerations that should be taken into account in the facility location decision. Most of these considerations are invisible boundaries that can be of great significance in the location decision.

Land may be zoned, which means that there are limits on how the land can be used. For example, a warehouse might be allowed only in areas set aside for wholesale or other specified commercial operations. Restrictions on manufacturing sites may be even more severe, especially if the operation might be viewed as an undesirable neighbor because of the fumes, noise, dust, smoke, or congestion it may create. Distribution facilities are often considered to be more desirable because the primary complaints tend to involve only traffic volume and congestion caused by the trucks that serve the facilities. If a community is attempting to encourage, or discourage, business activity, zoning classifications can be changed, although the process may be time consuming.

Union locals have areas of jurisdiction, and a firm's labor relations manager may have distinct preferences with which locals he or she is willing to deal. Even though an individual union may ratify national labor agreements, local supplemental agreements often reflect the unique characteristics of a particular area. The different supplemental agreements provide companies with differing levels of managerial flexibility (or inflexibility).

Once a precise site is under consideration, many other issues should be dealt with before beginning construction or operations. For example, a title search may be needed to make sure that a particular parcel of land can be sold and that there are no liens against it. Engineers should examine the site to ensure that it has proper drainage and to ascertain the load-bearing characteristics of the soil.

Environmental regulations may require that due diligence be carried out with respect to who previously owned a prospective site and how it was used. One key environmental issue in some economically developed countries involves the use of **brownfields**, or locations that contain chemicals or other types of industrial waste. Brownfields are an important locational issue because many are found in urban areas that are often desirable from a locational point of view. Brownfield developments in the United States continue to grow in popularity because of the emergence of environmental insurance as well as legislation that makes it easier and less costly to develop brownfield sites.[21]

Another specialized characteristic involves the weather, and location decisions can be influenced by the potential for tornadoes, floods, and hurricanes, among others. Unfortunately,

---

[20]Aparna Nancherla, "A New World of Development Potential," *T&D*, July 2010, 24.
[21]Kristin Gunderson Hunt, "Urban Squeeze Builds Fresh Interest in Developing Contaminated Land," *Business Insurance*, December 3, 2007, 23–24.

to date the twenty-first century has been characterized by tremendous weather extremes in the form of record drought, record precipitation, record temperatures, record hurricanes (cyclones), and record tornadoes, among others. One suggestion for dealing with these weather extremes is to hire experts to evaluate site-specific climate risks and the associated mitigation costs.[22]

Free Trade Zones

A highly specialized site in which to locate is a free trade zone, also known as *foreign trade zones, export processing zones*, or *special economic zones*. In a **free trade zone** nondomestic merchandise may be stored, exhibited, processed, or used in manufacturing operations without being subjected to duties and quotas until the goods or their products enter the customs territory of the zone country. Free trade zones have become extremely popular in recent years; as an example, India has approved over 575 new special economic zones since 2005.[23] Free trade zones are often located at, or near, water ports, although they can also be located at, or near, airports.

Free trade subzones refer to specific locations at an existing free trade zone—such as an individual company—where goods can be stored, exhibited, processed, or manufactured on a duty-free basis. There are over 500 free trade subzones in the United States, and they are particularly popular among automotive manufacturers. For example, 16 of the 19 subzones in Detroit, Michigan, involve automobile manufacturers.[24]

FINDING THE LOWEST-COST LOCATION

Many products are a combination of several material inputs and labor. Traditional site location theory can be used to show that one or several locations will minimize transportation costs. Figure 9.3 shows a laboratory-like piece of equipment that could be used to find the lowest-cost location, in terms of transportation, for assembling a product consisting of inputs from two sources and a market in a third area.

Although most solutions to locational problems currently involve computer analysis, such analysis may not be needed if the relevant parameters are not too complex. Thus, grid systems can be used to determine an optimal location (defined as the lowest cost) for one additional facility.

GRID SYSTEMS

Grid systems are important to locational analysis because they allow one to analyze spatial relationships with relatively simple mathematical tools. **Grid systems** are checkerboard patterns that are placed on a map, as in Figure 9.4, and the grid is numbered in two directions: horizontal and vertical. Recall from geometry that the length of the hypotenuse of a right triangle is the square root of the sum of the squared values of the right triangle's two legs. Grid systems are placed so that they coincide with north–south and east–west lines on a map (although minor distortion is caused by the fact that east–west lines are parallel, whereas north–south lines converge at both poles).

A **center-of-gravity approach** can be used for locating a single facility so that the distance to existing facilities is minimized. Figure 9.4 shows a grid system placed over a map of five existing retail stores. At issue is where a warehousing facility to serve these stores should be located. Assuming that each store receives the same volume and that straight-line distances are used, the best (lowest-cost) location for a warehousing facility to serve the five stores is determined by taking the average north–south coordinates and the average east–west coordinates of the retail stores.

---

[22]Wayne Labs, "Refining Location, Location, Location," *Food Engineering*, December 2011, 49–55.
[23]http://www.sezindia.nic.in/HTMLS/about.htm
[24]See www.foreign-trade-zone.com

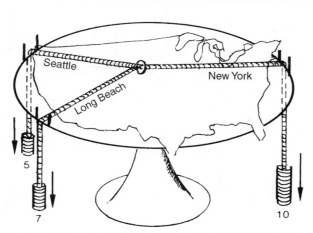

This is a simplified demonstration showing the various "pulls" which exist to determine the industrial location which minimizes the total ton miles of transportation used to transport both inputs and output. This method can be used for situations where there are "pulls" in three directions—either two sources of supply and one market, or one source of supply and two separate markets.

Assume we have two inputs, one produced in Long Beach and one produced in Seattle. The two inputs are combined to make a product which is sold in New York City. Assume further that to produce ten tons of the product consumed in New York, we must combine seven tons of the product which comes from Long Beach with five tons of the product which comes from Seattle. Assume finally that a transportation system is available anywhere and that the transport costs per ton mile are the same for either input or for the final product.

We take a circular table, placing a map of the U.S. on it and pairs of pegs on the table edge in the vicinity of Long Beach, Seattle, and New York as they are on the tabletop map. The pairs of pegs are so that a piece of string can pass between them.

We knot together three pieces of string, with all of them ending in one knot. To one of the pieces of string, which we pass through the pegs near Seattle on our map, we attach five identical metal washers (each one representing one ton). We attach seven washers to a second piece of string and pass it through the pegs in the vicinity of Long Beach on our tabletop map. To the third piece of string we attach ten washers and place it through the pegs in the vicinity of New York.

Then we take the knot and gently lift it to a point above the center of the table, with the washers on all three strings pulling down. We then drop the knot and it comes to rest at the spot on the map which represents the point in the U.S. where the manufacturing operation (for combining these two inputs into the single product) should locate. No other point will require less transportation effort—measured in ton-miles of freight moved.

(If transportation costs, or rates, differ on a per ton mile for each of the commodities or products involved, this can be taken into account by having the number of washers "weighted" to take into account the varying rates as well as the differences in weight being shippped. If for example in the situation described above carriers charged twice as much per ton mile to carry the finished product as they charged for carrying inputs, one would attach 20 washers (2×10) on the string reaching toward New York.)

Adapted from: Alfred Weber, *Theory of the Location of Industries,* translated by Carl J. Friedrich (Chicago: Univ. of Chicago Press, 1929).

FIGURE 9.3 Example of Transportation Forces Dictating Plant Location *Source:* Adapted from Alfred Weber, *Theory of the Location of Industries,* translated by Carl J. Friedrich (Chicago: Univ. of Chicago Press, 1929).

In Figure 9.4, the grid system has its lower left (southwest) corner labeled as point zero, zero (0,0). The vertical (north–south) axis shows distances north of point 0,0. The horizontal (east–west) axis shows distances to the east. In this example, the average distance north is $(3 + 1 + 3 + 2 + 3)$ or 12. This figure is divided by the number of stores (5), resulting in a north location of 12/5 or 2.4 miles. The average distance east is $(1 + 2 + 3 + 4 + 6)$ or 16; 16 divided

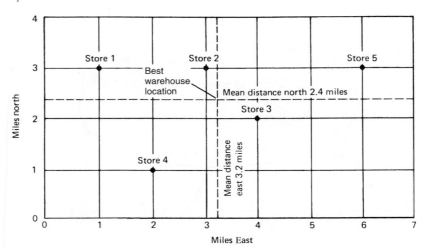

FIGURE 9.4 Center-of-Gravity Location for a Warehouse Serving Five Retail Stores

by 5 equals 3.2 miles. Thus, the best (lowest-cost) location is one with coordinates 2.4 miles north and 3.2 miles east of point zero.

Because it's not likely that each store will place equal demands on a prospective warehousing facility, the center-of-gravity approach can be easily modified to take volume into account— the *weighted center-of-gravity approach.* The idea behind the weighted center-of-gravity approach is that a prospective warehousing facility will be located closer to the existing sites with the greatest current demand.

To illustrate the weighted center-of-gravity approach, consider the preceding five-store example, but modify the assumption that each store receives the same volume. Assume that store 1 receives 3 tons of shipments per month, store 2 receives 5 tons, store 3 receives 4 tons, store 4 receives 2 tons, and store 5 receives 6 tons. To calculate the north weighted center-of-gravity location, each north coordinate is multiplied by the corresponding volume, and these values are summed; this total is then divided by the sum of the monthly volume. This procedure is repeated to calculate the east weighted center-of-gravity location.

The new data (see Table 9.2) indicate that the monthly volume for the five locations is 20 tons $(3 + 5 + 4 + 2 + 6)$ and that the weighted center-of-gravity location is 2.6 miles north and 3.7 miles east. Thus, the weighted approach locates a warehousing facility slightly more north and more east than what was determined in the basic center-of-gravity approach (2.4 miles north; 3.2 miles east).

The two approaches just described are relatively simple and straightforward, and the calculations can be done relatively quickly to provide approximate locations of centralized facilities,

| Table 9.2 | | Weighted Center-of-Gravity Example | | | |
Store	North Location	East Location	Monthly Volume (tons)	North × Volume	East × Volume
1	3	1	3	$(3 \times 3) = 9$	$(1 \times 3) = 3$
2	3	3	5	$(3 \times 5) = 15$	$(3 \times 5) = 15$
3	2	4	4	$(2 \times 4) = 8$	$(4 \times 4) = 16$
4	1	2	2	$(1 \times 2) = 2$	$(2 \times 2) = 4$
5	3	6	6	$(3 \times 6) = 18$	$(6 \times 6) = 36$
Total			20	52	74
Weighted average				2.6	3.7

at least in a transportation sense. Because neither the center-of-gravity nor the weighted center-of-gravity approach is very sophisticated, adjustments may have to be made to take into account real-world considerations such as taxes, wage rates in particular locations, volume discounts, the cost and quality of transport services, and the fact that transport rates taper with increased distances. These considerations increase the complexity, as well as the time, to do the necessary calculations and partially explain why some companies have turned to specialized software packages to help them with facility location decisions.

FACILITY RELOCATION AND FACILITY CLOSING

Two specialized situations conclude this discussion of location choice, one involving facility relocation (associated with business growth) and the other involving facility closing (associated with business contraction). More specifically, **facility relocation** occurs when a firm decides that it can no longer continue operations in its present facility and must move operations to another facility to better serve suppliers or customers. **Facility closing**, by contrast, occurs when a company decides to discontinue operations at a current site because the operations may no longer be needed or can be absorbed by other facilities.

A common reason for facility relocation involves a lack of room for expansion at a current site, often because of a substantial increase in business. In the United States, this has involved the relocation of industrial plants and warehousing facilities from aging and congested central cities to more attractive sites in suburban locations. Land costs and congestion in the central cities often make expansion difficult (or impossible), and transportation companies generally prefer the suburban sites because there is less traffic congestion to disrupt pickups and deliveries.

In theory, the relocation decision involves a comparison of the advantages and disadvantages of a new site to the advantages and disadvantages of an existing location. Although this inevitably involves quantitative comparisons, companies should also consider the potential consequences of relocation on their human resources—consequences that may not be easily quantified.

For example, plant relocations inevitably result in a plethora of employee-related questions, including the following: How many current employees will be offered positions at the new facility? Will the company use years of service, employee productivity, or other factors to decide who gets offered positions at the new facility? What happens to employee seniority? What percentage, if any, of relocation expenses will be paid by the employer? Will older employees be offered incentives to retire rather than relocate? Will employees who decide not to relocate be offered severance benefits?

Employers should keep current employees informed of planned relocations and how such relocations might affect them. Relocation information from other sources could lead to confusion, anger, and lower morale and could easily affect the productivity of the existing facility at a time when hiring replacements is likely to be very difficult. It's also important for employers to be cognizant of relevant legislation at the federal and state levels. For example, U.S. federal legislation in the form of the Worker Adjustment and Retraining Notification (WARN) Act mandates that employers give 60 days' notice about plant closings and mass layoffs. Many individual states have additional requirements concerning large-scale employee layoffs.

Companies should also recognize that, no matter how well planned beforehand, a relocation from one facility to another is rarely trouble free; at a minimum, relocation glitches can add to logistics costs and detract from customer service. For example, transferring equipment, furniture, and supplies from an old facility to a new one may take longer than expected. Also, a newly constructed plant or warehousing facility is likely to have flaws or shortcomings that are only discovered after occupancy.

Facility closings can occur for various reasons, such as eliminating redundant capacity in mergers and acquisitions, improving supply chain efficiency, poor planning, or an insufficient volume of business. Whatever the reason(s), it is imperative for an organization to clearly specify why a plant is being closed. As an example, Nestlé announced the closing of a coffee plant

the United States, Europe, the Far East, and the ⋯ freight and ensures the timely movement of cargo in Haves (a London suburb) by 2014 and the transfer of production elsewhere in the United

10 | WAREHOUSING MANAGEMENT

KEY TERMS

- Accumulating (bulk making)
- Allocating (bulk breaking)
- Assorting
- Contract (third-party) warehousing
- Cross-docking
- Distribution center
- Dunnage

- Fixed slot location
- Hazardous material(s)
- Multiclient warehousing
- Occupational Safety and Health Administration (OSHA)
- Private warehousing
- Public warehousing

- Regrouping function
- Sorting out
- Throughput
- Variable slot location
- Warehouse
- Warehouse automation
- Warehousing

LEARNING OBJECTIVES

- To discuss the role of warehousing in a logistics system
- To learn about public, private, contract, and multiclient warehousing

- To analyze select considerations when designing warehousing facilities
- To examine some prominent operational issues in warehousing

---

A recurring theme in previous chapters has been the changing nature of the logistics discipline and the individual functions that comprise it. In the systems approach of logistics, changes to one function affect other functions as well. Indeed, many of the changes described in previous chapters—such as electronic ordering, facility consolidation, and lean inventories—have especially affected warehousing management.

Many well-run companies today view warehousing as a strategic consideration—and thus a potential source of competitive advantage. For example, the continuing growth of e-commerce is causing some companies to shift away from warehousing's traditional cost focus to an emphasis on customer satisfaction in terms of rapid, and correct, order fulfillment.[1]

This chapter begins with an overview that defines what is meant by warehousing and discusses the role of warehousing in a logistics system. This is followed by analysis of public, private, contract, and multiclient warehousing. Next comes a section devoted to design considerations in warehousing, with particular attention to trade-offs in design considerations. The chapter concludes with an examination of some key operational issues in warehousing, such as productivity, safety, and security.

---

[1]Mary Shacklett, "The 21st Century Warehouse," *World Trade*, March 2011, 18–25.

THE ROLE OF WAREHOUSING IN A LOGISTICS SYSTEM

Warehousing, which refers to "that part of a firm's logistics system that stores products (raw materials, parts, goods-in-process, finished goods) at and between points of origin and point of consumption,"[2] and transportation are substitutes for each other, with warehousing having been referred to as "transportation at zero miles per hour." Figure 10.1, which presents an example of the trade-off between warehousing and transportation, indicates that placing a warehousing facility between the producer and customers adds a new layer of costs (those associated with warehousing) into the system. Moreover, the warehousing facility generates shorter-haul transportation routes (from the producer to the facility; from the facility to the customers); as a general rule, short-haul transportation tends to be more costly per mile than long-haul transportation. However, the increased costs of short-haul transportation may be offset by lower transportation costs per unit of weight associated with volume shipments.

If the introduction of warehousing into a supply chain simply shifts business costs across various logistics activities, then why is warehousing desirable? A key reason for warehousing is because patterns of production and consumption do not coincide, and warehousing serves to match different rates or volumes of flow. Canned fruits and vegetables are examples of one extreme in which production occurs during a relatively short period, but sales are spread throughout the year. The other extreme—sales concentrated in a relatively short time period, steady production rates throughout the year—is more likely to be addressed by having the production occur closer to the demand period.

Sometimes, larger quantities of goods are purchased than can be consumed in a short period of time, and warehousing space is needed to store the surplus product. This can occur for several reasons, such as guarding against anticipated scarcity or to benefit from a seller's advantageously priced deal.

Much of the preceding discussion could be viewed as a market-oriented approach to warehousing. However, warehousing management can also be relevant to production and raw materials considerations. For example, an automobile manufacturer might purchase extra amounts of steel in response to anticipated steel shortages.

Moreover, warehousing facilitates the **regrouping function** in a supply chain. This function involves rearranging the quantities and assortment of products as they move through the

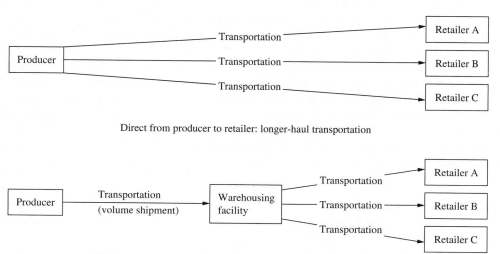

Direct from producer to retailer: longer-haul transportation

FIGURE 10.1 Adding a Warehousing Facility: Shorter-Haul Transportation

[2]Douglas M. Lambert, James R. Stock, and Lisa M. Ellram, *Fundamentals of Logistics Management* (New York: Irwin McGraw-Hill, 1998), Chapter 8.

supply chain and can take four forms—accumulating (also referred to as bulk making), allocating (also referred to as bulk breaking), assorting, and sorting out. Accumulating and allocating refer to adjustments associated with the *quantity of product*, whereas assorting and sorting out refer to adjustments associated with *product assortment*.

Thus, **accumulating** involves bringing together similar stocks from different sources, as might be done by a department store that buys large quantities of men's suits from several different producers. **Allocating**, by contrast, involves breaking larger quantities into smaller quantities; continuing with our suit example, whereas the department store might buy 5,000 suits in size 42 short, an individual store might only carry 15 or 20 suits in this size.

Assorting refers to building up a variety of different products for resale to particular customers; our department store example might want to supply individual stores with a number of different suit sizes (e.g., size 36, size 38, and size 40) and styles (e.g., two-button suits and three-button suits). **Sorting out** refers to "separating products into grades and qualities desired by different target markets."[3] For example, a department store chain may sell $1,000 men's suits only in stores located in high-income areas, whereas $600 men's suits might be the highest priced suit sold in less-affluent areas.

Warehousing can be provided by warehouses, distribution centers, or cross-docking facilities. **Warehouses** emphasize the storage of products, and their primary purpose is to maximize the usage of available storage space. **Distribution centers** emphasize the rapid movement of products through a facility, and thus they attempt to maximize **throughput** (the amount of product entering and leaving a facility in a given time period).

The increased emphasis on time reduction in supply chains has led to the growth of **cross-docking**, which can be defined as "the process of receiving product and shipping it out the same day or overnight without putting it into storage."[4] Indeed, the length of time a product is in a facility is one factor that differentiates distribution centers and cross-docks, with 24 hours (or less) of storage time increasingly being used to differentiate a cross-dock facility from a distribution center. Key benefits to cross-docking include improved service by allowing products to reach their destinations more quickly as well as reduced inventory carrying costs from less safety stock because of faster product delivery.[5]

The experiences of Saks Inc., an upscale retail department store, illustrate some of the potential benefits from cross-docking. For example, it takes just *seven minutes* to move a carton from the inbound dock to an outbound trailer at the Saks cross-dock facility. Moreover, on a daily basis the Saks cross-dock can handle four times as much product, with one-half the labor, of its predecessor facility; in other words, the cross-dock facility is approximately *eight times* as productive as its predecessor.[6]

Because cross-docking is predicated on time reduction, the design of cross-dock facilities is an important consideration. More specifically, cross-docks emphasize extremely rapid product movement, and they should be designed with a minimal amount of storage space and truck doors on two or more sides.[7] Figure 10.2 shows an "I-shaped" cross-dock design—rectangular, long, and as narrow as possible.[8] Other possible cross-dock designs include "H," "L," "T," "U," and "E," and their applicability depends on the spatial configuration of the land used to build the cross-dock as well as the number of docks to be used.[9]

---

[3]William D. Perreault, Jr., Joseph P. Cannon, and E. Jerome McCarthy, *Basic Marketing,* 16th ed. (New York: McGraw-Hill Irwin, 2008), Chapter 11.

[4]No author, "2008 Cross-Docking Trends Report," Saddle Creek Corporation, 2008.

[5]Mike DelBoro, "Cross-Docking Rediscovered," *Material Handling & Logistics,* May 2011, 34–37.

[6]Connie Robbins Gentry, "Distribution Utopia," *Chain Store Age,* November 2005, 70–72.

[7]DelBoro, "Cross-Docking Rediscovered."

[8]Maida Napolitano, *Making the Move to Cross-Docking* (Oak Brook, IL: Warehousing Education and Research Council, 2000).

[9]Jan Van Boelle, Paul Valckenaers, and Dirk Cattrysse, "Cross-Docking: State of the Art," *Omega* 40, no. 6 (2012): 827–846.

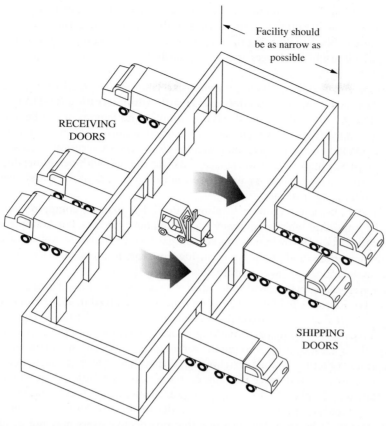

Facility should
be as narrow as
possible

RECEIVING
DOORS

SHIPPING
DOORS

FIGURE 10.2 Ideal Facility for Pure Supplier Consolidation (Full Pallet Movement) *Source:* Reprinted by permission of the Warehousing Education and Research Council.

PUBLIC, PRIVATE, CONTRACT, AND MULTICLIENT WAREHOUSING

In addition to understanding the distinctions among warehouses, distribution centers, and cross-dock facilities, organizations must decide the proper mix in terms of owning (private warehousing) or renting (public, contract, multiclient warehousing) warehousing space. Because companies have different strategies, goals, and objectives, there is no correct mix of owning or renting. Thus, one organization might only use public warehousing, another organization might use only private warehousing, and a third organization might use a mix of public, private, contract, and multiclient warehousing. Each has distinct characteristics that might be either attractive or unattractive to potential users and these characteristics are discussed in the following sections.

Public Warehousing

Public warehousing serves (is supposed to serve) all legitimate users and has certain responsibilities to those users. Public warehousing requires no capital investment on the user's part, which can certainly be an important consideration when the cost of borrowing money (interest rates) is high. With public warehousing, the user rents space as needed, thus avoiding the costs of unneeded space. A related advantage is that users should have a fairly exact determination of their warehousing costs since public warehousing space tends to be rented on a month-to-month basis.

Public warehousing can also be attractive to prospective users because other parties have responsibilities for personnel decisions and regulatory issues. As pointed out in Chapter 4, warehousing is one of two major sources of labor in logistics (the other is transportation), and warehousing employees are often unionized, thus adding to the managerial challenges. At a minimum, when using public warehousing the recruitment, selection, compensation, motivation, and evaluation of warehousing employees are the responsibility of the warehousing company and not the customer (user).

With respect to regulatory issues, warehousing labor safety practices in the United States are monitored by the **Occupational Safety and Health Administration (OSHA)**. From a managerial perspective, because OSHA standards are complex and lengthy, it can be quite costly and challenging to comply with OSHA regulations. It is worth pointing out that in recent years warehousing in the United States has been subjected to closer OSHA scrutiny because warehousing has been classified as a high-hazard workplace.[10] As was the case with personnel decisions, when using public warehousing regulatory issues are the responsibility of the warehousing provider and not the warehousing customer.

Public warehousing offers more locational flexibility than do company-owned facilities, and this can be important when a company is entering new markets. For example, an organization may want to start off slowly in new markets or may be uncertain how well its products will be received in these markets, and public warehousing can provide storage services in these markets without an overwhelming capital commitment.

Public warehousing may provide a number of specialized services that aren't available from other sources. For example, public warehousing is heavily involved in such value-added services as repackaging larger shipments into retail-size quantities and then shrink-wrapping them, assisting in product recalls, and doing price marking, product assembly, and product testing.

Perhaps the biggest drawback to public warehousing is the potential lack of control by the user. For example, sometimes public warehousing doesn't have the space availability required by a particular user. And even if space is available, users may have little say in where their goods are stored—they may be placed wherever space is available, which may result in part of a user's inventory being stored in one area and the remainder in another. Moreover, some public warehousing is not open 24 hours a day, meaning that prospective users may not be able to access their products as needed or that users may need to tailor their operations to fit those of the public warehouse.

Private Warehousing

Private warehousing is owned by the firm storing goods in the facility; private warehousing generates high fixed costs and thus should only be considered by companies dealing with large volumes of inventory. In so doing, the high fixed costs can be spread out over more units of inventory, thus reducing the cost per unit of storage. The largest users of private warehousing are retail chain stores; they handle large volumes of merchandise on a regular basis.

In addition to large volumes, private warehousing also tends to be feasible when demand patterns are relatively stable. Fluctuating demand patterns could at times lead to insufficient storage space for product, in which case the company might need to use public warehousing as a supplement, thus increasing total warehousing costs. At other times, by contrast, there could be too much space (excess capacity), which costs money as well.

Assuming both sufficient demand volume and stability of demand, private warehousing offers potential users a great deal of control over their storage needs. For example, the storage facility can be constructed to the user's specifications, which is a particularly attractive feature when a company has unique storage or handling requirements, as is the case with steel beams and gasoline. Moreover, in private warehousing, companies can control product placement

---

[10]No author, "OSHA Announces FY 2010 Inspection Plan to Target Industries with High Injury Rates," *HR Focus*, December 2010, 11.

within a facility; some products, for instance, should not be stored on the floor. Another aspect of control is that private warehousing offers access to products when an organization needs (or wants) them, as opposed to an organization having to tailor its activities to match a public facility's operating hours.

Private warehousing is also characterized by several important drawbacks, including the high fixed cost of private storage and the necessity of having high and steady demand volumes. In addition, a high-fixed-cost alternative such as private warehousing becomes less attractive in times of high interest rates because it is more costly to secure the necessary financing to build or lease the facility (to be fair, interest rates in some nations, such as the United States, have been relatively low in recent years).

Private warehousing may also reduce an organization's flexibility in responding to changes in the external environment. For example, companies that utilize private warehousing are susceptible to changing demand patterns, such as those experienced with the passage of multicountry trade alliances. Likewise, organizational flexibility can be affected by mergers with, or acquisitions of, other companies, as illustrated by the case of a multibillion-dollar company that acquired a competitor's production and private warehousing facilities. Although the production facilities added much-needed manufacturing capacity, the warehousing facilities were largely redundant in nature. Yet the acquiring company had little choice but to continue operating them because of substantial penalties (e.g., labor compensation) that would have been incurred if the facilities were closed.

Contract Warehousing

Organizations historically had two choices with respect to renting or owning warehousing facilities—public (renting) and private (owning). In the early 1990s, contract warehousing (also referred to as *third-party warehousing* or *dedicated warehousing*) emerged as a second option for renting warehousing space. Although **contract warehousing** has been defined in a number of different ways, in this text it refers to "a long term, mutually beneficial arrangement which provides unique and specially tailored warehousing and logistics services exclusively to one client, where the vendor and client share the risks associated with the operation."[11]

Contract warehousing expenditures in the United States are more than $25 billion annually and are expected to grow between 2 percent and 4 percent annually over the next few years, with this growth coming largely at the expense of public warehousing. More specifically, contract warehousing has embraced value-adding activities such as customization, reverse logistics, and repair and refurbishment to a greater degree than has public warehousing.[12] From a cost perspective, contract warehousing tends to be less costly than private warehousing but more costly than public warehousing.

Contract warehousing is a preferred alternative for many organizations because it simultaneously mitigates the negative aspects and accentuates the positive aspects of public and private warehousing. More specifically, contract warehousing allows a company to focus on its core competencies (what it does best), with warehousing management provided by experts—experts who solely focus on the client's needs and wants.[13] In addition, contract warehousing potentially offers the same degree of control as private warehousing because key specifications can be included in the contract. For example, if a certain product should not be stored on the floor, then this can be explicitly reflected in the particular contract.

With respect to changes in the external environment, contract warehousing is viewed as more flexible than private warehousing but less so than public warehousing. This flexibility

---

[11]Warehousing Education and Research Council, *Contract Warehousing: How It Works and How to Make It Work Effectively* (Oak Brook, IL: Author, 1993).
[12]William Hoffman, "Contract Warehousing Evolves," *Traffic World,* January 31, 2005, 16.
[13]John R. Johnson, "Bigger and Better," *Warehousing Management,* October 2000, 22–25.

depends in part on the length of the contract; as the contract length increases, the flexibility to respond to change decreases. Three- to five-year contracts appear to allow sufficient time for the warehousing provider to learn the client's business while allowing clients some flexibility in case the agreement fails to produce acceptable results.

Multiclient Warehousing

Another warehousing alternative, **multiclient warehousing**, which mixes attributes of contract and public warehousing, has become popular in the first part of the twenty-first century. For example, where contract warehousing is generally dedicated to just one customer and public warehousing may be used by any number of customers, a limited number of customers (at least two, but generally no more than one dozen) utilize a multiclient facility. In a similar fashion, the services in a multiclient facility are more differentiated than those in a public facility, but less customized than would be found in contract warehousing.

Furthermore, where public warehousing services are purchased on a month-to-month basis, multiclient warehousing services are purchased through contracts that cover at least one year. Multiclient facilities are particularly attractive to smaller organizations that don't have sufficient volumes to (1) build their own storage facilities or (2) use traditional one client contract warehousing services.[14] While we view multiclient warehousing as a distinct type of warehousing, some warehousing providers view "multiclient warehousing" as a synonym for "public warehousing."

DESIGN CONSIDERATIONS IN WAREHOUSING

General Considerations

One of the best pieces of advice with respect to the design of warehousing facilities is to use common sense, as illustrated by the businessperson who was convinced that warehouses were bland, boring, and visually unappealing. He decided to build a more aesthetically pleasing facility and designed a warehouse with black floors, reasoning that black floors would stand out compared to the floors in many other warehouses.

Although the black floor was certainly eye-catching, it was an unmitigated disaster in part because the floor showed more dirt than comparable facilities. Moreover, the black floor was extremely slippery—meaning that forklifts had a harder time stopping (some actually crashed into the walls!), and warehouse workers were more prone to falling. This anecdote provides an excellent example of form triumphing over function or style triumphing over substance. From a commonsense perspective, the primary design consideration should be the facility's function—be it long-term storage or product movement—in the relevant logistics system, with aesthetics a secondary consideration.

One commonsense piece of advice is that prior to designing a warehousing facility, the quantity and character of goods to be handled must be known. Indeed, one of the early challenges of online commerce for bricks-and-mortar organizations was that many of them attempted to fulfill online orders through warehousing facilities largely designed to supply retail store locations. Online orders tend to be much smaller than those going to retail stores; as a consequence, picking and assembling an order for one or two items is much different from picking and assembling an order for a pallet load of items.

A second commonsense piece of design advice is that it's important for an organization to know the purpose to be served by a particular facility because the relative emphasis placed on the storage and distribution functions affects space layout. As such, a storage facility with low rates of product turnover should be laid out in a manner that maximizes utilization of the cubic

---

[14]William Hoffman, "Dividing the Box," *Journal of Commerce*, February 25, 2008, 23.

capacity of the storage facility. Alternatively, a facility that emphasizes rapid product movement with limited time in storage should be configured to facilitate the flow of product into and out of it.

Trade-offs

Trade-offs must be made among space, labor, and mechanization with respect to warehousing design. Spaciousness may not always be advantageous because the distances that an individual or machine must travel in the storing and retrieving functions are increased. Moreover, unused space is excess capacity, and we know that excess capacity costs money. Alternatively, cramped conditions can lead to such inefficiencies as the product damage that can be caused by forklift puncture and movement bottlenecks caused by insufficient aisle width, to name but two.

Before layout plans are made, each item that will be handled should be studied in terms of its specific physical handling properties, the volume and regularity of movement, the frequency with which it is picked, and whether it is fast or slow moving compared to other items. For example, one frequently cited suggestion is to place fast-moving items close to pick locations, such as a conveyor, so as to reduce a picker's travel time.

Many trade-offs are inevitable when designing the structure as well as the arrangement of the relevant storage and handling equipment. Several of these trade-offs are discussed in this section, and these trade-offs are often more complex than they appear because individual trade-offs are not independent from one another. Although there may not be "right" or "wrong" answers with respect to warehousing design, an understanding of the various trade-offs might help managers make more efficient, as opposed to less efficient, decisions.

Fixed versus Variable Slot Locations for Merchandise

You might remember from Chapter 7 that order picking and assembly represents the best opportunity to improve the effectiveness and efficiency of the order cycle. One possible way to improve the effectiveness and efficiency of order picking and assembly involves figuring out where to store (slot) product in a warehouse or distribution center. A well-thought-out slotting plan can reduce labor costs, increase pick and replenishment efficiencies, and increase order accuracy.[15] To this end, organizations need to understand the attributes of fixed and variable slot locations for merchandise.

With a **fixed slot location**, each SKU has one or more permanent slots assigned to it (think of a parking garage that assigns particular parking spaces to certain individuals). This can provide stability in order picking in the sense that the company should always know where a specific SKU is located. However, this may result in low space utilization, particularly with seasonal products.

Alternatively, a **variable slot location** involves empty storage slots being assigned to incoming products based on space availability. One example of variable slot location is the closest available storage position, with "closest" defined as the shortest travel time to an entrance or exit point. Although variable slot location generally results in more efficient space utilization, from an order picking perspective it requires a near-perfect information system because there must be flawless knowledge of each product's location.

Build Out (Horizontal) versus Build Up (Vertical)

A general rule of thumb is that it's cheaper to build up than build out; building out requires more land, which can be quite expensive, particularly in certain geographic locations. Alternatively, although building costs decline on a cubic-foot basis as one builds higher, warehousing equipment costs tend to increase. Moreover, the build up versus build out issue illustrates the importance of understanding interfunctional trade-offs when thinking about warehousing design. For

---

[15]Paul Hansen and Kelvin Gibson, "Effective Warehouse Slotting," *The National Provisioner*, May 2008, 90, 92, 94.

example, the Midlands section of Britain, located between London and Birmingham, is a popular site for distribution centers—there is available land for development, and the land is reasonably priced. Having said this, Midlands' locational popularity is dependent on a highway system offering speedy, reliable, and cost-efficient transportation service.[16]

Order-Picking versus Stock-Replenishing Functions

Organizations must decide whether workers who pick outgoing orders and those who are restocking storage facilities should work at the same time or in the same area. Although the latter scenario may result in fewer managerial personnel being needed, it may also lead to congestion within the facility due to the number of workers. One suggestion to reduce congestion is for order pickers and stock replenishers to use different aisles for their respective activities; again, this requires a very good information system to identify where a given employee is at any time.

Two-Dock versus Single-Dock Layout

A two-dock layout generally has receiving docks on one side of a facility and shipping docks on the other side, with goods moving between them. In a one-dock system, each and every dock can be used for both shipping and receiving, typically receiving product at one time of the day and shipping it at another time. Viewed from overhead, the goods move in a u-shaped rather than a straight configuration. This alternative reduces the space needed for storage docks, but it requires carriers to pick up and deliver at specific times. In addition, this alternative may also result in an occasional mix-up in that received product is sometimes reloaded into the vehicle that delivered it.

Conventional, Narrow, or Very Narrow Aisles

Aisle width might seem like an arcane issue until you realize that as aisle space increases, the storage capacity of a facility decreases. For example, narrow aisles (defined as between 9.5 feet and 12 feet wide) can store 20 percent to 25 percent more product than conventional aisles (more than 12 feet wide), while very narrow aisles (defined as less than 8 feet) can store 40 percent to 50 percent more product than conventional aisles.[17] However, it is easier to operate mechanical equipment in wider aisles, and wider aisles reduce the chances of accidents and product damage.

Narrower aisles require specialized storage and handling equipment, such as narrow aisle forklifts, that are capable of simultaneously moving both vertically and horizontally, and which are more expensive to buy or lease than are conventional forklifts. Moreover, in many cases, very narrow aisle machines are custom made for specific situations, so they are not only quite expensive to purchase, but they also have limited, if any, resale value.[18]

Degree of Warehouse Automation

The degree of automation is another important consideration in warehousing design, and for our purposes **warehouse automation** will refer to utilizing mechanical or electronic devices to substitute for human labor. Examples of warehouse automation include narrow aisle forklifts, automated guided vehicles, automated storage and retrieval systems, and radio frequency identification, among others. Although warehouse automation offers the potential

---

[16]Stan Luxenberg, "Warehouses for Warsaw," *NREI,* October 2004, 28–30.

[17]Mary Aichlmayr, "Narrow-Aisle: Form Follows Lift-Truck Function," *Material Handling Management,* June 2009, 18–20.

[18]Malory Davies, "Time to Be Narrow-Minded," *Logistics Manager,* April 2009, 20–24.

to reduce labor costs and to improve warehouse productivity, it's important for managers to ensure that the automation results in noticeable improvement in warehousing effectiveness and efficiency. With respect to effectiveness, organizations should delineate the key benefits associated with automation and then evaluate whether any of the benefits could be achieved without automation (e.g., working smarter on particular tasks). As for efficiency, organizations must look beyond just the initial automated-related investment costs and factor in other expenditures, such as operating, repair, and maintenance costs as well as relevant personnel and management costs.[19]

Other Space Needs

Although many would assume that the primary role of warehousing involves the storage of product, one estimate suggests that only approximately *10 percent* of a facility's cubic capacity is actually occupied by product.[20] Because every warehousing facility sets aside areas for nonstorage activities, it's important to know about them. These nonstorage activities include, but are not limited to, the following:

1. An area where transport drivers and operators can wait while their equipment is loaded or unloaded
2. Staging, or temporary storage, areas for both incoming and outgoing merchandise
3. Employee washrooms, lunchrooms, and the like
4. Pallet storage and repair facilities (Facilities that receive unpalletized materials but ship on pallets may require a pallet-assembly operation.)
5. Office space, including an area for the necessary computer systems
6. An area designed to store damaged merchandise that is awaiting inspection by claim representatives
7. An area to salvage or repair damaged merchandise
8. An area for repacking, labeling, price marking, and so on
9. An area for accumulating and baling waste and scrap
10. An area for equipment storage and maintenance (For example, battery-powered lift trucks need to be recharged on a regular basis.)
11. Specialized storage for hazardous items, high-value items, warehousing supplies, or items needing other specialized handling (such as a freezer or refrigerated space)
12. A returned or recycled goods processing area

When designing warehousing facilities, it's also important to keep in mind external space-related needs, which unfortunately are sometimes overlooked. These include areas for vehicles waiting to be loaded and unloaded, space for vehicle maneuvering (e.g., turning, backing up), and employee parking.

WAREHOUSING OPERATIONS

Because operating a warehousing facility has many facets, efficient and effective warehousing management can be an exacting task. Workforce motivation can be difficult because of the somewhat repetitive nature of the work. It can also be strenuous and physically demanding, and on occasion warehousing facilities can be dangerous places. Some of the more prominent operational issues are discussed in the following sections.

---

[19]Sam Flanders, "6 Questions to Ask Before You Consider Distribution Center Automation," *Multichannel Merchant Executive Insight*, January 18, 2012, 2.
[20]No author, "Warehouses Must Balance Space and Time," *Modern Materials Handling*, June 2006, 21.

Warehousing Productivity Analysis

Recall from Chapter 4 that productivity is a measure of output divided by input, and although a number of different productivity metrics can be used to assess warehousing productivity, not all are relevant to all kinds of facilities. Representative measures of warehousing productivity include cases shipped per person, product lines shipped per person, pallets shipped per person, average warehouse capacity used, and forklift capacity used, among others. These and other productivity metrics can be utilized to provide comparisons within an organization through time.

In addition, external data may be available that can be used for benchmarking purposes depending on the relevant metrics being analyzed. Suppose, for example, that the cases picked and shipped per hour at a particular warehouse increased from 72 to 84 over a two-year period. Although this represents a 16.7 percent ([84–72]/72) productivity improvement over the two years, the 84 cases per hour might be viewed much differently when compared to recent warehousing industry data that show a median of 100 cases picked and shipped per hour and a best practice metric of more than 250 cases picked and shipped per hour.[21]

It's important to recognize that increases in warehousing productivity do not always require significant investment in technology or mechanized or automated equipment. For example, one suggestion for improving warehousing productivity involves a review of existing procedures and practices to identify the tasks that are creating the largest inefficiencies and then developing methods to reduce or eliminate the inefficiencies without adding to or upgrading present technology or equipment. Organizations can also examine their facility layouts; long horizontal runs and frequent backtracking could be symptoms of layout problems. Something as basic as adding cross aisles could reduce the length of horizontal runs as well as the length of backtracking. Another low-cost suggestion for improving warehousing productivity is to play music, if conditions permit; research suggests that worker productivity increases when music is playing.[22]

Safety Considerations

Warehouses, distribution centers, and cross-docking facilities can be dangerous places to work; in the United States, for example, the fatality rate in warehousing is higher than the average rate for all industries.[23] Figure 10.3 provides a listing of workplace safety issues, and many of these safety issues, such as falls and bodily reaction, are associated with warehousing facilities. You should recognize that many suggestions for dealing with warehousing safety are common sense—and low cost—in nature. Consider, for example, several of the Occupational Safety and Health Administration's (OSHA) suggestions to improve warehouse safety: "prohibit 'dock jumping' (jumping from dock plate to dock plate) by employees;" "prohibit stunt driving (of forklifts) and horseplay;" "keep floors clean and free of slip and trip hazards."[24]

Warehousing safety can be influenced by governmental regulations and in the United States, safety standards have been set for warehousing equipment and operations, and OSHA inspectors make frequent visits to industrial workplaces to ensure regulatory compliance. Forklift operations and equipment have received particular attention from OSHA in part because of the number of deaths and injuries associated with them. For example, only trained and certified warehousing employees are permitted to operate a forklift, and forklift operators must be recertified every three years.

---

[21]Karl B. Manrodt and Kate L. Vitasek, "DC Measures 2012," *WERC Watch,* Spring 2012.
[22]John Tufts, "9 Tips for Improving Warehouse Productivity," *Multichannel Merchant Executive Insight*, March 6, 2012, 1.
[23]Tommie Jones, "Warehousing & Storage Safety: Establishing a Comprehensive Safety Approach," *Professional Safety*, June 2010, 34–36.
[24]www.osha.gov/Publications/3220_Warehouse.pdf

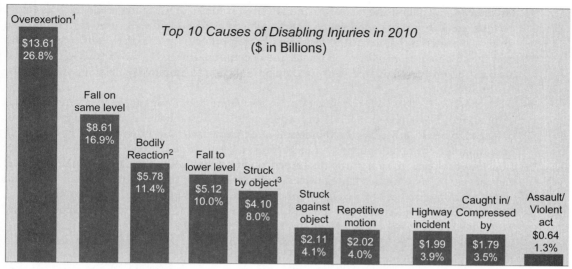

Top 10 Causes of Disabling Injuries in 2010
($ in Billions)

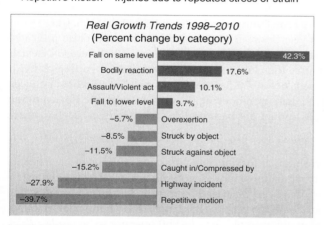

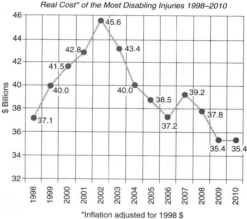

[1]Overexertion – Injuries from excessive lifting, pushing, pulling, holding, carrying, throwing
[2]Bodily reaction – Injuries from bending, climbing, reaching, standing, sitting, slipping or tripping without falling
[3]Struck by object – Such as a tool falling on a worker from above
[4]Struck against object – Such as a worker walking into a door
[5]Repetitive motion – Injuries due to repeated stress or strain

FIGURE 10.3 Workplace Safety Issues   *Source:* Reprinted with permission of Liberty Research Institute for Safety, August 30, 2012.

Warehouse safety considerations fall into three primary categories—employee, property, and motor vehicles[25]—and we'll discuss each of these in the paragraphs that follow. With respect to *employee safety,* consider one warehousing professional's advice: "It costs more to recruit, train, and replace a worker than to provide a safe environment."[26] Workers can be injured due to improper lifting procedures, trying to carry too heavy a load, failing to observe proper hand clearances, and the like. Back and shoulder injuries are the most frequent among warehousing personnel; back support belts and braces are becoming more widely used, but they are only of value if workers also receive adequate training in how to safely lift various loads.

---

[25]Joe Nowlan, "Safety Doesn't Have to Hurt Your Budget," *Industrial Distribution,* January 2008, 25–27.
[26]Ed Engel, "Getting a Lift from Safety," *Warehousing Management,* January–February 2001, 54–57.

PROPERTY   Warehousing facilities generate large volumes of waste materials, such as empty cartons, steel strapping, and broken pallets, as well as wood and nails used for crating and **dunnage** (material that is used to block and brace products inside carrier equipment to prevent the shipment from shifting in transit and becoming damaged). The various waste materials must be properly handled because they pose threats to employee safety and may also be fire hazards.

Moreover, even with the best of practices, some goods that are received, stored, and shipped will be damaged. Special procedures must be established for handling broken or damaged items, if only from the standpoint of employee safety. A broken bottle of household ammonia, for example, results in three hazards: noxious fumes, broken glass, and a slippery floor. Aerosol cans pose hazards that are affected by the product in the cans. For example, cans of shaving cream cause little problem in fires because if they explode, the shaving cream serves to extinguish the fire; that is not the case with aerosol cans containing paints or lacquers, and such cans are often kept in special cages because in a fire they might become burning projectiles.

Indeed, fires are a constant threat in warehousing, in part because many materials used for packaging are highly flammable. In addition, although plastic pallets last longer, are cleaner, and are less likely to splinter than wooden pallets, plastic pallets tend to be a greater fire risk. High-rise facilities are more susceptible to fires because the vertical spaces between stored materials serve as flues and help fires burn. You should recognize that warehouse fires may result in substantial property damage as well as injury or death, as illustrated by a 2008 warehouse fire in South Korea that injured 17 and killed 40 people.

A 2012 report by the National Fire Protection Association indicated that U.S. warehouses averaged approximately 1,300 fires per year between 2005 and 2009. The report also indicated that the most common causes of warehousing fires between 2005 and 2009 were (1) electrical failure or malfunction; (2) heat source too close to combustibles; and (3) cutting or welding too close to combustibles. Moreover, nearly 20 percent of all warehousing fires between 2005 and 2009 were set intentionally.[27] Many warehousing fires can be prevented by common sense; flammable products, for example, should not be stored near heat sources (such as space heaters).

MOTOR VEHICLES   We mentioned earlier that forklift operations and equipment have been a particular focus of governmental safety regulations. Indeed, according to OSHA, approximately 100 employees are killed and 95,000 injured every year while operating forklifts in warehousing facilities.[28] These deaths and injuries are caused by reckless operation of the equipment as well as poor communication. It is not unheard of, for example, for a forklift operator to be *inside a truck trailer* as it pulls away from a loading/unloading dock. This often results in a forklift accident, with the forklift falling from the trailer floor to the parking area.

There are other truck-related safety considerations in warehousing in addition to the forklift-inside-a-truck issue. For example, tractor-trailer drivers who are backing into loading/unloading docks should utilize a lookout person to alert the driver about employees who might be walking behind the vehicle. Moreover, wheel chocks—hard-rubber wedges that are inserted under truck tires—can guard against intentional or unintentional trailer movements.[29]

Hazardous Materials

Hazardous materials (hazmat) often receive special attention from logistics managers because of the injuries, death, and property damage they can cause. According to the Institute of Hazardous

---

[27]http://www.nfpa.org/assets/files//PDF/Warehousefactsheet.pdf
[28]http://www.osha.gov/Publications/3220_Warehouse.pdf
[29]Nowlan, "Safety Doesn't Have to Hurt Your Budget."

Materials Management, a **hazardous material** "is any item or agent (biological, chemical, physical) which has the potential to cause harm to humans, animals, or the environment, either by itself or through interaction with other factors."[30] Examples of hazardous materials include explosives, flammable liquids, and flammable solids.

Government regulations often require that shipping documents indicate the hazardous nature of the materials being transported. Warehouse employees should note these warnings when receiving materials and similarly should include such warnings on outbound shipping documents when materials leave warehouses. In the United States, government regulations also require organizations to create a safety data sheet (SDS) for each hazardous product to be stored in a facility. The SDS contains information about the physical and health hazards associated with a particular product as well information about its proper storage.[31]

Hazmat experts generally agree that the applicable regulations should only provide a starting point for proper storage of hazardous materials, in part because for some situations no regulations exist. These experts further suggest that hazmat storage can be managed effectively by answering four questions: *What* material is being stored? *Why* is it being stored? *Where* is it being stored? *How* is it being stored?[32]

A number of design elements must also be considered with the storage of hazardous materials. Buildings that store hazmat often have specially constructed areas so that materials can be contained in the case of an accident. Likewise, these facilities may have walls and doors that can withstand several hours of intense fire. It's also important for a hazmat storage facility to have proper sprinkling systems as well as excellent ventilation.

Warehousing Security

Interest in providing building security for warehouses and other distribution facilities is a primary concern for many organizations because, according to FreightWatch International, a company that specializes in logistics security, "Freight at rest is freight at risk."[33] Potential threats to warehousing security include theft, pilferage, heat and humidity, vandalism, fire, and loss of electricity, among others.[34] These threats can present a number of negative consequences such as lost sales and revenues, additional costs to enhance security, the time and costs to file the appropriate claims, and potential danger to the public.

Some of these consequences were well illustrated in the high-profile theft of nearly $80 million in pharmaceuticals from a Connecticut warehouse in 2010. For example, the pharmaceutical manufacturer instituted an immediate review of its warehouse security processes and procedures and is implementing more stringent (and more costly) security practices. In addition, pharmaceuticals that are sold outside of traditional channels can create potential safety risks (e.g., lack of refrigeration could contaminate some pharmaceuticals) and the revenues from such sales aren't realized by the manufacturer. And although the pharmaceuticals stolen from the Connecticut warehouse were eventually recovered, they became evidence in a criminal case and will be destroyed at the conclusion of all relevant legal proceedings—which means no revenues from their sale for the manufacturer.[35]

Warehousing security focuses on two primary issues, namely, protecting products and preventing their theft, and warehousing security can be enhanced by focusing on people, facilities, and processes. In terms of people, one area of focus should be the hiring process for warehousing workers; a starting point might be determining whether an individual facility even has a formal

---

[30]http://www.ihmm.org/dspWhatIsHazMat.cfm
[31]Maureen Brady, "Safe, Segregated and Secure: Are Your Hazardous Chemicals Properly Constrained?" *Industrial Safety & Hygiene News*, June 2012, 46.
[32]Todd Nighswonger, "Are You Storing Hazardous Materials Safely?" *Occupational Hazards*, June 2000, 45–47.
[33]FreightWatch, *US Cargo Theft: A Five-Year Review*, April 2011.
[34]Linda Pohle, "What to Do with a Warehouse," *SDM: Security Distribution and Management*, September 2008, 64–70.
[35]Diane Ritchey, "The $80 Million Theft," *Security: Solutions for Enterprise Security Leaders*, July 2012, 20–24.

Table 10.1 Possible Shortcomings in Warehousing Security

Shortcoming	Comment
Reluctance to pursue criminal charges against offending personnel	Fewer than 5 percent who commit crimes are prosecuted
Ineffective security tools	Security cameras aren't always turned on
Laissez-faire attitude toward theft	Don't wait until theft reaches an "unacceptable" level
Minimal (or no) penalties for on-the-job substance abuse	Approximately 90 percent of drug users either steal or deal to support their habit
Infrequent auditing of order checkers' performance	They may become complacent
Institutional roadblocks to reporting theft and substance abuse	Outsourcing the reporting may be more effective
Hiring personnel who are predisposed to theft	An ounce of prevention is worth a pound of cure

Source: Julia Kuzeljevich, "The SEVEN DEADLY SINS in Warehouse Security," *Canadian Transportation & Logistics*, April 2006, 44.

hiring process. One commonsense suggestion when hiring warehousing workers is to not hire people who might be predisposed to theft (e.g., people with substance abuse problems).

In terms of a facilities focus, experts recommend a combination of overt and covert surveillance methods. With respect to the former, electronic devices such as closed-circuit television systems can be helpful, particularly if they are monitored on a regular basis. One type of covert surveillance involves unannounced security audits that focus on shortages or overages of particular products.[36] You should recognize that there is virtually no limit to the sophistication or cost of devices and techniques that can be used to monitor warehousing security. Having said this, the more sophisticated security devices also tend to be more expensive, and organizations need to weigh the trade-off of whether the devices' benefits exceed their costs.

In terms of processes to improve warehousing security, the more times a shipment is handled, the greater the opportunities for loss or damage. Thus, logisticians would do well to reduce the number of times an individual shipment is handled. Table 10.1 highlights some possible shortcomings in warehousing security.

Cleanliness and Sanitation Issues

At first glance, cleanliness and sanitation might seem like issues that are more relevant to, say, restaurants and hospitals than to warehousing operations. However, warehousing cleanliness and sanitation are of paramount importance in many industries, such as the foodservice industry where clean and sanitary warehouses reduce the likelihood of food-borne illnesses. Moreover, clean and sanitary warehousing facilities can have a positive impact on employee safety, morale, and productivity while also reducing employee turnover.[37]

Fortunately, warehouse cleanliness and sanitation are not predicated on complex theories or costly technology, but rather on common sense and diligence. For example, one prominent warehousing consultant suggests that cleanliness and sanitation can be facilitated by putting the "junk and old stuff" at the back of a facility where it is out of the way (and often out of sight). Another suggestion is to purchase a powered sweeper and use it at least once a day.[38]

---

[36]Maria Hoffman, "Eight Ways to Prevent Cargo Theft," *Food Logistics*, July 2011, 5.
[37]Ned Bauhof, "Keeping It Clean," *Beverage World*, July 2007, 77.
[38]Jim Apple, "Have You Done Your Housekeeping Chores?" *Modern Materials Handling*, April 2004, 64.

Summary

This chapter focused on warehousing, the sites where inventories are stored for varying periods of time, and began with a discussion of why warehousing exists in a logistics system. A key reason for warehousing is that production and consumption may not coincide, and warehousing can help smooth out imbalances between them. The chapter discussed the differences among warehouses, distribution centers, and cross-docking facilities.

This chapter also discussed public, private, contract, and multiclient warehousing. Public warehousing has a number of established duties regarding the care of goods, and customers pay only for the space that is actually used to store their products. Private warehousing is owned by the firm using such facilities, and it is best used when an organization has large and steady demand patterns. Contract warehousing involves specially tailored warehousing services that are provided to one client on a long-term basis. Multiclient warehousing, a relatively new alternative, is a mixture of public and contract warehousing.

Various design considerations are relevant to warehousing, with trade-offs among them. For example, a decision to build up or out can affect a facility's utilization of labor, mechanization, and automation. Similarly, organizations that prefer a fixed slot location for merchandise may have to build larger facilities to have a sufficient number of storage slots.

The chapter concluded with an examination of some of the more prominent issues in warehousing operations. The material in this section emphasized that common-sense, low-cost approaches can facilitate effective and efficient management of warehousing operations. For example, warehousing safety could be enhanced if employees refrain from jumping from one dock plate to another.

Questions for Discussion and Review

10.1 Why does warehousing exist in a supply chain?

10.2 Explain the four ways that warehousing facilitates the regrouping function.

10.3 Distinguish among warehouses, distribution centers, and cross-docking facilities.

10.4 Discuss the disadvantages to public warehousing.

10.5 What are the advantages and disadvantages of private warehousing?

10.6 Discuss why contract warehousing is a preferred alternative for many organizations.

10.7 How does multiclient warehousing mix attributes of public and contract warehousing?

10.8 Explain how common sense can be helpful in terms of warehousing design.

10.9 In terms of warehousing design, give examples of trade-offs involving space, labor, and mechanization.

10.10 Distinguish between fixed and variable slot locations. How might they affect warehousing design?

10.11 Discuss the trade-offs associated with order-picking versus stock-replenishing functions.

10.12 Explain the relevance of aisle width in warehouse design.

10.13 Discuss some key considerations associated with warehouse automation.

10.14 What are some potential nonstorage space needs that might impact warehousing design?

10.15 How can warehousing productivity be improved without significant investment in technology or equipment?

10.16 What is OSHA's role in warehousing safety?

10.17 Discuss how fires are a constant threat in warehousing.

10.18 What is a hazardous material? What design elements should be considered when storing hazardous materials?

10.19 Discuss how warehousing security can be enhanced by focusing on people, facilities, and processes.

10.20 How are cleanliness and sanitation issues relevant to warehousing operations?

Suggested Readings

Armstrong, Richard D. "An Overview of Warehousing in North America." *Journal of Transportation Law, Logistics & Policy* 73, no. 1 (2006): 48–53.

Baker, Peter and Marco Canessa. "Warehouse Design: A Structured Approach." *European Journal of Operational Research* 193, no. 2 (2009): 425–436.

Bowen, John T. "Moving Places: The Geography of Warehousing in the U.S." *Journal of Transport Geography* 16, no. 6 (2008): 379–387.

Dhooma, José and Peter Baker. "An Exploratory Framework for Energy Conservation in Existing Warehouses." *International Journal of Logistics: Research & Applications* 15, no. 1 (2012): 37–51.

Franklin, Rod and Stefan Spinler. "Shared Warehouses: Sharing Risks and Increasing Eco-Efficiency." *International Commerce Review* 10, no. 1 (2011): 22–31.

Holmola, Olli-Pekka and Harri Lorentz. "Warehousing in Northern Europe: Longitudinal Survey Findings." *Industrial Management & Data Systems* 111, no. 3 (2011): 320–340.

Lu, Chin-Shan and Ching-Chao Yang. "Evaluating Key Logistics Capabilities for International Distribution Center Operators in Taiwan." *Transportation Journal* 45, no. 4 (2006): 9–27.

Ludwig, Timothy D. and David T. Goomas. "Real-Time Performance Monitoring, Goal-Setting, and Feedback for Forklift Drivers in a Distribution Centre." *Journal of Occupational and Organizational Psychology* 82, no. 2 (2009): 391–403.

Min, Hokey. "Application of a Decision Support System to Strategic Warehousing Decisions." *International Journal of Physical Distribution & Logistics Management* 39, no. 4 (2009): 270–281.

Van Belle, Jan, Paul Valckenaers, and Dirk Cattryse. "Cross Docking: State of the Art." *Omega* 40, no. 6 (2012): 827–846.

CASE

CASE 10.1   Minnetonka Warehouse

Wayne Schuller managed a warehouse in Minnetonka, Minnesota. His major concern was the number of workers to assign to his single unloading dock. After he began contracting with motor carriers for deliveries, he found that they were assessing him stiff penalties if their trucks had to wait to be unloaded. Wayne started adding larger crews at the unloading dock, but often they seemed idle because there were no trucks to unload. Wayne recalled from college that queueing theory might be applicable to such a problem.

The theory of queueing is an analysis of the probabilities associated with waiting in line, assuming that orders, customers, and so on arrive in some pattern (often a random pattern) to stand in line. A common situation is that on the average a facility may have excess capacity, but often it is more than full, with a backlog of work to be done. Often, this backlog has costs associated with it, including penalties to be paid or customers who walk away rather than wait. If a firm expands its capacity to reduce waiting times, then its costs go up and must be paid even when the facility is idle. Queueing theory is used to find the best level of capacity, the one that minimizes the costs of providing a service and the costs of those waiting to use the service.

After some further research specific to his firm, Wayne determined the following facts:

1. Trucks arrive randomly at the average rate of 4 per hour, with a deviation of plus or minus one.
2. A team of two warehouse workers can unload trucks at the rate of 5 per hour, or one every 12 minutes.
3. A team of three warehouse workers can unload trucks at the rate of 8 per hour, or one every 7.5 minutes.

4. A team of four warehouse workers can unload trucks at the rate of 10 per hour, or one every 6 minutes.
5. A team of five warehouse workers can unload trucks at the rate of 11 per hour, or one every 4.45 minutes.
6. The unloading times given in the preceding items (1–5) are average figures.
7. Each warehouse worker receives $14 per hour, must be paid for an entire shift, and—because of union work rules—cannot be assigned to other tasks within the warehouse.
8. Because of its contract with the carriers, the Minnetonka warehouse must pay the motor carriers that own idle trucks at the rate of $60 per hour while the trucks stand idle, waiting to be unloaded.

Use a software package that enables you to perform queueing operations. Note that the variable defined as number of servers (# servers) denotes number of teams of workers and accompanying equipment working as a complete server. In the situation described, the number of teams or servers is always 1, although the number varies in terms of costs and output.

Questions

1. For each of the four work team sizes, calculate the expected number of trucks waiting in the queue to be unloaded.
2. For each of the four work team sizes, calculate the expected time in the queue—that is, the expected time a truck has to wait in line to be unloaded.
3. For each of the four work team sizes, what is the probability that a truck cannot be unloaded immediately?
4. Which of the four work team sizes results in the lowest cost to Wayne?

5. Wayne is also considering rental of a forklift to use in truck unloading. A team of only two would be needed, but the hourly cost would be $38 per hour ($28 for the workers and $10 for the forklift). The two workers could unload a truck in 5 minutes. Should Wayne rent the forklift?

6. Disregard your answer to Question 5. Labor negotiations are coming up, and Wayne thinks he can get the union to give way on the work rule that prohibits warehouse workers on the unloading dock from being given other assignments when they are not unloading trucks. How much would Schuller save in unloading dock costs if he could reassign warehouse workers to other tasks when they are not unloading trucks, assuming that he has picked a good team of workers and each worker works 8 hours a day?

11 PACKAGING AND MATERIALS HANDLING

This chapter deals with the physical handling of products, and provides you with an example of the interconnectedness of logistics activities, with a particular emphasis on packaging and materials handling. You should keep in mind that packaging and materials handling decisions should not be made in isolation; rather, Chapter 10's discussion pointed out that certain warehousing decisions have distinct materials handling implications. For example, a decision to reduce aisle width to improve space utilization likely necessitates materials handling equipment capable of functioning in narrower aisles.

Each product has unique physical properties that, along with the normally accepted volumes or quantities in which it is traded or moved, determine how and when the product is packaged. A product may move in bulk from the manufacturer to a wholesaler, where the product may be placed into some type of container (e.g., barrel, box, or crate) prior to further distribution.

In turn, packaging attributes strongly influence materials handling concerns; nonpackaged products necessitate different handling than do packaged products. For example, bulk items (i.e., free flowing or loose) can be handled by pumps, shovels, or conveyor devices. Nonbulk materials can be placed in various types of containers and can be handled by such conveyances as carts, cranes, dollies, and forklifts.

This chapter begins with a discussion of product characteristics and how they might affect packaging and materials handling. Next, the chapter looks at several fundamentals of packaging, such as its promotional and protective functions as well as labeling considerations. This is followed by a discussion of select packaging issues that includes environmental protection and packaging inefficiencies. The chapter next examines unit loads and unit load platforms such as pallets and slip sheets. The chapter concludes with an examination of materials handling, with a particular emphasis on 10 materials handling principles and types of materials handling equipment.

PRODUCT CHARACTERISTICS

Various product characteristics can influence packaging and materials handling considerations. One is the product's physical characteristics; substances exist in three forms—solid, liquid, gas—and each form has specific packaging requirements. For instance, metal cylinders are one method for the packaging of gases, whereas metal pails can be used for the packaging of liquids. Another physical characteristic is the product's ability to withstand the elements; coal piles can be exposed to rain, whereas salt piles cannot. In a similar vein, some products can be exposed to freezing conditions, but others cannot. Product density (weight per volume) is yet another physical characteristic that can affect packaging considerations.

The physical characteristics of some goods change while they are moving in the logistics channel. Fresh fruits and vegetables are the best-known examples. Even after they are picked, they continue to give off gases and moisture and to generate heat—a process known as *respiration*. Fruits and vegetables are harvested before they are ripe so they will reach the retail stores as they ripen. Ripening processes can be delayed through the use of lower temperatures or application of gases.

Products such as fresh produce, meats, fish, and baker's yeast are referred to as *perishables*. They require special packaging, loading, storage, and monitoring as they are moved from source to customer. The growth in popularity of washed, cut lettuce sold in plastic bags is an example of how packaging can benefit several members of the supply chain. The lettuce grower benefits because smaller, misshaped heads can be used, and not merely the eye-pleasing, "perfect" heads. Both the retailer and the customer benefit because the shelf life is much longer for bagged lettuce than for head lettuce (bagged lettuce also carries a higher markup than does head lettuce).

Tropical fish are carried in plastic bags with enough water to cover them, but no more than necessary, to keep weight down. The area in the bag above the water is filled with oxygen. Sometimes tranquilizers are added to water to keep fish calm. The bag is sealed and placed in a plastic foam cooler, similar to a picnic cooler, which is then placed inside a cardboard box. Fish must be transported within 36 hours, although the time can be extended if oxygen is added to the bags.

In addition to physical characteristics, products also possess chemical characteristics that affect the manner in which they should be handled. Certain pairs of products are incompatible. For example, commodities that are sensitive to ethylene, such as broccoli, lettuce, and watermelon, should never be held for more than a few hours in the same area as products that emit ethylene, such as apples, pears, and tomatoes. Prolonged exposure to ethylene can cause ethylene sensitive products to yellow, soften, and decay.

The various properties of goods must also be made known to consumers to help them make the correct buying decision and care for the product properly. For example, Figure 11.1 is a portion of a fabric-care label that goes on Levi's jeans sold in Japan. Figure 11.2 is used for marking lumber and indicates that the (a) position is for the trademark of the accrediting agent, such as the National Hardwood Lumber Association or the Pacific Lumber Inspection Bureau; (b) identifies the specific mill; (c) indicates whether lumber is heat treated; and (d) is for the country of origin, which is necessary if the lumber is exported. In recent years, interest has grown in having an additional symbol that indicates the wood used for packing was free of insects. Nations in various parts of the world are concerned that untreated wood and wood materials used in packing carries a wide variety of unwanted insects.

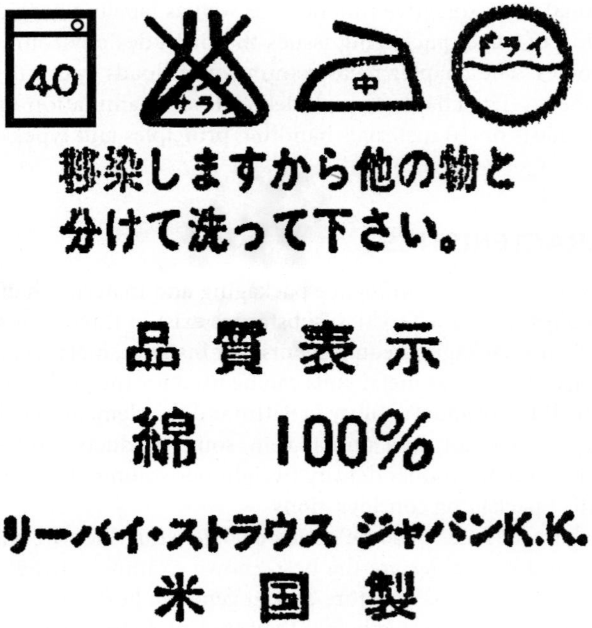

洗染しますから他の物と
分けて洗って下さい。

品 質 表 示

綿   100%

リーバイ・ストラウス ジャパンK.K.
米 国 製

FIGURE 11.1 Portion of Fabric-Care Label for Levis Jeans Sold in Japan
From left to right the pictures say, Wash at 40 degree centigrade, use no chlorine bleach, iron at the medium temperature setting; the jeans can be dry cleaned. The text below the label gives the fabric content, the nation of origin, and the name *Levi Strauss.*   *Source:* Courtesy of Levi Strauss Japan K.K.

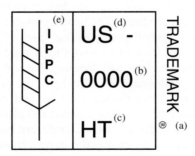

a. *Trademark*—the identifying symbol, logo, or name of the accredited agency
b. *Facility Identification*—product manufacturer name, brand, or assigned facility number
c. *Heat Treated* mark
d. *Country Code*—the two letter ISO country abbreviation
e. Approved International symbol for compliant wood packaging material
f. Indication for use as dunnage (may be abbreviated or spelled out fully)

FIGURE 11.2 Lumber Markings   *Source:* American Lumber Standard Committee, Inc.

PACKAGING FUNDAMENTALS

Packaging, which refers to materials used for the containment, protection, handling, delivery, and presentation of goods,[1] can be thought of in terms of the **building-blocks concept**, where a very small unit is placed into a slightly larger unit, which then might be placed into a larger unit, and so on. Consider the various bags, cans, cartons, jars, and so on that the customer sees on the shelves of a grocery store. These units were likely unpacked from some larger container, such as

---

[1]*Logistics Dictionary*, www.tntfreight.com

a crate or box, and these crates or boxes might have been delivered to the store on a unit load (which will be discussed later in the chapter).

The building-blocks hierarchy is important to remember because each of the different building blocks is inside another, and their total effect should be to protect the product. They function in a complementary sense. When the consumer-size package is very solid, the larger packaging elements require less-sturdy packaging materials because the smaller packages are themselves sturdy. Alternatively, when the smallest package isn't very solid (e.g., the retail packaging for lightbulbs), the larger packaging elements will require very sturdy packaging materials and/or careful arrangement of the smallest product to minimize damage.

There are a number of packaging fundamentals that organizations should be aware of and we'll discuss three of them—functional trade-offs, package testing and monitoring, and labeling—in this section.

Functional Trade-offs

Packaging serves three general functions, namely, to promote, to protect, and to identify the relevant product. These disparate functions mean that packaging design decisions involve a number of separate departments within an organization, such as engineering, manufacturing, marketing, quality control, transportation, and warehousing. Moreover, upstream and downstream supply chain members can also be involved in packaging design decisions; the departments and supply chain members tend to pursue different packaging design objectives.[2]

With so many potential entities involved in packaging decisions, a natural question involves which entity(ies) drive the packaging design process?[3] For example, the marketing department and retailers might prefer packaging designs that are attractive and that encourage consumers to purchase the product. Alternatively, quality control might be interested in packaging design that minimizes loss and damage. As such, while attractive packaging might encourage consumers to purchase a product, the attractive packaging might increase the chances of a product being stolen. As another example, transportation and warehousing might be interested in packaging designs that minimize the amount of a package container's excess space—so that purchasing additional transportation or warehouse space might be minimized. Doing so, however, might lead to an overwhelming number of different-sized packaging containers—which would create an entirely different set of issues.

Package Testing and Monitoring

To properly design a protective packaging system requires three important kinds of information: the severity of the distribution environment, the fragility of the product to be protected, and the performance characteristics of various cushion materials. When new products or new packaging techniques are about to be introduced, it is sometimes advisable to have the packages pretested. Various packaging material manufacturers and trade organizations provide free package testing, and independent testing laboratories can also be used. The packages are subject to tests that attempt to duplicate all the expected various shipping hazards: vibrations, dropping, horizontal impacts, compression (having too much weight loaded on top), overexposure to extreme temperatures or moisture, and rough handling.

In addition to the testing of new products or new packages, shippers should keep detailed records on all loss and damage claims. Statistical tests can be applied to the data to determine whether the damage pattern is randomly distributed. If it is not, efforts are made toward providing additional protection for areas in the package that are overly vulnerable. Some carriers also offer packaging test applications for their customers. For example, FedEx customers can ship a sample test package to FedEx Packaging Services, which tests the package at no cost to the

---

[2]Jack Ampuja, "Finding the Right Package for Your Chain," *Material Handling & Logistics*, September 2011, 26–29.
[3]Ibid.

customer. FedEx Packaging Services will report the testing results within five to seven days of receiving the package.[4]

Related to package testing is actual monitoring of the environment the package must pass through. This is done by enclosing recording devices within cartons of the product that are shipped. The measuring devices may be very simple, such as hospital-like thermometers that record only temperature extremes and springs that are set to snap only if a specified number of g's (a measure of force) are exceeded. More sophisticated devices record a series of variables over time, such as temperature, humidity, and acceleration force and duration (in several directions). Acceleration force and duration are usually recorded along three different axes, making it possible to calculate the precise direction from which the force originated.

Sophisticated monitors are expensive, but they may be necessary to solve a problem of recurrent in-transit damage. Less-complicated devices are used to record temperatures and may be used aboard a shipper's own equipment to ensure quality control. For example, large shipments of apples are accompanied by a mechanical temperature recorder, which provides the receiver with a greater workable knowledge of each load, such as information on temperature variation that may affect the speed at which the receiver should handle and merchandise the apples.

Labeling

Packaging is usually done at the end of the assembly line, so package labeling also occurs there because using this location avoids accumulating an inventory of preprinted packages. This is also a key point for control because this is where there is an exact measure of what comes off the assembly line. As the packaged goods are moved from the end of the assembly line, they become stocks of finished goods and become the responsibility of the firm's outbound logistics system. Near the point where product packaging occurs, it is necessary to maintain a complete inventory of all the packages, packing materials, and labels that will be used.

Once the material being packaged is placed into the box and the cover is closed, the contents are hidden. At this point, it becomes necessary to label the box. Whether words, pictures, or code numbers are used depends on the nature of the product and its vulnerability to pilferage. Retroflective labels that can be read by optical scanners may also be applied. Batch numbers are frequently assigned to food and drug products, so they may be more easily traced in case of a product recall. Figure 11.3 shows a small sampling of labels that can be purchased for individual placement on cartons or pallets.

Many regulations govern the labeling of packaging, including the labeling of weight, specific contents, and instructions for use. Today, much of this information must also be placed outside the larger cartons as well, because some retail outlets sell in carton lots, and the buyer does not see the consumer package until he or she reaches home. In an increasingly global economy, it is important to recognize that labeling regulations differ from country to country. As a general rule, labeling requirements and enforcement tend to be more stringent in economically developed countries than in economically developing ones.

Moreover, labeling requirements within a particular country can differ from state to state (or province to province). In the United States, the liquor (alcoholic beverage) industry is heavily regulated and states have liquor control boards that are responsible for regulating liquor-related activities, including labeling, within state borders. The labeling guidelines for liquor can be quite detailed and specific with respect to font type, font size, and label placement, among others. Failure to comply with the relevant labeling guidelines can result in surcharges, administrative fees, or penalty charges.

HAZARDOUS MATERIALS. It's also important to realize the special labeling requirements associated with hazardous materials. Although hazardous materials were defined and discussed in

---

[4]http://images.fedex.com/us/services/pdf/PKG_Packaging_Test_Application.pdf

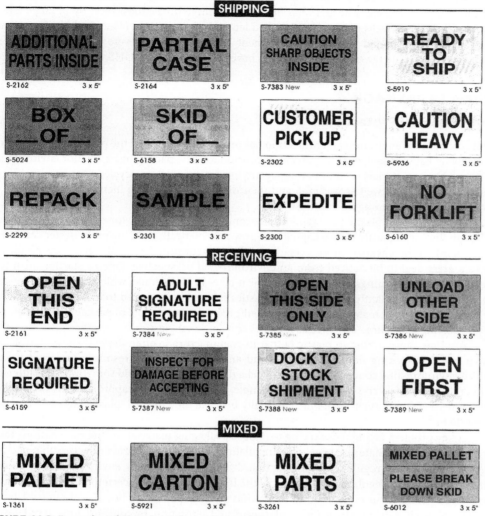

FIGURE 11.3 Examples of Shipping Labels *Source:* Uline.

Chapter 10, almost any material can possess hazardous qualities under certain conditions; for example, flour dust can explode and grain in elevators can self-ignite and burn. Special care is needed to handle these and many other substances.

Governmental regulations address labeling of hazardous materials, and while the specific requirements differ for each hazardous commodity, all of the requirements involve labeling, packaging and repackaging, placing warnings on shipping documents, and notifying transportation carriers in advance. For example, a common requirement on transferring flammable materials is that the vehicle and the receiving or discharging device both be electrically grounded. Care must be taken to properly clean tanks, pumps, hoses, and cleaning apparatus to avoid contamination of the next cargo that is handled. Shipping documents must also indicate whether the cargo is of hazardous nature, and sometimes additional documentation is required. Packages, containers, trailers, and railcars carrying hazardous materials must carry distinct signs, or placards, identifying the hazard.

Because hazardous materials are increasingly being stored and transported across country borders, the United Nations (UN) has played an active role in developing a global system to classify and label hazardous materials. One of the UN's more recent efforts in this area involved its **Globally Harmonized System of Classification and Labeling of Chemicals (GHS)** which was first adopted in 2002. The GHS has been revised three times, most recently in 2010, and it provides three key pieces of classification and labeling information: (1) a symbol; (2) a signal word (e.g., "danger"); and (3) a hazard statement (e.g., "explosion; severe projection hazard").[5] Unfortunately, to date fewer than 70 countries have implemented the GHS.

ISSUES IN PACKAGING

Environmental Protection

Public concern for environmental protection has profoundly impacted the packaging industry on a worldwide basis; in fact, over 80 percent of consumers view packaging as a major environmental issue.[6] Many materials used in packaging are increasingly being recycled; disposable packing materials are often viewed as wasteful, and their disposal is becoming increasingly expensive as costs increase for dumping in landfill sites.

In recent years, plastic packaging has become a frequent target for environmental critics. Although the use of plastic for packaging has grown dramatically over the past quarter century—plastic tends to be cheaper, more versatile, and more consumer friendly than paper—plastic leaves a great deal to be desired from an environmental perspective. One of plastic's most frequently cited shortcomings is the length of time it takes to biodegrade, which can be up to *several hundred years*. Importantly, biodegradable plastics (sometimes referred to as bioplastics), which are derived from plant material, have found their greatest usage to date in packaging applications, despite costing approximately twice as much as conventional plastics.[7]

Another shortcoming to plastic is that its manufacture is often dependent on petroleum, which is a diminishing natural resource (and an extremely costly resource in recent years). A third environmental concern with plastic packaging involves litter, and sometimes this litter has unintended ecological consequences. For example, it is estimated that approximately one million birds and 100,000 sea turtles are killed annually because they mistake plastic bags for food and ingest them.[8]

A key problem facing those trying to choose packaging materials is that each nation's (and, for that matter, each state's or province's) regulations can differ in terms of acceptable packaging. One reason that regulations differ is that different entities view environmental problems differently and enact regulations that address the issues of current concern to them. For instance, some jurisdictions focus on legislation that reduces plastic packaging because of litter-related as well as ecological considerations. Other plastic-related legislation, by contrast, aims to reduce the amount of packaging material that ends up in landfills.

Firms can adopt any number of environmentally friendly packaging strategies, and we'll look at several of them. One strategy is to reduce the amount of packing materials used, but this is tempered by the fact that, as pointed out earlier, transportation carriers may have a great deal of influence on packaging specifications for goods they are transporting. Possible suggestions to reduce the amount of packing materials include the use of just one material, which should improve recyclability, as well as changing a product or format to minimize packaging waste.[9] One of the most noteworthy examples of packaging reduction is Germany's Packaging Ordinance that was enacted in the early 1990s. This legislation attempted to address Germany's solid waste problem by requiring manufacturers, as opposed to consumers, to take

---

[5]http://www.unece.org/trans/danger/publi/ghs/ghs_rev02/English/06e_annex2.pdf
[6]Rosie Baker, "When Less is Moreish," *In-Store*, January 2009, 25–26.
[7]Lou Reade, "A Growing Biodegradable Plastics Industry," *Chemicals & Industry*, July 27, 2009, 14–16.
[8]Gina M. Hernandez, "Bill Seeks to Ban Plastic Shopping Bags," *Caribbean Business*, December 3, 2009, 36.
[9]Trish Lorenz, "No More Pass the Parcel," *Design Week*, April 14, 2005, 9.

back and either reuse or recycle postconsumer packaging. Similar legislation was adopted by the European Union in the mid-1990s.

A second packaging strategy is to use environmentally friendly packaging materials. For example, although plastic tends to be an environmentally unfriendly product, some plastics are less environmentally friendly than others. Polyvinyl chloride (PVC), commonly referred to as vinyl, is an extremely unfriendly plastic because it produces dioxin, a highly carcinogenic (cancer-causing) chemical. Moreover, mushroom blocks, made from the roots of mushrooms, have emerged in recent years as an environmentally friendly packaging alternative. Crate and Barrel, a retailer of housewares, furniture, and home accessories, currently uses mushroom-based packaging, as does Dell, the computer manufacturer.[10]

A third strategy is to use reusable containers, such as refillable glass beverage bottles. This cannot be done for all products, because problems arise when goods in reused containers are contaminated by traces of whatever product had been carried earlier. As an example, dressed poultry (i.e., the removal of blood and feathers after slaughter) often carries salmonella organisms (which are killed in cooking), and the organisms survive in the wooden crates used by the poultry processor and then may spread to vegetables if they are transported later in the same crate. As a result, the U.S. Food and Drug Administration (FDA) issued an order restricting the reuse of such containers to avoid food contamination.

An increasing number of companies currently utilize returnable containers of some type in their operations. For example, Do it Best, a hardware and lumber retailer, utilizes plastic containers to ship items such as light bulbs, batteries, and tools from its distribution centers to its retail stores. In addition to being reusable over long periods of time, the plastic containers can be stacked up to six layers high and provide better overall protection than traditional corrugated packaging.[11]

A fourth environmentally friendly packaging strategy is to retain or support services that collect used packaging and recycle it. This strategy is well suited for companies that receive large quantities of packaged products; if sufficient units of waste material can be collected, it is easier to process for reuse. Recycling companies can specialize in plastic bottles, wooden pallets, cardboard cartons, aluminum cans, and glass bottles, among others.

Note that both the third and fourth strategies add a returned packaging loop to the supply chain and are examples of **closed-loop systems**, or those that consider the return flow of products, their reuse, and the marketing and distribution of recovered products.

Before concluding our look at packaging and environmental protection, you should recognize that dust and vapors produced during bulk-cargo transfer operations are also being scrutinized more closely by public agencies. Coal dust can be blown for several miles from a large coal pile. In port areas, bulk materials that were once stored outside are now in enclosed structures. For products still left outside, elaborate vacuum systems are used to capture the dust created by handling, and ditches around the facility capture rainwater runoff so that it can be run through filters. Some states require handlers of petroleum products, including retail gasoline stations, to install vapor recovery systems. For liquids with vapor-escape problems, the transfer processes are redesigned so that tanks and other receptacles are loaded from the bottom rather than the top.

Metric System

The United States, along with Liberia and Myanmar (formerly Burma), are the only three countries in the world that do not currently use the metric system of measurement. Although this lack of uniformity might have been a relatively minor nuisance 30 years ago, economic globalization has led to increasing pressure on U.S. exporters to market their products overseas in metric units.

[10]http://www.usatoday.com/money/smallbusiness/story/2012-03-10/mushrooms-as-eco-firendly-packing-materials/53441606/1
[11]Sara Pearson Spector, "Do it Best Relies on Reusables," *Modern Materials Handling*, April 2009, 32.

Indeed, some importing nations levy fines against products that are not sold in metric measurements. More and more products are being packaged and sold in metric units, with the nonmetric equivalents printed in smaller type. For example, residents of the United States used to be able to purchase soft drinks in 16-ounce containers. Today, by contrast, the 16-ounce beverage container has been replaced by the .5-liter (approximately 16.9 ounces) beverage container.

One U.S. industry that has prominently embraced the metric system is the liquor-producing industry. This industry's conversion to the metric system, which began in the 1970s, illustrates several of the potential challenges that might stand in the way of the United States formally adopting the metric system. As pointed out earlier in the chapter, the liquor industry is heavily regulated in the United States, and one example of this regulation is the high taxes that are applied to alcoholic beverages. These taxes became an issue in converting to the metric system because they were drawn up to be applicable to half pints, pints, quarts, and other English units of measure, as opposed to half liters and liters. Moreover, the liquor industry's adoption of the metric system also caused some short-term packaging issues because the cartons that were used for transporting and storing quart bottles were in some cases just a bit too small to hold one-liter bottles.

Identifying Packaging Inefficiencies

We introduced the building-blocks concept of packaging earlier in this section, and to refresh your memory, this means that a very small unit is placed into a slightly larger unit, which is then placed into a larger unit, and so on. The building-blocks concept is also useful for analyzing packaging inefficiency in the sense that packaging inefficiency tends to be compounded as one moves from a very small unit to a smaller unit, to a small unit, and so on. Packaging inefficiency can have a number of undesirable logistics consequences, to include increased loss, increased damage, slower materials handling, higher storage costs, and higher transportation costs.

The compounding nature of packaging inefficiency is illustrated in the hypothetical example involving desktop tape dispensers that is presented in Table 11.1. According to Table 11.1, less than one-third of the available case cube is occupied by actual product, while approximately three-quarters of available pallet space is occupied by cases. Multiplying the case efficiency

Table 11.1	A Hypothetical Example of Packaging Inefficiency
Product:	One (1) Desktop tape dispenser (cube = 30 inches) 12 dispensers per carton
Product cube per carton:	30 cubic inches × 12 dispensers = 360 cubic inches
Carton dimensions:	1,140 cubic inches
Carton efficiency:	Product cube per carton divided by carton cube 360 / 1,140 = 31.6%
60 cartons can be put on a pallet Pallet capacity:	90,720 cubic inches
Carton cube per pallet:	1,140 cubic inches per carton × 60 cartons = 68,400 cubic inches
Pallet load efficiency:	Carton cube per pallet divided by pallet capacity 68,400 / 90,720 = 75.4%
Carton efficiency times pallet load efficiency = the amount of pallet cube that is actually product:	31.6% × 75.4% = 23.8%

(31.6 percent) by the pallet load efficiency (75.4 percent) means that less than 25 percent (23.8 percent) of available pallet space is occupied by actual product. One implication of this level of inefficiency is that an increased number of pallets will be needed, which in turn leads to higher storage and transportation costs.

The identification of packaging inefficiencies is important because these inefficiencies have been described as the "last frontier" of logistics savings opportunities. Moreover, there can be impressive cost savings as well as service improvements from improved packaging efficiency. For example, a footwear manufacturer reduced transportation spending by 25 percent and warehousing costs by 35 percent through improved packaging. Similar to the example presented in Table 11.1, this company's savings resulted from optimizing carton efficiency as well as pallet load efficiency. The improved packaging efficiency has also led to a substantial reduction in damaged product for the manufacturer.[12]

Packaging's Influence on Transportation Considerations

Carriers' tariffs and classifications influence the type of packaging and packing methods that must be used. In freight classification documents, the type of packaging is specified. The commodity is listed, followed by a comma and then by a phrase—such as "in machine-pressed bales," "in barrels," "in bales compressed in more than 18 lb. per square foot," "folded flat, in packages," "celluloid covered, in boxes," "SU" (setup), or "KD" (knocked down—or disassembled and packed so that it occupies two-thirds or less of the volume it would occupy in its setup state).

The carriers established these different classifications for two main reasons. First, packaging specifications determined by product density encourage shippers to tender loads in densities that make the best use of the equipment's weight and volume capabilities. IKEA, the Swedish-based home furnishings chain, designs many of its products so that they can be shipped in a dense form. Such products are often displayed unassembled in retail stores, and customers realize that they can easily take them home in their automotive vehicles.

Second, carrier specifications for protective packaging reduce the likelihood of damage to products while they are being carried; this, in turn, reduces the amount of loss and damage claims placed against the carrier. Figure 11.4 shows the type of label (the "box maker's certificate," or BMC) that motor carriers and railroads require on fiber boxes used for shipping freight. It is the fiber box manufacturer's assurance to the motor carriers and railroads that the boxes will be sturdy enough to meet their handling specifications. Note that a number of measures are used. For example, the size limit shown, 75 inches, means that the material should not be used in a package where the total length, width, and height, when added together, exceed 75 inches.

It is difficult to know exactly how much carrier tariffs and classifications control shippers' packaging. Responsibility for damage in transit is one issue subject to carrier–shipper contract negotiation; if the carrier remains liable, the carrier specifies the level of packaging protection to be used. If the shipper assumes responsibility, the shipper may choose the type of packaging to use. Carrier deregulation has allowed corrugated packaging manufacturers and their customers to innovate with performance outside the traditional carrier packaging rules. As specific contract rates are negotiated between individual carriers and shippers, packaging requirements may, of course, be one element of negotiation.

Airlines, express delivery companies, and the U.S. Postal Service also have packaging requirements, although they are somewhat less detailed than those used by rail and motor common carriers. With respect to international shipments, the International Air Transport Association regulates the packaging of air shipments, and limited packaging requirements apply to ocean shipments. However, exporters nearly always buy additional insurance coverage for their export shipments, and the type of packaging influences the insurance rates.

---

[12]William Hoffman, "Thinking Inside the Box," *Traffic World,* December 11, 2006, 17.

FIGURE 11.4 Boxmaker's Guarantee
Source: Courtesy of the American Trucking Association.

UNIT LOADS IN MATERIALS HANDLING

As mentioned earlier in the chapter, the packaging of materials is based on the building-blocks concept of putting products in containers that will provide efficient yet manageable units. This section discusses unit loads, an extension of the building-blocks concept to very large quantities. A **unit load (unitization)** refers to consolidation of several units (cartons or cases) into larger units to improve efficiency in handling and to reduce shipping costs.[13] Handling efficiency can be facilitated by mechanical devices such as a pallet jack or forklift as well as by using a **pallet** or **skid** (a small platform made of plastic, metal, or wood on which goods are placed for handling by mechanical means). Figure 11.5 shows a unit load resting on an automatic guided vehicle.

The unit load offers several advantages, one of which is additional protection to the cargo because the cartons are secured to the pallet by straps, shrink-wrapping, or some other bonding device that provides a sturdier building block. A second unit load advantage is that pilferage is discouraged because it can be difficult to remove a single package or its contents. Also, a pallet can be stacked so that the cartons containing the more valuable or more fragile items are on the inside of the unit load. The major advantage of the unit load is that it enables mechanical devices to be substituted for manual labor and numerous machines have been devised that can quickly build up or tear down a pallet load of materials. Robots can be used when more sophisticated integrated movements are needed for loading or unloading pallets.

The unit load does have its limitations, however. It represents a larger quantity of an item than a single box—often 30–50 times as much. Therefore, it is of limited value to companies that deal in small quantities. And, although one unit load advantage is that mechanical devices can be substituted for manual labor, these mechanical devices cost money to purchase or lease. Manual pallet jacks (trucks) can range in price from $275 to $4,500, whereas conventional forklifts can range in price from $7,500 to $30,000. Moreover, routine maintenance (another expense) should be performed on forklifts to keep them in optimal operating condition.

---

[13]http://cscmp.org/digital/glossary/glossary.asp

FIGURE 11.5 Automatic Guided Vehicle *Source:* Courtesy of Dematic Corp., Rapistan Division, Grand Rapids, MI.

Yet another drawback to the unit load is the lack of standardization in terms of pallet sizes. Although the International Standards Organization (ISO) has established six international pallet size standards (see Table 11.2)—four in metric units, two in English units—literally hundreds of different pallet sizes are used by companies in the United States. If these shipments are exported from the United States, they must be repalletized, which means an increase in manual labor, and thus a diminution in potential advantages to the unit load concept.[14]

The discussion in this chapter thus far has emphasized the building of loads from small blocks into large blocks. However, the reverse is also true; that is, the large units or blocks must be broken down into their smaller component blocks, with the very smallest unit being the single item that the retail customer carries home.

The Unit Load Platform

An important issue with respect to unit loading concerns the platform (basic unit) on which to place the unit load. As mentioned before, the pallet is generally viewed as the basic unit in unit loading. In the United States, the wooden pallet has long been the backbone of the unit load in

---

[14]"Marshall White on the State of Pallets," *Modern Materials Handling*, March 2006, 53–58.

Table 11.2 ISO Pallet Standards	
Dimensions Millimeters **(width × length)**	**Dimensions Inches** **(width × length)**
1219 × 1016	48.00 × 40.00
1000 × 1200	39.37 × 47.24
1165 × 1165	44.88 × 44.88
1067 × 1067	42.00 × 42.00
1100 × 1100	43.30 × 43.30
800 × 1200	31.50 × 47.24

Source: ISO Standard 6780: Flat Pallets for Intercontinental Materials Handling.

the sense that the vast majority (between 90 and 95 percent) of pallets are made of wood. Pallets can also be constructed from plastic, wood composites (such as fiberboard), paper, and metal. The choice of pallet material has increased in importance, in part because highly mechanized and automated materials handling systems subject pallets to greater stress than when materials handling involved less mechanization and automation.[15]

Each pallet material has its advantages and disadvantages, with price being a major drawback to both plastic and metal pallets. For example, a new 48" by 40" wood pallet costs around $20, whereas a new 48" by 40" plastic pallet costs approximately $80; a new 48" by 40" metal pallet costs approximately $125. However, one potential advantage to plastic and metal is their longevity relative to wood; wood pallets might last only one use, and their maximum life span is three years (and only with gentle use). Plastic pallets, by contrast, last at least five years, and life spans of over 10 years are not uncommon, whereas metal pallets can last for over 20 years. Another shortcoming of wood pallets is that they can break and splinter, which could pose safety dangers to workers and also necessitates pallet repairs (assuming the pallet is salvageable). Neither plastic nor metal pallets are likely to break and splinter, thus improving worker safety and resulting in minimal repair costs.

Another important consideration is pallet weight, with a typical 48-inch-by-40-inch wood pallet weighing approximately 40 pounds, compared to 30 pounds for a similar-sized plastic pallet and 65 pounds for a similar-sized metal pallet. Fifty pounds is a significant weight in many logistics systems because it represents the approximate weight at which there is a noticeable increase in injuries, particularly back injuries, from manual handling. Furthermore, wood and plastic are much more flammable than is metal; you might recall from Chapter 10 that fires are a regular threat in warehousing.

Although pallets are a popular unit load platform, one disadvantage (regardless of material) is their height, and when goods are loaded aboard pallets into railcars, trailers, or containers, the space occupied by the pallet (approximately five inches) is unproductive. One alternative to the pallet is a **slip sheet**, a flat sheet of either fiberboard material or plastic, which is placed under the unit load. From a space utilization perspective, one pallet occupies 80 times more space than a plastic slip sheet.[16]

Shrink-wrap (plastic wrapping that when heated shrinks in size to form a cover over the product) or banding straps are used to attach the unit load to the slip sheet. Until the early part of the twenty-first century, one major drawback was high product damage rates due to the fragility of the slip sheets. However, advances in technology have created stronger plastics to construct slip sheets as well as improved materials handling equipment for moving slip sheets. As a result, the damage rates for slip sheeted products are much improved.

---

[15] April Terriri, "Balancing Cost, Quality, Strength, Service," *Food Logistics*, April 2009, 24–27.
[16] www.desicant-solution.com

Beyond the Unit Load

The next step in the building-blocks process is to stow the unit load pallets into a waiting truck trailer, railcar, or container van. Increasingly this stowage is based upon load-planning software, and Figure 11.6 shows a computer printout from this type of software. The load-planning software depicted in Figure 11.6 suggests how to load a container with different sizes of cartons and tells where the loads for several customers should be loaded. The software recognizes, for example, that some cartons cannot be laid on their sides or cannot have other cartons placed on top of them. The software also takes into account the load's center of gravity and the allowable weights on axles. When planning for refrigerated loads, the software will also take into account the need for air spaces.

Slight clearances must be maintained between pallets to allow for the loading and unloading processes. Bracing or inflatable dunnage bags (see Figure 11.7) are used to fill narrow empty spaces, and when inflated, they fill the void space and function as both a cushion and a brace.

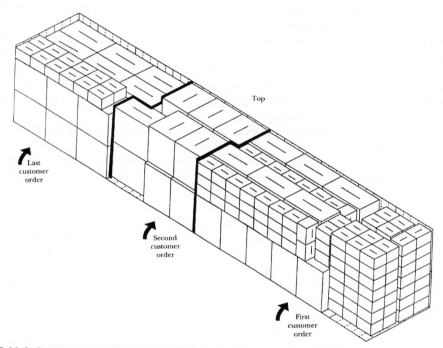

FIGURE 11.6 Computer-Generated Load Plan   *Source:* Courtesy of TOPS Software Corp.

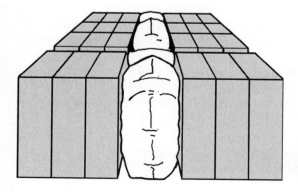

FIGURE 11.7 Inflated Dunnage Bags between Pallets   *Source:* Courtesy of Sea-Land Service Inc.

A problem involved with any bracing or cushioning device is that the load is subjected to forces from all directions. Even when cargoes are properly braced, various forces such as vibration, pitch, and roll can still cause damage: Continued vibrations may loosen screws on machinery or cause the contents of some bags or packages to settle, changing the type of support they give to the materials packed above them. For products that present this problem, special preloading vibrators are used to cause the load to settle immediately.

Some goods are so heavy that they utilize the railcar's, trailer's, or container's weight capacity without filling its cubic capacity (a situation called **weighing out**). These loads, such as heavy machinery, must be carefully braced, and the weight must be distributed as evenly as possible. In highway trailers, for example, it is dangerous to have one side loaded more heavily than the other. In addition, the load should be distributed evenly over the axles.

MATERIALS HANDLING

As a supply chain is linked together, one of the concerns of those involved with logistics is the physical transfer of the product from one party to another: How will product be handled? In what form will it be? In what quantities? What kind of equipment is needed to handle or to store product? Materials handling processes generally receive little public attention, although there are periodic exceptions, such as the baggage-handling system at Heathrow (London, United Kingdom) Airport's Terminal 5 which opened in March, 2008. Within one week of Terminal 5's opening, approximately 30,000 pieces of luggage were "misplaced," due to software and hardware glitches, and this malfunction forced the bags to be sent to airports *outside the United Kingdom* to be sorted and returned to their rightful owners!

For our purposes, **materials handling (also referred to as material handling)** will be defined as "short-distance movement that usually takes place within the confines of a building such as a plant or DC and between a building and a transportation service provider."[17] This short-distance movement distinguishes materials handling from transportation (which will be discussed in Chapters 12 and 13).

Nearly all products that are packaged—often in consumer-size boxes, bottles, or cans—are handled by the building-block concept of packaging that has been described previously. The other way that products, especially large quantities of products, are handled is in *bulk*. Bulk materials are in loose rather than in packaged form and are handled by pumps, shovel devices, conveyor belts (see Figure 11.8), or the mere force of gravity. The decision must be made as to where in the supply chain the bulk materials should be placed into smaller containers for further sale or shipment. Sometimes, bagged and bulk quantities of the same material are part of the same shipment; for example, bagged rice is placed on top of bulk rice to provide load stability on ocean vessels.

Bulk cargoes have various handling characteristics, one of which is *density*. Consider three different bulk materials, namely, iron ore, coal, and grain, each of which is characterized by a different density. One particular type of ship uses only two-thirds of its cubic capacity when carrying iron ore, yet the 15,800 tons of ore lower the vessel to its maximum allowable draft of 24 feet, 8 inches. Alternatively, when loaded with coal, the vessel **cubes out**; that is, the cubic capacity is filled before reaching its weight capacity, and the vessel is lowered to only 20 feet, 6 inches. Grain loads are lower density than either coal or iron ore; the ship's draft when full of grain is slightly less than 20 feet.[18]

A material's *angle of repose* is the size of angle that would be formed by the side of a conical stack of that material. The greater the angle, the higher the pile of materials that can be placed on a specific land area. Anthracite coal has an angle of repose of approximately 27 degrees, whereas

[17]John J. Coyle, C. John Langley, Jr., Brian J. Gibson, Robert A. Novack, and Edward J. Bardi, *Supply Chain Management: A Logistics Perspective*, 8th ed. (Mason, OH: South-Western Cengage Learning, 2009), Appendix 11-A.
[18]Correspondence from the Reiss Steamship Company to the authors.

FIGURE 11.8 Conveyor Belt *Source:* Shutterstock Photo.

for iron ore the angle is 35 degrees. This means more cubic yards of ore can be stockpiled on a given site and that the ore can be carried on a slightly steeper, narrower conveyor belt.

Bulk liquids also have unique handling characteristics. Resistance to flow is measured as viscosity, which can be lowered by increasing the temperature of a liquid. Molasses, cooking oils, and many petroleum products are heated before an attempt is made to pump them.

Gases have unique handling properties, although most of them are handled within completely enclosed pipeline systems. An exception is liquefied natural gas, or LNG, which is cooled and compressed into liquid form that is 1/630 of its volume in gaseous state. In its liquefied, highly pressurized state, it is transported by oceangoing vessels in special tanks.

The handling process itself may change the characteristics (or quality) of the product. Rice grains cannot fall far without being broken. This influences the design of loading and unloading facilities so that the grains of rice never drop more than a few feet at any one time. When sugar is handled, a dust is formed because of abrasion between sugar crystals. This dust is also sugar, but it is in much finer form and has different sensitivities to moisture. The dust must be separated from the rest of the sugar, or the quality of the final bakery product in which the sugar is used will be affected.

An ideal equipment configuration for one bulk cargo may not be able to handle another. Another consideration is the size of particle of the cargo in question; costs are involved in pulverizing to a uniform size so it can be handled by pneumatic or slurry devices.

Materials Handling Principles[19]

The Material Handling Institute, a leading nonprofit trade association that represents the materials handling industry, has developed a list of 10 materials handling principles. The principles are particularly important when laying out the design of a warehousing facility or when

---

[19]The material in this section comes from "The Ten Principles of Material Handling," www.mhia.org.

troubleshooting to learn why a system is not performing well. The Material Handling Institute suggests that these principles can facilitate an organization's productivity, customer service, and profitability. We'll list and briefly describe each of the 10 material handling principles.

1. The *planning principle*. Materials handling processes and procedures should be the result of careful planning and not just an afterthought.
2. The *standardization principle*. Standardization of equipment and operating procedures can improve an organization's performance in part by reducing cost redundancies.
3. The *work principle*. Work smarter, not harder; unnecessary work reduces organizational productivity and negatively impacts customer service.
4. The *ergonomic principle*. **Ergonomics** refers to the interaction between workers and workplace conditions, and the ergonomic principle aims to design material handling systems that facilitate worker health (both mental and physical) and organizational performance.
5. The *unit load principle*. Unit loads consolidate smaller units into larger ones in order to improve efficiency in handling and to reduce logistics costs.
6. The *space utilization principle*. Organizations should maximize the utilization of existing space; unused or poorly utilized space reduces organizational productivity.
7. The *system principle*. Materials handling is one component in a logistics system and must be coordinate with other components in a logistics so as to meet customer requirements and expectations.
8. The *automation principle*. Organizations should take advantage of mechanization and automation opportunities to improve customer service as well as organizational productivity.
9. The *environmental principle*. Materials handling processes and procedures should be designed to minimize their short-term and long-term environmental impacts.
10. The *life cycle cost principle*. The total cost of ownership—acquisition costs, purchase price, usage costs, and end-of-life costs—should be used to evaluate materials handling equipment and systems.

Materials Handling Equipment

A comprehensive discussion of materials handling equipment is beyond the scope of this text. Having said this, it's important to recognize that decisions about materials handling equipment can affect the effectiveness, efficiency, and safety of logistics systems. Although forklifts, for example, facilitate the effective and efficient handling of unit loads, forklifts can be dangerous, and tens of thousands of forklift-caused injuries occur annually in the United States.

Moreover, it is important that the materials handling equipment be aligned with an organization's objectives, customers, and products. This seems to be common sense, but the authors are aware of a consumer products company that redesigned one of its storage facilities with the primary purpose to be a state-of-the-art showcase in terms of materials handling equipment. Less than a year later, the storage facility had to be redesigned because the state-of-the-art materials handling equipment was inconsistent with the types of products sold by the company as well as with its customers' ordering requirements.

Materials handling equipment can be divided into two categories—storage equipment and handling equipment. Examples of storage equipment include shelves, racks, and bins, whereas examples of handling equipment include conveyor systems, lift trucks, carts, and cranes. Although storage and handling equipment are very different, the choice of one often influences the choice of the other. For example, the use of storage racks allows for narrow aisles, but narrow aisles require specialized handling equipment capable of moving both vertically and horizontally.

Materials handling equipment can also be categorized in terms of whether they are labor intensive, mechanized, or automated. True automation, such as automatic guided vehicles (AGVs), refers to an absence of human intervention, whereas mechanization refers to equipment that complements, rather than replaces, human contact (e.g., forklift).[20] A key trade-off among labor, mechanization, and automation involves the relevant volumes; because automation is a very high fixed cost option, sufficient volume is needed to make it cost effective. It has been suggested that automation becomes economically viable only when a facility handles at least 50,000 cartons a day.[21]

Decisions as to materials handling equipment can also be influenced by an organization's order picking and assembly system. In **picker-to-part systems**, an order picker goes to where a product is located, such as with a forklift, whereas in **part-to-picker systems**, the pick location is brought to the picker, such as with carousels. These two systems involve trade-offs between travel time; recall that travel time accounts for between 60 and 80 percent of total order picking time.

Summary

Many considerations, such as a product's physical characteristics, must be taken into account when thinking about packaging and materials handling decisions. Packaging can be thought of in terms of the building-blocks concept where a very small unit is placed into a slightly larger unit, and so on. The chapter looked at a number of packaging issues and began by distinguishing between packaging's protective and promotional functions. We also learned that correct package labeling can impact the effectiveness and efficiency of logistics systems. Packaging has important environmental consequences and several environmentally friendly packaging strategies were identified and discussed.

Unit loads (unitization) were also discussed, with a particular emphasis on the characteristics of wood, plastic, and metal pallets. The chapter then turned to an examination of materials handling and identified some of the challenges associated with handling the various types of bulk products. Ten materials handling principles were identified and described, and these principles can improve the effectiveness and efficiency of logistics systems. The chapter concluded with a discussion of materials handling equipment, and this equipment should be aligned with an organization's objectives, customers, and products.

Questions for Discussion and Review

11.1 How do product characteristics influence packaging and materials handling considerations?

11.2 What is the building-blocks concept? How is it applied to the handling of packaged goods?

11.3 What are the three general functions of packaging? How might they come into conflict?

11.4 What information is needed to design a protective package properly?

11.5 Describe some of the devices that are used to monitor conditions during the journey that a shipment makes.

11.6 Why is it important to recognize that labeling requirements may differ from country to country?

11.7 Discuss some of the labeling requirements associated with hazardous materials.

11.8 What are some environmental disadvantages to plastic packaging?

11.9 What environmentally friendly packaging strategies might a firm adopt?

11.10 Discuss some of the potential challenges to adopting the metric system in the United States.

11.11 How can reducing packaging inefficiencies improve the performance of a logistics system?

11.12 How do transportation tariffs and classifications influence the type of packaging and packing methods?

11.13 Discuss the advantages and disadvantages of the unit load.

11.14 What trade-offs exist between wood, plastic, and metal pallets?

11.15 What issues does the logistics manager face once unit loads have been placed onto a transportation vehicle?

11.16 Distinguish between weighing out and cubing out and explain how these concepts impact the logistician's job.

11.17 Discuss the various handling characteristics associated with bulk cargoes.

11.18 Of the 10 materials handling principles discussed in the chapter, which two are most surprising to you? Why?

11.19 Why is it important that materials handling be aligned with an organization's objectives, customers, and products?

11.20 How might an organization's order picking and assembly system influence its decisions on materials handling equipment?

[20]Mary Aichlmayr, "Making a Case for Automation," *Transportation & Distribution*, June 2001, 85–90.
[21]Ibid.

Suggested Readings

Buehlmann, Urs, Matthew Bumgardner, and Tom Fluharty. "Ban on Landfilling of Wooden Pallets in North Carolina: An Assessment of Recycling and Industry Capacity." *Journal of Cleaner Production* 17, no. 2 (2009): 271–275.

Garcia-Arca, Jesus and Jose Carlos Prado. "Packaging Design Model from a Supply Chain Approach." *Supply Chain Management Review* 13, no. 5 (2008): 375–380.

Guzman-Siller, Christina, Diana Twede, and Diane Mollenkopf. "Differences in the Perception of Pallet Systems between U.S. and Canadian Grocery Retailers." *Journal of Food Distribution Research* 41, no. 3 (2010): 84–97.

Hellstrom, Daniel and Fredrik Nilsson. "Logistics-Driven Packaging Innovation: A Case Study at IKEA." *International Journal of Retail & Distribution Management* 39, no. 9 (2011): 638–657.

Minami, Chieko, Davide Pellegrini, and Munchiko Itoh. "When the Best Packaging Is No Packaging." *International Commerce Review* 9, no. 1 & 2 (2010): 58–65.

Newmann, W.P. and L. Medbo. "Ergonomic and Technical Aspects in the Redesign of Material Supply Systems: Big Boxes vs. Narrow Bins." *International Journal of Industrial Ergonomics* 40, no. 3 (2010): 541–548.

Nunes, Isabel L., Pedro M. Arezas, A. Sergio Miguel, and Ana S. Colim. "Manual Materials Handling: Knowledge and Practices among Portuguese Health and Safety Practitioners." *Work* 39, no. 4 (2011): 385–395.

Qalyoubi-Kemp, Rula. "Packaging Recycling Index." *Journal of Economic Issues* 43, no. 2 (2009): 457–465.

Rokka, Joonas and Liisa Uusitalo. "Preference for Green Packaging in Consumer Product Choices—Do Consumers Care?" *International Journal of Consumer Studies* 32, no. 5 (2008): 516–525.

Roodbergen, Kees Jan and Iris F.A. Vis. "A Survey of the Literature on Automated Storage and Retrieval Systems." *European Journal of Operational Research* 194, no. 2 (2009): 343–362.

Williams, Helen, Fredrik Wikstrom, Tobias Otterbring, Martin Lofgren, and Anders Gustafson. "Reasons for House Food Waste with Special Attention to Packaging." *Journal of Cleaner Production* 24 (2012): 141–148.

CASE

CASE 11.1   Let There Be Light Lamp Shade Company

Located 60 miles from Chicago, Illinois, the Let There Be Light Lamp Shade Company, which designs and builds custom lamp shapes and lamp globes, historically derived all of its sales from customers in the United States and Canada. Recently, an architectural firm that often contracted with Let There Be Light was commissioned to design several large public buildings in the People's Republic of China (China). These buildings would require Let There Be Light to supply 8,100 identical lights, and the relevant terms of sale would include delivery to the Port of Shanghai where the architectural firm would take possession.

Let There Be Light designed a prototype cylindrical lamp shade that measured 11 inches high and 11 inches in diameter and would be packed into cartons that measured 12 inches by 12 inches by 12 inches. (We refer to these shades as Style A.) The Style A lamp shades would cost $4 each to manufacture and weighed nine pounds each; each carton cost 60 cents and weighed one pound, meaning that each loaded Style A carton weighed 10 pounds.

In an effort to reduce packaging costs and also enhance the company's commitment to environmental logistics, Let There Be Light also developed two prototype lamp shades (referred to Style B and Style C) in the shape of a cone, rather than a cylinder. One advantage to conical shades is that they can be nested, that is, stacked inside each other, meaning that, unlike Style A, multiple lamp shades could be packed into a single carton. Moreover, the nested shades would also help protect each other, although a slight bit of padding would be needed between the nested shades. The production costs for the conical lamp shades would be higher than those for the cylindrical shades.

Let There Be Light determined that each Style B lamp shade would cost $4.50 to manufacture and could be shipped nested, with six lamp shades per carton. The carton dimensions were 12 inches by 12 inches by 40 inches, and when holding six shades, a carton weighed 62 pounds. Each Style B carton cost $2.00, and this included padding between the shades. Each Style C lamp shade would cost $5 to make and could be shipped nested, with 10 lamp shades per carton. The carton dimensions were 12 inches by 12 inches by 48 inches, and when holding 10 shades, a carton weighed 101 pounds. Each carton cost $2.25, including padding between the individual shades.

The lamp shades would be loaded into intermodal containers and transported by rail to the Port of Vancouver. The transportation cost to Vancouver was $1,400 per 40-foot container, without regard to weight, although the total shipment weight could not exceed 44,000 pounds per container because of highway weight restrictions. The interior dimensions of the intermodal container were 8 feet wide by 8.5 feet high by 40 feet long. Insurance costs were 2 percent of the value of the shipment ready to be loaded aboard ship in Vancouver (i.e. all of the company's costs up to this point). Let There Be Light learned that the transportation cost from the Port of Vancouver to the Port of Shanghai were $800 for a 40-foot container.

Questions

1. How many Style A shades can be loaded into a 40-foot container?
2. How many Style B shades can be loaded into a 40-foot container?
3. How many Style C shades can be loaded into a 40-foot container?
4. What are the total costs of delivering the Style A shades to the Port of Shanghai?
5. What are the total costs of delivering the Style B shades to the Port of Shanghai?
6. What are the total costs of delivering the Style C shades to the Port of Shanghai?
7. Which style would you recommend? Why?

12 | TRANSPORTATION

Transportation, which can be defined as the actual, physical movement of goods and people between two points, is pivotal to the successful operation of any supply chain because it carries the goods, literally, as they move along the chain. Transportation influences, or is influenced by, the logistics activities discussed in previous chapters to include:

1. Transportation costs are directly affected by the location of the firm's plants, warehouses, vendors, retail locations, and customers.
2. Inventory requirements are influenced by the mode of transport used. High-speed, high-priced transportation systems require smaller amounts of inventories in a logistics system, whereas slower, less-expensive transportation requires larger amounts of systemwide inventory.
3. The transport mode selected influences the packaging required, and carrier classification rules dictate package choice.

4. The type of carrier used dictates a manufacturing plant's materials handling equipment, such as loading and unloading equipment and the design of the receiving and shipping docks.

5. An order management philosophy that encourages maximum consolidation of shipments between common points enables a company to give larger shipments to its carriers and take advantage of volume discounts.

6. Customer service goals influence the type and quality of carrier and carrier service selected by the seller.

This chapter begins with a brief look at the transportation infrastructure in various countries throughout the world, and this is followed by a thorough discussion of the five different types, or modes, of transportation: air, motor carrier (truck), pipeline, rail, and water (listed in alphabetical order). The chapter also discusses intermodal transportation and transportation specialists and concludes with an examination of transportation regulation and the legal classification of carriers.

In keeping with past practice in this and other basic logistics texts, the discussion of transportation will primarily be presented from the perspective of the United States and will primarily focus on domestic (within the United States) transportation. Having said this, readers should recognize that an individual country's topology, economy, infrastructure, and other macroenvironmental factors could result in a different transportation system than that found in the United States. Moreover, the globalization of the world's economy means that an increasing number of shipments are being transported between multiple countries (international transportation), a topic that will be discussed in Chapter 14.

COMPARING AND CONTRASTING TRANSPORTATION INFRASTRUCTURE

Because readers of this text increasingly reside outside of the United States, we believe it would be helpful to present a brief comparison of the transportation infrastructure that exists in five highly populated countries located on various continents. This infrastructure data, which appear in Table 12.1, indicate wide disparities in the various infrastructures; at a minimum, a lack of infrastructure makes it difficult to use that mode in domestic (within-country) transportation.

Table 12.1	Infrastructure Statistics in Several Countries				
	Brazil	**China**	**Germany**	**Nigeria**	**United States**
Air[a]	7	68	14	10	189
Highway (paved)	212,798 km	3,453,890 km	644,480 km	28,980 km	4,374,784 km
Pipeline (oil)	4,835 km	23,072 km	2,826 km	4,441 km	244,620 km
Broad-gauge (1.676 m) rail	5,627 km				
Standard-gauge (1.435 m) rail	194 km	86,000 km	41,722 km		224,792 km
Narrow-gauge (1.000 m) rail	22,717 km		220 km	3,505 km[b]	
Water (inland)	50,000 km	110,000 km	7,467 km	8,600 km	41,009 km

[a]Number of paved runways over 3,047 m (approximately 10,000 feet).
[b]gauge = 1.067 m.

Source: The World Factbook, www.cia.gov, 2013.

The relevant infrastructure statistic for air transportation in Table 12.1 is the number of paved runways over 3,047 meters (approximately 10,000 feet). This length is significant because a 10,000-foot runway has generally been viewed as adequate for accommodating the largest existing wide-body aircraft; wide-body aircraft are essential to long-haul international movements of both freight and passengers. According to Table 12.1, the United States by far has the most airports with paved runways of at least 10,000 feet, an indication that the United States is well positioned to participate in long-haul international movements. Although China currently reports nearly 70 airports with 10,000 foot runways, this number is expected to increase dramatically because the country plans to construct nearly 100 new commercial airports by 2020.

The infrastructure statistics for highway, pipeline, and water, presented in kilometers (1 kilometer is equivalent to approximately 0.62 miles), provide some interesting findings. For example, although Brazil and China are approximately the same geographic size, China currently has about 32 times more paved highway kilometers than Brazil. (It's worth noting that China has added more than *1,500,000 kilometers* of paved highways since this text's previous edition, published in 2011.) The data also indicate that oil pipelines are much more prevalent in the United States, and that China has much more extensive inland waterways, relative to the four other countries listed in Table 12.1.

The information in Table 12.1 on **rail gauge** (the distance between the inner sides of two parallel rail tracks) is also enlightening. Both China and the United States use only one size— standard—rail gauge (1.435 meters) in their rail infrastructure. Brazil, by contrast, uses broad gauge (1.676 meters), standard gauge, *and* narrow gauge (1.000 meter) in its rail infrastructure, whereas Nigeria uses only narrow-gauge rail—with Nigeria's narrow gauge measured at 1.067 meters rather than 1.000 meters. The data on rail gauge are important because nonuniform rail gauge within a country, or between neighboring countries, means that shipments moving by rail will need to be transferred from one vehicle to another, which adds to both delivery time and costs. For example, China and India share a common border and, as mentioned above, China uses standard-rail gauge; India, by contrast, uses broad- and narrow-rail gauge.

TRANSPORTATION MODES

Each of the five modes of transportation exists because of certain attributes that provide one or more advantages over the other modes of transportation. The attractiveness of a particular mode depends on the following attributes[1]:

- Cost (price that a carrier charges to transport a shipment)
- Speed (elapsed transit time from pickup to delivery)
- Reliability (consistency of delivery)
- Capability (amount of different types of product that can be transported)
- Capacity (volume that can be carried at one time)
- Flexibility (ability to deliver the product to the customer)

It is important to recognize that public policy can affect a mode's performance on these attributes. Railroads, for example, were the dominant mode, as measured by **ton miles** (the number of tons multiplied by the number of miles transported) and revenues, in the United States from the nineteenth century through the middle part of the twentieth century. However, the development of the U.S. Interstate Highway System allowed motor carriers to improve their speed, reliability, and flexibility, and although railroads still have the largest share of ton miles, motor carriers now account for the majority of freight revenues. From a public policy perspective, construction costs of the Interstate Highway System were primarily paid for by the U.S. government

---

[1]Drawn from David J. Bloomberg, Stephen LeMay, and Joe B. Hanna, *Logistics* (Upper Saddle River, NJ: Prentice Hall, 2002), Chapter 7.

(90 percent), with the remaining construction costs paid for by state governments. This funding by both the federal and state governments is significant because U.S. railroads have been responsible for the construction costs of their track systems, whereas rail construction costs in other nations are often covered by the national government. As such, the U.S. railroads have a substantial cost disadvantage relative to motor carriers, and this cost disadvantage must be captured in railroad pricing practices.

We'll take a rather detailed look at each of the five modes in this section and the discussion will be presented alphabetically by mode, beginning with airfreight.

Airfreight

When one thinks of air transportation, one immediately thinks of speed, particularly on the **line-haul** (terminal-to-terminal movement of freight or passengers); modern jet aircraft are capable of traveling between 500 and 600 miles per hour, a speed that far exceeds any other form of transportation. Indeed, air is generally the fastest mode of transportation for shipments exceeding 600 miles although some motor carriers now offer overnight service of between 600 and 700 miles.

However, air transportation is a quite expensive form of transportation, and the line-haul cost of airfreight service is regarded as its primary disadvantage; many companies simply cannot afford to have their shipments travel by air. Moreover, because most shippers and **consignees** (receivers of freight) are not located at an airport, this requires transportation from the shipper to the origin airport as well as from the destination airport to the consignee. This **accessorial service** (transportation service that is supplemental to the line-haul) adds to both transportation costs and transit time and also increases the number of times a shipment is handled (thus increasing handling costs and the opportunities for loss and damage).

Unlike other forms of transportation, the great majority of airfreight is carried in the freight compartments of passenger airplanes (so called belly freight). This belly freight limits the capacity available for air shipments and is particularly problematic with respect to narrow-body (single-aisle) aircraft. A narrow-body Boeing 737-800, offers approximately 1,850 cubic feet of belly space, whereas a wide-body Boeing 777-200 offers approximately 5,950 cubic feet of belly space.[2] However, wide-body aircraft devoted to all-cargo service have impressive carrying capacity; the latest version of an all-cargo Boeing 747 can carry almost 150 tons of freight. The cost, speed, and capacity attributes mean that, for the most part, airfreight is best suited to carry high-value, lower-volume products that are of a perishable nature or otherwise require urgent or time-specific delivery. Airfreight rates discourage bulky cargo and use **dimensional weight (also called dim weight)**, which considers a shipment's density (the amount of space occupied in relation to actual weight) to determine a shipment's billable weight.[3] Examples of products that move by air include the following:

- Auto parts and accessories
- Cut flowers and nursery stock
- Electronic or electrical equipment, such as cell phones and iPods
- Fruits and vegetables
- Machinery and parts
- Metal products
- Photographic equipment, parts, and film
- Printed matter
- Wearing apparel

The reliability of airfreight is somewhat problematic. On the one hand, air's tremendous speed relative to the other modes offers the potential to "make up lost time" that isn't possible

---

[2]Data derived from www.boeing.com, About Our Products.
[3]http://www.ups.com/content/us/en/resources/ship/packaging/dim_weight.html?srch_pos=1&srch_phr=dim+weight

with the other modes. Alternatively, because so much airfreight is belly freight, the increasing congestion and resultant delays associated with air passenger transportation mean congestion and delays for airfreight. Moreover, weather conditions such as fog, snow, and thunderstorms can have an adverse effect on the reliability of airfreight transportation. Indeed, FedEx located its first (and still primary) air cargo hub in Memphis, Tennessee, in part because Memphis rarely experiences foggy conditions.

Motor Carriers

The backbone of the U.S. highway system is the Interstate Highway System (its formal name is the Dwight D. Eisenhower System of Interstate and Defense Highways), which was approved by federal legislation in 1956. This nearly 47,000-mile, high-speed, limited-access highway system has had a profound impact on economic development in the United States over the past 50 years. From a logistics perspective, many companies began to locate manufacturing, assembly, and distribution facilities in close proximity to interstate highways. Indeed, accessibility to highways consistently ranks as the most important factor in annual surveys of corporate location decisions.[4]

The most important business user of the highway system is the motor carrier (trucking) industry. One way of classifying motor carriers is according to whether they carry less-than-truckload (LTL) or truckload (TL) traffic. **Less-than-truckload (LTL)** shipments range from about 150 to 10,000 pounds; they are often too big to be handled manually, yet they do not fill an entire truck. Trucks that carry LTL freight have space for and plan to carry shipments of many other customers simultaneously. Unlike TL carriers, LTL carriers operate through a system of **terminals** (a facility where freight is shifted between vehicles), and from each terminal small trucks go out to customers, delivering and picking up shipments. These shipments are then taken to a terminal, where they are loaded aboard line-haul trucks, which are driven to a terminal near the freight's destination. The goods are unloaded from the line-haul carrier, move through the terminal, and are loaded aboard a small truck for local delivery. Prominent LTL carriers include ABF Freight System, FedEx Freight, UPS Freight, and YRC Freight.

Truckload (TL) carriers focus on shipments of greater than 10,000 pounds, and although the exact weight depends on the product, it is close to the amount that would physically fill a truck trailer. For glassware, this might be 18,000 pounds; for canned goods, it might be 40,000 pounds. Although TL traffic may involve only one customer, it is possible that large shipments (greater than 10,000 pounds) from several customers can be consolidated into a truckload shipment. Whereas LTL shipments are routed through terminals, TL shipments tend to move directly from the shipper's location to the consignee's location. Prominent TL carriers include Schneider National, J.B. Hunt, Swift Transportation, and Werner Enterprises.

Although LTL companies tend to be limited in the type of freight that they haul—primarily dry freight such as apparel, books, greeting cards, among others—TL companies can carry a plethora of freight types. These include, but are not limited to, dry freight, foodstuffs, refrigerated products, liquid products, animals and livestock, automobiles, and steel. Overall, although motor carriers have the ability to haul many different kinds of freight, their capacity is limited by highway weight and size (width, length) restrictions. For example, motor carriers using the Interstate Highway System are limited to a maximum gross vehicle weight of 80,000 pounds. With respect to size considerations, truck trailers can be a maximum of 102 inches wide; the maximum length for tractor–trailer combinations varies from state to state. You should recognize that some countries do not have size and weight restrictions for motor carriers.

Although U.S. motor carriers can travel wherever there are roads, their length of haul is mitigated by several factors, such as speed limits and hours-of-service (HOS) rules. HOS rules

---

[4]"25th Annual Corporate Survey," *Area Development*, 2011.

have been the subject of near-constant legislation in the United States since the beginning of the twenty-first century, and rather than trying to articulate the relevant rules, suffice it to say that—unlike automobile drivers—truck drivers are limited in terms of the number of hours that can be driven in a 24-hour period, as well as the number of hours that can be driven in a one-week period.

Both HOS and highways speed limits have long been justified on the basis of safety concerns, and several states (e.g., Indiana, Washington) mandate a two-tier speed limit policy in which the maximum speed for motor carriers is lower than for noncommercial vehicles. Having said this, several U.S. states have eliminated, or are in the process of eliminating, the lower maximum speed limit for truckers, which could potentially increase motor carriers' length of haul. Readers should recognize that each country may have its own hours of service rules for motor carrier operators as well as its own speed limits. Canada, for example, has different hours of service rules depending on whether one is driving north or south of 60 degrees north latitude. In addition, 110 kilometers per hour (approximately 68 miles per hour) is the maximum speed limit in Canada's Manitoba province, compared to 100 kilometers per hour in the province of Ontario.

Without question, the primary advantage for motor carriers is flexibility, or the ability to deliver the product to the customer (or where the customer has relatively easy access to it). For example, if you bought this textbook at your university's bookstore, this book was delivered there by some type of motor carrier, perhaps an LTL carrier. If you bought this textbook from an online site, then it was most likely delivered to your residence by a truck, perhaps a small package truck. Indeed, a longtime slogan of the American Trucking Associations (a trade group that represents motor carrier interests) was, "If you have it, it moved by truck."

As was the case with airfreight, weather considerations also affect the reliability of motor carrier delivery, and relevant weather considerations include ice, fog, snow, flooding, and high winds (which can affect bridge crossings). The reliability of motor carrier service is also affected by highway congestion, which is caused by increased travel demand, weather, roadway incidents (e.g., disabled vehicle, accident), and construction. Highway congestion tends to be most severe in major metropolitan areas and is not likely to be alleviated by additional highway construction. Rather, technology-based approaches, such as intelligent transportation systems and computer routing software that factors in congestion, are being used to deal with road congestion.

Although the cost of motor carrier service is lower than for airfreight, motor carriers tend to be more costly than the remaining modes of transportation. Moreover, there can be significant cost variation depending on the type of motor carrier service that is purchased. Expedited trucking, such as provided by Panther Transportation and FedEx Custom Critical, tends to have the highest cost per *hundredweight* (100 pounds), whereas truckload transportation tends to have the lowest cost per hundredweight.

These cost variations highlight the importance of understanding the trade-offs between logistical activities that have been discussed throughout the text. For example, suppose an organization manufactures 8,000 pounds of crayons per day. The company could have one 8,000-pound LTL shipment each day, or the company could accumulate five days of crayons into one 40,000-pound TL shipment. This would be done to take advantage of the lower TL rate per hundredweight; however, to receive the lower TL rate, the company will need to hold an inventory of crayons, thus increasing inventory and storage costs.

Pipelines

Pipelines are a unique mode of transportation because it is the only one without vehicles, and this is significant for several reasons. First, there is no need for vehicle operators, an important consideration, given that vehicle operators in some modes, such as airplane pilots and ship captains, can achieve annual compensation in excess of $100,000. In addition, vehicle operators sometimes engage in work stoppages (e.g., strikes) and can be the cause of accidents. The lack of vehicles also means that pipeline transportation is one way; other modes have two-way transportation, a fronthaul and a backhaul. The backhaul is often a significant source of excess capacity, or unused available space.

Pipelines' lack of vehicles means that it is the most reliable form of transportation in part because there aren't vehicle-related disruptions (such as accidents), and pipelines are virtually unaffected by adverse weather conditions. Having said this, pipelines tend to be the slowest form of transportation; the lack of vehicles means that the relevant product needs to be forced through the pipeline, often by pumping stations. The slow speed for pipelines is significant because this increases overall transit times and thus necessitates additional inventory in the logistics system.

From a capability perspective, pipelines are quite limited in the sense that products must be liquid, liquefiable, or gaseous in nature. Indeed, pipelines are probably best known for transporting petroleum products, and petroleum pipelines are characterized as either crude oil or product pipelines. *Gathering lines*, which are 6 inches or smaller in diameter, start at each well and carry crude oil to concentration points. *Trunk lines* carry crude oil from gathering-line concentration points to the oil refineries. Their diameter varies from 3 to 48 inches; 8- to 10-inch pipe is the most common size. Product pipelines carry products such as gasoline or aviation fuel from the refineries to tank farms (storage tanks) located nearer to customers. These products are stored at the tank farms and then delivered to customers by truck or by rail, an indication that pipelines have limited delivery flexibility.

Slurry systems allow bulk commodities to become liquefiable by grinding the solid material to a certain particle size, mixing it with a liquid to form a fluid muddy substance, pumping that substance through a pipeline, and then decanting the liquid and removing it, leaving the solid material. Although water is the most common liquid used in slurry systems, other liquids, such as methanol, can be used. The Black Mesa pipeline, which transports pulverized coal from northern Arizona to an electric-generating station, is probably the best-known slurry pipeline currently in operation; other slurry pipelines in current operation transport phosphate, limestone, copper concentrate, and iron concentrate.

Although pipelines tend to have limited capabilities with respect to the products that can be transported, pipelines are capable of transporting very large product volumes. For example, the 48-inch Trans-Alaska pipeline, which is 789 miles long, has a discharge capacity of two million barrels of oil per day. Moreover, pipelines are quite costly to construct and thus have high fixed costs; however, because these fixed costs can be spread over rather large capacities, pipelines offer their users a relatively low cost per unit.

Railroads

Although approximately 560 freight railroads operate in the United States, over 90 percent of the rail industry's revenues and ton-miles are accounted for by the seven Class I (2011 revenues of approximately $433 million) freight railroads.[5] Moreover, the U.S. railroad industry is dominated by four freight carriers, the Burlington Northern (BN), CSX, Norfolk Southern (NS), and Union Pacific (UP); the BN and UP dominate rail freight transportation west of the Mississippi River, whereas CSX and NS have a similar position east of the Mississippi River.

This level of market concentration and domination isn't found in the other modes, and from a practical perspective it can create limited service and pricing options for potential customers. One possible manifestation of limited service options might be seen in the railroads' rather uneven reliability in recent years, some of which can be linked to adverse weather conditions. In recent years, major U.S. railroads have dealt with blizzards, severe flooding, tornadoes, and tropical storms that have damaged and destroyed many miles of rail track.

U.S. freight railroads present an intriguing paradox in the sense that they are not either the "best" or "worst" on any of the six attributes (capability, capacity, cost, flexibility, reliability, speed)

---

[5]www.aar.org

that we're using as a basis of comparison for the five transport modes. For example, although freight railroads have the potential to transport many different kinds of products (capability), they tend to transport lower-value, high-volume shipments of bulk-type commodities such as coal, chemicals, farm products, and nonmetallic minerals. Having said this, the growth of inter-modal transportation (which will be more fully discussed later in the chapter) has given railroads access to manufactured and packaged products, which tend to be higher value. Overall, railroads are superior to air, motor, and pipeline, but inferior to water, in terms of their ability to transport different kinds of products.

Similarly, rails possess less flexibility (ability to deliver the product to the customer) than motor carriers, unless the customer is located on a rail line or has a rail siding (a track that runs from a main line to a particular facility). However, rails generally have greater flexibility than air, water, and pipeline. In terms of the volume that can be carried at any one time (capacity), rails are superior to air and motor, but not as good as pipeline or water. Boxcars (used to carry general freight), hopper cars (used to carry products like coal and minerals), and tank cars (used for liquid or liquefiable products) have usable carrying capacities of approximately 110 tons. Although this dwarfs the 25-ton capacity of a typical truck trailer, consider that the carrying capacity of one dry bulk **barge** (flatboard boat used to transport heavy products) is about 1,750 tons.[6]

Freight railroads are also right in the middle of the five modes when it comes to cost (price that a carrier charges to transport a shipment) and speed (elapsed transit time from pickup to delivery) considerations. Although railroads are less expensive than air and motor, they are more expensive than pipeline and water. Alternatively, railroads are faster than both pipeline and water, but slower than air and truck.

Water

Freight moves by water on the Great Lakes, using vessels called lake freighters (lakers), as well as on inland waterways, using barges. Waterborne commerce also moves via oceangoing vessels between the mainland states (Lower 48) and Alaska, Hawaii, and Puerto Rico. Our discussion will focus on the inland waterways, primarily rivers, which are dredged to a depth of nine feet—the minimum depth required for most barges. Although minimum dredging depths might appear to be a rather mundane topic, it is actually quite important in the sense that inland water transportation is somewhat unreliable due to weather-related conditions such as drought and icing.

Drought creates problems because when water levels drop below acceptable levels, barges are forced to reduce their loads, or barge traffic might be halted altogether, situations that require alternate means of transportation. During 2012, for example, drought conditions closed an 11-mile stretch of the Mississippi, costing barge operators approximately $1 million per day.[7] Flooding is another weather-related consideration that can affect the reliability of inland water transportation. For example, severe flooding along the Ohio River in April and May 2011 caused substantial delays to the delivery of coal by barge transportation.[8] Icing is a problem in northern states such as Minnesota and Wisconsin; the ice closes the rivers and prevents year-round operation. Because of this, customers can stockpile inventories in the fall to last through winter months or can use alternate methods of transportation.

However, not all of the unreliability associated with U.S. inland water transportation is weather related. More specifically, the waterways' **lock** system (a lock raises or lowers barges so they can meet the river's level as they move upstream or downstream) also contributes to transport unreliability. Many locks on the U.S. inland waterway system are quite old, with some locks dating to the 1930s, and their maintenance needs tend to increase as a function of age. With

---

[6]Center for Ports and Waterways, *A Modal Comparison of Domestic Freight Transportation Effects on the General Public* (College Station, TX: Texas Transportation Institute, 2009).
[7]Josh Sanburn, "As Barges Sit Idle Along the Mississippi, the Economic Costs Grow," *business.time.com*, August 22, 2012.
[8]http://www.eia.gov/todayinenergy/detail.cfm?id=1590

preventive maintenance of locks currently the exception rather than the rule, when a lock malfunctions the related repairs can take months to complete—a situation with potentially adverse consequences for shippers and barge operators.[9]

Inland water transportation in the United States is also characterized by slow average speeds of approximately six miles per hour. It should be noted that transit times will be affected by the direction of travel; upstream movements that go against the prevailing current will be slower than downstream movements. In addition, inland waterways can be circuitous in nature, which can add to transit time. And, as previously pointed out, transit times may be extended because of lock-related maintenance considerations.

In terms of positive attributes, inland water transportation is relatively inexpensive to users. At one time inland water transportation was considered to be the least expensive form of transportation, but fuel taxes that were imposed on inland water transportation in the 1980s permitted pipelines to become the least expensive mode. Nevertheless, inland water transportation is quite inexpensive when compared to rail and motor carrier transportation. As a general guideline, on a ton-mile basis, rail costs are approximately two to three times as high as inland water carriers, whereas truck costs are approximately 20–30 times higher than inland water carriers.

Although inland water carriers tend to focus on lower-value bulk commodities that can be handled by mechanical means such as pumps, scoops, and conveyors, many different kinds of products can be carried. The predominant commodity moved by barge is petroleum and petroleum-related products, followed by coal. Other products that move extensively in the inland waterway system include food and farm products, industrial chemicals, and minerals and stone. And, as pointed out in the previous section, inland water carriers can carry much greater volumes than can rail and truck.

INTERMODAL TRANSPORTATION

We have discussed each mode as if it acts in isolation from the other modes, but in an increasingly global economy, multiple modes are used to transport a shipment from its origin to its destination. For our purposes, **intermodal transportation** refers to transportation when using a container or other equipment that can be transferred from the vehicle of one mode to the vehicle of another mode without the contents being reloaded or disturbed.[10] With intermodal transportation two or more modes work closely together in an attempt to utilize the advantages of each mode while at the same time minimizing their disadvantages. For example, a company might use **piggyback transportation**, that is, either truck trailer-on-flatcar or container-on-flatcar, to take advantage of rail's low transportation costs on the line-haul along with truck's ability to provide door-to-door service.

As evident in our defintion, the container is an important type of equipment in intermodal transportation. Containers are moved by mechanical devices such as container cranes, and companies need only handle a container and not the freight inside it, thus providing a dramatic reduction in freight handling costs. Because the container is interchangeable among rail, truck, and water carriers, containers can be used in intermodal applications and provide the advantages offered by each of several modes. Both ocean carriers and railroads have developed methods of handling multiple containers at one time, thereby reducing the number of individual lifting and storage moves.

Containers are generally 8 feet wide, 8 feet high, and between 10 and 53 feet long. Most containers are dry-cargo boxes, although some are insulated and come with temperature-controlling

[9]www.mvs.usace.army.mil/floodfight/L-D/LD21.pdf
[10]This definition comes from Barton Jennings and Mary C. Holcomb, "Beyond Containerization: The Broader Concept of Intermodalism," *Transportation Journal* 35, no. 3 (1995): 5–13.

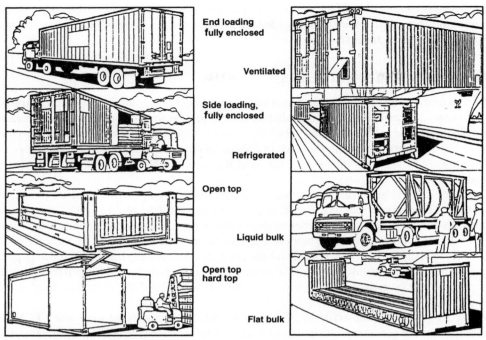

**End loading
fully enclosed**

Ventilated

**Side loading,
fully enclosed**

Refrigerated

Open top

Liquid bulk

**Open top
hard top**

Flat bulk

FIGURE 12.1 Various Types of Intermodal Surface Containers   *Source: Ports of the World,* 14th ed.,
CIGNA Property & Casualty Companies.

devices. Specialized intermodal containers are also available that carry tanks for holding liquids
or gases as well containers that hold insulated or refrigerated cargo. Figure 12.1 shows several different types of containers.

Airfreight containers, often referred to as **unit load devices (ULDs)**, are constructed of
lightweight metals and come in different sizes. Unlike the containers in Figure 12.1, airfreight
ULDs have somewhat irregular shapes, dictated by the contours of the fuselage into which they
must fit.

Although intermodal containers can range between 10 and 53 feet in length, a commonly used metric is **TEU**, which stands for 20-foot equivalent unit, and volumes of
intermodal traffic are commonly expressed as so many TEUs, meaning they would fill that
many 20-foot containers. Water ports, for example, are often ranked in terms of the number of
TEUs that are handled in a particular period of time. Likewise, containerships are measured
by the number of TEUs that can be carried, and containership capacity continues to increase
over time. Consider that in 1995—a time when many of today's college undergraduates
were younger than five years of age—the largest capacity containership was approximately
5,000 TEUs. By contrast, Maersk Line, a major ocean transportation company, began operating
an *18,000 TEU* vessel in July 2013.

Not only did the container revolutionize freight handling, it also spurred cooperation
between various modes to develop more effective and efficient transport offerings, such as **land
bridge** services. Rather than all water service between two ports, land bridge services involve the
use of surface transportation—usually rail transportation—between the origin and destination
port. Consider, for example, a shipment of pineapples from Hawaii to Europe. Rather than the
shipment going by water from Hawaii through the Panama Canal and then on to Europe, under
land bridge service, the pineapples would move by containership from Hawaii to a U.S. West
Coast water port. From this port, the containers of pineapple would be placed on railcars and
shipped across the United States to an East Coast port, where the containers would be loaded

onto a vessel for continuation of the shipment to Europe. Although the land bridge adds to total transportation costs, the primary advantage to land bridge service is the reduction in total transit time from the origin to destination port.

TRANSPORTATION SPECIALISTS

In addition to the five basic modes and intermodal transportation, a number of different transportation specialists can provide value-added services to prospective customers and we'll discuss several transportation specialists in the paragraphs that follow. **Freight forwarders** are not modes, but from the shipper's viewpoint, they are analogous to other carriers. There are two types of domestic freight forwarders—surface and air—and they can best be thought of as consolidators of freight.

Surface carriers give volume discounts to customers shipping large quantities of freight at one time. For example, the LTL rate from city A to city B might be $5 per 100 pounds for shipments less than 20,000 pounds, whereas the TL rate might be $2 per 100 pounds when shipments of 20,000 pounds or more are tendered. Truckload rates are lower than LTL rates for three reasons: (1) the shipper loads the goods, and the consignee unloads the trailer; (2) the load goes directly from shipper to consignee without passing through terminals; and (3) paperwork, billing, and other administrative costs are little more for a 25,000-pound shipment than they would be for a 250-pound shipment.

The freight forwarder exists by offering a service to shippers that must use LTL rates because they do not generate enough volume to use TL rates. Without the freight forwarder, the shipper has to use the $5 LTL rate. The freight forwarder, however, offers the same transportation service for a rate between the LTL and TL rate—say, $4 per 100 pounds. This is possible because the freight forwarder consolidates enough small shipments to reach a volume of at least 20,000 pounds and thus qualifies for the $2 per 100 pound TL rate. The freight forwarder typically offers pickup and delivery service but does not perform the line-haul service, which is done by motor carriers or railroads (in terms of intermodal service).

The air forwarding industry works with the air carriers and air forwarders to consolidate shipments and tender them in containers that are ready for aircraft loading. This results in significant ground-handling savings for the airlines. Therefore, airlines encourage forwarder traffic because it results in an agreeable division of labor: The forwarders provide the retailing function and deal with each individual shipper and consignee, and the airline concentrates on wholesaling, moving the forwarders' loaded containers among major cities.

Some forwarders specialize in certain cargoes. A common example is in the garment industry, in which many small garment firms send large numbers of a few garments each to retail shops in most large cities. The garment forwarders use special containers in which the garments are on hangers and thus ready for display on arrival. Another specialized forwarder relocates house pets. The firm handles health inspection prior to shipment, arranges for cages and quarantines (if required), books flights, and handles all documentation.

Shippers' associations perform basically the same function as surface and airfreight forwarders, except that they do not operate as profit-making organizations. Shippers' associations are membership cooperatives where membership can be based on different considerations, such as shipping a particular commodity or commodities, belonging to a particular industry, or being located in a particular area. Although shippers' associations tend to be thought of as providing a large number of transportation-related services for their members (full-service associations), some shippers' associations are primarily focused on achieving the lowest rates for their members ("rate negotiator" associations). The main benefit of shippers' associations, whether they are full service or rate negotiators, is transportation cost savings for its members.[11]

---

[11]Information from the Web site of the American Institute for Shippers' Associations.

Brokers are another type of transportation specialist; they are companies that look to match a shipper's freight with a carrier to transport it. Brokers look to secure the best transportation rate and service package available for shippers, while attempting to ensure that carriers operate as close as possible to maximum capacity. Brokers can handle both LTL and TL shipments; those handling LTL shipments consolidate them and then turn them over to motor carriers, freight forwarders, or shippers' associations. With respect to TL shipments, brokers will retain a particular carrier and receive a portion of the transportation charges as compensation.

In some cases, third-party logistics companies are involved in arranging transportation services. They try to find clients with complementary transportation needs so that equipment utilization can be increased, which should reduce transportation costs to the respective clients. As an example, Exel Logistics was able to persuade Chrysler and Ford to share space on trucks that were delivering repair parts to both Chrysler and Ford dealerships in a particular geographic area. Exel was able to show both Chrysler and Ford that dedicated equipment (i.e., equipment carrying only Chrysler or only Ford parts) led to additional equipment, additional shipments, and excess capacity for each party—thus increasing the costs of distributing the repair parts.

Much of the discussion up to this point has assumed that we are dealing with shipments that weigh at least several hundred pounds. We'll conclude our discussion of transportation specialists by looking at **parcel carriers**, companies that specialize in transporting parcels, which are often referred to as packages that weigh up to 150 pounds. Parcel shippers have a variety of potential options available to them, one of which is Parcel Post, a service of the U.S. Postal Service that was specifically established to send packages through the mail system. Parcel Post has size (130 inches in combined length and girth) and weight limitations (70 pounds), with transportation charges based on weight, distance, and shape.[12] In most cases, a parcel must be transported to the post office by the shipper, but it will be delivered to the receiver's actual mailing address.

Another option for parcel shippers is United Parcel Service (UPS), which financially dwarfs any other transportation company in the United States (2012 revenues of approximately $54 billion). UPS was able to attract customers in its early years because it offered certain services, such as automatic daily pickups, multiple delivery attempts, and the return of undeliverable packages, that were not available from competitors such as Parcel Post—and UPS was able to offer this service at rates that were competitive with Parcel Post. Unlike the Parcel Post, UPS rates include both pickup and delivery, and today UPS offers a range of parcel services via several modes of transport, including truck, rail, and air.

Whereas UPS started as a package delivery company that emphasized line-haul movement by truck and in the 1980s expanded into air transportation, Federal Express (now FedEx Express) started as a package delivery company that emphasized service by air transportation and later expanded into line-haul movement by truck. Both UPS and FedEx now offer package shippers service options that include same-day service involving air transportation, next-day service involving air or truck, and second-day service involving air or truck, among others. The size and weight limitations for packages shipped by UPS and FedEx are similar, with both carriers limiting package sizes to a maximum of 108 inches in length and 165 inches in girth. And while the maximum package weight for UPS and FedEx is 150 pounds, both carriers mandate special guidelines and procedures when shipping packages that weigh more than 70 pounds (UPS) or 75 pounds (FedEx).

Package services are also available from Greyhound Lines (called Greyhound Package Express), which is the primary intercity bus company in the United States. As is the case with UPS and FedEx, several service options are available for package delivery, such as same-day service (which generally uses a courier company) and standard service (where the packages travel in special compartments on the bus). Packages that are sent via Greyhound Package Express are limited to a maximum weight of 100 pounds.[13]

---

[12]http://www.usps.com/ship/parcel-post.htm
[13]http://www.shipgreyhound.com/faq/#package_1

domestic water transportation, and the rates and services of pipelines that are not regulated by the Federal Energy Regulatory Commission.[22]

From a logistics perspective, the economic deregulation of transportation is important because it has allowed transportation companies much greater freedom with respect to pricing and service options—two attributes that are at the heart of the tailored logistics concept that was presented in Chapter 1. In addition, the economic deregulation that occurred in the United States spurred economic deregulation (sometimes called "liberalization") in many other countries, and this movement has been particularly noticeable with respect to air transportation.

LEGAL CLASSIFICATION OF CARRIERS

Although there has been a dramatic reduction in U.S. economic regulation since the late 1970s, the legal classification of carriers continues to be relevant. More specifically, transportation carriers are classified as either for hire or private, and for-hire carriers can be further subdivided into common, contract, and exempt carriers. The legal classification of carriers is important because of the varying levels of economic regulation that are applicable to the different carriers (e.g., common carriers have more extensive economic regulation than contract carriers). However, all carriers, regardless of their legal classification, must comply with the relevant environmental and safety regulations.

The key factor that separates a **common carrier** from other forms of transportation is that the common carrier has agreed to serve the general public. To ensure that the general public is adequately serviced, common carriers assumed four specific obligations: to serve, to deliver, to charge reasonable rates, and to avoid discrimination in pricing and service. The service obligation means that common carriers are supposed to serve all customers who request service, so long as the commodity and origin/destination are within a carrier's scope of service. For example, a motor carrier that specializes in dry van, general freight service would not be expected to transport a shipment of liquid chemicals. Even though a company might not want to carry certain types of freight, its undesirability (see Figure 12.2) is not a legitimate reason to avoid the obligation to serve. To this end, in recent years the major U.S. freight railroads have tried to convince the Surface Transportation Board to waive their common carrier obligations associated with the transportation of hazardous chemicals such as chlorine.[23]

The obligation to deliver requires that a carrier provide timely pickup and delivery as well as ensure that the delivered shipment is in the same condition as the picked up shipment (i.e., the avoidance of lost or damaged freight). The obligation to charge reasonable rates has long been viewed as offering protection for both carriers and users; the idea of reasonable rates guards against rates so low that carriers are unable or unwilling to carry freight, and it guards against rates so high that users are unwilling or unable to tender freight to carriers. The obligation to avoid discrimination in pricing and service suggests that similarly situated customers (e.g., customers that ship the same product, customers that ship to the same origin and destination point) should receive identical treatment. One of the key provisions of the ICC Termination Act of 1995 was the elimination of the reasonable rate obligation (hence also the obligation to avoid discrimination in pricing and service) for many types of motor carriers.

A **contract carrier** offers a specialized service to customers on a contractual basis, and the contract specifies the compensation to be received, the services to be provided, and the type of equipment to be used, among others. Unlike the common carrier, the contract carrier is under no obligation to render services to the general public and only has to serve customers with whom it

---

[22]http://www.stb.dot.gov/stb/about/overview.html
[23]John D. Boyd, "A Toxic Rate Battle," *The Journal of Commerce*, June 22, 2009, 62.

"IT'S CARRYING A LOAD OF FERTILIZER."

FIGURE 12.2 Undesirable Cargo *Source:* Reproduced by permission of *Jet Cargo News.*

has contracts. Moreover, the contract carrier is under no obligation to treat its customers on an equal basis. Because each contract can be tailored to the specifications of individual customers, contract carriage is viewed as offering many of the advantages of private transportation (such as control over service) while avoiding many of the disadvantages of private transportation (e.g., the hiring of drivers, owning equipment).

Exempt carriers are for-hire carriers that have been exempted from economic regulation through provisions in various pieces of legislation; the appropriate rates and services must be negotiated directly between the carrier and user. For example, the Transportation Act of 1940, which brought domestic water carriers under economic regulation, exempted liquid bulk commodities from economic regulation, as well as dry-bulk commodities, so long as no more than three dry-bulk commodities were moved in a particular tow.[24] In a similar fashion, the Motor Carrier Act of 1935, which brought motor carriers under economic regulation, exempted unprocessed agricultural commodities from economic regulation; the Motor Carrier Act of 1980, which lessened economic regulation for motor carriers, exempted agricultural seeds and plants from regulation.[25]

Private carriers, which are exempt from any economic regulation, are companies whose primary business is other than transportation and provide their own transportation service by operating trucks, railcars, barges, ships, or airplanes. Private transportation is most prevalent in the trucking industry, accounting for over 50 percent of the U.S. highway mileage for trucks.[26] Prominent private truckers in the United States include Frito-Lay, Kraft Foods, Marathon Petroleum, and Walmart, among others.

One advantage to private transportation is that the equipment can serve as a rolling billboard that allows an organization to promote itself. Operational control is another advantage to private transportation, in part because shipments can move at a time convenient for the company,

---

[24]Harper, *Transportation in America.*
[25]Ibid.
[26]http://www.nptc.org/index.php?option=com_content&view=article&id=39&Itemid=457

Advances in technology, and their impact on logistics management, have been a recurring theme throughout the text. Rate determination (to be more fully discussed in the next section) provides one example of how advances in technology have impacted transportation management. As recently as the 1980s, all rates were published in tariffs (a phonebook-like manual that contained rate information), and it wasn't uncommon for a transportation manager to refer to multiple tariffs to determine the applicable rate—a process that led to numerous incorrect rate determinations. Today, by contrast, many carriers provide rating information online and a transportation manager may need to enter little more than origin and destination zip codes and the relevant shipment weight to receive an estimated rate.

For our purposes, **transportation management** will refer to the buying and controlling of transportation services by either a shipper or consignee.[1] Today more than ever before, organizations are concerned about transportation management because transportation represents a major expense item. In general terms, freight transportation accounts for approximately 6 percent of U.S. gross domestic product. Moreover, as we've emphasized throughout, transportation is the most costly logistics activity for many organizations, and as pointed out in Chapter 12, transportation is pivotal to the successful operation of any supply chain.

Similar to Chapter 12, the discussion in the chapter will be approached from the perspective of the transportation manager in the United States. Keep in mind that a particular country's transportation system, the degree of government involvement in transportation, and a country's technological development will influence the nature of transportation management in that country. For example, in some countries there may be only one government-run transportation company in a particular mode; thus the transportation manager wouldn't need to be concerned with carrier selection considerations for that particular mode.

Although the majority of this chapter will focus on several of the transportation manager's key responsibilities, it should be pointed out that transportation managers are also involved with many other operations of the firm. They can assist marketing by quoting freight rates for salespeople, suggesting quantity discounts that can be based on transportation savings, and selecting carriers and routes for reliable delivery of products. Transportation managers can help manufacturing by advising on packaging and materials handling and making certain that an adequate supply of transportation is available when it is needed. Transportation managers can aid the outbound shipping process by providing simplified shipping or routing guides, drawing up transportation documents, and encouraging shipment consolidations. Finally, they can help purchasing by advising about methods to control the costs and quality of inbound deliveries and by tracking and expediting lost or delayed shipments of important inputs.

Our discussion in the remainder of the chapter will focus on some of a transportation manager's primary responsibilities. We'll first analyze rate (pricing) considerations, with a particular emphasis on rate determination. Next, the chapter will discuss modal and carrier selection and this will be followed by a discussion of documentation considerations. The chapter will also look at making and receiving shipments and concludes with an examination of transportation service quality.

RATE (PRICING) CONSIDERATIONS

Rate Determination

As we've seen throughout this text, logistics has discipline-specific terminology, and to this end, one key responsibility of transportation managers involves rate considerations, with **rate** being the logistics term that signifies the price charged for freight transportation ("fare" refers to the

---

[1]John J. Coyle, Edward J. Bardi, and Robert A. Novack, *Transportation*, 6th ed. (Mason, OH: South-Western, 2006).

prices charged for passenger transportation). Rate determination is essential to calculating the appropriate transportation cost, according to the following formula:

$$\text{Weight} \times \text{rate} = \text{transportation charge}$$

Moreover, transportation rates are based on three primary factors—product, weight, and distance—which will be discussed next:

- Relationships between *different products,* in terms of their handling characteristics, for example, the difference between carrying 2,000 pounds of ballpoint pens and 2,000 pounds of live chickens
- Relationships between shipments of *different weights*, for example, shipments of 10 pounds each versus shipments of 1,000 pounds each versus shipments of 10,000 pounds each
- Relationships between *different distances* the products are carried, for example, from Boston, Massachusetts, to Albany, New York, versus from Atlanta, Georgia, to Spokane, Washington

Rate determination has to define all three relations in numeric form and then has to devise methods of tying those numbers into a rate for a specific shipment. The three relationships just mentioned are of continual importance to the transportation manager because if they are altered, the total transportation charges will be altered.

One approach to rate making is to determine one specific rate for every possible combination of product, weight, and distance—in other words, a **commodity rate**. Although a commodity rate is very good for dealing with demand-specific situations, the number of commodity rates quickly becomes overwhelming (and potentially counterproductive) when you consider how many different products, weights, and distances exist. For example, because there are over 30,000 "important" shipping and receiving points in the United States, in the commodity rate system there would need to be separate rates for all possible combinations of shipping and receiving points—a number that is in the trillions of trillions![2]

When you consider that the transportation rate structure dates to the time of economic regulation in the late 1800s—a time when "office automation" might have meant a *manual typewriter*—it becomes clear that the transportation community needed a way to simplify rate determination. This was accomplished through the **class rate system**, which simplified each of the three primary rate factors—product, weight, and distance. One widely used system for simplifying the number of products is the National Motor Freight Classification (NMFC), which has 18 separate ratings, or classes, from 50 to 500[3]; the higher the rating, the greater the relative charge for transporting the commodity. Classification numbers are very important because they are code words that describe cargo in a manner that carriers and shippers understand, and classification descriptions also specify the packaging that must be used and that carriers require. Figure 13.1 shows a page of the National Motor Freight Classification; note the detail. *NOI* stands for "not otherwise indexed by number" (i.e., one cannot find a definition that fits more closely). Packages are referred to by number; they are described in great detail in the classification document.

Four factors are used to determine a product's freight classification, namely, *density, stowability, ease of handling,* and *liability to damage and theft*. **Density**, which refers to how heavy a product is in relation to its size, is viewed as the primary factor for setting a product's classification, in part because of the opportunity costs associated with it. That is, a product with low density (i.e., low weight per cubic foot), such as foam rubber, can easily fill a vehicle's usable capacity (cubing out) before the reaching the maximum weight (weighing

---

[2]Ibid.
[3]http://www.nmfta.org/Pages/Nmfc.aspx

NATIONAL MOTOR FREIGHT CLASSIFICATION 100-AM

ITEM	ARTICLE	CLASS
	GLASS: subject to item 86500	
86560	**Automobile or Boat Glass,** including **Windshield Glass,** cut to shape, see Note, item 86566, in Packages 772, 2146, 2147, 2223, 2261 or 2483:	
Sub 1	Not bent, in boxes or crates:	
Sub 2	120 united inches or less	70
Sub 3	Exceeding 120 united inches	85
Sub 4	Bent, other than tempered:	85
Sub 5	Nested, in boxes, crates or Packages 304, 305, 315, 2347 or 2348	85
Sub 6	Not nested, in boxes or Packages 1180, 1247 or 2034	125
Sub 7	Bent, tempered, in boxes, crates or Packages 304, 305, 315, 774, 2347 or 2348, or when not nested, in Packages 1180 or 2034	85
86566	NOTE—Applies only on glass in specific sizes or shapes for installation in automobile bodies or in or on boats.	
86580	**Building Slabs,** opaque glass, NOI, with or without backing, in boxes or crates:	85
Sub 1	$5/16$ inch thick or less	65
Sub 2	Over $5/16$ inch thick,	50
86600	**Cullet (Broken Glass),** in boxes or drums	55
86650	**Glass,** crushed, ground or powdered, not including enamel or frit, in bags, boxes, drums or Package 2453	85
86660	**Glass,** faceted, in panels, see Note, item 86662, in boxes or crates	
86662	NOTE—Applies on glass, plain or colored, set in cement, concrete or plastic resins to form designs, patterns or pictures.	
86670	**Glass,** flashed or ruby, not framed nor leaded, in boxes	85
86700	**Glass,** flat, NOI, see Note, item 86701:	
Sub 1	Bent, in boxes or crates:	85
Sub 2	220 united inches or less	100
Sub 3	Exceeding 220 united inches but not exceeding 15 feet in length nor 9 feet in width	250
Sub 4	Exceeding 15 feet in length or 9 feet in width	
Sub 5	Not bent, see Note, item 86702, in boxes, crates or Packages 195, 198, 235, 785, 2008, 2025, 2147, 2149, 2160, 2239, 2245, 2281 or 2497:	65
Sub 6	220 united inches or less	100
Sub 7	Exceeding 220 united inches but not exceeding 15 feet in length nor 9 feet in width	200
Sub 8	Exceeding 15 feet in length or 9 feet in width	
86701	NOTE—The term 'flat' applies to glass known as sheet, plate, polished prism, rolled, window or float glass, whether or not polished, laminated, colored, opalescent, opaque, chipped, decorated, wired, etched, figured, acid dipped, ground, sandblasted, metalized (sprayed with atomized metal while glass is hot) or tempered, but not when silvered for mirrors, nor flashed, nor framed or leaded (set in or framed by lead or other metal).	
86702	NOTE—Flat glass, not bent, may also be cut to size, edges beveled or ground, or holes cut or drilled.	
86750	**Glass,** leaded, see Note, item 86752, in boxes:	200
Sub 1	With landscape, pictorial or religious designs,	100
Sub 2	With curved, angled or straight line patterns, or with designs other than landscape, pictorial or religious	
86752	NOTE—The term 'leaded glass' means glass either colored or clear, set in lead or in other metal.	
86770	**Glass,** microscope slide or slide cover, see Note, item 86771, in boxes	70
86771	NOTE—Does not apply on microscope slides or slide cover glasses. Applies only on the glass from which these articles are manufactured. For provisions applicable to microscope slides or slide cover glasses, see item 88535.	
86830	**Glass,** rolled, overlaid with aluminum strips with metal terminals attached, in boxes or crates	77.5
86840	**Glass,** rolled, overlaid with aluminum strips, NOI, in boxes or crates	70
86900	**Glass,** silvered for mirrors, not framed, nor backed nor equipped with hangers or fastening devices:	
Sub 1	Shock (window glass, silvered), in boxes, see Note, item 86902	85
Sub 2	Other than shock glass, in packages shown:	
Sub 3	Bent, in boxes:	
Sub 4	Not exceeding 15 feet in length nor 9 feet in breadth	100
Sub 5	Exceeding 15 feet in length or 9 feet in breadth	250
Sub 6	Not bent, see Package 785:	
Sub 7	120 united inches or less, in boxes, crates or Packages 198 or 235	70
Sub 8	Exceeding 120 united inches but not exceeding 15 feet in length nor 9 feet in breadth, in boxes or crates	100
Sub 9	Exceeding 15 feet in length or 9 feet in breadth, in boxes or crates	200
86902	NOTE—Glass, silvered for mirrors, which has been framed or backed, or equipped with hangers or fastening devices, is subject to the classes for mirrors, NOI.	
86940	**Glass,** window, other than plate, with metal edging other than sash or frames, in boxes	77.5
86960	**Glazing Units,** glass, not in sash, see Note, item 86966, in boxes, crates or Packages 2149 or 2281	70
86966	NOTE—Applies on units consisting of sheets of glass separated by air or vacuum, sealed at all edges with same or other materials.	
87100	**Glass Factory Flattening Stones, Floats, Gathering Rings or Pot Rings or Glasshouse Pots,** clay, in boxes, crates or drums or on skids	85
87500	**GLASSWARE GROUP:** Articles consist of Glassware or Glass Articles, see Note, item 87512, as described in items subject to this grouping.	
87512	NOTE—All articles of glassware which are plated, mounted or trimmed with gold or silver will be subject to the provisions provided for glassware, gold or silver deposit, gold or silver mounted or gold or silver trimmed.	
87520	**Ampoules (Ampuls),** in boxes or Package 2362	100
87540	**Aquariums or Terrariums,** capacity over $1/2$ gallon, see Note, item 87552, in boxes or crates:	
Sub 1	Each in individual fiber box, two or more smaller sizes nested within one larger	85
Sub 2	NOI	150

FIGURE 13.1 Page from National Motor Freight Classification *Source:* Reprinted from the National Motor Freight Classification © ATA 2013.

out). As a result, low-density products are assigned a higher classification; for example, at the time of this book's publication, products with densities of less than one pound per cubic foot are assigned to Class 400, while densities of one pound but less than two pounds per cubic foot are assigned to Class 300.[4]

---

[4]Freight Class Calculator: Freight Class Chart & Density Calculator—Freightquote.

Stowability refers to how easy the commodity is to pack into a load, and possible considerations involve the commodity's ability to be loaded with hazardous materials and ability to load freight on top of the commodity. *Ease or difficulty of handling* refers to challenges to handling that might be presented by a commodity's size, weight, and so on. Finally, the *liability for loss and damage* considers, among others, a commodity's propensity to damage other freight, its perishability, and its value.

Just as the freight classification is used to simplify the number of commodities, shipment weight is simplified through weight groups (e.g., less than 500 pounds; 500–999 pounds; 1,000–1,999 pounds). The rate for shipments weighing less than 500 pounds will be higher than that for shipments between 500 and 999 pounds, and so on. Distances are simplified in a similar fashion and historically distances were classified according to a rate basis number, and the higher the rate basis number, the greater the distance between origin and destination. Increasingly, rate basis numbers are being replaced by the zip codes of a particular shipment's origin and destination.

An example of rate determination using the class rate system is presented in Table 13.1. Before proceeding with a discussion of the class rate system, note that the rates are expressed in terms of hundredweight (100 pounds), rather than per pound. Shipment 1 in Table 13.1 will serve as our reference point for looking at changes in commodity classification, weight, and distance.

As shown in Table 13.1, the commodity classification is the only difference between Shipment 1 (class 100) and Shipment 2 (class 200). As pointed out earlier, a higher class rating takes a higher rate and Shipment 2's rate per hundredweight ($504.22) is noticeably high than Shipment 1's rate per hundredweight ($269.74). With respect to the class rate system and weight, Shipment 1 weighs 500 pounds versus 1,500 for Shipment 3, and the rate per hundredweight is lower for Shipment 3 than for Shipment 1. Finally, Shipments 1 and 4 differ in terms of the destination zip code, and because Shipment 4 is traveling much farther than Shipment 1, Shipment 4's rate per hundredweight is higher than Shipment 1's.

A commodity's freight classification is developed and maintained by the Commodity Classification Standards Board, which consists of at least three but no more than seven full-time employees of the National Motor Freight Traffic Association. There is often a natural tension between shippers and carriers with respect to a product's classification; shippers tend to prefer a lower classification number (which translates into a lower rate), whereas carriers tend to prefer a higher classification number. Transportation managers can appeal a commodity's classification, and Figure 13.2 shows a proposal for a new classification for soft contact lenses.

Referring to Figure 13.2, the proposal begins with the present classification provisions, followed by the proposed classification provisions. Figure 13.2 indicates that the proposal does not seek to change the classification of existing items; rather, the proposal advocates the creation of a new item—contact lenses, soft—and a corresponding rate class. The majority of the content presented in Figure 13.2 provides the proponent's rationale for the proposed classification. Note that the "Transportation Characteristics" section in Figure 13.2 focuses on the four-product attributes—density, stowability, handling, and liability—that were discussed earlier in this chapter.

Table 13.1 Example of the Class Rate System

Shipment	Commodity Classification	Weight (pounds)	Distance (using zip codes)	Rate Per Hundred weight (cwt)[a]
1	Class 100	500	44023 to 32169	$269.74
2	Class 200	500	44023 to 32169	$504.22
3	Class 100	1,500	44023 to 32169	$206.82
4	Class 100	500	44023 to 90210	$344.68

[a]Rates are representative as of late 2012 and do not include the applicable discount or fuel surcharge.
Source: Data derived from a sample rate calculator for Old Dominion Freight Lines http://www.odfl.com/MyRate/.

Unfortunately, the carrier selection procedure is more challenging than that for modal selection, in part because there can be tens, hundreds, or even thousands of carriers from which to choose in a particular mode. It might not be realistic to expect a transportation manager to be aware of every possible carrier in a particular mode or to know about each carrier's service and operating characteristics.

Carrier selection is also less straightforward due to a lack of agreement on the number of relevant factors that might be used in carrier selection. For example, the number of carrier selection factors evaluated in academic research studies has ranged from less than 10 to over 150. As was the case with rate and service negotiation, it's not possible to provide a comprehensive list of all possible factors that might be used in the carrier selection decision. Representative carrier selection factors include total transit time, transit time reliability, competitive rates, and loss and damage performance, among others.

Modal and carrier selection has become even murkier in recent years with the rise in what we'll call the **amodal shipper**. An amodal shipper refers to a transportation manager who purchases a prespecified level of transportation service (e.g., two-day delivery for a particular price) and is indifferent to the mode(s) and/or carrier(s) used to provide the actual transportation service. Indeed, research indicates that shippers are exhibiting more interest in transportation metrics such as transit time and transit time dependability than in transportation modes. One reason for the growth of amodalism is that nonasset-based third-party logistics companies have the ability to develop multimodal solutions to a client's transportation problems.[6] Amodalism is also aided by companies such as UPS and FedEx that own companies that provide different types of transportation services (e.g., air, expedited, LTL, parcel).

DOCUMENTATION

The definition of logistics presented in Chapter 1 refers to the *management of information* and the documents associated with transportation shipments, or **documentation**, are one important source of logistics information. Transportation documentation serves both a practical function (e.g., what, where, and how much is being transported) as well as potentially providing legal recourse if something goes awry with a particular shipment. Our discussion here will focus on the documents associated with domestic shipments; the documentation for international shipments is presented in Chapter 14.

The transportation department is responsible for completing all the documents needed to transport the firm's products. Today, many carriers provide software that enables the shipper to use computers to generate all the commonly used documents. Some shippers also have their own order processing software that is capable of generating transportation documents.

Bill of Lading

The most important single transportation document is the **bill of lading**, which is the basic operating document in the industry. The bill of lading functions as a delivery receipt when products are tendered to carriers. On receipt of the freight, the carrier signs the bill of lading and gives the original to the shipper. The signed original of the bill of lading is the shipper's legal proof that the carrier received the freight. The bill of lading is a binding contract, specifying the duties and obligations of both carrier and shipper. The bill of lading contract for surface carriers is basically standardized by law and greatly simplifies the transportation manager's job because it specifies exactly the duties of the shipper and carrier.

[6]"Transport Buying Shifts from Mode to Metrics," *Transportation and Distribution,* January 2006, 34–35.

There are two types of bills of lading: the straight bill of lading and the order bill of lading. On a *straight bill of lading*, which is printed on white paper, the name of the consignee is stated in the appropriate place, and the carrier is under a strict legal obligation to deliver the freight to the named consignee and to no one else. Ownership of the goods is neither stated nor implied. On the *order bill of lading*, which is printed on yellow paper, the name of the consignee is not specified. For example, assume that a lumber company in Washington state has loaded a boxcar of plywood that it has not yet sold. It would use an order bill and tender the shipment to the Burlington Northern Railroad, which would start the car moving toward Chicago. Once a buyer for the plywood is found, the shipper would send the original copy of the order bill by mail to a bank near the buyer and would also tell the buyer which bank had possession of the order bill. The buyer would go to the bank and pay for the plywood, and the bank would give the original copy to the buyer. The buyer would take it to the railroad, and the railroad would deliver the carload of plywood. Order bills can also be used when faced with slow-paying customers because the order bill guarantees that the customer must pay for the products prior to receipt.

An additional classification for bills of lading is the specific form: long, short, or preprinted. The *long-form bill of lading*, which may be either an order or straight bill, contains the standard information on the face of the bill (see Figure 13.3), and on the reverse side it contains the entire contract between carrier and shipper. The reverse side is printed in extremely small print. Because of the difficulty of reading the long-form contract and the printing costs of including the contract on all bills, in 1949 the railroads and motor carriers adopted the short-form bill of lading. The short form has the following statement on its face: "Every service to be performed hereunder shall be subject to all the terms and conditions of the Uniform Domestic Straight Bill of Lading."

Another kind of bill of lading—which may be long, short, order, or straight—is preprinted. In theory, the bill of lading is prepared and issued by the carrier. In fact, however, most shippers buy their bills of lading and then have them preprinted with a list of the products they regularly ship. Shippers go to the expense of buying and printing their own bills because, in practice, they frequently prepare them prior to calling the carrier. The preprinted bill can be prepared more rapidly and with less chance of error; for example, the shipper can insert the correct classification rather than letting the carrier determine it.

A few shippers are adopting their own bills of lading, which carriers may be reluctant to accept because the carriers may be subject to new liabilities specified in the documents. Carriers are advised to supply drivers with stickers to place on the bills of lading indicating that their signature means only that they have picked up the freight.

Freight Bill

Another basic document that the transportation manager must be familiar with is the **freight bill**, which is an invoice submitted by the carrier requesting to be paid. Often, the transportation manager must approve each freight bill before it is paid, and carriers must be paid within a specific number of working days. In an attempt to meet these time limits, many transportation managers now participate in automated *freight bill-paying services*. Once the transportation manager initiates the program with the payment service, the carriers submit their freight bills directly to the service. The payment service treats the freight bills as checks drawn on the shipper's freight account and then pays the carriers.

One continuing issue with freight bills involves companies being charged too much (overcharges) for transportation services. To detect current errors that result in overcharges and to correct these errors in the future, shippers conduct *internal audits* (work is performed by employees of the company) of their freight bills. Some shippers also conduct *external audits* (work is performed by an independent third party) of their freight bills. Figure 13.4 is an example of one

FIGURE 14.1 Some of the Symbols Used for Packing Export Shipments

through the implementation of just-in-time systems. Other countries, however, have very different time orientations. Some countries, for example, view time as circular, rather than linear, and under this perspective, today isn't much different from yesterday; similarly, tomorrow isn't much different from today. From an operational perspective, a circular time orientation means that what doesn't get accomplished today can be accomplished tomorrow and thus "time schedules" (e.g., production schedules, pickup and delivery schedules) are often viewed as guidelines, rather than as absolutes.

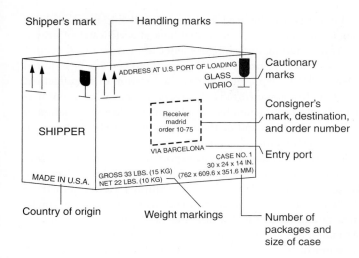

FIGURE 14.2 A Package Marked for Export *Source:* From *Ports of the World,* 15th ed., a publication of CIGNA Property & Casualty.

Table 14.1	Beginning Dates for the Chinese New Year 2015–2020
Year	**Beginning Date**
2015	February 19
2016	February 8
2017	January 28
2018	February 16
2019	February 5
2020	February 14

Source: www.apples4theteacher.com/holidays/chinese-new-year/when-is-chinese-new-year.html.

INTERNATIONAL DOCUMENTATION[10]

International logistics involves a system in which documentation flows are as much a part of the main logistical flow as the flow of the product. Companies that export products from their home country for sale in other countries soon find that preparing the requisite documentation, assembling the documentation, and ensuring that the documentation arrives where and when they are needed is quite a challenge. Although domestic shipments might only require several pieces of documentation, export shipments typically require approximately 10 documents, and for some cross-border trades, more than 100 separate documents can be required!

Documentation can act as a nontariff barrier in the sense that all the necessary documents are required at the point of importation. Failure to do this can cause delays or, in some cases, result in the shipment being seized by the customs authority of the importing country. Moreover, simply having all required documentation is often just a starting point; the exporting organization may be given specific instructions, such as the relevant languages as well as appropriate font types and sizes, for completing the documentation.

---

[10]This material in this section is drawn from Donald F. Wood, Anthony Barone, Paul R. Murphy, and Daniel L. Wardlow, *International Logistics,* 2nd ed. (New York: Amacom, 2002), Chapter 12.

Given the vast array of documents that can be used for international shipments, it's only possible to discuss several of the most commonly used, and we'll look at certificates of origin, commercial invoices, shipper's export declaration, and shipper's letter of instruction. A **certificate of origin** specifies the country(ies) in which a product is manufactured and can be required by governments for control purposes or by an exporter to verify the location of manufacture. A **commercial invoice** is similar in nature to a domestic bill of lading in the sense that a commercial invoice summarizes the entire transaction and contains (should contain) key information to include a description of the goods, the terms of sale and methods of payment (to be discussed in the next section), the shipment quantity, the method of shipment, and so on.

A **shipper's export declaration (SED)** contains relevant export transaction data such as the transportation mode(s), transaction participants, and description of what is being exported. SEDs often serve as the basis for a country's official export statistics. A **shipper's letter of instruction (SLI)** often accompanies an SED and provides explicit shipment instructions. For example, an SLI might indicate which parties should receive which documents, the method or route of shipment, what types of insurance to purchase, and which insurance company(ies) to use.

Before concluding our discussion of the documentation requirements associated with international shipments, mention should be made about free trade agreements. Although some free trade agreements have led to a decrease in documentation requirements, others actually result in an *increase* in documentation, which could defeat the primary purpose of these agreements, namely, facilitating trade between participating countries.

Consider, for example, the U.S. and Central America Free Trade Agreement (CAFTA), which went into effect in 2005. To receive the favorable tariffs specified in this agreement, organizations provide extensive documentation, beginning with a detailed certificate of origin that is supported by sworn affidavits from various supply chain participants such as suppliers and producers. By contrast, there is much less documentation required for products imported from China.[11]

TERMS OF SALE

Choosing the **terms of sale** involves parties working within the negotiations channel, looking at the possible logistics channels, and determining when and where to transfer the following between buyer and seller:

1. The physical goods (the logistics channel)
2. Payment for the goods, freight charges, and insurance for the in-transit goods (the financing channel)
3. Legal title to the goods (the ownership channel)
4. Required documentation (the documentation channel)
5. Responsibility for controlling or caring for the goods in transit, say, in the case of livestock (the logistics channel)

Transfer can be specified in terms of calendar time, geographic location, or completion of some task. One must think in terms of both time and location.

In the 1930s, the International Chamber of Commerce developed, and then has periodically revised, terms of sale for international shipments. In the recent past, these terms of sale, commonly referred to as **Incoterms**, were implemented at the beginning of a new decade, such as Incoterms 1990 and Incoterms 2000. The most recent revision, Incoterms 2010, became effective on January 1, 2011 and it reflects the rapid expansion of global trade with a particular focus on improved cargo security and new trends in cross-border transportation.[12]

---

[11]Alan M. Field, "Too Complex?" *The Journal of Commerce*, May 16, 2005, 16–18.
[12]*Export.gov—Incoterms* 2010.

Two key changes with Incoterms 2010 involve (1) organizing the terms by modes of transport and (2) using the terms in both international and domestic transportation. With respect to the former, Incoterms are now characterized as Group 1 (apply to any mode of transport) and Group 2 (apply to sea and inland waterway transport only). These two groups, and their respective Incoterms, will be listed and described in the following paragraphs.[13]

GROUP 1: TERMS THAT APPLY TO ANY MODE OF TRANSPORT

EXW (ExWorks)

The seller fulfills his obligation by having the goods available for the buyer to pick up at his premises or another named place (i.e., factory, warehouse, etc.). The buyer bears all risk and costs starting when he picks up the products at the seller's location until the products are delivered to his location.

FCA (Free Carrier)

The seller delivers the goods export cleared to the carrier stipulated by the buyer or another party authorized to pick up goods at the seller's premises or another named place. The buyer assumes all risks and costs with delivery of goods to final destination including transportation after delivery to carrier and any customs fees to import the product into a foreign country.

CPT (Carriage Paid To)

The seller clears the goods for export and delivers them to the carrier or another person stipulated by the seller at a named place of shipment. The seller is responsible for the transportation costs associated with delivering goods to the named place of destination but is not responsible for purchasing insurance.

CIP (Carriage and Insurance Paid To)

The seller clears the goods for export and delivers them to the carrier or another person stipulated by the seller at a named place of shipment. The seller is responsible for the transportation costs associated with delivering goods and purchasing minimum insurance coverage to the named place of destination.

DAT (Delivered at Terminal)

The seller clears the goods for export and bears all risks and costs associated with delivering the goods and unloading them at the terminal at the named port or place of destination. The buyer is responsible for all costs and risks from this point forward including clearing the goods for import at the named country of destination.

DAP (Delivered at Place)

The seller clears the goods for export and bears all risks and costs associated with delivering the goods to the named place of destination not unloaded. The buyer is responsible for all costs and risks associated with unloading the goods and clearing customs to import the goods into the named country of destination.

---

[13]This information comes from *Export.gov—Incoterms* 2010.

DDP (Delivered Duty Paid)

The seller bears all risks and costs associated with delivering the goods to the named place of destination ready for unloading and clearing for import.

GROUP 2: TERMS THAT APPLY TO SEA AND INLAND WATERWAY TRANSPORT ONLY

FAS (Free Alongside Ship)

The seller clears the goods for export and delivers them when they are placed alongside the vessel at the named port of shipment. The buyer assumes all risks and costs for goods from this point forward.

FOB (Free on Board)

The seller clears the goods for export and delivers them when they are onboard the vessel at the named port of shipment. The buyer assumes all risks and costs for goods from this moment forward.

CFR (Cost and Freight)

The seller clears the goods for export and delivers them when they are onboard the vessel at the port of shipment. The seller bears the cost of freight to the named port of destination. The buyer assumes all risks for goods from the time goods have been delivered on board the vessel at the port of shipment.

CIF (Cost, Insurance, and Freight)

The seller clears the goods for export and delivers them when they are onboard the vessel at the port of shipment. The seller bears the cost of freight and insurance to the named port of destination. The seller's insurance requirement is only for minimum coverage. The buyer is responsible for all costs associated with unloading the goods at the named port of destination and clearing goods for import. The risk passes from seller to buyer once the goods are onboard the vessel at the port of shipment.

Although Incoterms use is not mandatory, they are generally accepted by legal authorities as well as buyers and sellers worldwide. In addition, it is acceptable to use previous versions of Incoterms, but both parties should clearly indicate which version is being used (e.g., Incoterms 2010, Incoterms 2000, Incoterms 1990).

METHODS OF PAYMENT[14]

With respect to international transactions, **methods of payment** refer to the manner by which a seller will be paid by a buyer and methods of payment are much more challenging in international logistics than in domestic logistics. The goals of international buyers and sellers are pretty much the same as those for domestic buyers and sellers—buyers want to receive the product that was paid for, and sellers want to get paid. However, the vagaries of international trade, such as delayed transportation and the economic and political riskiness of particular countries, impact the likelihood of successfully achieving these goals. Moreover, incorrect documentation for international shipments as well as documentation with incorrect information can cause sellers not to be paid by buyers.

---

[14]The material in this section is largely drawn from Jim Sherlock and Jonathan Reuvid, eds., *The Handbook of International Trade* (Edinburgh, UK: GMB Publishing, 2005), Part 8.

Four distinct international methods of payment exist—cash in advance, letters of credit, bills of exchange, and the open account—and similar to terms of sale, the different payment methods offer varying amounts of risk to the involved parties. For example, although cash in advance is of minimal risk to the seller, it is extremely risky to the buyer—what if the paid-for product is never received? Alternatively, an **open account**, where a seller sends the goods and all documents directly to the buyer and trusts the buyer to pay by a certain date, involves tremendous potential risk for the seller and minimal risk for the buyer.

The continuing worldwide economic uncertainty has resulted in a pronounced reduction in credit availability for open account financing and generated renewed usage of letters of credit as an international payment method.[15] A **letter of credit** is issued by a bank and guarantees payment to a seller provided that the seller has complied with the applicable terms and conditions of the particular transaction. A sample letter of credit appears in Figure 14.3; note the specific terms such as duplicate certificates of origin and duplicate packing lists, among others.

The method of payment for international shipments should be established at the time that a shipment price is decided upon and the payment method can be influenced by key factors such as the country the product is to be sold in and the seller's assessment of buyer risk. For example, with respect to the country the product is to be sold in, buyers located in countries characterized by political and/or economic instability would likely need to pay via cash in advance. The seller's assessment of buyer risk can be based on previous experience with the buyer, references from other companies that trade with the buyer, and the buyer's credit rating, if available.

INTERNATIONAL TRADE SPECIALISTS

Few companies involved in international logistics rely solely on in-house personnel to manage all shipping operations. Specialist firms have developed, and most companies involved in international trade eventually use one or more services that these specialists provide. Several international trade specialists will be discussed in this section.

International Freight Forwarders

International freight forwarders specialize in handling either vessel shipments or air shipments, yet their functions are generally the same. Some of their principal functions are discussed in the following paragraphs.

ADVISING ON ACCEPTANCE OF LETTERS OF CREDIT When a client receives a letter of credit, the document contains many conditions that the seller must meet. The forwarder determines whether the client can meet these conditions, and, if it cannot, it will advise the client that the letter of credit must be amended. The buyer and buyer's bank must be notified before the order can be processed further.

BOOKING SPACE ON CARRIERS Space is frequently more difficult to obtain on international carriers than on domestic carriers for several reasons. Vessel or aircraft departures are less frequent, and the capacities of planes or ships are strictly limited. Connections with other carriers are more difficult to arrange, and the relative bargaining strength of any one shipper with an international carrier is usually weaker than it is with respect to domestic carriers. Forwarders are experienced at keeping tabs on available carrier space, and because they

---

[15]Bernie Hart, "Risks and Rewards," *Gulf Shipper*, January 12, 2009, 58–60.

IRREVOCABLE COMMERCIAL LETTER OF CREDIT

Since 1852

WELLS FARGO BANK, N.A.

FORMERLY WELLS FARGO BANK AMERICAN TRUST COMPANY
HEAD OFFICE: 464 CALIFORNIA STREET, SAN FRANCISCO, CALIFORNIA 94104

INTERNATIONAL DIVISION — COMMERCIAL L/C DEPARTMENT — CABLE ADDRESS WELLS

OUR LETTER OF CREDIT NO. 27724 — AMOUNT: US$12,288.00 — DATE: April 1, 19
THIS NUMBER MUST BE MENTIONED ON ALL DRAFTS AND CORRESPONDENCE

- The Japan Co.
- Box X 25
- Tokyo, Japan

S P E C I M E N

- Wells Fargo Bank N.A.
- Fuji Bldg., 2-3, 3-chome
- Marunouchi, Chiyoda-ku
- Tokyo, Japan

GENTLEMEN:

BY ORDER OF Wards, Oakland, California

AND FOR ACCOUNT OF same

WE HEREBY AUTHORIZE YOU TO DRAW ON us

UP TO AN AGGREGATE AMOUNT OF Twelve Thousand Two Hundred Eighty Eight and No/100 U.S. Dollars

AVAILABLE BY YOUR DRAFTS AT sight

ACCOMPANIED BY
Commercial Invoice and two copies certifying merchandise is in accordance with Purchase Order No. 08142.
Signed Special Customs Invoice in duplicate.
Certificate of Origin in duplicate.
Packing List in duplicate.
Full set clean ocean bills of lading to order shipper, blank endorsed, freight collect, notify Wards, Oakland, California, dated on board not later than May 25, 19 .

Relating to: Transistor Radios from FOB vessel Japanese Port to San Francisco Bay Port.

Partial shipments permitted. Insurance to be effected by buyers
Transhipment is not permitted.

Negotiating bank is to forward all documents attached to the original draft in one airmail envelope.

Courtesy Wells Fargo Bank

DRAFTS MUST BE DRAWN AND NEGOTIATED NOT LATER THAN June 5, 19
ALL DRAFTS DRAWN UNDER THIS CREDIT MUST BEAR ITS DATE AND NUMBER AND THE AMOUNTS MUST BE ENDORSED ON THE REVERSE SIDE OF THIS LETTER OF CREDIT BY THE NEGOTIATING BANK.
WE HEREBY AGREE WITH THE DRAWERS, ENDORSERS AND BONA FIDE HOLDERS OF ALL DRAFTS DRAWN UNDER AND IN COMPLIANCE WITH THE TERMS OF THIS CREDIT, THAT SUCH DRAFTS WILL BE DULY HONORED UPON PRESENTATION TO THE DRAWEE.
THIS CREDIT IS SUBJECT TO THE UNIFORM CUSTOMS AND PRACTICE FOR DOCUMENTARY CREDITS (1962 REVISION), INTERNATIONAL CHAMBER OF COMMERCE BROCHURE NO. 222.

W/ SPECIMEN
AUTHORIZED SIGNATURE

FIGURE 14.3 Letter of Credit *Source:* Courtesy of Wells Fargo Bank.

represent more business to the carrier than an individual shipper does, they have more success when finding space is difficult.

PREPARING AN EXPORT DECLARATION An export declaration is required by the U.S. government for statistical and control purposes and must be prepared and filed for nearly every shipment.

PREPARING AN AIR WAYBILL OR BILL OF LADING The international air waybill is a fairly standardized document; the ocean bill of lading is not. The latter may differ between ocean lines, coastal areas through which the shipments are moving, and for a variety of other circumstances. Ocean bills of lading are frequently negotiable, which means that whoever legally holds the document may take delivery of the shipment. Because nearly every ocean vessel line has its own bill of lading, a forwarder's expertise is necessary to fill it out accurately.

OBTAINING CONSULAR DOCUMENTS Consular documents involve obtaining permission from the importing country for the goods to enter. Documents are prepared that the importing country uses to determine duties to be levied on the shipment as it passes through customs.

ARRANGING FOR INSURANCE Unlike domestic shipments, international shipments must be insured. Either the individual shipment must be insured or the shipper (or forwarder) must have a blanket policy covering all shipments. International airlines offer insurance at nominal rates. Rates on vessel shipments are higher, and the entire process is complex because of certain practices that are acceptable at sea. For example, if the vessel is in peril of sinking, the captain may have some cargo jettisoned (thrown overboard) to keep the vessel afloat. The owners of the surviving cargo and the vessel owner must then share the costs of reimbursing the shippers whose cargo was thrown overboard.

PREPARING AND SENDING SHIPPING NOTICES AND DOCUMENTS The financial transaction involving the sale of goods is carefully coordinated with their physical movement, and rather elaborate customs and procedures have evolved to ensure that the seller is paid when the goods are delivered. The international freight forwarder handles the shipper's role in the document preparation and exchange stages, and it is necessary to have certain documents available as the shipment crosses international boundaries.

SERVING AS GENERAL CONSULTANT ON EXPORT MATTERS Questions continually arise when dealing with new products, terms of sale, new markets, or new regulations, and a good international freight forwarder knows the answers or how to find them. A conscientious forwarder also advises a shipper as to when certain procedures, such as similar shipments to the same market, become so repetitive that the shipper can handle the procedures in its own export department at a cost lower than the fees charged by the forwarder.

International freight forwarders' income comes from three sources. Similar to domestic forwarders, they buy space wholesale and sell it retail. By consolidating shipments, they benefit from a lower rate per pound. In addition, most carriers allow the forwarders a commission on shipping revenues they generate for the carriers. Also, forwarders charge fees for preparing documents, performing research, and the like. Figures 14.4 and 14.5 show forms used by forwarders. Figure 14.4 is used to prepare cost estimates for the client to use when quoting a price to a potential overseas buyer while Figure 14.5 is the form that a forwarder uses to bill a client for handling a shipment.

Nonvessel-Operating Common Carriers

Another international logistics intermediary, the **nonvessel-operating common carrier** (NVOCC), is often confused with the international freight forwarder, because both intermediaries consolidate freight from different shippers and leverage this volume to negotiate favorable transportation rates from ocean carriers. The United States requires both NVOCCs and international freight forwarders to be licensed as ocean transportation intermediaries by the Federal Maritime Commission. According to the Federal Maritime Commission, NVOCCs are common carriers and thus have common carrier obligations to serve and deliver, among others. From the shipper's perspective, an NVOCC is a carrier; from an ocean carrier's perspective, an NVOCC is a shipper.

Although a company can simultaneously hold both NVOCC and international freight forwarder licenses, it cannot act as an NVOCC and international freight forwarder on the same shipment. Currently, three key factors differentiate NVOCCs from international freight forwarders: (1) NVOCCs can issue their own bills of lading; (2) NVOCCs can set their own rates for ocean and intermodal shipments; and (3) NVOCCs can enter into service contracts with ocean carriers to purchase transportation services.[16]

---

[16]James E. Devine, Jr., "10 Steps for FMC Licensing as an OTI," *Florida Shipper*, February 18, 2008, 11, 74.

EXPORT QUOTATION WORKSHEET

DATE_____ REF/PRO FORMA INVOICE NO._____
COMMODITY_____ EXPECTED SHIP DATE_____
CUSTOMER_____ PACKED DIMENSIONS_____
COUNTRY_____ PACKED WEIGHT_____
PAYMENT TERMS_____ PACKED CUBE_____

PRODUCTS TO BE SHIPPED FROM_____
                                    TO_____

SELLING PRICE OF GOODS: $_____

SPECIAL EXPORT PACKING:
    $_____   quoted by_____
    $_____   quoted by_____
    $_____   quoted by_____ $_____

INLAND FREIGHT:
    $_____   quoted by_____
    $_____   quoted by_____
    $_____   quoted by_____ $_____
    Inland freight includes the following charges:
    ☐ unloading   ☐ pier delivery   ☐ terminal   ☐_____

OCEAN FREIGHT			AIR FREIGHT		
quoted by		tariff item		quoted by	spec code
$_____ _____		#_____	$_____ _____		#_____
$_____ _____		#_____	$_____ _____		#_____
$_____ _____		#_____	$_____ _____		#_____

Ocean freight includes the following surcharges: Air freight includes the following surcharges:

☐ Port congestion   ☐ Heavy lift   ☐ Fuel adjustment
☐ Currency adjustment ☐ Bunker   ☐ Container stuffing
☐ Container rental   ☐ Wharfage   ☐ _____
☐ _____   ☐ _____

INSURANCE ☐ includes war risk   ☐ INSURANCE ☐ includes war risk
rate:_____ per $100 or $_____   rate:_____ per $100 or $_____

TOTAL OCEAN CHARGES $_____   **TOTAL AIR CHARGES** $_____ $_____
notes: notes:

FORWARDING FEES: $_____
Includes: ☐ Courier Fees ☐ Certification Fees ☐ Banking Fees ☐ _____

CONSULAR LEGALIZATION FEES: $_____

INSPECTION FEES: $_____

DIRECT BANK CHARGES: $_____

OTHER CHARGES: _____ $_____
                _____ $_____

TOTAL: ☐ FOB_____   ☐ C & F_____
        ☐ FAS_____   ☐ CIF_____ $_____

Form 10-020 Printed and Sold by *UNZ&CO* 190 Baldwin Ave., Jersey City, NJ 07306 • (800) 631-3098

FIGURE 14.4 A Forwarder's Export Quotation Sheet Showing Factors to Include When Determining the Price to Quote a Potential Buyer of a Product   *Source:* Reprinted with permission of Unz & Co., 190 Baldwin Ave., Jersey City, NJ.

			INVOICE NO.	

DATE

YOUR REF. NO.

CONSIGNEE:

FROM:			CARRIER:
TO:	☐ AIR	☐ OCEAN	B/L OR AWB NO.

INLAND FREIGHT/LOCAL CARTAGE		$
EXPORT PACKING		
AIR FREIGHT CHARGES		
OCEAN FREIGHT/TERMINAL CHARGES		
CONSULAR FEES		
INSURANCE/CERTIFICATE OF INSURANCE		
CHAMBER OF COMMERCE		
BROKERAGE FEES		
FORWARDING		
HANDLING AND EXPEDITING		
DOCUMENT PREPARATION		
MESSENGER FEES		
POSTAGE		
TELEPHONE		
CABLES		
CERTIFICATE OF ORIGIN		
BANKING: (LETTER OF CREDIT/SIGHT DRAFT)		
MISCELLANEOUS		
	TOTAL	$

As amended by the United States Shipping Act of 1984.

_____ has a policy against payment, solicitation, or receipt of any rebate, directly or indirectly, which would be unlawful under the United States Shipping Act, 1916, as amended

FIGURE 14.5 Invoice Form Used by a Freight Forwarder to Bill Client for Handling an Export Shipment *Source:* Reprinted with permission of Unz & Co., 190 Baldwin Ave., Jersey City, NJ.

Export Management Companies

Sometimes the manufacturer seeking to export retains the services of an **export management company** (EMC), a firm that acts as the export sales department for a manufacturer. EMCs can provide a variety of value-added activities to include marketing research in prospective countries, developing appropriate distribution channels, handling sales correspondence in foreign languages, ensuring that foreign labeling requirements are met, among others. When handling the overseas sales for a U.S. firm, the export management firm either buys and sells on its own account or provides credit information regarding each potential buyer to the U.S. manufacturer, which can judge whether to take the risk.

Export management companies often specialize by product (products) or by country (regions). For example, Five Star NDT exports, markets, and sells U.S.-manufactured products to grocery chains and retail stores in Mexico. To this end, Five Star represents U.S. manufacturers like Mrs. Fields Cookies and Sun Dish Detergent whose products are sold in Mexican retailers such as Benavides, Calimax, and Walmart de Mexico.[17]

---

[17]http://www.soldinmexico.com/

Export Packers

Export packers custom pack shipments when the exporter lacks the equipment or the expertise to do so itself. Export packaging involves packaging for two distinct purposes, in addition to the sales function of some packaging. The first is to allow goods to move easily through customs. For a country assessing duties on the weight of both the item and its container, this means selecting lightweight packing materials. For items moving through the mail, it might mean construction of an envelope with an additional small flap that a customs inspector could open and look inside without having to open the entire envelope. For crated machinery, this might involve using open slats rather than completely closed construction (the customs inspectors would likely satisfy their curiosity by peering and probing through the openings between the slats).

The second purpose of export packing is to protect products in what almost always is a more difficult journey than they would experience if they were destined for domestic consignees. For many firms, the traditional ocean packaging method is to take the product in its domestic pack and enclose it in a wooden container. Ocean shipments are subject to more moisture damage and more extreme temperature variations than are domestic shipments. For example, because canned goods moving through hot areas sweat, causing the cans to rust and the labels to become unglued, Campbell's Soup adds desiccants to its cartons of soup; otherwise specks of rust will appear on the cans during their sea voyage.[18]

TRANSPORTATION CONSIDERATIONS IN INTERNATIONAL LOGISTICS

In many cases the distances associated with international shipments are often much greater than those associated with domestic shipments. Because these increased distances often mean that the buyer or seller must choose water or air transportation, we'll take a somewhat detailed look at ocean shipping and international air transportation in this section. This will be followed by a discussion of surface transportation in international logistics.

Before beginning our discussion of ocean shipping and international air transportation, you should recognize the transit time/cost trade-offs between them. For example, a shipment from Shanghai to Los Angeles might take one day by air transportation and two weeks by water transportation. On the other hand, the cost of air transportation for this shipment can be 8–10 times more expensive than sending it by water.[19]

Moreover, international transportation can't be effective or efficient without fairly identical handling equipment being in place at each end of the trip. Thus, containerization isn't feasible unless both the origin and destination ports are equipped with the appropriate container handling equipment. Having said this, there continue to be countries where certain products are still stowed or unloaded by stevedores carrying individual bags on their shoulders (or heads) and walking up and down gangplanks. Although this manual loading and unloading is inefficient because of increasing loading or unloading times, the nations in which this practice occurs are often very poor, and manual cargo handling can be a means for providing jobs (and thus income) to many people.

Ocean Shipping

If you don't live near a seaport, you might not have an appreciation for the importance of water transportation in international trade; a frequently cited statistic is that approximately 60 percent of cross-border shipments moves by water transportation. Another example of the importance of water transportation in international trade can be seen in Table 14.2, which provides data on the

---

[18]American Shipper, September 2001, 26.
[19]Cameron McWhirter and Shelley Banjo, "Tentative Deal Averts Port Strike," *The Wall Street Journal*, Saturday/Sunday, December 29–30, 2012, B1–B2.

Table 14.2	World's Busiest Container Ports (2012)	
Port	**Country**	**TEU Throughput**
Shanghai	China	32,529,000
Singapore	Singapore	31,649,400
Hong Kong	China	23,097,000
Shenzhen	China	22,941,300
Pusan	South Korea	17,030,000
Ningbo	China	16,830,000
Guangzhou	China	14,743,600
Qingdao	China	14,500,000
Dubai	United Arab Emirates	13,280,000
Tianjin	China	12,300,000

Source: www.daily-cargo.com/english/2013/0221.

world's 10 busiest container ports in 2012, as measured by twenty-foot equivalent units (TEU) throughput. As pointed out in Table 14.2, Shanghai, the world's busiest container port, handled over 32 million TEUs in 2012; moreover, 9 of the 10 busiest container ports are located in Asia, with 7 of the ports located in China. Note that no European ports, and no U.S. ports, rank among the 10 busiest container ports.

In addition, you might not be aware of the variety of ship types available for transporting international shipments by water. For example, dry-bulk cargoes, such as grain, ores, sulfur, sugar, scrap iron, coal, lumber, and logs, usually move in complete vessel-load lots on chartered vessels. A bulk carrier is shown in Figure 14.6. There are also large, specialized dry cargo ships that are often owned by shippers. Nissan Motor Company of Japan, for example, owns auto-carrying ships, which can carry between 1,200 and 1,900 vehicles. Liquid bulk cargoes, such as

FIGURE 14.6 An Ocean Bulk Carrier Being Loaded with Export Coal Carried by a Mechanical Device at Far Left *Source:* Shutterstock Photo.

petroleum, are transported by tankers that are either owned by oil companies or leased (chartered) by them from individuals who invest in ships.

Another type of vessel that combines aspects of several vessel types is the parcel tanker, which has over 50 different tanks, ranging from 350 to 2,200 cubic meters. Each can carry a different liquid and is loaded and unloaded through a separate piping system. The tanks have different types of coating; some are temperature controlled. Some of the vessels go on round-the-world voyages and carry palm oil, coconut oil, chemicals, and refined petroleum products.

Finally, containerships dominate the traffic between Europe and the United States, Europe and Asia, and the United States and Asia. Shippers or forwarders tender full containers, and if a shipper tenders a less-than-container lot, the vessel operator must load all the less-than-container lots into containers so that the cargo can be loaded aboard the containership. In large containerships, some of the containers are carried above the level of the deck, which increases the vessel's cubic-carrying capacity.

We pointed out in an earlier chapter that the carrying capacity of containerships continues to increase, and this increased vessel size is one contributor to the growth of **load centers**, or major ports where thousands of containers arrive and depart each week. As vessel sizes increase, it becomes more costly to stop (call) at multiple ports in a geographic area, and as a result operators of larger containerships prefer to call at only one port in a geographic area. Load centers might affect the dynamics of international transportation in the sense that some ports will be relegated to providing feeder service to the load centers. In addition, load centers might affect supplemental transportation providers, such as truck and rail, particularly if the existing road and rail infrastructure is insufficient to accommodate the higher volumes that will be associated with the megaports.

Shipping Conferences and Alliances

Beginning in the mid-1860s, ocean rates were determined by **shipping conferences**, or cartels of all ocean vessel operators operating between certain trade areas such as Asia and Europe. Historically, shipping conferences provided both rate stability and guaranteed space availability due in large part to the ability of member carriers to collectively set rates and service levels without fear of antitrust prosecution.

The relationship between buyers (shippers) and sellers (carriers) and groups of sellers (conferences or alliances) has changed dramatically over the last 20 years, and these relationships are currently very fluid. In certain regions, this commercial relationship has moved from a tightly regulated environment to a largely unregulated environment wherein shippers and carriers are free to work out whatever commercial relationship best suits them in confidential contractual agreements.

In particular, the influence of shipping conferences has been on the wane in the United States and Europe since the late 1990s. For example, although the U.S. Ocean Shipping Reform Act (OSRA) of 1998 did not explicitly prohibit shipping conferences, OSRA allowed ocean shippers and carriers to negotiate confidential contracts—which severely undermined conferences' power and lessened their appeal. Moreover, in late 2008 the European Union removed the shipping conferences' antitrust immunity for collective ratemaking for ocean shipments between EU countries. This dissolution of European shipping conferences has caused Asian shippers to push for the end of shipping conferences in their region.[20]

In the mid-1990s, **ocean carrier alliances**, in which carriers retain their individual identities but cooperate in the area of operations, began forming in the container trades. There are presently three major ocean carrier alliances: the Grand Alliance II [consisting of Hapag-Lloyd, Nippon Yusen Keisha (NYK) Line, and Orient Overseas Container Line (OOCL)];

---

[20]No author, "Asia Shippers Push for Ban on Liner Conferences," *The Journal of Commerce*, September 12, 2011, 6.

the New World Alliance [consisting of American President Lines (APL), Hyundai Merchant Marine, and Mitsui O.S.K. Lines (MOL)]; and CYKH Group (consisting of China Ocean Shipping Company (Cosco), Hanjin, "K" Line, and Yang Ming). A newly formed alliance, the P3 (consisting of Maersk Lines, Mediterranean Shipping Company, and CMA CGM), is set to begin service during 2014.

These alliances provide two primary benefits to participating members, namely, the sharing of vessel space and the ability to offer shippers a broader service network (i.e., ports of call). Although alliances are not conferences, their size allows the alliances to exercise considerable clout in their dealings with shippers, port terminal operators, and connecting land carriers.

International Airfreight

Three types of international airfreight operations exist: chartered aircraft, integrated air carriers that specialize in carrying parcels, and scheduled air carriers. Chartering an entire aircraft is, of course, expensive, but sometimes the expense can be justified. For example, chartered aircraft can be used in the transport of livestock and pedigreed animals and one particular shipment involved carrying 7,000 cattle from Texas to southern Chile. Nineteen charter flights were involved, each lasting 15 hours. The comparable time by sea was 20 days, and past experience showed that the sea journey was hard on the cattle, causing either lung damage or long delays before the animals could be bred.

A second type of international airfreight focuses on parcel services offered by well-known carriers such as UPS, FedEx, and DHL International. These companies provide land pickup and delivery services for documents and small parcels and are called *integrated carriers* because they own all their vehicles and the facilities that fall in between. These parcel services are of special significance to international logistics because they often provide the fastest service between many major points. They are also often employed to carry the documentation that is generated by—and is very much a part of—the international movement of materials, although many international trade documents can now be transferred electronically. The integrated carriers also handle documentation services for their clients.

The principal function of scheduled airlines is to carry passengers; freight tends to be a secondary consideration and is often carried in the bellies of passenger aircraft. Having said this, some scheduled airlines use all-freight aircraft (called *freighters*) in certain markets. For example, Lufthansa, a German airline, flies nonstop freighters between Frankfurt, Germany, and Shanghai, China, as well as between Frankfurt and Delhi, India, among other city pairs.

Historically, the routes of scheduled international air carriers were established by negotiations between nations and these negotiations generally involved two countries (called *bilateral agreements*). The types of issues that could be negotiated in these bilateral agreements included the number of flights between the two nations, the types of aircraft to be used, the total number of seats to be offered, the regions or cities to be served, the carriers that were to serve particular regions or city pairs, among others.

While the traditional bilateral air agreements provided an important stimulus to international air transportation, these agreements tended to be quite restrictive in nature as illustrated in the previous paragraph. To this end, **open skies agreements**, which liberalize international aviation opportunities and limit federal government involvement, have become increasingly popular in the twenty-first century. Perhaps the most prominent open skies treaty is the Open Aviation Area agreement between the United States and 27 European Union member states that went into effect in March 2008. A key provision of this agreement is that any EU airline as well as any U.S. airline can fly between any point in the EU and any point in the United States.[21]

---

[21]Cathy Buyck, "A Slow Opening," *Air Transport World*, March 2008, 24–30.

Surface Transport Considerations

While ocean shipping and air transportation play a key role in international trade, particularly among shipments that move long distances, an understanding of surface transportation considerations is also important. For example, highway freight transportation is accomplished by trucks (motor carriers) in certain countries; alternatively, highway freight transportation can be provided by bicycles or some type of animal and cart combination in certain countries.

Surface transportation considerations in international logistics include an understanding of both a country's infrastructure and its modal operating characteristics. As an example of infrastructure characteristics, the United States ranks first in the world in terms of highway mileage (approximately 6.5 million kilometers), followed by China (approximately 4.1 million kilometers) and India (approximately 3.3 million kilometers). However, only 2,000 kilometers of Indian highways are classified as expressways, compared to 75,000 for the United States and 85,000 kilometers for China.[22]

The relative paucity of expressways in India suggests that motor carrier transit times might be slower than in other countries, and indeed one report suggested that Indian truckers rarely travel more than 300 kilometers a day (compared to over 1,000 kilometers a day in some Western countries). Moreover, a truck trip from Delhi to Kolkata (formerly Calcutta), which is approximately 1,500 kilometers, can take more than four days to complete.[23] By contrast, several U.S. motor carriers promise transit times of approximately 30 hours for a 1,500 kilometer trip.

In addition to infrastructure characteristics, it's also important to understand a country's modal operating characteristics for surface transportation. For example, a motor carrier shipment from Cleveland, Ohio, to Orlando, Florida experiences virtually no delays when moving across state borders (e.g., from Ohio into West Virginia; from West Virginia into Virginia). Alternatively, multistate motor carrier shipments in other countries can be subject to lengthy delays when moving across state borders. One source of delays is that certain countries limit a motor carrier's operations to within a particular state's borders; as a result, multistate shipments must be transferred from one company's vehicle to another company's vehicle whenever crossing into another state. Another source of delays is that certain countries conduct inspections of trucks as they move from one state to another. This can include physical counting and inspection of all shipments, inspection of documentation, vehicle inspection, as well as driver inspection. Keep in mind that delays, whatever their source, result in slower transit times and increased costs.

Service performance is another important modal operational characteristic associated with surface transportation in other countries. For example, freight is given lower priority than passengers in rail transportation in China. Railroad transportation in China is also plagued by poor handling techniques, resulting in higher damage than if shipments moved by truck. In addition, the theft of rail freight is quite common in China and in some cases shippers provide their own security guards on trains to protect their goods from theft![24]

An alternative to surface transport in some nations is **short-sea shipping** (SSS), which refers to waterborne transportation that utilizes inland and coastal waterways to move shipments from domestic ports to their destination.[25] SSS is more widely accepted and practiced in Europe (see Figure 14.7), and the European Union has championed a Motorways of the Sea concept that specifies four well-defined short-sea shipping lanes involving EU member nations. Potential benefits to SSS include reduced rail and truck congestion, reduced highway damage, a reduction in truck-related noise and air pollution, and improved waterways utilization.

---

[22]Highway data taken from *The CIA World Factbook*, 2013.
[23]http://forbesindia.com/printcontent/32618
[24]Christina Wu, "China Logistics Profile," *USDA Foreign Agricultural Service GAIN Report*, 2003.
[25]www.marad.dot.gov

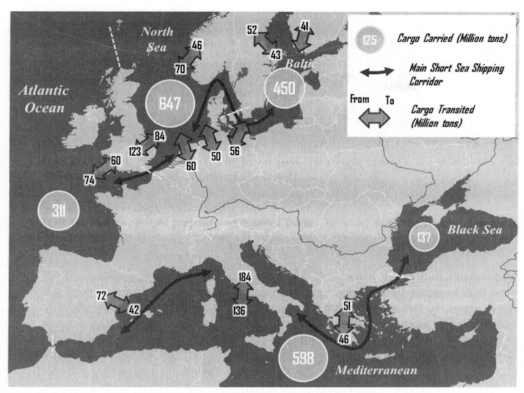

FIGURE 14.7 The European Short Sea Shipping Network *Source:* Courtesy of Dr. Jean-Paul Rodrigue, *The Geography of Transport Systems*, 2nd edition, Routledge, 2013.

Although the short-sea concept has received some attention in North America, a short-sea service that linked Halifax, Nova Scotia, to several Northeast U.S. ports ceased operations in early 2012 after only nine months in operation. The fact that this service failed—and failed in such a short period of time—makes it highly unlikely that SSS will be a viable North American transportation option in the coming years.[26]

INTERNATIONAL TRADE INVENTORIES

Even under the best conditions, the movement of products in an international supply chain is never as smooth as a comparable domestic movement. Because greater uncertainties, misunderstandings, and delays often arise in international movements, safety stocks must be larger. In addition, inventory valuation is difficult because of continually changing exchange rates. If goods are valued in the currency of where they are produced, that value can fluctuate with respect to the currency value of where the product is being stored. When a nation's (or the world's) currency is unstable, investments in inventories may increase because they are believed to be less risky than holding cash or securities.

Firms involved in international trade must give careful thought to their inventory policies, in part because inventory available for sale in one nation may not necessarily serve the needs of markets in nearby nations. Consider, for example, that electrical voltages, electrical plugs, and electrical sockets differ across countries. As a result, a 120-volt electrical product designed for use in the United States would need both a voltage converter and a plug adapter in order to be used in Europe.

---

[26]Peter T. Leach, "Marine Highway Suffers a Blowout," *The Journal of Commerce*, May 7, 2012, 38, 40.

Product return (reverse logistics) policies are another concern with respect to international inventory management. One issue is that, unlike the United States where products can be returned for virtually any reason, some countries don't allow returns unless the product is defective in some respect. A second challenge with international returns is that it may be unreasonable or impractical to tell buyers to return a defective item to the country where it was produced.

Warehousing is another inventory-related consideration associated with international logistics. Whereas warehousing facilities in economically developed countries have been developed to meet the requirements of contemporary logistics systems (e.g., high ceilings, sufficient lighting), warehousing facilities in other countries can be more problematic. For example, a report commissioned by the Indian government in 2011 indicated that only about 20 percent of the country's warehousing facilities were mechanized—with mechanized being defined as either *hand pallet trucks or forklifts.*[27]

LOGISTICS PERFORMANCE INDEX[28]

We'll conclude this chapter with a look at a relatively new international logistics concept, the **Logistics Performance Index (LPI)** that was first introduced in 2007 and then updated in 2010 and again in 2012. The LPI was created in recognition of the importance of logistics in global trade and measures a country's performance across six logistical dimensions (seven logistical dimensions were evaluated in 2007):

- Efficiency of the clearance process (i.e., speed, simplicity, and predictability of formalities) by border control agencies, including customs
- Quality of trade and transport-related infrastructure (e.g., ports, railroads, roads, information technology)
- Ease of arranging competitively priced shipments
- Competence and quality of logistics services (e.g., transport operators, customs brokers)
- Ability to track and trace consignments
- Timeliness of shipments in reaching destination within the scheduled or expected delivery time

The LPI incorporates data for approximately 155 countries using a score of 1 (lowest possible score) to 5 (highest possible score) to rate each of the six dimensions. Singapore (LPI score = 4.13) and Hong Kong (LPI score = 4.12) were the two top-ranked countries in the 2012 LPI, while Burundi (LPI score = 1.61) and Djibouti (LPI score = 1.80) were the two lowest-ranked countries.

The LPI is a potentially valuable international logistics tool because the data can be analyzed from several different perspectives. First, the LPI can be analyzed for all countries according to the overall LPI score as well as according to scores on each of the six dimensions. For example, while Hong Kong ranks second in terms of the overall 2012 LPI score, it ranks first in terms of the "ease of arranging competitively priced shipments" dimension.

Second, the LPI can be analyzed in terms of an individual country's performance (1) over time, (2) relative to its geographic region, and (3) relative to its income group. For example, one can compare Argentina's overall and dimension-specific LPI scores (1) in 2007, 2010, and 2012, (2) to Latin American and Caribbean countries, and (3) to upper-middle-income countries. The 2012 LPI also allows for comparisons to the top performing country in a geographic region as well as the top performing country in an income group. Thus, Chile was the top-performing Latin American and Caribbean country while Taiwan was the top-performing upper-middle-income country.

---

[27]*Report of Working Group on Warehousing Development and Regulation* (New Delhi, India: Government of India, October, 2011).
[28]The material in this section is based on *Logistics Performance Index*, http://lpisurvey.worldbank.org/

Summary

This chapter covered various aspects of international logistics, which differs from domestic logistics in many respects, such as by having a requirement for numerous documents as well as by greater distances between origin and destination points. Macroenvironmental influences can provide significant challenges for international logistics; the chapter discussed three specific macroenvironmental factors: political, economic, and cultural.

From a political perspective, we learned that international trade can be influenced through tariff and nontariff barriers and that federal governments are actively involved in cross-border trade. The chapter also mentioned that different economic factors, such as currency fluctuations and economic integration, can impact international logistics. In terms of culture, a country's time orientation can influence the use of schedules as well as the emphasis placed on on-time performance.

The chapter also looked at three key operational issues—documentation, terms of sale, and methods of payment—in international logistics. Several key pieces of international documentation, including the certificate of origin and shipper's export declaration, were examined and international terms of sale—Incoterms—were discussed. And because international logistics is complex, many firms rely on specialists, such as international freight forwarders and export packers, to help with export and import transactions.

The chapter also examined transportation and inventory considerations in international distribution. We looked at ocean shipping, international airfreight, and surface transportation, and we learned that the greater uncertainties associated with international shipments necessitate higher inventory levels. The chapter concluded with a discussion of a relatively new international logistics concept, the Logistics Performance Index.

Questions for Discussion and Review

14.1 Discuss some of the key political restrictions on cross-border trade.

14.2 How might a particular country's government be involved in international trade?

14.3 Discuss how a nation's market size might impact international trade and, in turn, international logistics.

14.4 How might economic integration impact international logistics?

14.5 How can language considerations impact the packaging and labeling of international shipments?

14.6 What is a certificate of origin, a commercial invoice, and a shipper's export declaration?

14.7 Discuss international terms of sale and Incoterms.

14.8 Name the four methods of payment for international shipments. Which method is riskiest for the buyer? For the seller?

14.9 Discuss four possible functions that might be performed by international freight forwarders.

14.10 What is an NVOCC?

14.11 What are the two primary purposes of export packing?

14.12 Discuss the importance of water transportation for international trade.

14.13 Explain the load center concept. How might load centers affect the dynamics of international transportation?

14.14 Discuss the role of ocean carrier alliances in international logistics.

14.15 How do integrated air carriers impact the effectiveness and efficiency of international logistics?

14.16 How do open-skies agreements differ from bilateral agreements?

14.17 Discuss the potential sources of delays in certain countries with respect to motor carrier shipments that move across state borders.

14.18 Define what is meant by short-sea shipping (SSS), and discuss some advantages of SSS.

14.19 What are some challenges associated with inventory management in cross-border trade?

14.20 What is the Logistics Performance Index? How can it be used?

Suggested Readings

Cui, Lianguang, Ivan Shong-Lee Su, and Suzanne Hertz. "Logistics Innovation in China." *Transportation Journal* 51, no. 1 (2012): 98–117.

Douet, Marie and Jean Francois Cappuccilli. "A Review of Short Sea Shipping Policy in the European Union." *Journal of Transport Geography* 19, no. 4 (2011): 968–976.

Jayaram, Jayanth and Balram Avittathur. "Insights into India." *Supply Chain Management Review* 16, no. 4 (2012): 34–41.

Kumar, Sameer. "Logistics Routing and Flexibility and Lower Freight Costs through Use of Incoterms." *Transportation Journal* 49, no. 3 (2010): 48–56.

Liu, Xiaohong. "Competitiveness of Logistics Service Providers: A Cross-National Examination of Management Practices in China and the U.K." *International Journal of Logistics: Research & Applications* 14, no. 4 (2011): 251–269.

Martin, Juan Carlos. "Transportation Changes in Europe." *Transportation Journal* 50, no. 1 (2011): 109–124.

Paixao Casaca, Ana C. "Motorway of the Sea Port Requirements: The Viewpoint of Port Authorities." *International Journal of Logistics: Research & Applications* 11, no. 4 (2008): 279–294.

Tan, Albert Wee-Kan and Olli-Pekka Hilmola. "Future of Transshipment in Singapore." *Industrial Management & Data Systems* 112, no. 7 (2012): 1085–1100.

Tongzon, Jose. "Liberalization of Logistics Services: The Case of ASEAN." *International Journal of Logistics: Research & Applications* 14, no. 1 (2011): 11–34.

Wagner, Stephan M. "Innovation Management in the German Transportation Industry." *Journal of Business Logistics* 29, no. 2 (2008): 215–231.

Winston, Evelyn, Charlene A. Dadzie, and Kofi Q. Dadzie. "How Managers Handle Conflict in Supply Chain Collaborative Relationships in Ghana." *Journal of African Business* 10, no. 2 (2009): 203–217.

Xavier, Wescley Silva and Ricardo S. Martins. "Logistics Strategy and Organizational Structure in Brazilian Small and Medium-Sized Enterprises (SMES)." *Organizations and Markets in Emerging Economies* 2, no. 2 (2011): 91–116.

CASE

CASE 14.1 Nürnberg Augsburg Maschinenwerke (N.A.M.)

The Nürnberg Augsburg Maschinenwerke, one of Germany's most successful manufacturing companies, enjoys a long tradition. It dates from 1748, when the St. Antony Iron Mill opened in Oberhausen (located in the heart of the Ruhrgebiet industrial region) during the beginning years of German industrialization. The owners soon founded additional iron and coal mills, and then established the firm as Gute Hoffungshuette (GHH). Shortly following, in Augsburg and Nürnberg, several companies joined together to form Nürnberg Augsburg Maschinenwerke (N.A.M.). These two firms, GHH and N.A.M., would ultimately merge in the early twentieth century.

In the interim, N.A.M. had distinguished itself through the work of Rudolf Diesel, who invented his famous engine and then brought it to N.A.M. late in the nineteenth century. The diesel engine competed with the internal combustion engine in early automotive design and today powers heavy trucks, turbines, railroad engines, and ships. Based on this success, N.A.M. swiftly expanded manufacturing operations and distribution across the globe, only to have its foreign operations compromised by international politics on two occasions. First, N.A.M. lost most of its foreign property in the wake of World War I, a setback that, among other adjustments, encouraged its merger with GHH in 1920. Second, N.A.M. lost all of its foreign property again after World War II and had to rebuild and restructure much of its domestic operation as well. In 1955, the company opened a truck unit in Munich, which would later become the new company headquarters.

By 2003 the company had reclaimed its preeminence as a global player in heavy truck and bus design, engineering, and manufacturing, as well as in print technology, rocket, and energy science. It had reestablished both its plants and sales offices across the globe, and is one of the largest diesel engine makers in the world. Karl Huber was the N.A.M. regional vice president of sales for South America, and he supervised a team of local sales representatives in the countries of that continent, plus a small group of people in the Munich headquarters.

On August 15, Huber received an e-mail from Leopold Escabar in Caracas, who had just returned from an important meeting with local authorities in charge of redesigning the local public transportation systems for the Brazilian cities of São Paulo and Rio de Janeiro. Escabar had attended the meeting along with salespeople from competing truck and bus companies. Escabar gave Huber some good news and some bad news. Escabar had been told N.A.M. was favored to receive an order for 224 N.A.M. class #4-G two-section articulated buses (or "accordion" buses, as Escabar liked to call them), with the possibility of securing a contract for an additional 568 buses. To win the business, however, N.A.M. would have to meet cost and timing guarantees.

The customers first required that N.A.M. must match or beat the total price per unit, including shipping, that N.A.M. had received for a shipment of 233 buses to the transit district of Buenos Aires, six months earlier. That price was € 124,500 per bus. Huber had built in a small extra profit margin on the Buenos Aires deal, so he felt confident that to meet their pricing demand he could shave profit a little, if necessary, in this case.

The second guarantee, however, was more worrisome: The Brazilian authorities were feeling political heat because they were badly behind schedule in implementing their transportation plan and needed proof to show the public that their new programs were under way. So they had made this offer to N.A.M. on strict condition that the company could ensure delivery of the first 25 buses to Santos, the port that serves São Paulo, by November 15 (only three months away). If N.A.M. delivered this initial 90-day order on time, the company would receive a contract for the remaining 199 vehicles to be delivered in full within the following 15 months. The follow-on order for 568 more vehicles was, essentially, contingent on meeting terms of the initial contract to the letter, with regard to the 224 buses. All buses were to be delivered to the Port of Santos.

Huber whistled softly to himself as he read Escabar's e-mail. This would be a major order. In a single stroke, it could move him ahead of his regional sales targets for several quarters to come. Huber immediately sent back an e-mail, instructing Escabar to tentatively accept the offer, assuring the local authorities that they'd have their 25 buses in 90 days and the rest within 18 months. N.A.M. would formally agree to the proposal within five working days. Then he scratched his head and tried to figure out how. Huber had four days before the next managing director's meeting, at which time he would present the project and, with the vice president for production, propose a plan to accomplish it. Huber lunged for the phone and, scarcely glancing at the number pad, his fingers automatically dialed 4823.

Dieter Berndsen, the production V.P., listened as his old friend Huber described the opportunity, jotting down notes as he went. He explained to Huber that the factory in Munich was already producing to its limits, and the two other German facilities were also facing a backlog of orders through the fourth quarter. So Berndsen offered two immediate possibilities. First, he considered wait listing a 40-bus order from the Thai military at the Munich plant. He said he was reluctant to do this, however, because the Thais had ordered several product modifications, and the Munich line had been already set up to handle them. Second, Berndsen suggested sending the new Brazil order to N.A.M.'s Prague facility. Prague was the smallest of all the European plants and had the oldest, slowest assembly lines, but they were just finishing up manufacture of an order of #4-G's and, due to

a recent order cancellation, would now be working at only 70 percent capacity through year-end. Within eight weeks, figured Berndsen, Prague could easily handle the order for Brazil's first 25 buses.

Huber eagerly agreed, as Berndsen decided to recommend Prague for this assignment. The problem was that this facility could not produce fast enough to fulfill more than 20 percent of the rest of the contract (for the 224 buses), which meant that he would have to coordinate production and delivery on the rest of this order from other plants. Sighing audibly over the phone line, Berndsen said, "Thanks a lot for the new headache, Hubie. Let me mull this one over for a bit before I call you back. But don't worry, we'll make your deadline—and you will make your bonus. Just remember to cut me in for a piece."

Huber chuckled, thanked him, and hung up.

Berndsen decided to split the full order (224 buses) among the factories in Prague and the much larger plant in Munich. To finalize both scheduling and pricing, he now needed to estimate the time it would take to fulfill the order, as well as the cost of transportation. He was inclined to use the Deutsche Bundesbahn to transport the buses by train to the North Sea port of Bremerhaven, but he wasn't sure that this was the best solution for each of the plants involved.

Berndsen's immediate problem was the first shipment of buses, which would be ready to leave Prague on October 15. Berndsen asked Marcus Weiss, his supply-chain analyst, to create a worksheet that would show all costs and times required to get the buses from the Prague factory to the port of Bremerhaven, and he also asked Weiss to identify viable alternatives. (Europe possesses an extensive network of rivers and channels that connect together its network of commercial waterways. In fact, the European Union champions a Waterways of the Seas concept that specifies four short-sea shipping lanes that involve its member nations.) Consequently, the Prague plant sometimes transported buses on barges via the Elbe, north to Hamburg. The German plants occasionally shipped north to Bremerhaven or Hamburg, via a network of industrial waterways, or westward, over the River Rhein, to the port of Rotterdam in the Netherlands. (See Exhibit 14.A.)

Following is some of the information Weiss assembled for Berndsen:

- By train, the geographic distances between plants and ports were as follows: Prague to Hamburg 490 kilometers, Prague to Rotterdam 640 kilometers.

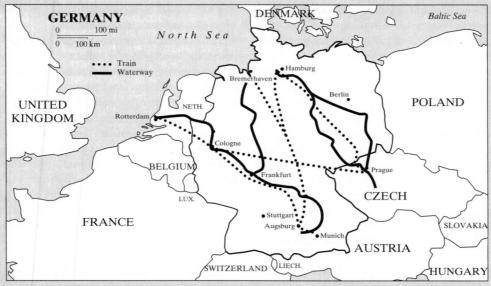

EXHIBIT 14.A Map of Central Europe

- N.A.M. would need three days to get the buses from the factories in Prague to the Port of Bremerhaven or Hamburg by train and four or five days to reach Rotterdam. The advantage of Rotterdam comes, however, in the shipping time from there to Santos, which saves a day versus Bremerhaven or Hamburg, and ocean shipping charges are 5 percent less.
- The Czech railway could transport the load to the border with Germany, where the Deutsche Bundesbahn would take over the flatcars, which carry two buses each. The Bundesbahn quotes a price of € 1,643 per flatcar from Prague to Hamburg, which includes the service by its Czech partner. If rail were used from Prague to Rotterdam, the cost per flatcar would be € 1,943. In either port, it costs another € 45 per bus to have it unloaded and driven to alongside the vessel. The vessel line can load and pack 20 buses per day, charging € 25 per bus and up to 30 buses with overtime charges. The overtime charges would amount to an additional € 15 per bus (for buses 21, 22, etc.). All charges per bus included detaching the two halves.
- Using the waterways instead of trains to reach the Hamburg port from Prague would decrease the transportation cost by € 48 per bus. Waterway transportation would increase the transport time necessary by three days to Hamburg.

- For transoceanic shipping on any of these routes, N.A.M. works with Hapag-Lloyd AG. Hapag-Lloyd is able to offer a cheap and flexible commodity cost, through its alliance with NYK, and OOCL, for the ocean transport of the buses. One vessel could carry up to 125 buses as deck cargo, but they would have to be disassembled at their accordion junctions and then reassembled again at their destination.
- The cost per bus (in shipments of 20 buses or more) from Bremerhaven or Hamburg to Santos is quoted at € 6,000, and the trip requires 18 days. Hapag-Lloyd indicates that deck space is available for the initial shipment of 25 buses on vessels departing Hamburg on October 24, October 27, October 31, and November 3. Hapag-Lloyd also has space on vessels leaving from Rotterdam to Santos on October 23, October 28, and November 2.
- Handling (unloading) in Santos is estimated to cost another € 94 per bus, and this includes reattaching the two halves.
- The interest for N.A.M.'s line of credit is 10 percent.

Questions

1. Assume that you are Weiss. How many viable alternatives do you have to consider regarding the initial shipment of 25 buses?

2. Which of the routing alternatives would you recommend to meet the initial 90-day deadline for the 25-bus shipment? Train or waterway? To which port(s)? What would it cost?

3. What additional information would be helpful for answering Question 2?

4. How important, in fact, are the transport costs for the initial shipment of 25 buses?

5. What kinds of customer service support must be provided for this initial shipment of 25 buses? Who is responsible?

6. The Brazilian buyer wants the buses delivered at Santos. Weiss looks up the International Chamber of Commerce's Incoterms and finds three categories of "delivered" terms:

   • *DAT (Delivered at Terminal).* In this type of transaction, the seller clears the goods for export and bears all risks and costs associated with delivering the goods and unloading them at the terminal at the named port or place of destination. The buyer is responsible for all costs and risks from this point forward including clearing the goods for import at the named country of destination.

   • *DAP (Delivered at Place).* The seller clears the goods for export and bears all risks and costs associated with delivering the goods to the named place of destination not unloaded. The buyer is responsible for all costs and risks associated with unloading the goods and clearing customs to import goods into the named country of destination.

   • *DDP (Delivered Duty Paid).* The seller bears all risks and costs associated with delivering the goods to the named place of destination ready for unloading and clearing for import.

   How should he choose? Why?

7. Would you make the same routing recommendation for the second, larger (199 buses) component of the order, after the initial 90-day deadline is met? Why or why not?

8. How important, if at all, is it for N.A.M. to ship via water to show its support of the European Union's Motorways of the Seas concept?

GLOSSARY

ABC analysis of inventory   Concept that recognizes that because inventories are not of equal value to a firm, they should not be managed in the same way.

Accessorial service   Transportation service that is supplemental to line-haul transportation.

Accumulating (bulk making)   Bringing together inventory from different sources.

Activity-based costing (ABC)   A technique that seeks to better understand the cost of a product by identifying what activities drive particular costs.

Agglomeration (industry cluster)   Refers to the net advantage which can be gained by a sharing of common locations by various enterprises.

Agile supply chain   Focuses on an organization's ability to respond to changes in demand with respect to volume and variety.

Allocating (bulk breaking)   Breaking larger quantities into smaller quantities.

Amodal shipper   A transportation manager who purchases a prespecified level of transportation service and is indifferent to the mode(s) or carrier(s) used to provide the actual transportation service.

Application-specific software   Refers to software that has been developed for managers to deal with specific logistics functions or activities (e.g., transportation management systems).

Assets   Are what a company owns and include current assets and long-term assets.

Asset turnover   In the Strategic Profit Model, asset turnover measures the efficiency of capital employed to generate sales.

Assorting   Building up a variety of different products for resale to a particular customer.

Back order   Placing an order for an item that is out of stock.

Balance of payments   Systems of accounts that record a country's international financial transactions.

Balanced Scorecard (BSC)   A strategic planning and performance management system that evaluates a business from four distinct perspectives: customers, internal business processes, learning and growth, and financial.

Balance sheet   Reflects an organization's assets, liabilities, and owners' equity at a given point in time.

Barge   Flatboard boat used to transport heavy products.

Benchmarking   Using measures of another organization's performance to judge one's own performance.

Big-box retailer   Stores with large amounts of both floor space and products for sale.

Big data   The collection of large amounts of near real-time data collected through a variety of sources, such as sensors, smart phones, RF tags and business-to-business data exchanges.

Bill of lading   The most important single transportation document that is the basic operating document in the industry.

Bribes   Money paid before an exchange.

Broker   A company that helps both shipper and carrier achieve lower freight rates and more efficient utilization of carrier equipment. Brokers also help match carriers to loads.

Brownfields   Locations that contain chemicals or other types of industrial wastes.

Building-blocks concept   Combining smaller packages into larger units that can be more efficiently handled at one time.

Bullwhip effect   Characterized by variability in demand orders among supply chain participants.

"C-level" position   Refers to corporate officers such as a chief executive officer (CEO), chief operating officer (COO), or chief financial officer (CFO).

Cargo preference   Requires a certain percentage of traffic to move on a nation's flag vessels.

Cause and effect (associative) forecasting   Assumes that one or more factors are related to demand, and the relationship between cause and effect can be used to estimate future demand.

Center-of-gravity approach   An approach for locating a single facility that minimizes the distance to existing facilities.

Centralized logistics organization   An organization maintains a single logistics department that administers the related activities for the entire company from the home office.

Certificate of origin   Specifies the country(ies) in which a product is manufactured.

Class rate system   A system that simplifies each of the three primary rate factors—product, weight, and distance.

Closed-loop systems   Refers to systems that consider the return flow of products, their reuse, and the marketing and distribution of recovered products.

Cloud computing   See on-demand software.

Co-branding   Refers to an alliance that allows customers to purchase products from two or more name-brand retailers at one store location.

Collaborative planning, forecasting, and replenishment (CPFR)   Retail industry initiative where trading partners share planning and forecasting data to better match supply and demand.

Commercial invoice   A document used in cross-border trade that summarizes the entire transaction and contains key information such as a description of the goods, the terms of sale and payment, and so on.

Commodity rate   A specific rate for every possible combination of product, weight, and distance.

Common carrier   Transportation carrier that has agreed to serve the general public and assumes four legal obligations: service, delivery, reasonable rates, and avoidance of discrimination.

Complementary products Inventories that are used or distributed together (e.g., razor blades and razors).

Concealed loss or damage Loss or damage that is not apparent until after a shipment has been unpacked and inspected.

Consignee The receiver of a shipment.

Container Security Initiative (CSI) An agreement in which the world's ports agree to allow U.S. customs agents to identify and inspect high-risk containers bound for the United States before they are loaded onto ships.

Container A uniform sealed reusable metal "box" in which goods are shipped.

Contract carrier A contract carrier provides specialized service to each customer based on a contractual arrangement.

Contract logistics See third-party logistics (logistics outsourcing).

Contract (third-party) warehousing A type of contract logistics that focuses on providing unique and specially tailored warehousing services to particular clients.

Cost leadership strategy Requires an organization to pursue activities that will enable it to become the low-cost producer in an industry for a given level of quality.

Cost trade-offs Changes to one logistics activity cause some costs to increase and others to decrease.

Cross-docking A process where product is received in a facility, occasionally married with product going to the same destination, and then shipped at the earliest opportunity, without going into long-term storage.

Cubes out Occurs when a cargo takes up a vehicle's or a container's cubic capacity before reaching its weight capacity.

Current ratio A financial ratio that measures how well an organization can pay its current liabilities by using only current assets.

Customer profitability analysis (CPA) Refers to the allocation of revenues and costs to customer segments or individual customers to calculate the profitability of the segments or customers.

Customer service The ability of logistics management to satisfy users in terms of time, dependability, communication, and convenience.

Customs Trade Partnership Against Terrorism (C-TPAT) A program in which public and private organizations work together to prevent terrorism against the United States through imports and transportation.

Cycle (base) stock Inventory needed to satisfy demand during an order cycle.

Data Facts or recorded measures of certain phenomena.

Data mining Utilizes sophisticated quantitative techniques to find hidden patterns in large volumes of data.

Data warehouse A central repository for all relevant data collected by an organization.

Dead inventory (dead stock) Product for which there is no demand.

Decentralized logistics organization Logistics-related decisions are made separately at the divisional or product group level and often in different geographic regions.

Demand management The creation across the supply chain and its markets of a coordinated flow of demand.

Demurrage A charge assessed by rail carriers to users that fail to unload and return vehicles or containers promptly.

Density A measure of how heavy a product is in relation to its size.

Department of Transportation (DOT) U.S. federal government body with primary responsibility for transportation safety regulation.

Detention A payment from a shipper or consignee to a truck carrier for having kept the carrier's equipment too long.

Differentiation strategy Entails an organization developing a product and/or service that offers unique attributes that are valued by customers and that the customers perceive to be distinct from competitor offerings.

Dimensional (dim) weight Considers a shipment's density (the amount of space occupied relative to weight) to determine a shipment's billable weight.

Disintermediation The removal of levels (layers) from a channel of distribution.

Distribution center A warehouse with an emphasis on quick throughput, such as is needed in supporting marketing efforts.

Documentation The documents associated with transportation shipments.

Dunnage Material that is used to block and brace products inside carrier equipment to prevent the shipment from shifting in transit and becoming damaged.

Economic order quantity (EOQ) An order size that minimizes the sum of carrying and ordering costs.

Economic utility Refers to the value or usefulness of a product in fulfilling customer needs and wants.

Electronic data interchange (EDI) Computer-to-computer transmission of business data in a structured format.

Electronic procurement (e-procurement) Uses the Internet to make it easier, faster, and less expensive for an organization to purchase goods and services.

Embargoes Prohibition of trade between particular countries.

Enterprise resource planning (ERP) system Lets a company automate and integrate the majority of its business processes, share common data and practices across the enterprise, and produce and access information in a real-time environment.

Ergonomics The science that seeks to adapt work or working conditions to suit the abilities of the worker.

Excess capacity Unused available space.

Excess (surplus) materials Stock that exceeds the reasonable requirements of an organization.

Exempt carrier A for-hire carrier that has been exempted from economic regulation through provisions in various pieces of legislation.

Expatriate workers   Employees who are sent to other countries for extended periods of time.

Expediting   The need to rapidly move a shipment to its final destination.

Expenses (costs)   Provide a dollar value for the costs incurred in generating revenues during a given period of time.

Export management company   Firm that acts as the export sales department for a manufacturer.

Export packers   An international logistics specialist that custom packs shipments when the exporter lacks the equipment or expertise to do so itself.

Facility closing   A company discontinues operations at a current site because the operations are no longer needed or can be absorbed by other facilities.

Facility location   Refers to choosing the locations for distribution centers, warehouses, and production facilities to facilitate logistical effectiveness and efficiency.

Facility relocation   A firm must move operations to another facility to better serve suppliers or customers.

Fast supply chain   Emphasizes a speed or time component.

Fixed order interval system   Inventory is replenished on a constant, set schedule and is always ordered at a specific time; the quantity ordered varies depending on forecasted sales before the next order date.

Fixed order quantity system   Inventory is replenished with a set quantity every time it is ordered; the time interval between orders may vary.

Fixed slot location   Each product is assigned a specific location in a warehouse and is always stored there.

FOB destination   A transportation term that signifies that the seller retains title and control of a shipment until it is delivered.

FOB origin   A transportation term that signifies that the buyer assumes title and control of a shipment at the point of pickup.

Focus strategy   Concentrates an organization's effort on a narrowly defined market to achieve either a cost leadership or differentiation advantage.

Form utility   Refers to a product's being in a form that (1) can be used by the customer and (2) is of value to the customer.

Fourth-party logistics (lead logistics provider)   General contractor that ensures that third-party logistics companies are working toward relevant supply chain goals and objectives.

Fragmented logistics structure   Logistics activities are managed in multiple departments throughout an organization.

Free trade zone   An area, usually near a port or an airport, where goods can be stored or processed before entering through the importing nation's customs inspections.

Freight bill   An invoice submitted by a transportation carrier requesting to be paid.

Freight claims   A document that notifies a transportation carrier of wrong or defective deliveries, delay, or other delivery shortcoming.

Freight forwarder   Consolidates freight shipments and buys transportation services in volume rates.

Global positioning systems (GPS)   Use satellites that allow companies to compute vehicle positions, velocity, and time.

Global procurement (sourcing)   Refers to buying components and inputs anywhere in the world.

Globally Harmonized System of Classification and Labeling of Chemicals (GHS)   An effort by the United Nations to classify and label hazardous materials that provides three key pieces of information: (1) a symbol; (2) a signal word; and (3) a hazard statement.

Grid systems   A location technique utilizing a map or grid, with specific locations marked on the north–south and east–west axes. Its purpose is to find a location that minimizes transportation costs.

Gross world product   The sum of the gross domestic product of all countries.

GSCF model   A framework that identifies eight relevant processes, such as customer relationship management, demand management, and order fulfillment, associated with supply chain management.

Hazardous material(s)   Any item or agent (biological, chemical, physical) that has the potential to cause harm to humans, animals, or the environment, either by itself or through interaction with other factors.

Humanitarian logistics   The process and systems involved in mobilizing people, resources, skills, and knowledge to help people who have been affected by either a natural or human-made disaster.

Import quota   Absolute limits to the quantity of a product that can be imported into a country during a particular time period.

Importer Security Filing (ISF) rule   Also known as "10 + 2"; a regulation that stipulates that importers are required to file 10 pieces of information, and carriers two pieces of information, before cargo is loaded at non-U.S. water ports.

Income statement   Shows revenues, expenses, and profit for a period of time.

Incoterms   Terms of sale for international transactions that represent, from the seller's viewpoint, the different locations, or stages, for quoting a price to an overseas buyer.

Information   A body of facts in a format suitable for decision making.

Intermodal competition   Refers to the number of transportation modes available to prospective users.

Intermodal transportation   Using a container that can be transferred from the vehicle of one mode to a vehicle of another, and with the movement covered under a single bill of lading.

International freight forwarders   An international trade specialist that can handle either vessel shipments or air shipments and that offers a number of different functions such as booking space on carriers, obtaining consular documents, and arranging for insurance, among others.

International logistics Refers to logistical activities associated with goods that move across national boundaries.

Intramodal competition Refers to competition among carriers within a particular mode.

Inventory Stocks of goods and materials that are maintained for many purposes.

Inventory carrying (holding) costs The costs of holding an inventory, such as interest on investment, insurance, deterioration, and so on.

Inventory shrinkage Refers to the fact that more items are recorded entering than leaving warehousing facilities.

Inventory tax Analogous to personal property taxes paid by individuals, an inventory tax is based on the value of inventory that is held by an organization on the assessment date.

Inventory turnover The number of times an inventory is used or replaced each year.

Investment recovery Identifies opportunities to recover revenues or reduce costs associated with scrap, surplus, obsolete, and waste materials.

ISO 9000 A set of generic standards used to document, implement, and demonstrate quality management and assurance systems.

Judgmental forecasting Refers to forecasting that involves judgment or intuition and is preferred in situations where there is limited, or no, historical data.

Just-in-time (JIT) approach Seeks to minimize inventory by reducing (if not eliminating) safety stock, as well as having the required amount of materials arrive at the production location at the exact time they are needed.

Kickbacks Money paid after an exchange.

Kraljic's Portfolio Matrix A technique used by many managers to classify corporate purchases in terms of their importance and supply complexity with a goal of minimizing supply vulnerability and getting the most out of the firm's purchasing power.

Land bridge services Refers to a combination of water transportation and surface transportation between an origin and destination port.

Landed costs Price of the product at its source plus transportation costs to its destination.

Leagility Combines agility and leanness as a way to focus part of one's supply chain on a timely response to customer orders and/or product variety and another part of the supply chain on leveling out the planning requirements to smooth production output.

Lean manufacturing (lean) Focuses on the elimination of wastes and the increase of speed and flow.

Lean Six Sigma Integrates the goals and methods of the lean and Six Sigma approaches and recognizes that organizations cannot focus only on quality or speed.

Lean supply chain Focuses on eliminating all waste, including time, and ensuring a level schedule.

Less-than-truckload (LTL) carrier Shipments that range from about 150 to 10,000 pounds; they are often too big to handle manually, yet they do not fill an entire truck.

Letter of credit An international payment option that is issued by a bank and guarantees payment to a seller provided that the seller has complied with the applicable terms and conditions of the particular transaction.

Liabilities Financial obligations that a company owes to another party.

Line-haul Terminal-to-terminal movement of freight or passengers.

Load centers A major port where thousands of containers arrive and depart per week. These ports specialize in the efficient handling of containers.

Locavore strategy Refers to food companies that purchase locally grown or produced foods.

Lock Raises or lowers barges so that they can meet the river's level as they move upstream or downstream.

Logistics According to the Council of Supply Chain Management Professionals, that part of supply chain management that plans, implements, and controls the efficient, effective forward and reverse flow and storage of goods, services, and related information between the point of origin and the point of consumption to meet customers' requirements.

Logistics information system (LIS) People, equipment, and procedures to gather, sort, analyze, evaluate, and distribute needed, timely, and accurate information to logistics decision makers.

Logistics optimization models Utilize spreadsheet software and add-ins to help logisticians make complex judgments and decisions about key logistics issues at strategic, tactical, operational and collaborative levels.

Logistics Performance Index (LPI) An index that is designed to measure a country's performance across six logistical dimensions.

Logistics service quality Refers to a firm's ability to deliver products, materials and services without defects or error to both internal and external customers.

Logistics social responsibility Refers to corporate social responsibility issues that relate directly to logistics.

Logistics Uncertainty Pyramid Model A model that identifies uncertainty sources that can affect the risk exposure for logistics activities.

Macroenvironmental influences The uncontrollable forces and conditions facing an organization and include cultural, demographic, economic, natural, political, and technological factors.

Make-to-order Products are produced after receiving a customer order.

Make-to-stock Products are produced prior to receiving a customer order.

Maquiladora Manufacturing plants that exist just south of the U.S.–Mexican border.

Marketing channels A set of institutions necessary to transfer the title to goods and to move goods from the point of production to the point of consumption and, as such, which consists of all the institutions and all the marketing activities in the marketing process.

Mass logistics   A one-size-fits-all approach in which every customer gets the same type and levels of logistics service.

Materials handling (material handling)   The short-distance movement of material between two or more points.

Materials management   The movement and storage of materials into a firm.

Methods of payment   With respect to international transactions refers to the manner by which a seller will be paid by a buyer.

Multichannel marketing systems   Refers to separate marketing channels to serve customers.

Multiclient warehousing   Mixes attributes of public and contract warehousing; services are more differentiated than a public facility but less customized than in a contract facility.

Multiple sourcing   A procurement philosophy that suggests that by having more than one supplier, increased amounts of competition, greater supply risk mitigation and improved market intelligence can arise.

Near-sourcing   Refers to procuring products from suppliers closer to one's own facilities.

Net profit margin   Measures the proportion of each sales dollar that is kept as profit.

Nontariff barriers   Restrictions other than tariffs that are placed on imported products.

Nonvessel-operating common carrier (NVOCC)   In international trade, a firm that provides carrier services to shippers but owns no vessels itself.

Obsolete materials   Refer to materials that are not likely to ever be used by the organization that purchased it.

Occupational Safety and Health Administration (OSHA)   A U.S. federal agency that regulates workplaces to ensure the safety of workers.

Ocean carrier alliances   Refers to an alliance in the container trades in which ocean carriers retain their individual identities but cooperate in the area of operations.

On-demand software (software-as-a-service)   Refers to software that users access on a per-use basis instead of software they own or license for installation.

Open account   A method of payment for international transactions where a seller sends the goods and all documents directly to the buyer and trusts the buyer to pay by a certain date.

Open skies agreement   Refers to an agreement between two or more countries that liberalize international aviation opportunities and limit federal government involvement.

Order cycle   Elapsed time between when a customer places an order and when the goods are received.

Order delivery   The time from when a transportation carrier picks up the shipment until it is received by the customer.

Order fill rate   The percentage of orders that can be completely and immediately filled from existing stock.

Order management   The management of the various activities associated with the order cycle.

Order picking and assembly   Includes all activities from when an appropriate location is authorized to fill an order until goods are loaded aboard an outbound carrier.

Order processing   The time from when the seller receives an order until an appropriate location is authorized to fill the order.

Order to cash cycle   The length of time it takes an organization to receive payment for an order.

Order transmittal   The time from when the customer places or sends the order to when the seller receives it.

Order triage   Classifying orders according to preestablished guidelines so that a company can prioritize how orders should be filled.

Ordering costs   The costs associated with ordering inventory, such as order costs and setup costs.

Owners' equity   Difference between what a company owns and what it owes at any particular point in time.

Packaging   Materials used for the containment, protection, handling, delivery, and presentation of goods.

Pallet (skid)   A small platform (made of plastic, steel, or wood) on which goods are placed for handling by mechanical means.

Parcel carriers   Companies that specialize in transporting parcels.

Part-to-picker system   The pick location is brought to the picker (e.g., carousels).

Perfect order   An order that simultaneously achieves relevant customer metrics.

Physical distribution   Storage of finished product and movement to the customers.

Pick-to-light technology   The orders to be picked are identified by lights placed on shelves or racks.

Picker-to-part system   An order picker goes to where the product is located (e.g., a forklift).

Piggyback transportation   Truck trailers on flatcars, also referred to as TOFC.

Pilferage   Employee theft.

Pipeline (in-transit) stock   Inventory that is in route between various nodes in a logistics system.

Place utility   Having products available where they are needed by customers.

Possession utility   Refers to the value or usefulness that comes from a customer being able to take possession of a product.

Postponement   The delay of value-added activities such as assembly, production, and packaging to the latest possible time.

Private carrier   Companies whose primary business is other than transportation provide their own transportation service by operating truck, railcars, barges, ships, or airplanes.

Private warehousing   A warehousing facility that is owned by the firm using it.

Procurement (purchasing)   Raw materials, component parts, and supplies brought from outside organizations to support a company's operations.

Procurement cards (p-cards) Are similar to credit cards for personal use, only p-cards are used for organizational purchases.

Productivity The amount of output divided by the amount of input.

Psychic stock Inventory that stimulates demand in the sense that customer purchases are stimulated by inventory that they can see.

Public warehousing Serves all legitimate users and has certain responsibilities to those users.

Pure materials Materials that lose no weight in processing.

Quality-of-life considerations Their intent is to incorporate nonbusiness factors (e.g., cost of living, crime rate, educational opportunities) into the decision of where to locate a plant or distribution facility.

Radio-frequency identification (RFID) The use of radio frequency to identify objects that have been implanted with an RFID tag.

Rail gauge The distance between the inner sides of two parallel rail tracks.

Rate The price charged for freight transportation.

Regrouping function Involves rearranging the quantities and assortment of products as they move through the supply chain.

Reorder (trigger) point (ROP) The level of inventory at which a replenishment order is placed.

Return on assets (ROA) Indicates what percentage of every dollar invested in the business ultimately is returned to the organization as profit.

Revenues (sales) A dollar value of all the products and/or services an organization provides to their customers during a given period of time.

Reverse auction A buyer invites bids from multiple sellers, and the seller with the lowest bid is often awarded the business.

Reverse logistics Goods that flow from the consumer to the manufacturer (e.g., product recalls and product recycling).

Right-to-work laws State laws that specify that a worker does not have to join the union to work permanently at a facility.

Routing The process of determining how a shipment will be moved between consignor and consignee or between place of acceptance by the carrier and place of delivery to the consignee.

Routing guide Provides guidance in terms of a preferred list of carriers for shipments moving between two points.

Safety (buffer) stock Inventory that is held in addition to cycle stock to guard against uncertainties in supply and/or lead time.

SCOR model A framework that identifies five key processes—plan, source, make, deliver, return—associated with supply chain management.

Scrap materials These are materials that are no longer serviceable, have been discarded, or are a by-product of the production process.

Service parts logistics Involves designing a network of facilities to stock service parts, deciding upon inventory ordering policies, stocking the required parts, and transporting parts from stocking facilities to customers.

Service recovery A process for returning a customer to a state of satisfaction after a service or product has failed to live up to expectations.

Shippers' associations Nonprofit membership cooperatives that perform basically the same function as freight forwarders.

Shipper's export declaration (SED) Contains relevant export transaction data such as the transportation mode(s), transaction participants, and description of what is being exported.

Shipper's letter of instruction (SLI) Often accompanies an SED and provides explicit shipment instructions.

Shipping conferences Cartels of all ocean vessel operators operating between certain trade areas.

Short-sea shipping Refers to waterborne transportation that utilizes inland and coastal waterways to move shipments from domestic ports to their destination.

Shrink-wrap Plastic wrapping that when heated shrinks in size to form a cover over the product.

Simulation A technique that models a real-world system, typically using mathematical equations to represent the relationships among components of the real-world system.

Single sourcing A procurement philosophy that consolidates purchase volume with a single supplier with the hopes of enjoying lower costs per unit and increased cooperation and communication in the supply relationship.

Six Sigma A practice that emphasizes the virtual elimination of business errors that strives to achieve 3.4 defects, deficiencies, or errors per one million opportunities.

Slip sheet A flat sheet of either fiberboard material or plastic that is placed under the unit load.

Slurry systems Transport products that are ground into a powder, mixed with water, and then shipped in slurry form through a pipeline.

Sorting function Bridges the discrepancy between the assortment of goods and services generated by the producer and the assortment demanded by the customer.

Sorting out Separating products into grades and qualities desired by different target markets.

Speculative stock Inventory that is held for several reasons such as seasonal demand, projected price increases, and potential product shortages.

Stock-keeping units (SKUs) Each separate type of item that is accounted for in an inventory.

Stockouts Being out of an item at the same time there is a willing buyer for it.

Stockout costs The costs to a seller when it is unable to supply an item to a customer ready to buy.

Stowability Refers to how easy a commodity is to pack into a load.

Strategic Profit Model Provides the framework for conducting return on assets analysis by incorporating revenues and expenses to generate a net profit margin, as well as an inclusion of assets to measure asset turnover.

Substitute products   Products that customers view as being able to fill the same need or want as another product.

Supplier audits   Involve assessments of the supplier's structure (management, people, quality, innovation), resources (technology, processes), health (financials, risk) and responsibility (social, environmental).

Supplier development (reverse marketing)   A degree of aggressive procurement involvement not normally encountered in supplier selection.

Supplier parks   Key suppliers locate on, or adjacent to, automobile plants, which helps reduce shipping costs and inventory carrying costs.

Supplier scorecards   Are used by companies to report performance information to their suppliers.

Supply chain   All activities associated with the flow and transformation of goods from the raw material stage, through to the end user, as well as the associated information flows.

Supply chain analytics   Combines technology with manual employee effort to identify trends, perform comparisons and highlight opportunities in supply chain processes, even when large amounts of data are involved.

Supply chain collaboration   Cooperative, formal or informal supply chain relationships between manufacturing companies and their suppliers, business partners, or customers, developed to enhance the overall business performance of both sides.

Supply chain management (SCM)   According to the Council of Supply Chain Management Professionals, SCM encompasses the planning and management of all activities involved in sourcing and procurement, conversion, and all logistics management activities. Importantly, it also includes coordination and collaboration with channel partners, which can be suppliers, intermediaries, third-party service providers, and customers. In essence, supply chain management integrates supply and demand management within and across companies.

Supply chain partnership   Refers to a tailored business relationship between two supply chain members.

Supply management   A relational exchange approach involving a limited number of suppliers.

Surface Transportation Board (STB)   A U.S. government agency with primary responsibility for regulating railroad pricing and service.

Sustainable procurement   Refers to the integration of social and environmental considerations into all stages of the purchasing process with the goal of minimizing the impact of procurement activities on human health and the environment.

Sustainable products   Refers to products that meet present needs without compromising the ability of future generations to meet their needs.

Sweatshops   Organizations that exploit workers and that do not comply with fiscal and legal obligations toward employees.

Systems approach   A company's objectives can be realized by recognizing the mutual interdependence of the major functional areas of the firm, such as marketing, production, finance, and logistics.

Tachograph   A recording instrument that is installed inside a truck and produces a continuous, timed record of the truck, its speed, and its engine speed.

Tailored logistics   Groups of customers with similar logistical needs and wants are provided with logistics service appropriate to those needs and wants.

Tariffs   Taxes that governments place on the importation of certain items.

TEU   Twenty-foot equivalent unit; a measure of the number of 20-foot containers that are used or handled.

Terminal   A carrier or public facility where freight (or passengers) is shifted between vehicles or modes.

Terms of sale   For international transactions, refers to determining when and where to transfer between buyer and seller, the physical goods, the payment for goods, legal title, required documentation as well as responsibility for controlling and caring for goods while in transit.

Theft (stealing)   Taking and removing personal property with the intent to deprive the rightful owner of it.

Third-party logistics (logistics outsourcing; contract logistics)   The general idea behind these concepts is that one company (e.g., a manufacturer) allows a specialist company to provide it with one or more logistics functions (e.g., warehousing, outbound transportation).

Throughput   Refers to the amount of product entering and leaving a facility in a given time period.

Time series forecasting   A group of forecasting techniques that is based on the idea that future demand is solely dependent on past demand.

Time utility   Having products available when they are needed by customers.

Ton miles   The number of tons times the number of miles.

Total cost approach   Concept that suggests that all relevant activities in moving and storing products should be considered as a whole (i.e., their total cost), not individually.

Total cost of ownership (TCO)   Refers to an approach where firms consider all the costs that can be assigned to the acquisition, use and maintenance of a purchase.

Tracking   A carrier's attempt to determine a shipment's location during the course of its move.

Transportation   Actual physical movement of goods and people between two points.

Transportation management   The buying and controlling of transportation services by either a shipper or consignee.

Transportation management system (TMS)   A software package that automates the process of building orders, tending loads, and tracking shipments, audits, and payments.

Transportation Worker Identification Credential (TWIC)   A common credential that is used to identify workers across all modes of transportation.

Truckload (TL) carrier   A motor carrier that focuses on shipments of greater than 10,000 pounds.

Unified logistics structure   Multiple logistics activities are combined into, and managed as, a single department.

Unit load (unitization)   Consolidation of several units (cartons or cases) into larger units to improve efficiency in handling and to reduce shipping costs.

Unit load devices (ULD)   An alternative name for airfreight containers.

Variable slot location   A system in which products are stored wherever there is empty space available in a warehouse.

Vendor-managed inventory (VMI)   A system in which the size and timing of replenishment orders into a retailer's system are the manufacturer's responsibility.

Voice-based order picking   The use of speech to guide order-picking activities.

Warehouse   Emphasize the storage of products and their primary purpose is to maximize usage of available storage space.

Warehouse automation   The utilization of mechanical or electronic devices to substitute for labor.

Warehouse management system (WMS)   Software packages that control the movement and storage of materials within a warehousing facility.

Warehousing   That part of a firm's logistics system that stores products at and between points of origin and point of consumption.

Waste materials   These are materials that have been spoiled, broken, or otherwise rendered unfit for further use or reclamation.

Weighing out   Cargo reaches a vehicle's or a container's weight capacity without filling its cubic capacity.

Weight-gaining product characteristics   A product that gains weight in processing; the processing point should be close to the market.

Weight-losing product characteristics   A product that loses weight during the production process; the processing point should be as near to its origin as possible.

Wireless communication   Refers to communication without cables and cords, and includes infrared, microwave, and radio transmissions.

NAME INDEX

Note: Locators followed '*n*' refer to footnotes.

SUBJECT INDEX

Note: Locators followed by '*f*' and '*t*' refer to figures and tables.